A Custom Edition | Elaine N. Marieb | Pamela B. Jackson

Essentials of Human Anatomy & Physiology

Laboratory Manual

Taken from:

Essentials of Human Anatomy & Physiology: Laboratory Manual
Seventh Edition
by Elaine N. Marieb and Pamela B. Jackson

Cover Art: Courtesy of design36/Shutterstock.

Taken from:

Essentials of Human Anatomy and Physiology: Laboratory Manual, Seventh Edition
by Elaine N. Marieb and Pamela B. Jackson
Copyright © 2018, 2015, 2012 by Pearson Education, Inc.
New York, New York 10013

This special edition published in cooperation with Pearson Education, Inc.

Pearson Education, Inc., 330 Hudson Street, New York, New York 10013
A Pearson Education Company
www.pearsoned.com

Printed in the United States of America

000200010272166422

CC

ISBN 10: 0-135-35439-0
ISBN 13: 978-0-135-35439-1

8 2022

Contents

iv   Contents

10 Joints and Body Movements   111

THE MUSCULAR SYSTEM

11 Microscopic Anatomy and Organization of Skeletal Muscle   121

12 Gross Anatomy of the Muscular System   131

REGULATORY SYSTEMS: NEURAL AND ENDOCRINE

13 Neuron Anatomy and Physiology   151

14 Gross Anatomy of the Brain and Cranial Nerves   163

15 Spinal Cord and Spinal Nerves   183

16 Human Reflex Physiology   193

17 The Special Senses   201

18 Functional Anatomy of the Endocrine Glands   229

Preface

Students in particular health-related programs, such as LPN, medical records, and dental technician programs, typically encounter a fast-paced anatomy and physiology course that leaves little time for laboratory study, and yet hands-on laboratory experiences are highly desirable to clarify the lecture. This challenge provided the impetus for writing this brief laboratory manual, meant to be used in short A&P lab courses.

Basic Pedagogical Approach

The Seventh Edition offers a variety of lab activities that give the instructor flexibility to choose which ones will best supplement the topics that are taught in lecture. While it is based on the concepts and terminology in Elaine Marieb and Suzanne Keller's *Essentials of Human Anatomy & Physiology,* Twelfth Edition, text, this manual is a stand-alone resource that can complement any textbook. Each activity is preceded by pertinent background information so that students will not need to carry their textbooks to lab.

Although length and content have been rigorously controlled, the 27 exercises in this manual still provide fairly complete coverage of the most common topics of human anatomy and physiology. The manual also includes a complete exercise on microscope care and use (see Appendix A).

Pedagogy and Special Features

1. Each exercise is preceded by a list of materials needed for conducting the lab activities, followed by brief directives to help students prepare for the lab experience.

2. Key terms appear in boldface print, and each term is defined when introduced.

3. Learning objectives precede key passages in each exercise to focus the student's attention on the important lessons to "take home" from the exercise.

4. Large illustrations, now in full color, highlight and differentiate important structures and help students recognize important structure/function relationships.

5. Histology and isolated organ specimen photos supplement the diagrams, where useful.

6. The Histology Atlas features 55 histology photomicrographs, and students are referred to relevant photos in the Atlas throughout the manual.

7. Body structures are presented from simple to complex and allow ample opportunity for student observation, manipulation, and experimentation. Histology lessons will be facilitated by instructor-set-up-slides at demonstration areas for student viewing so students don't have to spend time finding the "right" section. These, along with physiology experiments, can be conducted in limited time periods and with inexpensive, widely available equipment and supplies.

8. All exercises involving body fluids (blood, saliva, etc.) incorporate current Centers for Disease Control and Prevention

guidelines for handling body fluids. A safety icon alerts students to observe special precautions.

9. An Instructor's Guide can be downloaded from the "Instructor Resources" area of MasteringA&P for Marieb and Keller, *Essentials of Human Anatomy & Physiology,* Twelfth Edition. Prepared by co-author Pamela Jackson, the Guide provides answers to activity and review sheet questions along with helpful teaching suggestions for the lab.

New to the Seventh Edition

- **All of the black and white figures in previous editions are now in full-color,** making it easier than ever for students and instructors to quickly and easily identify structures.

- **Improved tear-out review sheets and in-exercise questions** are more closely aligned with the content in the lab exercises.

- **Updated terminology and streamlined content** makes selected content more accessible for today's students.

- **New, full-color design** is more intuitive, making it easier for learners to differentiate "big picture" concepts and learning objectives from supporting details.

For information on creating a custom version of this manual, visit www.pearsoncollections.com or contact your Pearson representative for details.

Also Available

- *The Anatomy & Physiology Coloring Workbook,* Twelfth Edition (by Elaine N. Marieb and Simone Brito) (0-134-45936-9)

- *The Physiology Coloring Book,* Second Edition (by Wynn Kapit, Robert Macey, and Esmail Meisami) (0-321-03663-8)

- *The Anatomy Coloring Book,* Fourth Edition (by Wynn Kapit and Lawrence Elson) (0-321-83201-9)

Acknowledgments

Many thanks to the Pearson editorial team of Lauren Harp, Sr. Acquisitions Editor, and Managing Producer, Nancy Tabor. Kudos as usual to Mangelli Productions and to David Novak, Art and Production Coordinator for this project. Thanks also to Content Developers Kari Hopperstead and Alice Fugate, to Accuracy Reviewer Carla Perry, and to Copyeditor Sally Peryrefitte.

As always, we invite users of this edition to send us their comments and suggestions for subsequent editions.

Elaine N. Marieb
Pamela B. Jackson
Pearson Education, A & P
1301 Sansome Street
San Francisco, CA 94111

The Language of Anatomy

Materials

☐ Human torso model (dissectible)
☐ Human skeleton
☐ Demonstration area:
   Station 1: Sectioned and labeled kidneys (three separate kidneys uncut or cut so that (a) entire, (b) transverse, and (c) longitudinal sectional views are visible)
   Station 2: Gelatin-spaghetti molds, scalpel

Pre-Lab Quiz

1. Circle True or False. In the anatomical position, the body is recumbent (lying down).

2. The term *superficial* refers to a structure that is:
   a. attached near the trunk of the body
   b. toward or at the body surface
   c. toward the head
   d. toward the midline

3. The _____ plane runs longitudinally and divides the body into right and left parts.
   a. frontal   c. transverse
   b. sagittal   d. ventral

Most of us are naturally curious about our bodies. This curiosity is apparent even in infants when they gaze in fascination at their own waving hands or their mother's nose. Unlike the infant, however, an anatomy student must learn to identify body structures formally.

This exercise presents some of the most important anatomical terms you will be using to describe the body and introduces you to **gross anatomy,** the study of body structures you can see with your naked eye. As you become familiar with this **anatomical terminology,** you will have a chance to examine the three-dimensional relationships of body structures using illustrations and models.

Anatomical Position

OBJECTIVE 1   Describe the anatomical position verbally or by demonstrating it.

When doctors refer to specific areas of the human body, they do so relative to a standard position called the **anatomical position.** In the anatomical position, the human body is erect, with head and toes pointed forward and arms hanging at the sides with palms facing forward (see Figure 1.3 on page 4).

Activity 1

Demonstrating the Anatomical Position

Stand and assume the anatomical position. Notice that it is not particularly comfortable, because you must hold your hands unnaturally forward instead of allowing them to hang partially cupped toward your thighs.

Surface Anatomy

OBJECTIVE 2   Demonstrate ability to use anatomical terms describing body landmarks, directions, planes, and surfaces.

Body surfaces provide a number of visible landmarks that can be used to study the body. Several of these are described on the following pages.

Activity 2

Locating Body Landmarks

Anterior Body Landmarks

Identify and use anatomical terms to correctly label the following regions in **Figure 1.1a**:

Abdominal: The anterior body trunk region inferior to the ribs.

Antecubital: The anterior surface of the elbow.

Axillary: The armpit.

Brachial: The arm.

Buccal: The cheek.

Carpal: The wrist.

Cervical: The neck region.

Coxal: The hip.

Deltoid: The roundness of the shoulder caused by the underlying deltoid muscle.

Digital: The fingers or toes.

Femoral: The thigh.

Fibular: The side of the leg.

Inguinal: The groin.

Mammary: The breast.

Manus: The hand.

Nasal: The nose.

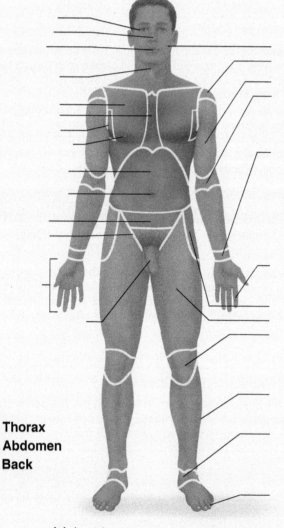

■ **Thorax**
■ **Abdomen**
■ **Back**

(a) Anterior

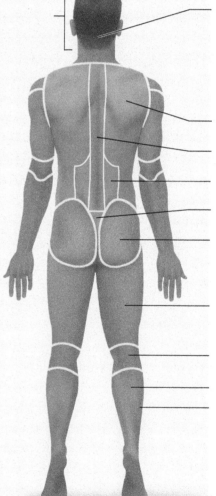

(b) Posterior

Figure 1.1 Surface anatomy. (a) Anterior body landmarks. **(b)** Posterior body landmarks.

Oral: The mouth.

Orbital: The bony eye socket (orbit).

Patellar: The anterior knee (kneecap) region.

Pelvic: The pelvis region.

Pubic: The genital region.

Sternal: The region of the breastbone.

Tarsal: The ankle.

Thoracic: The chest.

Umbilical: The navel.

Posterior Body Landmarks

Identify and appropriately label the following body surface regions in Figure 1.1b:

Cephalic: The head.

Femoral: The thigh.

Fibular: The side of the leg.

Gluteal: The buttocks, or rump.

Lumbar: The area of the back between the ribs and hips; the loin.

Occipital: The posterior aspect of the head or base of the skull.

Popliteal: The back of the knee.

Sacral: The area between the hips.

Scapular: The scapula or shoulder blade area.

Sural: The calf or posterior surface of the leg.

Vertebral: The area of the spinal column.

Body Orientation and Direction

Study the terms below, referring to **Figure 1.2**. Notice as you read that certain terms have a meaning for a four-legged animal that is different from the meaning for a human.

Superior/inferior *(above/below):* These terms refer to the location of a structure along the long axis of the body. Superior structures appear above other structures, and inferior structures are always below other body parts.

Anterior/posterior *(front/back):* In humans the most anterior structures are those that are most forward—the face, chest, and abdomen. Posterior structures are those toward the backside of the body.

Medial/lateral *(toward the midline/away from the midline or median plane):* Medial structures are closer to the body midline than are lateral structures.

The terms described above assume the person is in the anatomical position. The next four pairs of terms are more absolute. They do not relate to a particular body position, and they have the same meaning in all vertebrate animals.

Cephalad/caudad (caudal) *(toward the head/toward the tail):* In humans, these terms are used interchangeably with *superior* and *inferior*. But in four-legged animals, they are synonyms of *anterior* and *posterior*, respectively.

Dorsal/ventral *(backside/belly side):* Meaning "back," the term *dorsal* refers to the animal's back or the *back*side of any other structures. The term *ventral*, meaning "belly," always refers to the belly side of animals. In humans the terms *ventral* and *dorsal* are used interchangeably with the terms *anterior* and *posterior*, but in four-legged animals *ventral* and *dorsal* mean *inferior* and *superior*, respectively.

Proximal/distal *(nearer the trunk or attached end/farther from the trunk or point of attachment):* These terms locate various areas along the body limbs or an elongated organ such as the intestine. For example, the fingers are distal to the elbow; the knee is proximal to the toes.

Superficial/deep *(toward or at the body surface/away from the body surface or more internal):* These terms locate body organs according to their relative closeness to the body surface. For example, the skin is superficial to the skeletal muscles.

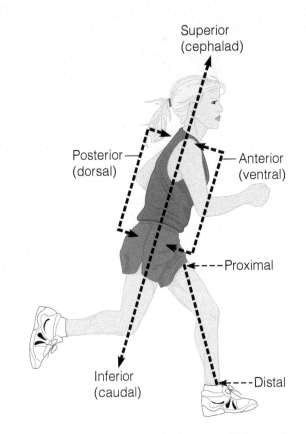

Figure 1.2 Anatomical terminology describing body orientation and direction in a human.

Activity 3

Practicing Using Correct Anatomical Terminology

Before continuing, use a human torso model, a skeleton, or your own body to specify the relationship between the following structures.

1. The wrist is _____ to the hand.

2. The trachea (windpipe) is _____ to the spine.

3. The brain is _____ to the spinal cord.

4. The kidneys are _____ to the liver.

5. The nose is _____ to the cheekbones.

6. The chest is _____ to the abdomen.

7. The skin is _____ to the skeleton.

Planes and Sections

The body is three-dimensional. So, to observe its internal parts, it often helps to make use of a **section**, or cut made along an imaginary surface or line called a **plane.** There are three planes of space (**Figure 1.3**), or sections, that lie at right angles to one another.

Sagittal plane: A plane that runs lengthwise or longitudinally down the length of the body, dividing it into right and left parts, is a sagittal plane. If it divides the body into equal parts, down the midline of the body, it is called a **median plane,** or **midsagittal plane** (Figure 1.3a).

Frontal (coronal) plane: A longitudinal plane that divides the body (or an organ) into anterior and posterior parts (Figure 1.3b).

Transverse plane: A plane that runs horizontally, dividing the body into superior and inferior parts (Figure 1.3c). These sections are also commonly called **cross sections.**

As shown in **Figure 1.4**, a sagittal or frontal section of any nonspherical object, be it a banana or a body organ, provides quite a different view from a transverse section.

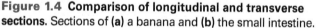

Longitudinal sections   **Transverse sections**

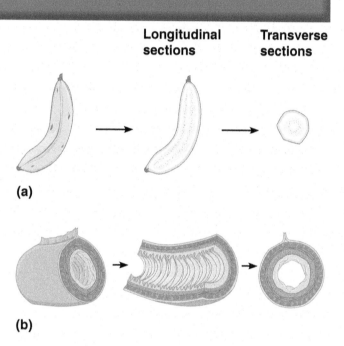

(a)

(b)

Figure 1.4 Comparison of longitudinal and transverse sections. Sections of **(a)** a banana and **(b)** the small intestine.

Figure 1.3 Planes of the body.

(a) Median (midsagittal) plane   **(b)** Frontal (coronal) plane   **(c)** Transverse plane

Activity 4

Observing Sectioned Specimens

1. Go to the demonstration area and observe the entire (uncut) kidneys and the transversely and longitudinally cut kidneys at station 1. Pay close attention to the different structural details you can see in the samples.

2. After completing step 1, obtain a gelatin-spaghetti mold and a scalpel, and bring them to your laboratory bench. (Essentially, this is just cooked spaghetti added to warm gelatin that is then allowed to gel.)

3. Cut through the gelatin-spaghetti mold along any plane, and examine the cut surfaces. You should see spaghetti strands that have been cut transversely and longitudinally.

4. Draw the appearance of each of these spaghetti sections below, and verify the accuracy of your section identifications with your instructor.

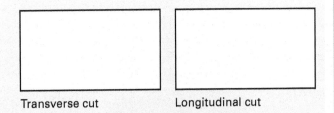

Transverse cut   Longitudinal cut

Body Cavities

OBJECTIVE 3   Name the body cavities, and indicate important organs in each cavity.

The axial portion of the body has two main cavities (**Figure 1.5**): the **dorsal body cavity** and the **ventral body cavity.**

Dorsal Body Cavity

The dorsal body cavity consists of the cranial and spinal cavities. The **cranial cavity,** within the rigid skull, contains the brain. The **spinal cavity,** which runs within the bony vertebral column, protects the spinal cord. The spinal cord is a continuation of the brain, and the cavities containing them are continuous with each other.

Ventral Body Cavity

Like the dorsal cavity, the ventral body cavity is subdivided. The superior **thoracic cavity** is separated from the rest of the ventral cavity by the muscular diaphragm. The heart and lungs, located in the thoracic cavity, are protected by the bony rib cage. The cavity inferior to the diaphragm is the **abdominopelvic cavity.** Although there is no further physical separation of this part of the ventral cavity, some describe the abdominopelvic cavity in terms of a superior **abdominal cavity,** the area that houses the stomach, intestines, liver, and other organs, and an inferior **pelvic cavity,** which is partially enclosed by the bony pelvis and contains the reproductive organs, bladder, and rectum. Notice in Figure 1.5 that the pelvic cavity tips away from the abdominal cavity in a posterior direction.

Abdominopelvic Quadrants and Regions

The abdominopelvic cavity is quite large and contains many organs, so it is helpful to divide it up into smaller areas for study. The medical scheme divides the abdominal surface (and the abdominopelvic cavity deep to it) into four approximately equal regions called **quadrants,** named according to their relative position—that is, *right upper quadrant, right lower quadrant, left upper quadrant,* and *left lower quadrant* (**Figure 1.6a**). (**Note:** These directions refer to the patient's left and right—not yours!)

Another scheme, commonly used by anatomists, divides the abdominal surface and abdominopelvic cavity into nine separate regions by four planes, as shown in Figure 1.6b. Although the names of these nine regions are unfamiliar to you now, with a little patience and study they will become easier to remember. Read through the descriptions of these nine regions that follow and locate them in the figure. Notice the organs they contain by referring to Figure 1.6c.

Umbilical region: The centermost region, which includes the umbilicus.

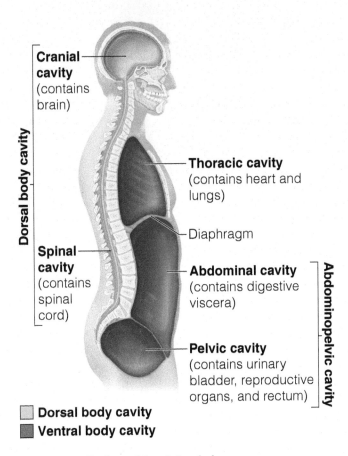

Cranial cavity (contains brain)

Thoracic cavity (contains heart and lungs)

Diaphragm

Spinal cavity (contains spinal cord)

Abdominal cavity (contains digestive viscera)

Pelvic cavity (contains urinary bladder, reproductive organs, and rectum)

Dorsal body cavity

Abdominopelvic cavity

▢ **Dorsal body cavity**
◼ **Ventral body cavity**

Figure 1.5 Body cavities, lateral view.

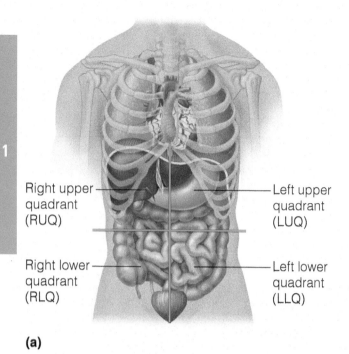

Right upper quadrant (RUQ)

Left upper quadrant (LUQ)

Right lower quadrant (RLQ)

Left lower quadrant (LLQ)

(a)

Epigastric region: Immediately superior to the umbilical region; overlies most of the stomach.

Hypogastric (pubic) region: Immediately inferior to the umbilical region; encompasses the pubic area.

Iliac (inguinal) regions: Lateral to the hypogastric region and overlying the superior parts of the hip bones.

Lumbar regions: Between the ribs and the flaring portions of the hip bones; lateral to the umbilical region.

Hypochondriac regions: Flanking the epigastric region laterally and overlying the lower ribs.

Activity 5

Locating Abdominal Surface Regions

Locate the regions of the abdominal surface on a torso model and on yourself before continuing.

(b)

Right hypochondriac region

Epigastric region

Left hypochondriac region

Right lumbar region

Umbilical region

Left lumbar region

Right iliac (inguinal) region

Hypogastric (pubic) region

Left iliac (inguinal) region

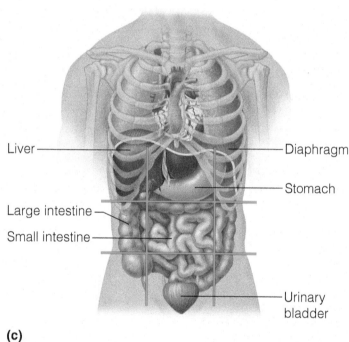

Liver

Diaphragm

Stomach

Large intestine

Small intestine

Urinary bladder

(c)

Figure 1.6 Abdominopelvic surface and cavity. (a) The four quadrants. **(b)** Nine regions delineated by four planes. The superior horizontal plane is just inferior to the ribs; the inferior horizontal plane is at the superior aspect of the hip bones. The vertical planes are just medial to the nipples. **(c)** Anterior view of the ventral body cavity showing superficial organs in the nine abdominopelvic regions.

REVIEW SHEET
The Language of Anatomy

Name _____ LabTime/Date _____

Surface Anatomy

1. Match each of the following descriptions with a key term, and record the term in front of the description.

Key: brachial   carpal   deltoid   patellar
         buccal   cervical   digital   scapular

_____ 1. cheek   _____ 5. anterior aspect of knee

_____ 2. referring to the fingers _____ 6. referring to the arm

_____ 3. shoulder blade region   _____ 7. curve of shoulder

_____ 4. wrist area   _____ 8. referring to the neck

Body Orientation, Direction, Planes, and Sections

2. Several incomplete statements are listed below. Correctly complete each statement by choosing the appropriate anatomical term from the key. Record the key terms on the correspondingly numbered blanks below.

Key: anterior   inferior   posterior   superior
         distal   lateral   proximal   transverse
         frontal   medial   sagittal

   In the anatomical position, the umbilicus and knees are on the 1 body surface; the buttocks and shoulder blades are on the 2 body surface; and the soles of the feet are the most 3 part of the body. The ears are 4 and 5 to the shoulders and 6 to the nose. The breastbone is 7 to the vertebral column (spine) and 8 to the shoulders. The elbow is 9 to the shoulder but 10 to the fingers. The thoracic cavity is 11 to the abdominopelvic cavity and 12 to the spinal cavity. In humans, the ventral surface can also be called the 13 surface; however, in quadruped animals, the ventral surface is the 14 surface.

   If an incision cuts the brain into superior and inferior parts, the section is a 15 section; but if the brain is cut so that anterior and posterior portions result, the section is a 16 section. You are told to cut a dissection animal along two planes so that the lungs are observable in both sections. The two sections that meet this requirement are the 17 and 18 sections.

1. _____   7. _____   13. _____

2. _____   8. _____   14. _____

3. _____   9. _____   15. _____

4. _____   10. _____   16. _____

5. _____   11. _____   17. _____

6. _____   12. _____   18. _____

3. A nurse informs you that she is about to give you a shot in the lateral femoral region. What portion of your body should you uncover?

   _____

4. Correctly identify each of the body planes by inserting the appropriate term for each on the answer line below the drawing.

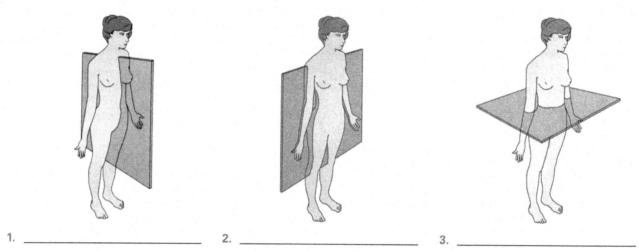

1. _____   2. _____   3. _____

Body Cavities

5. Which body cavity would have to be opened for the following types of surgery? Insert the key term(s) in the same-numbered blank. More than one choice may apply.

   Key: abdominopelvic   dorsal   thoracic
             cranial   spinal   ventral

   1. surgery to remove a cancerous lung lobe   1. _____

   2. removal of an ovary   2. _____

   3. surgery to remove a ruptured disk   3. _____

   4. appendectomy   4. _____

   5. removal of the gallbladder   5. _____

6. Correctly identify each of the described areas of the abdominal surface by inserting the appropriate term in the answer blank preceding the description.

   _____ 1. overlies the lateral aspects of the lower ribs

   _____ 2. surrounds the "belly button"

   _____ 3. encompasses the pubic area

   _____ 4. medial region overlying the stomach

7. What are the bony landmarks of the abdominopelvic cavity? _____

   _____

8. Which body cavity affords the least protection to its internal structures? _____

Organ Systems Overview

Materials

☐ Freshly killed or predissected rat (if available)
☐ Probes
☐ Forceps
☐ Scissors
☐ Dissecting pins or twine
☐ Dissecting trays
☐ Disposable gloves
☐ Human torso model (dissectible)

Pre-Lab Quiz

1. Name the basic unit, or building block, of all living things. _____

2. The _____ system is responsible for maintaining homeostasis of the body via rapid transmission of electrical signals.

3. The _____ system keeps the blood continuously supplied with oxygen while removing carbon dioxide.

4. The kidneys are part of the _____ system.

5. The thin muscle that separates the thoracic and abdominal cavities is the _____.

The building block of all living things is the **cell.** Cells fall into four different groups according to their structures and functions. Each of these corresponds to one of the four **tissue** types: epithelial, muscular, nervous, and connective. An **organ** is a structure composed of two or more tissue types that performs a specific function for the body. For example, the small intestine, which digests and absorbs nutrients, contains all four tissue types.

An **organ system** is a group of organs that act together to perform a particular body function or functions. For example, digestive system organs work together to break down foods moving through the digestive system and absorb the nutrients into the bloodstream. These nutrients are required by all of the body's cells.

Activity 1

Studying the Organ Systems of the Body and Their Functions

In all, there are 11 organ systems, which are described in Table 2.1. Read through this summary before beginning the rat dissection.

DISSECTION

Rat Dissection and/or Observation

OBJECTIVE 1   Identify several organs of the various organ systems on a dissected rat.

Many of the external and internal structures of the rat are similar in structure and function to those of humans, so a study of the gross anatomy of the rat should help you understand your own physical structure.

The following instructions direct your dissection and observation of a rat. In addition, the general instructions for observing external structures can easily be adapted to guide human cadaver observations if cadavers are available.

Note that you won't be studying four of the organ systems listed in Table 2.1 (integumentary, skeletal, muscular, and nervous), because they require microscopic study or more detailed dissection.

2

Table 2.1	Overview of Organ Systems of the Body	
Organ system	**Major component organs**	**Function**
Integumentary	Skin, nails, and hair; cutaneous sense organs and glands	• Protects deeper organs from injury due to bumps, chemicals, bacteria, and dehydration (drying out) • Excretes salts and urea • Helps regulate body temperature • Produces vitamin D
Skeletal	Bones, cartilages, tendons, ligaments, and joints	• Supports and protects internal organs • Provides levers for muscular action • Stores minerals (calcium and others) • Cavities provide a site for blood cell formation
Muscular	Muscles attached to the skeleton	• Skeletal muscles contract, or shorten; in doing so, they move bones to allow motion (running, walking, etc.), grasping and manipulating the environment, and facial expression • Generates heat
Nervous	Brain, spinal cord, nerves, and special sense organs	• Allows body to detect changes in its internal and external environment and to respond to such information by activating appropriate muscles or glands • Helps maintain short-term homeostasis of the body via rapid transmission of electrical signals
Endocrine	Pituitary, thyroid, parathyroid, adrenal, and pineal glands; ovaries, testes, and pancreas	• Promotes growth and development; produces chemical "messengers" (hormones) that travel in the blood to exert their effect(s) on various target organs of the body • Plays a role in regulating long-term homeostasis
Cardiovascular	Heart, blood vessels, and blood	• Primarily a transport system that carries blood containing oxygen, carbon dioxide, nutrients, wastes, ions, hormones, and other substances to and from the cells where exchanges are made; pumping action of the heart propels blood through the blood vessels • Protects body with blood clots, antibodies, and other protein molecules in the blood
Lymphatic/immune	Lymphatic vessels, lymph nodes, spleen, thymus, and tonsils	• Picks up fluid leaked from the blood vessels and returns it to the blood • Cleanses blood of pathogens and other debris • Houses cells (lymphocytes and others) that act in the immune response to protect the body from foreign substances (antigens)
Respiratory	Nose, pharynx, larynx, trachea, bronchi, and lungs	• Keeps the blood continuously supplied with oxygen while removing carbon dioxide • Contributes to the acid-base balance of the blood via its carbonic acid/bicarbonate buffer system
Digestive	Mouth, esophagus, stomach, small and large intestines, and accessory structures (teeth, salivary glands, liver, gallbladder, and pancreas)	• Breaks down ingested foods to tiny particles, which can be absorbed into the blood for delivery to the body's cells • Undigested residue leaves the body as feces
Urinary	Kidneys, ureters, urinary bladder, and urethra	• Filters the blood and then rids the body of nitrogen-containing wastes (urea, uric acid, and ammonia), which result from the breakdown of proteins and nucleic acids by the body's cells • Maintains water, electrolyte, and acid-base balance of blood
Reproductive	Male: testes, scrotum, penis, and duct system, which carries sperm to the body exterior	• Produces germ cells (sperm) for producing offspring
	Female: ovaries, uterine tubes, uterus, and vagina	• Produces germ cells (eggs) for producing offspring; the female uterus houses a developing fetus until birth

Activity 2

Observing External Structures

1. If a predissected rat is available, go to the demonstration area to make your observations. Alternatively, if you and/or members of your group will be dissecting the specimen, obtain a preserved or freshly killed rat (one for every two to four students), a dissecting tray, dissecting pins or twine, scissors, forceps, and disposable gloves and bring them to your laboratory bench.

⚠ 2. Don the gloves before beginning your observations. This precaution is particularly important when you are handling freshly killed animals, which may harbor internal parasites.

3. Observe the major divisions of the animal's body—head, trunk, and extremities. Compare these divisions to those of humans.

Activity 3

Examining the Mouth (Oral Cavity)

Examine the structures of the mouth or oral cavity, the most superior part of the digestive system. Identify the teeth and tongue. Observe the hard palate (the part supported by bone) and the soft palate (immediately posterior to the hard palate and with no bony support). Notice that the posterior end of the oral cavity leads into the throat, or pharynx, a passageway used by both the digestive and respiratory systems.

Activity 4

Opening the Ventral Body Cavity

1. Pin the animal to the wax of the dissecting tray by placing its dorsal side down and securing its extremities to wax, as shown in **Figure 2.1a**. If the dissecting tray

Text continues on next page. →

Figure 2.1 Rat dissection: Securing for dissection and the initial incision.
(a) Securing the rat to the dissection tray with dissecting pins. **(b)** Using scissors to make the incision on the median line of the abdominal region. **(c)** Completed incision from the pelvic region to the lower jaw. **(d)** Reflecting (folding back) the skin to expose the underlying muscles.

(a)

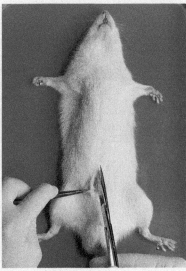

(b)

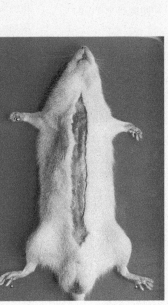

(c)

(d)

is not waxed or if the specimen has been preserved, you will need to secure the animal with twine; to do so, make a loop knot around one upper limb, pass the twine under the tray, and secure the opposing limb. (Repeat for the lower extremities.)

2. Lift the abdominal skin with a forceps, and cut through it with the scissors (Figure 2.1b). Close the scissor blades, and insert them under the cut skin. Moving in a cephalad direction, open and close the blades to loosen the skin from the underlying connective tissue and muscle. Once you have completed this skin-freeing procedure, cut the skin along the body midline, from the pubic region to the lower jaw (Figure 2.1c). Make a lateral cut about halfway down the ventral surface of each limb. Complete the job of freeing the skin with the scissor tips, and pin the flaps to the tray (Figure 2.1d) if possible. The underlying tissue that is now exposed is the skeletal musculature of the body wall and limbs, which allows voluntary body movement. Notice that the muscles are packaged in sheets of pearly white connective tissue (fascia), which protect the muscles and bind them together.

3. Carefully cut through the muscles of the abdominal wall in the pubic region, avoiding the underlying organs. Remember, *to dissect* means "to separate"—not mutilate! Now, hold and lift the muscle layer with a forceps, and cut through the muscle layer from the pubic region to the bottom of the rib cage. Make two lateral cuts through the rib cage (**Figure 2.2**). A thin membrane attached to the inferior boundary of the rib cage should be obvious: this is the **diaphragm**, which separates the

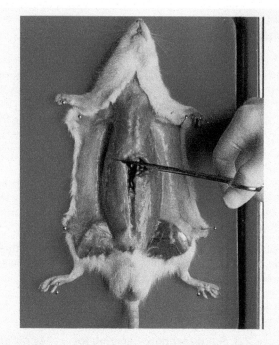

Figure 2.2 Rat dissection: Opening the ventral body cavity. Making lateral cuts at the base of the rib cage.

thoracic and abdominal cavities. Cut the diaphragm away to loosen the rib cage, and cut through the rib cage on either side. You can now lift the ribs to view the contents of the thoracic cavity.

Activity 5

Examining the Ventral Body Cavity

1. Examine the structures of the thoracic cavity, starting with the most superficial structures and working deeper. As you work, refer to **Figure 2.3**, which shows the superficial thoracic organs.

Thymus: An irregular mass of glandular tissue overlying the heart.

With a probe, push the thymus to the side to view the heart.

Heart: Medial oval structure that lies between the lungs.

Lungs: Multilobed organs flanking the heart on either side.

Now observe the throat region to identify the trachea.

Trachea: Tubelike "windpipe" running medially down the throat; part of the respiratory system.

Follow the trachea into the thoracic cavity. Notice where it divides into two branches—these are the bronchi.

Bronchi: Two passageways that plunge laterally into the tissue of the two lungs.

To expose the esophagus, push the trachea to one side.

Esophagus: A food chute; the part of the digestive system that transports food from the pharynx (throat) to the stomach.

Diaphragm: A thin muscle attached to the inferior boundary of the rib cage; separates the thoracic and abdominopelvic cavities.

Follow the esophagus through the diaphragm to its junction with the stomach.

Stomach: A C-shaped organ important in food digestion and temporary food storage.

2. Examine the superficial structures of the abdominopelvic cavity. Lift the *greater omentum,* an apronlike membrane fold that covers the abdominal organs. Continuing from the stomach, trace the rest of the digestive tract (Figure 2.3).

Small intestine: A long coiled tube connected to the stomach and ending just before the saclike cecum.

Large intestine: A large muscular tube coiled within the abdomen.

Follow the course of the large intestine, which begins at the saclike cecum, frames the small intestine, and ends at the rectum. Notice that it is partially covered by the urinary bladder.

Rectum: Terminal part of the large intestine; continuous with the anal canal.

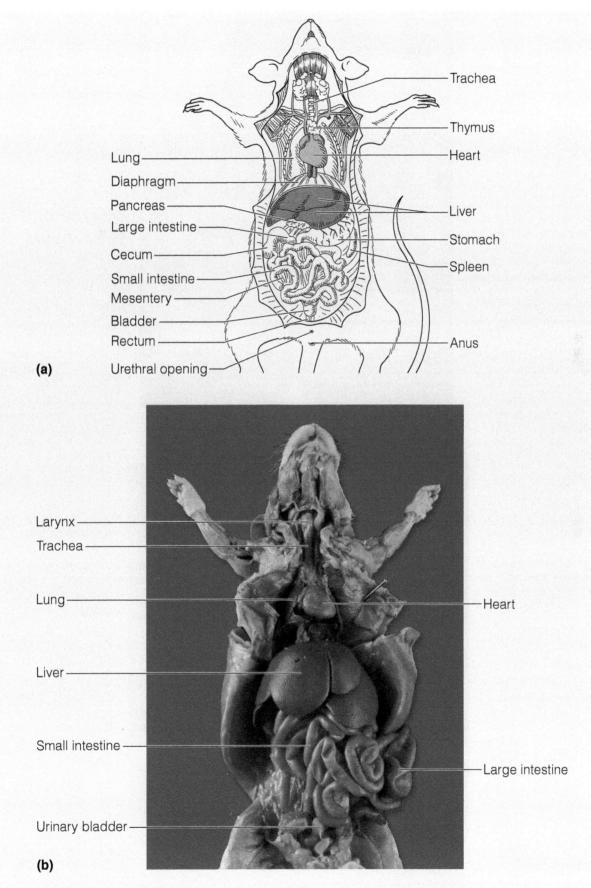

Figure 2.3 Rat dissection: Superficial organs of the thoracic and abdominal cavities.
(a) Diagrammatic view. **(b)** Photograph.

Text continues on page 15. →

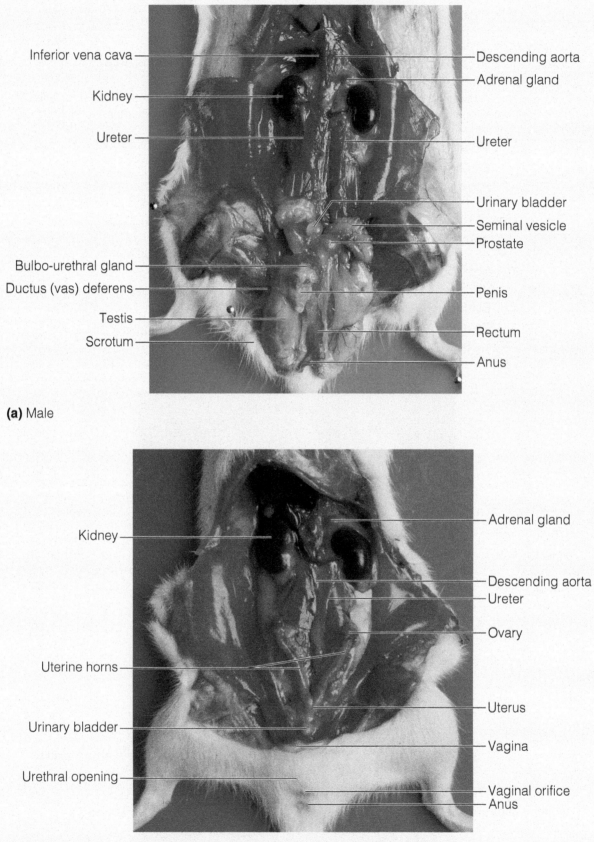

(a) Male

Inferior vena cava
Kidney
Ureter
Bulbo-urethral gland
Ductus (vas) deferens
Testis
Scrotum

Descending aorta
Adrenal gland
Ureter
Urinary bladder
Seminal vesicle
Prostate
Penis
Rectum
Anus

(b) Female

Kidney
Uterine horns
Urinary bladder
Urethral opening

Adrenal gland
Descending aorta
Ureter
Ovary
Uterus
Vagina
Vaginal orifice
Anus

Figure 2.4 Rat dissection: Deeper organs of the abdominal cavity and the reproductive structures.

Anus: The opening of the digestive tract (anal canal) to the exterior.

Now lift the small intestine with the forceps to view the mesentery.

Mesentery: A delicate membrane; suspends the small intestine in the abdominal cavity. Notice that it is heavily invested with blood vessels and is most likely riddled with fat deposits.

Locate the remaining abdominal structures.

Pancreas: A diffuse gland; rests posterior to and between the first portion of the small intestine and the stomach. You will need to lift the stomach to view the pancreas.

Spleen: A dark red organ curving around the left lateral side of the stomach; considered part of the lymphatic system.

Liver: Large and brownish red; the most superior organ in the abdominal cavity, directly inferior to the diaphragm.

3. To locate the deeper structures of the abdominopelvic cavity, move the stomach and the intestines to one side with the probe. (Refer to **Figure 2.4** as you work.)

Examine the posterior wall of the abdominal cavity to locate the two kidneys.

Kidneys: Bean-shaped organs; secured to the posterior wall of the body trunk.

Adrenal glands: Large glands that sit on the superior margin of each kidney; considered part of the endocrine system.

Carefully strip away part of the membrane covering a kidney with forceps. Attempt to follow the course of one of the ureters to the bladder.

Ureter: Tube running from the indented region of a kidney to the urinary bladder.

Urinary bladder: The sac in the pelvis that serves as a reservoir for urine.

4. In the midline of the body cavity lying between the kidneys are the two principal abdominal blood vessels. Identify each.

Inferior vena cava: The large vein that returns blood to the heart from the lower regions of the body.

Descending aorta: Deep to the inferior vena cava; the largest artery of the body; carries blood away from the heart down the midline of the body.

5. You will perform only a cursory examination of reproductive organs. First determine whether the animal is a male or female. Observe the ventral body surface beneath the tail. If a saclike scrotum and a single body opening are visible, the animal is a male. If three body openings are present, it is a female. (See Figure 2.4.)

Male Animal

Make a shallow incision into the **scrotum.** Loosen and lift out the oval **testis.** Pull very gently on the testis to identify the slender **ductus deferens,** or sperm duct, which carries sperm from the testis superiorly into the abdominal cavity and joins with the urethra. The urethra runs through the penis of the male and carries both urine and sperm out of the body. Identify the **penis,** extending from the bladder to the ventral body wall. Figure 2.4a indicates other glands of the male reproductive system, but you don't need to identify them at this time.

Female Animal

Inspect the pelvic cavity to identify the Y-shaped **uterus** lying against the dorsal body wall and beneath the bladder (Figure 2.4b). Follow one of the uterine horns superiorly to identify an **ovary,** a small oval structure at the end of the uterine horn. (The rat uterus is quite different from the uterus of a human female, which is a single-chambered organ about the size and shape of a pear.) The inferior undivided part of the rat uterus opens into the **vagina,** which leads to the body exterior. Identify the **vaginal orifice** (external vaginal opening).

OBJECTIVE 2   Identify several organs on a dissectible human torso model, and, given a list of organs, assign each to the correct organ system.

Activity 6

Examining the Human Torso Model

1. Examine a human torso model to identify the organs listed below. If a torso model is not available, **Figure 2.5** may serve as a reference for part of this exercise. Some model organs will have to be removed for you to see deeper organs.

Dorsal body cavity: Brain, spinal cord.

Thoracic cavity: Heart, lungs, bronchi, trachea, esophagus, diaphragm, thyroid gland.

Abdominopelvic cavity: Liver, gallbladder, stomach, pancreas, spleen, small intestine, large intestine, rectum, kidneys, ureters, bladder, adrenal glands, uterus, descending aorta, inferior vena cava.

2. Before continuing, identify each organ with a leader line in Figure 2.5 on page 16.

3. Assign each of the organs you identified on Figure 2.5 to one of the following organ system categories.

Digestive: _____

_____

Urinary: _____

_____

Cardiovascular: _____

_____

Text continues on next page. →

Endocrine: _____

_____

Reproductive: _____

Respiratory: _____

_____

Lymphatic: _____

Nervous: _____

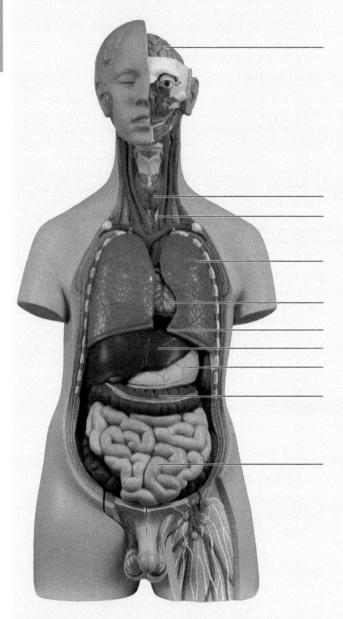

Figure 2.5 Human torso model.

REVIEW SHEET
Organ Systems Overview

Name _____ Lab Time/Date _____

1. Using the key choices, indicate the body systems that match the following descriptions. (Some choices may be used more than once.) Then, circle the organ systems (in the key) that are present in all subdivisions of the ventral body cavity (thoracic, abdominal, and pelvic cavities).

   Key: cardiovascular   integumentary   nervous   skeletal
           digestive   lymphatic   reproductive   urinary
           endocrine   muscular   respiratory

   _____ 1. rids the body of nitrogen-containing wastes

   _____ 2. is affected by removal of the adrenal gland

   _____ 3. protects and supports body organs; provides a framework for muscular action

   _____ 4. includes arteries and veins

   _____ 5. controls the body by means of chemicals called hormones

   _____ 6. external body covering

   _____ 7. houses cells involved in the body's immune response

   _____ 8. breaks down ingested food into its absorbable units

   _____ 9. loads oxygen into the blood

   _____ 10. uses blood as a transport vehicle

   _____ 11. generates body heat and provides for movement of the body as a whole

   _____ 12. regulates water and acid-base balance of the blood

   _____ and _____ 13. necessary for childbearing

   _____ 14. is damaged when you fall and scrape your knee

2. Using the above key, choose the *organ system* to which each of the following sets of organs or body structures belongs:

   _____ 1. lymph nodes, spleen, lymphatic   _____ 5. trachea, bronchi, alveoli
                     vessels
                                                            _____ 6. uterus, ovaries, vagina
   _____ 2. bones, cartilages, ligaments
                                                            _____ 7. arteries, veins, heart
   _____ 3. thyroid, thymus, pituitary
                                                            _____ 8. esophagus, large intestine, rectum
   _____ 4. skin, nails, hair

3. Using the key below, place the following organs in their proper body cavity:

   Key: abdominopelvic   cranial   spinal   thoracic

   _____   1. stomach   _____   6. urinary bladder

   _____   2. esophagus   _____   7. heart

   _____   3. large intestine _____   8. trachea

   _____   4. liver   _____   9. brain

   _____   5. spinal cord   _____ 10. rectum

4. Using the organs listed in item 3 above, record, by number, which would be found in the following abdominal regions:

   _____   1. hypogastric region   _____   4. epigastric region

   _____   2. right lumbar region   _____   5. left iliac region

   _____   3. umbilical region   _____   6. left hypochondriac region

5. The five levels of organization of a living body, beginning with the cell, are as follows: cell, _____,

   _____, _____, and organism.

6. Define *organ:* _____

   _____

7. Using the terms provided, correctly identify all of the body organs provided with leader lines in the drawings below.
   Then name the organ systems by entering the name of each on the answer blank below each drawing.

   Key: blood vessels   heart   nerves   spinal cord   urethra
            brain   kidney   sensory organ   ureter   urinary bladder

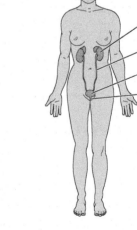

   1. _____   2. _____   3. _____

The Cell—Anatomy and Division

Materials

☐ Three-dimensional model of the "composite" animal cell or laboratory chart of cell anatomy

☐ Pipe cleaners and chalk

☐ Three-dimensional models of mitotic stages

☐ Demonstration area:

Station 1: Compound microscopes set up and focused on slides of four tissue samples for student observation (simple squamous epithelium [AgNO₃ stain], teased smooth muscle, human blood cell smear, and sperm)

Station 2: Compound microscopes set up and focused with pointers on whitefish blastula cells exhibiting the major phases of mitosis (prophase, metaphase, anaphase, and telophase)

Pre-Lab Quiz

1. Define *cell.* _____

_____

2. When a cell is not dividing, the genetic material is loosely dispersed throughout the nucleus in a threadlike form called:
   a. chromatin   c. cytosol
   b. chromosomes   d. ribosomes

3. Name the organelles that are the sites of protein synthesis. _____

_____

4. Which organelles are responsible for providing the bulk of ATP needed by the cell and are therefore often referred to as the "powerhouses" of the cell?
   a. centrioles   c. mitochondria
   b. lysosomes   d. ribosomes

5. Circle the correct term. During cytokinesis / interphase, the cell grows and carries out its usual activities.

6. DNA replication occurs during:
   a. cytokinesis   c. metaphase
   b. interphase   d. prophase

The **cell,** the structural and functional unit of all living things, is very complex. Differences in size, shape, and internal makeup of the cells of the human body reflect their specific roles in the body. Nonetheless, cells do have many common features and functions. For example, all cells maintain their boundaries, metabolize, digest nutrients and dispose of wastes, grow and reproduce, move, and respond to a stimulus. The structures of the cell allow it to carry out all of these functions. Cell division, or cell replication, is essential to the survival of almost all cells. In this exercise, we will focus on the structures typical of the "composite," or "generalized," cell, the functions of those structures, and the pathway of cell division.

Anatomy of the Composite Cell

OBJECTIVE 1   Name, identify, and list the major function(s) of the various cell structures.

All animal cells have three major regions, or parts: **nucleus, plasma membrane,** and **cytoplasm.** The nucleus is typically a round or oval structure near the center of the cell. It is surrounded by cytoplasm, which in turn is enclosed by the plasma membrane. Within the cytoplasm, even smaller cell structures—organelles—have been identified. **Figure 3.1** is a diagram of the internal structure of the composite cell.

Nucleus

The nucleus is the control center of the cell and is necessary for cell division, or cell replication. A cell that has lost or ejected its nucleus (for whatever reason) is programmed to die.

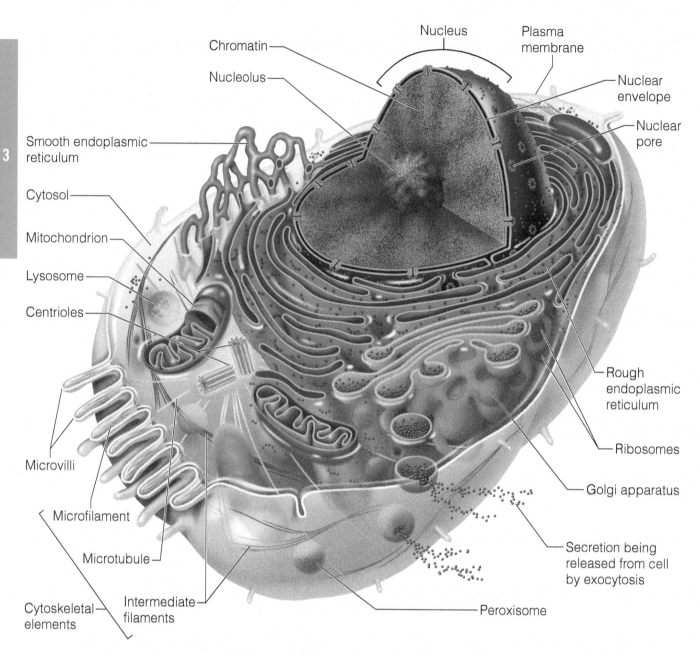

Figure 3.1 **Structure of the generalized cell.** Not all cells contain all the structures shown.

The nucleus is the structure that houses and protects the DNA (genetic material). When the cell is not dividing, that genetic material is in a threadlike form called **chromatin.** When a cell is dividing to form daughter cells, the chromatin coils and condenses to form darkly staining rodlike bodies called **chromosomes**—much in the way a stretched spring becomes shorter and thicker when it is released. (Cell division is discussed later in this exercise.)

The nucleus also contains one or more small round bodies, called **nucleoli** (singular: **nucleolus**). The nucleoli are assembly sites for ribosomes (particularly abundant in the cytoplasm), which are the actual protein-synthesizing "factories."

The nucleus is bound by a double-layered porous membrane, the **nuclear envelope,** or **nuclear membrane.** The nuclear membrane is similar to other cellular membranes, but it has particularly large *nuclear pores,* which permit large molecules such as protein and RNA molecules to pass easily.

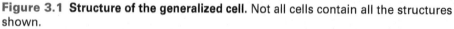

Identifying Parts of a Cell

Locate the nuclear membrane, chromatin, nucleoli, and the nuclear pores in Figure 3.1.

Plasma Membrane

The **plasma membrane** separates cell contents (its "inside") from the surrounding environment (its "outside"). The plasma membrane is made of a phospholipid bilayer. The membrane also contains some proteins. These proteins can allow for cell adhesion, cellular transport, and communication. The proteins can have other molecules attached, such as carbohydrates (**Figure 3.2**). Cholesterol molecules scattered here and there in the fluid phospholipid bilayer help to stabilize it.

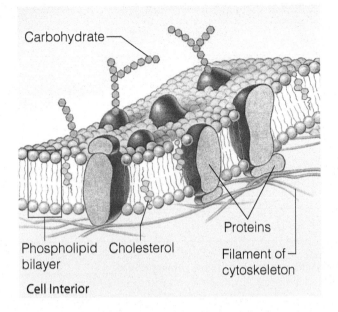

Carbohydrate

Proteins

Phospholipid   Cholesterol

Filament of cytoskeleton

Cell Interior

Figure 3.2 Structure of the plasma membrane.

Besides protecting the cell, the plasma membrane determines which substances may enter or leave the cell and in what amount. In some cells, the membrane has **microvilli,** very small fingerlike projections that greatly increase the

surface area of the cell. Increased surface area allows the cell to have greater absorption or secretion.

Activity 2

Identifying Components of a Plasma Membrane

Identify the phospholipid and protein parts of the plasma membrane in Figure 3.2. Also locate the sugar side chains and cholesterol molecules. Identify the microvilli in Figure 3.1.

Cytoplasm and Organelles

The cytoplasm is the cell contents outside the nucleus and is the major site of most activities carried out by the cell. Suspended in the **cytosol,** the fluid part of the cytoplasm, are tiny structures called **organelles** (literally, "small organs"). The organelles (Table 3.1) are the metabolic machinery of the cell, and they are highly organized to carry out specific activities for the cell as a whole.

The cell cytoplasm contains various other substances and structures, including stored foods (glycogen granules and lipid droplets), pigment granules, crystals of various types, water vacuoles, and ingested foreign materials. But these are not part of the active metabolic machinery of the cell and are therefore called **inclusions.**

Table 3.1	Summary of Structure and Function of Cytoplasmic Organelles
Organelle	**Location and function**
Ribosomes	Tiny spherical bodies composed of RNA and protein; actual sites of protein synthesis; seen floating free or attached to a membranous structure (the rough ER) in the cytoplasm
Endoplasmic reticulum (ER)	Membranous system of tubules that extends throughout the cytoplasm; two varieties: (1) rough ER—studded with ribosomes (tubules of the rough ER provide an area for proteins made on the ribosomes to be transported to other cell areas; external face synthesizes phospholipids and cholesterol) and (2) smooth ER—a site of steroid and lipid synthesis, lipid metabolism, and drug detoxification (no protein synthesis–related function)
Golgi apparatus	Stack of flattened sacs with swollen ends and associated small vesicles; found close to the nucleus; plays a role in packaging proteins or other substances for export from the cell or incorporation into the plasma membrane and in packaging lysosomal enzymes
Lysosomes	Various-sized membranous sacs containing digestive enzymes (acid hydrolases); act to digest worn-out cell organelles and foreign substances that enter the cell; if ruptured, they have the capacity to totally destroy the cell
Peroxisomes	Small lysosome-like membranous sacs containing oxidase enzymes that detoxify alcohol, hydrogen peroxide, and other harmful chemicals
Mitochondria	Generally rod-shaped bodies with a double-membrane wall; inner membrane is thrown into folds, or cristae; contain enzymes that oxidize foodstuffs to produce cellular energy (ATP); often referred to as "powerhouses of the cell"
Centrioles	Paired, cylindrical bodies lie at right angles to each other, close to the nucleus; direct the formation of the mitotic spindle during cell division; form the bases of cilia and flagella
Cytoskeletal elements: microtubules, intermediate filaments, and microfilaments	Provide cellular support; function in intracellular transport; microtubules form the internal structure of the centrioles and help determine cell shape; intermediate filaments, stable elements composed of a variety of proteins, resist mechanical forces acting on cells; microfilaments (formed largely of actin, a contractile protein) are important in cell mobility (particularly in muscle cells)

3

Activity 3

Locating Organelles

• Read through the material in Table 3.1, and then locate the organelles in Figure 3.1.

• Once you have located all of the structures in Figure 3.1, examine the cell model (or cell chart) to repeat and reinforce your identifications. Try not to look at the figure as you make your identifications.

OBJECTIVE 2   Compare and contrast specialized cells to generalized cells.

Activity 4

Observing Differences and Similarities in Cell Structure

1. Go to station 1 of the demonstration area, and examine the slides of simple squamous epithelium, sperm, teased smooth muscle cells, and human blood.

2. Observe each slide under the microscope carefully, noting similarities and differences in the four kinds of cells. Notice the cell shape and position of the nucleus in each case. When you look at the human blood smear, direct your attention to the red blood cells, the pink-stained cells that are most numerous. Sketch your observations in the circles provided below.

3. How do these four cell types differ in shape?

_____

_____

_____

_____

_____

_____

How might cell shape affect cell function?

_____

_____

_____

_____

_____

_____

Which cells have visible projections? _____

How do these projections relate to the function of these cells?

_____

_____

Do any of these cells lack a plasma membrane? If so, which?

_____

A nucleus? _____

Were you able to observe any of the organelles in these cells?

_____ Why or why not? _____

_____

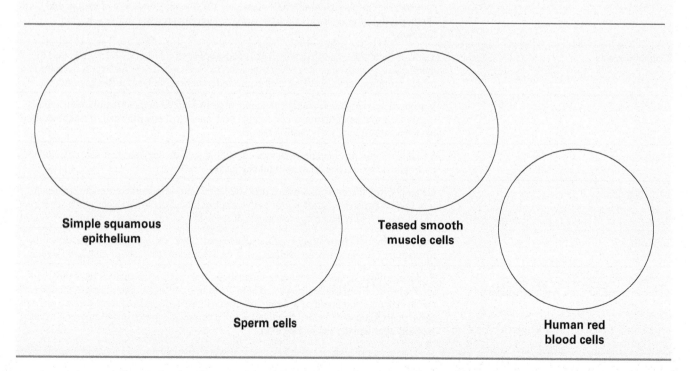

Simple squamous epithelium

Sperm cells

Teased smooth muscle cells

Human red blood cells

Cell Division: Mitosis and Cytokinesis

OBJECTIVE 3 Define *interphase, mitosis,* and *cytokinesis,* and list and describe (and/or identify) the stages of mitosis.

The **cell cycle** is a series of events that most cells complete during their life span. It includes two stages—**interphase,** the longer period when the cell grows and carries out its usual activities, and **cell division,** when the cell reproduces itself by dividing. In an interphase cell about to divide, the genetic material (DNA) is replicated. Once this important event has occurred, cell division occurs.

Cell division in all cells other than bacteria consists of a series of events collectively called mitosis and cytokinesis. **Mitosis** is nuclear division; **cytokinesis** is the division of the cytoplasm, which begins after mitosis is nearly complete. Although mitosis is usually accompanied by cytokinesis, sometimes division of the cytoplasm does not occur, and binucleate (or multinucleate) cells are formed. This is relatively common in the human liver and during embryonic development of skeletal muscle cells.

The products of **mitosis** are two daughter nuclei that are genetically identical to the mother nucleus. The function of

mitotic cell division in the body is to increase the number of cells for growth and repair.

The stages of mitosis illustrated in **Figure 3.3** include the following events:

Prophase (Figure 3.3b and c): As cell division begins, the chromatin threads coil and shorten to form densely staining, short, barlike **chromosomes.** By the middle of prophase, the chromosomes are obviously double-stranded structures (each strand is a **chromatid**) connected by a buttonlike body called a **centromere.** The centrioles separate from one another and direct the assembly of a system of microtubules called the **mitotic spindle** between them. The spindle acts as a scaffolding to which the chromosomes attach and are moved along during later mitotic stages. Meanwhile, the nuclear envelope and the nucleolus break down and disappear.

Metaphase (Figure 3.3d): In this brief stage, the chromosomes line up along the central plane, or metaphase plate.

Anaphase (Figure 3.3e): During anaphase, the centromeres split, and the chromatids (now called chromosomes again) separate from one another and then move slowly toward

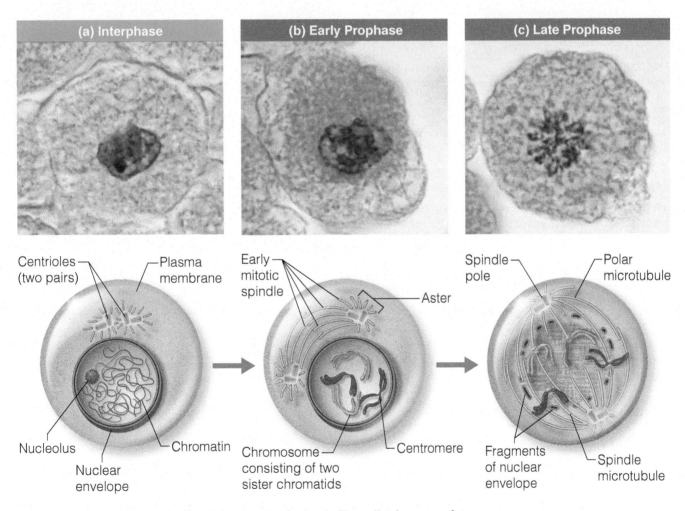

Figure 3.3 The interphase cell and the stages of mitosis. The cells shown are from an early embryo of a whitefish. Photomicrographs are above; corresponding diagrams are below. (Micrographs approximately 1600×.)

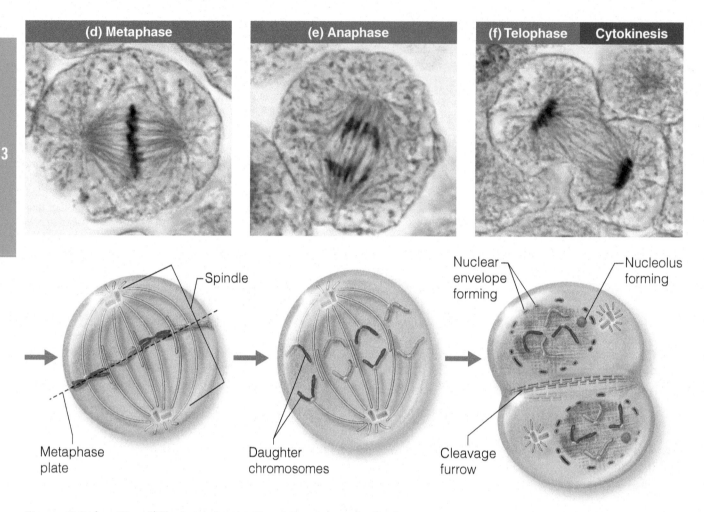

Figure 3.3 *(continued)* **The interphase cell and the stages of mitosis.**

opposite ends of the cell with their "arms" dangling behind them. Anaphase is complete when poleward movement ceases.

Telophase (Figure 3.3f): Events of prophase are reversed. The chromosomes uncoil and resume the chromatin form, the spindle breaks down and disappears, a nuclear envelope forms around each chromatin mass, and nucleoli appear in the daughter nuclei.

Cytokinesis typically begins in late anaphase and continues through telophase (Figure 3.3f) and provides a good clue for where to look for the mitotic structures visible in telophase. In animal cells, a *cleavage furrow* begins to form approximately over the equator of the spindle and eventually pinches the original cytoplasmic mass into two parts. Once formed, the daughter cells grow and carry out the normal spectrum of metabolic processes until it is their turn to divide.

Activity 5

Identifying the Mitotic Stages

1. Use the three-dimensional models of dividing cells to identify each of the mitotic states.

2. Go to station 2 of the demonstration area, where slides of whitefish blastulae are set up for your microscopic study of mitosis. The cells of each *blastula* (a stage of embryonic development consisting of a hollow ball of cells) are at approximately the same mitotic stage, so it is necessary to observe more than one blastula to view all the mitotic stages. A good analogy for a blastula is a soccer ball in which each of the multisided leather pieces making up the ball's surface represents an embryonic cell.

Examine the slides carefully, identifying the four mitotic stages and the process of cytokinesis. Compare your observations with Figure 3.3.

Activity 6

Creating Mitotic Figures

1. Obtain a packet of pipe cleaners and a piece of chalk from the supply area, and bring them to your bench.

2. Using the chalk, draw three representations of mitotic spindles on the bench top. Then bend pipe cleaners as necessary to create the typical appearance and location of chromosomes in (1) prophase, (2) metaphase, and (3) anaphase by placing them on your spindle drawings.

3. Have your instructor check your figures of mitosis before you clean up your bench top.

REVIEW SHEET
The Cell—Anatomy and Division

Name _____   LabTime/Date _____

Anatomy of the Composite Cell

1. Define the following:

   Organelle: _____

   _____

   Cell: _____

2. Identify the following cell parts:

   _____ 1. external boundary of cell; regulates flow of materials into and out of the cell

   _____ 2. contains digestive enzymes of many varieties; can destroy the entire cell

   _____ 3. scattered throughout the cell; major site of ATP synthesis

   _____ 4. slender extensions of the plasma membrane that increase its surface area

   _____ 5. stored glycogen granules, crystals, pigments

   _____ 6. membranous system consisting of flattened sacs and vesicles; packages proteins for export

   _____ 7. control center of the cell; necessary for cell division and cell life

   _____ 8. two rod-shaped bodies near the nucleus; the basis of cilia

   _____ 9. dense, darkly staining nuclear body; packaging site for ribosomes

   _____ 10. contractile elements of the cytoskeleton

   _____ 11. membranous system that has "rough" and "smooth" varieties

   _____ 12. attached to membrane systems or scattered in the cytoplasm; synthesize proteins

   _____ 13. threadlike structures in the nucleus; contain genetic material (DNA)

   _____ 14. site of detoxification of alcohol, hydrogen peroxide, and harmful chemicals

3. In the following diagram, label all parts provided with a leader line.

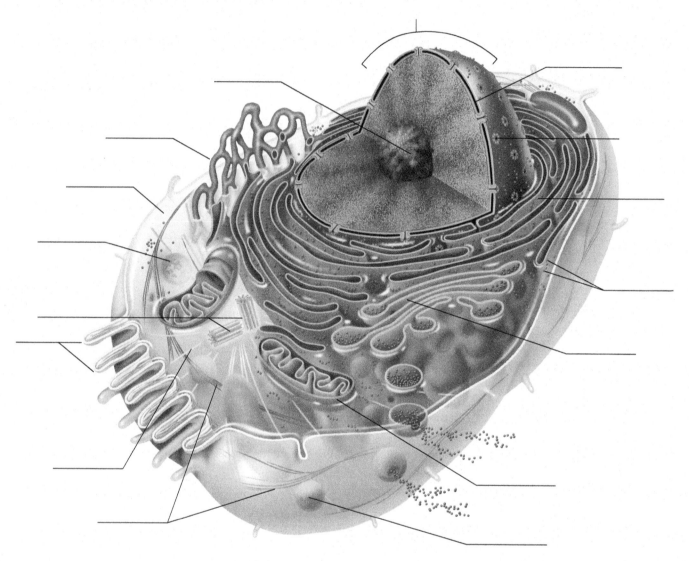

Differences and Similarities in Cell Structure

4. For each of the following cell types, on line (a) list *one* important *structural* characteristic observed in the laboratory. On line (b), write the *function* that the structure complements or ensures.

squamous epithelium   a. _____

                       b. _____

sperm   a. _____

                       b. _____

smooth muscle   a. _____

                       b. _____

red blood cells   a. _____

                       b. _____

5. What is the significance of the red blood cell being anucleate (without a nucleus)? _____

_____

Cell Division: Mitosis and Cytokinesis

6. What is the importance of mitotic cell division? _____

_____

7. Identify the three phases of mitosis shown in the following photomicrographs, and select the events from the key choices that correctly identify each phase. Write the key letters on the appropriate answer line.

Key:

a. Chromatin coils and condenses, forming chromosomes.

b. The chromosomes (chromatids) are V-shaped.

c. The nuclear envelope re-forms.

d. Chromosomes stop moving toward the poles.

e. Chromosomes line up in the center of the cell.

f. The nuclear envelope fragments.

g. The spindle forms.

h. DNA synthesis occurs.

i. Chromosomes first appear to be double.

j. Chromosomes attach to the spindle fibers.

k. The nuclear envelope(s) is absent.

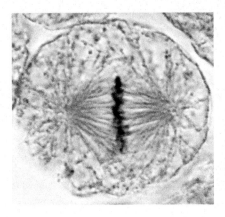
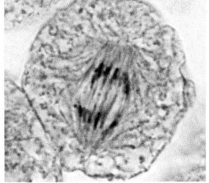

1. Phase: _____   2. Phase: _____   3. Phase: _____

   Events: _____   Events: _____   Events: _____

Cell Membrane Transport Mechanisms

Materials

Diffusion of Dye Through Agar Gel

☐ Forceps
☐ Petri dishes (2) containing 12 ml of 1.5% agar-agar
☐ 3.5% methylene blue solution (approximately 0.1 M)
☐ 1.6% potassium permanganate solution (approximately 0.1 M)
☐ Millimeter-ruled graph paper
☐ Medicine dropper

Diffusion Through Nonliving Membranes

☐ Four lengths of dialysis tubing or small "alligator" sandwich bags
☐ 15-ml graduated cylinders
☐ Four beakers (250 ml)
☐ Distilled water
☐ 40% glucose solution
☐ Fine twine or dialysis tubing clamps
☐ 10% NaCl solution
☐ 40% sucrose solution colored red with Congo red dye
☐ Laboratory balance
☐ Hot plate and large beaker for water bath
☐ Benedict's solution in dropper bottle
☐ Four test tubes in racks, test tube holder
☐ Wax marker
☐ Small syringes (without needles)
☐ Silver nitrate ($AgNO_3$) in dropper bottle
☐ Lugol's iodine solution in dropper bottle

Diffusion Through Living Membranes

☐ Three microscopes with blood cells suspended in the following:
  1. Physiological saline
  2. 1.5% saline
  3. Distilled water

Pre-Lab Quiz

1. Circle the correct term. A passive process, <u>diffusion</u> / <u>osmosis</u> is the movement of solute molecules from an area of their greater concentration to an area of their lesser concentration.

2. Circle the correct term. In <u>pinocytosis</u> / <u>phagocytosis</u>, parts of the plasma membrane and cytoplasm expand and flow around a relatively large or solid material and engulf it.

3. Circle the correct term. In <u>active</u> / <u>passive</u> processes, the cell provides energy in the form of ATP to power the transport process.

Because of its molecular makeup, the plasma membrane has **selective permeability.** The plasma membrane allows nutrients to enter the cell but keeps out undesirable substances. At the same time, valuable cell proteins and other substances are kept within the cell, and excreta, or wastes, pass to the exterior. Transport through the plasma membrane occurs in two basic ways. In **active transport,** the cell provides energy (ATP) to power the transport process. In **passive transport,** the transport process is driven by particle concentration or pressure differences. In this exercise we will observe several examples of passive transport processes.

Passive Transport Processes

OBJECTIVE 1 Define *diffusion,* and indicate the factors that determine the direction and speed of diffusion.

The two important types of passive membrane transport are *diffusion* and *filtration.* Diffusion is an important means of transport for every cell in the body. By contrast, filtration usually occurs only across capillary walls. Only diffusion will be considered here.

Diffusion

Molecules possess *kinetic energy* and are in constant motion. As molecules move about randomly, they collide and ricochet off one another, changing direction with each collision.

When a **concentration gradient** (difference in concentration) exists, the net effect of this random molecular movement is that the molecules eventually become evenly distributed throughout the environment. **Diffusion** is the movement of molecules from a region of their higher concentration to a region of their lower concentration. Its driving force is the kinetic energy of the molecules themselves. The rate of diffusion depends on the size of the molecule, the temperature, and the steepness of the concentration gradient. Smaller molecules, an increase in temperature, and the greater the steepness of the concentration gradient will all increase the rate of diffusion.

The diffusion of particles into and out of cells is controlled by the plasma membrane, a physical barrier. In general, molecules diffuse passively through the plasma membrane if they are small enough to pass through its pores or if they can dissolve in the lipid portion of the membrane (as in the case of CO_2 and O_2). The diffusion of solutes (particles dissolved in water) through a semipermeable membrane is called **simple diffusion.** The diffusion of water through a semipermeable membrane is called **osmosis.**

Molecules diffuse through a nondense medium (such as water) faster than through a denser or more viscous substance (e.g., agar gel). The next activity examines this relationship in the diffusion of two dyes.

Activity 1

Observing Diffusion of Dye Through Agar Gel

1. Obtain a Petri dish containing agar gel, millimeter-ruled graph paper, dropper bottles of methylene blue and potassium permanganate stain, and a medicine dropper. Bring these items to your bench.

2. Place the Petri dish on the graph paper.

3. Create a well in the center of each section using the medicine dropper (**Figure 4.1a**). To do this, squeeze the bulb of the medicine dropper, and push the tip of the dropper down into the agar. Release the bulb as you slowly pull the dropper out of the agar. This should remove an agar plug, leaving a well in the agar that goes all the way down to the bottom of the Petri dish.

4. Carefully fill one well with the methylene blue solution and the other with potassium permanganate solution (Figure 4.1b).

Record the time: _____.

5. At 15-minute intervals, measure the distance the dye has diffused from *each* solution source. Continue these observations for 1 hour, and record the results in the Activity 1 chart.

Which dye diffused more rapidly? _____

What is the relationship between molecular weight and rate of molecular movement (diffusion)?

_____

Why did the dye molecules move? _____

_____

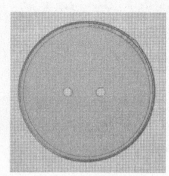

(a)

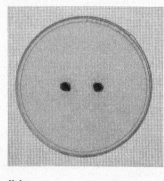

(b)

Figure 4.1 Setup for comparing the diffusion rates of molecules of methylene blue and potassium permanganate through an agar gel.

Compute the rate of diffusion of the potassium permanganate molecules in millimeters per minute (mm/min), and record.

_____ mm/min

Compute the rate of diffusion of the methylene blue molecules in mm/min, and record.

_____ mm/min

How would applying heat affect the rate of diffusion of

the dyes? _____

In molecular terms, what is the basis of this effect?

_____

_____

	Activity 1: Diffusion of Dye Through Agar Gel	
Time (min)	Diffusion of methylene blue (mm) at room temperature	Diffusion of potassium permanganate (mm) at room temperature
15		
30		
45		
60		

OBJECTIVE 2   Determine the direction of passive movement through a selectively permeable membrane (given appropriate information on concentration differences).

Activity 2

Observing Diffusion Through Nonliving Membranes

This experiment provides information on the diffusion of water and solutes through semipermeable membranes, which may be applied to the study of membrane transport in living cells.

1. Obtain four sections of dialysis tubing,* a small syringe, a graduated cylinder, a wax marker, fine twine or dialysis tubing clamps, and four beakers (250 ml). Number the beakers 1 to 4 with the wax marker. Fill beakers 1, 3, and 4 halfway with distilled water. Fill beaker 2 halfway with the 40% glucose solution (**Figure 4.2**).

2. Prepare the dialysis sacs one at a time. Close one end of the dialysis tubing by folding it over and securing it closed by tying it with twine or with a clamp (Figure 4.2). Using the syringe, half fill each with 10 ml of the specified

*Dialysis tubing is a selectively permeable membrane with pores of a particular size. The selectivity of living membranes depends on more than just pore size, but using the dialysis tubing will allow you to examine selectivity that is due to this factor.

liquid: 40% glucose solution for sacs 1 and 2; 10% NaCl solution for sac 3; and 40% sucrose solution with Congo red dye for sac 4 (see Figure 4.2). Press out the air, fold over the open end of the sac, and tie it securely with fine twine or clamp it. Before proceeding to the next sac, rinse it under the tap, and quickly and carefully blot the sac dry by rolling it on a paper towel. Weigh it with a laboratory balance. Record the weight, and then drop the sac into the corresponding beaker. Be sure the sac is completely covered by the beaker solution, adding more solution if necessary.

- Sac 1: 40% glucose solution. Weight: _____ g
- Sac 2: 40% glucose solution. Weight: _____ g
- Sac 3: 10% NaCl solution. Weight: _____ g
- Sac 4: Congo red dye in 40% sucrose. Weight: _____ g

Allow the sacs to remain undisturbed in the beakers for 1 hour. (Use this time to continue with other experiments.)

3. After an hour, get a beaker of water boiling on the hot plate. Obtain the supplies you will need to determine your experimental results: dropper bottles of Benedict's solution, silver nitrate solution, Lugol's iodine, a test tube rack, four test tubes, and a test tube holder.

Text continues on next page. →

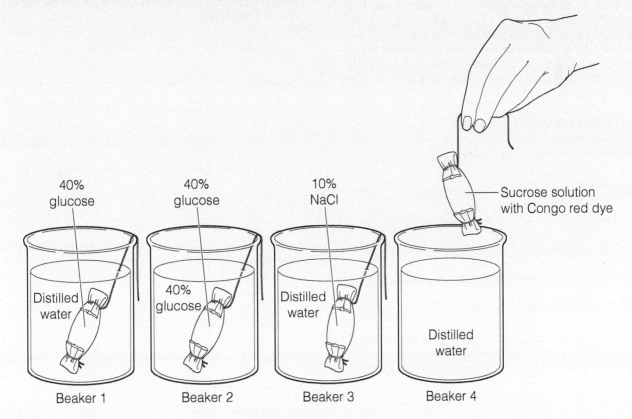

Figure 4.2 Setup for observing diffusion through nonliving membranes.

Table 4.1	Reagent Testing Solutions	
Testing solution	**Positive result**	
Benedict's solution	A green, yellow, or rusty red color indicates the presence of glucose	
Silver nitrate	A white precipitate or cloudiness indicates the presence of salt	
Lugol's iodine	A blue-black color indicates the presence of starch	

4. Quickly and gently blot sac 1 dry, and weigh it. (**Note:** Do not squeeze the sac during the blotting process.)

Weight of sac 1: _____ g

Has there been any change in weight? _____

Conclusions: _____

_____

_____

Place 2.5 ml of Benedict's solution in each of two test tubes. Put 2 ml of the fluid from beaker 1 into one test tube, and 2 ml of the fluid from sac 1 into the other. Mark the tubes for identification, and then place them in the beaker containing boiling water. Boil test tubes for 2 minutes, and then cool them slowly. (See Table 4.1 to interpret test results.)

Was glucose still present in the sac? _____

Was glucose present in the beaker? _____

Conclusions: _____

_____

_____

5. Blot gently and weigh sac 2: _____ g

Was there an *increase* or *decrease* in weight?_____

With 40% glucose in the sac and 40% glucose in the beaker, would you expect to see any net movements of water (osmosis) or of glucose molecules (simple diffusion)?

_____ Why or why not? _____

_____

6. Blot gently and weigh sac 3: _____ g

Was there any change in weight? _____

Conclusions: _____

_____

Take a 3-ml sample of beaker 3 solution, and put it in a clean test tube. Add a drop of silver nitrate. (See Table 4.1 to interpret results.)

Results: _____

Conclusions: _____

7. Blot gently and weigh sac 4: _____ g

Was there any change in weight? _____

Did the water turn pink? _____

Put a 1-ml sample of beaker 4 solution into a test tube, and put the test tube in boiling water in a hot water bath. Add 5 drops of Benedict's solution to the tube, and boil for 5 minutes. Benedict's solution detects the presence of glucose, a hydrolysis product of sucrose. (See Table 4.1.)

Based on this test, did sucrose from sac 4 diffuse into the beaker 4 solution?

_____ Explain your conclusion. _____

_____

8. In which of the test situations did net osmosis occur?

_____

In which of the test situations did net simple diffusion occur?

_____

What conclusions can you make about the relative size of glucose, sucrose, NaCl, Congo red, and water molecules?

_____

_____

_____

_____

With what cell structure can the dialysis sac be compared?

_____

Activity 3

Investigating Diffusion Through Living Membranes

Isotonic solution has the same concentration of solutes as the fluid found inside the cell.

Hypertonic solution has a higher concentration of solutes than the fluid found inside the cell.

Hypotonic solution has a lower concentration of solutes than the fluid found inside the cell.

To examine permeability properties of cell membranes, conduct the following microscopic study.

1. Go to the demonstration area, where three red blood cell suspensions have been prepared for microscopic observation. In slide 1, the red blood cells are suspended in physiological saline; in slide 2 they are bathed in 1.5% saline (NaCl), and in slide 3, the cells are suspended in distilled water. (Note that physiological saline is *isotonic* to the cells.)

2. View slide 1 to see whether any changes in the normal disclike shape of the red blood cells have occurred.

Observation: _____

3. Observe slide 2. What has happened to the red blood cells in this preparation?

_____

A solution of 1.5% saline is *hypertonic* to red blood cells. Based on what you know about the effect of such solutions on living cells, explain your observation.

_____

_____

4. Observe slide 3. What has happened to the cells in this preparation?

_____

Explain. _____

Active Transport Processes

OBJECTIVE 3   Compare active transport processes to passive processes studied relative to energy source and types of substances transported.

Whenever a cell uses the energy of ATP to move substances across its boundaries, the process is *active*. Substances moved by active means are generally unable to pass by diffusion. They may not be lipid soluble; they may be too large to pass through the membrane channels; or they may have to move against the concentration gradient. There are two types of active processes: *active transport* and *vesicular transport*.

Active transport requires carrier proteins that combine specifically with the transported substance. In most cases, the substances move against concentration or electrical gradients or both. Substances moved into the cells by such carriers include amino acids and some sugars. Both solutes are insoluble in lipid and too large to pass through membrane channels but are necessary for cell life. Sodium ions (Na^+) are ejected from cells by active transport. Carrier-mediated active transport is difficult to study in an anatomy and physiology laboratory and will not be considered further here.

Large particles and molecules are transported across the membrane by **vesicular transport.** Movement may be into the cell (**endocytosis**) or out of the cell (**exocytosis**).

In the type of endocytosis called **phagocytosis** ("cell eating"), parts of the plasma membrane and cytoplasm expand and flow around a relatively large or solid material (for example, bacteria or cell debris) and engulf it (**Figure 4.3a**). The membranous sac thus formed, called a *phagosome*, is then fused with a lysosome, and its contents are digested.

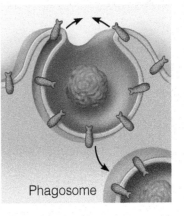

Phagosome

(a) Phagocytosis

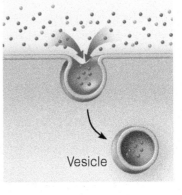

Vesicle

(b) Pinocytosis

Figure 4.3 Two types of endocytosis.
(a) Phagocytosis is a major means of moving large particles or molecules into the cell. **(b)** Pinocytosis moves liquids into the cell.

In the human body, phagocytic cells are mainly found among the white blood cells and macrophages that act as scavengers and help protect the body from disease-causing microorganisms and cancer cells.

In **pinocytosis** ("cell drinking"), the cell membrane sinks beneath the material to form a small vesicle, which then pinches off into the cell interior (see Figure 4.3b). Pinocytosis is most common for taking in liquids containing protein or fat.

EXERCISE 4

REVIEW SHEET

Cell Membrane Transport Mechanisms

Name _____ Lab Time/Date _____

Choose all answers that apply to items 1 and 2, and place their letters on the response blanks.

1. The motion of molecules _____.
   a. reflects the kinetic energy of molecules
   b. reflects the potential energy of molecules
   c. is ordered and predictable
   d. is random and erratic

2. The speed of molecular movement _____.
   a. is higher in larger molecules
   b. is lower in larger molecules
   c. increases with increasing temperature
   d. decreases with increasing temperature
   e. reflects kinetic energy

3. What is the relationship between density of the medium and diffusion rate? _____

   _____

4. The following refer to Activity 2, "Observing Diffusion Through Nonliving Membranes":

   Sac 1: 40% glucose suspended in distilled water

   Did glucose pass out of the sac? _____ Test used to determine presence of glucose: _____

   Did the sac weight change? _____ If so, explain the reason for its weight change: _____

   _____

   Sac 2: 40% glucose suspended in 40% glucose

   Was there net movement of glucose in either direction? _____

   Explanation: _____

   Did the sac weight change? _____ Explanation: _____

   _____

   Sac 3: 10% NaCl suspended in distilled water

   Was there net movement of NaCl out of the sac? _____

   Test used to determine the presence of NaCl: _____

   Direction of net osmosis: _____

Sac 4: Sucrose and Congo red dye suspended in distilled water

Was there net movement of dye out of the sac? _____

Was there net movement of sucrose out of the sac? _____

Explanation: _____

Test used to determine the movement of sucrose into the beaker: _____

Direction of net osmosis: _____

5. What single characteristic of the semipermeable membranes used in the laboratory determines the substances that

can pass through them? _____

In addition to this characteristic, what other factors influence the passage of substances through living membranes?

_____

6. A semipermeable sac containing 4% NaCl, 9% glucose, and 10% albumin is suspended in a solution with the following composition: 10% NaCl, 10% glucose, and 40% albumin. Assume that the sac is permeable to all substances except
albumin. State whether each of the following will (a) move into the sac, (b) move out of the sac, or (c) not move.

glucose _____   water _____   albumin _____   NaCl _____

7. The diagrams below represent three microscope fields containing red blood cells. Arrows show the direction of net
osmosis.

Which field contains a hypertonic solution? _____

The cells in this field are said to be _____.

Which field contains an isotonic bathing solution? _____Which field contains a hypotonic solution?_____

What is happening to the cells in this field? _____

(a)   **(b)**   **(c)**

8. Define *diffusion:* _____

_____

9. What determines whether a transport process is active or passive? _____

_____

10. Contrast phagocytosis and pinocytosis. _____

_____

Classification of Tissues

Materials

☐ Demonstration area with four microscope stations set up:

Station 1: Prepared slides of simple squamous, simple cuboidal, simple columnar, stratified squamous (nonkeratinized), pseudostratified ciliated columnar, and transitional epithelia

Station 2: Prepared slides of adipose, areolar, reticular, and dense regular (tendon) connective tissue; of hyaline cartilage; and of bone (cross section)

Station 3: Prepared slides of skeletal, cardiac, and smooth muscle (longitudinal sections)

Station 4: Prepared slide of nervous tissue (spinal cord smear)

Pre-Lab Quiz

1. How many primary tissue types are found in the human body? _____

2. Epithelial tissues can be classified according to cell shape. _____ epithelial cells are scalelike and flattened.
   a. Columnar   c. Squamous
   b. Cuboidal   d. Transitional

3. This type of epithelium lines the digestive tract from stomach to rectum.
   a. simple cuboidal   c. stratified squamous
   b. simple columnar   d. transitional

4. All the following are examples of connective tissue *except:*
   a. bones   c. neurons
   b. ligaments   d. tendons

5. Circle the correct term. Of the two major cell populations in nervous tissue, neurons / neuroglial cells are highly specialized to receive stimuli and conduct waves of excitation to all parts of the body.

6. This type of muscle tissue is found in the walls of hollow organs. It has no striations, and its cells are spindle-shaped. It is:
   a. cardiac muscle   b. skeletal muscle   c. smooth muscle

Cells are the building blocks of life. In humans and other multicellular organisms, cells depend on one another and cooperate to maintain homeostasis in the body.

With a few exceptions, even the most complex animal starts out as a single cell, the fertilized egg, which divides almost endlessly. The resulting trillions of cells then specialize for a particular function. Some become supportive bone, others skin cells, and so on. Thus a division of labor exists, with certain groups of cells highly specialized to perform functions that benefit the organism as a whole. Cell specialization provides for sophisticated functions but involves certain hazards, because when a small, specific group of cells is indispensable, any inability to function on its part can paralyze or destroy the entire body.

Groups of cells that are similar in structure and function are called **tissues.** The four primary tissue types—epithelial, connective, muscular, and nervous—have distinct structures, patterns, and functions.

To perform specific body functions, the tissues are organized into **organs** such as the heart, kidneys, and lungs. Most organs contain several representatives of the primary tissues, and the arrangement of these tissues determines the organ's structure and function. The main objective of this exercise is to familiarize you with the major similarities and dissimilarities of the primary tissues. Because we will not consider epithelium and some types of connective tissue again, we emphasize them more than muscle, nervous tissue, and bone (a connective tissue), which we cover in greater depth in later exercises.

Epithelial Tissue

OBJECTIVE 1   List the general structural characteristics, functions, and locations of epithelia in the body and identify the subcategories when presented with a diagram or slide.

Epithelial tissues, or **epithelia,** cover or line surfaces. For example, epithelia cover the external body surface (as the epidermis), line its cavities, and generally mark off our "insides" from our outsides. Because glands of the body almost always develop from epithelial membranes, glands too are classed as epithelia.

Epithelial functions include protection, absorption, filtration, excretion, secretion, and sometimes sensory reception. For example, the epithelium covering the body protects against bacterial invasion and chemical damage; that lining the respiratory tract is ciliated to sweep dust and other foreign particles away from the lungs. Secretion is a specialty of the glands, and taste receptors are epithelial cells.

Epithelia generally exhibit these characteristics:

• Cells fit closely together to form membranes, or sheets of cells, and are bound together by specialized junctions.

• The membranes always have one exposed surface or free edge, called the *apical surface.*

• The cells are attached to and supported by an adhesive **basement membrane,** a material secreted collectively by the epithelial cells and the connective tissue cells that lie next to each other.

• Epithelial tissues have no blood supply of their own (are avascular), but depend on diffusion of nutrients from the underlying connective tissue. (The exception is glandular epithelial tissue, which is very vascular.)

• If well nourished, epithelial cells can easily regenerate themselves. This is an important characteristic because many epithelia are subjected to a good deal of friction and other types of trauma.

The covering and lining epithelia are classified according to two criteria—relative number of layers and cell shape (height) (**Figure 5.1**). In regard to the number of layers, epithelia are classified as follows:

• **Simple** epithelia consist of one layer of cells attached to the basement membrane.

• **Stratified** epithelia consist of two or more layers of cells.

Based on cell shape, epithelia are classified into three categories:

• **Squamous** (scalelike)
• **Cuboidal** (cubelike)
• **Columnar** (column-shaped)

The terms denoting shape and arrangement of the epithelial cells are combined to describe the epithelium fully. *Stratified epithelia are named according to the cells at the apical surface of the epithelial membrane, not those resting on the basement membrane.*

There are also two less easily categorized types of epithelia. **Pseudostratified epithelium** is actually a simple columnar epithelium (one layer of cells with all cells attached to the basement membrane), but its cells extend varied distances from the basement membrane, so it gives the false appearance of being stratified. **Transitional epithelium** is a rather peculiar stratified squamous epithelium formed of rounded, or "plump," cells with the ability to slide over one another to allow the organ to be stretched. Transitional epithelium is found only in urinary system organs. The superficial cells are flattened (like true squamous cells) when the organ is distended, or full, and are rounded when the organ is empty.

The most common types of epithelia, their characteristic locations in the body, and their functions are described in **Figure 5.2**.

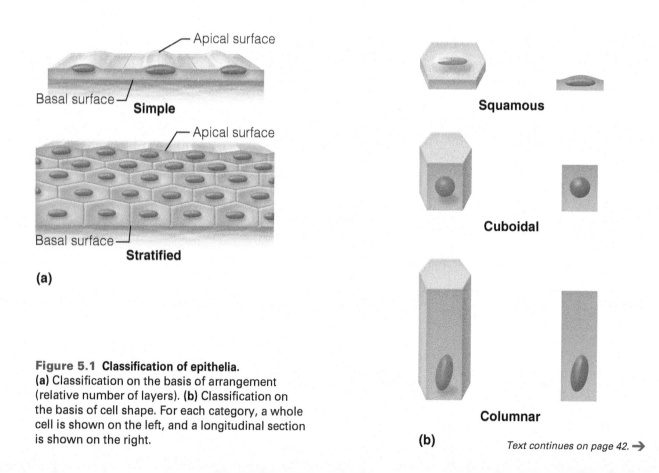

Figure 5.1 Classification of epithelia.
(a) Classification on the basis of arrangement (relative number of layers). **(b)** Classification on the basis of cell shape. For each category, a whole cell is shown on the left, and a longitudinal section is shown on the right.

Text continues on page 42. →

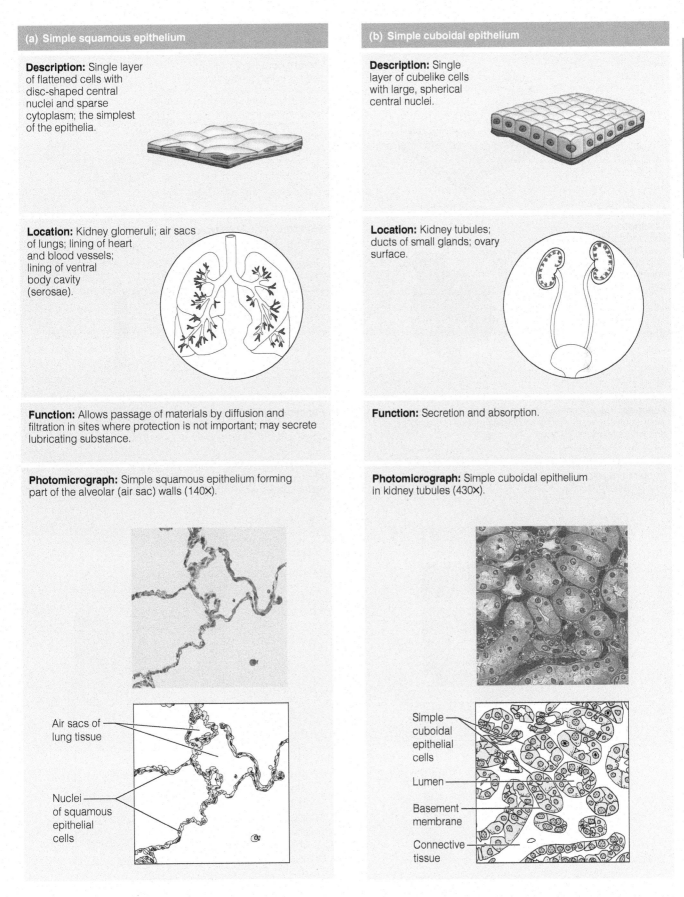

(a) Simple squamous epithelium

Description: Single layer of flattened cells with disc-shaped central nuclei and sparse cytoplasm; the simplest of the epithelia.

Location: Kidney glomeruli; air sacs of lungs; lining of heart and blood vessels; lining of ventral body cavity (serosae).

Function: Allows passage of materials by diffusion and filtration in sites where protection is not important; may secrete lubricating substance.

Photomicrograph: Simple squamous epithelium forming part of the alveolar (air sac) walls (140×).

Air sacs of lung tissue

Nuclei of squamous epithelial cells

(b) Simple cuboidal epithelium

Description: Single layer of cubelike cells with large, spherical central nuclei.

Location: Kidney tubules; ducts of small glands; ovary surface.

Function: Secretion and absorption.

Photomicrograph: Simple cuboidal epithelium in kidney tubules (430×).

Simple cuboidal epithelial cells

Lumen

Basement membrane

Connective tissue

Figure 5.2 Epithelial tissues. Simple epithelia **(a and b).**

Figure continues on next page. →

5

(c) Simple columnar epithelium

Description: Single layer of tall cells with *round* to *oval* nuclei; some cells bear cilia; layer may contain mucus-secreting goblet cells.

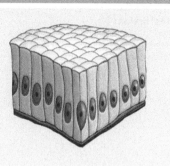

Location: Nonciliated type lines most of the digestive tract (stomach to rectum) and gallbladder; ciliated variety lines small bronchi and uterine tubes.

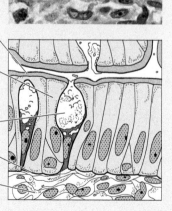

Function: Absorption; secretion of mucus, enzymes, and other substances; ciliated type propels mucus (or reproductive cells) by ciliary action.

Photomicrograph: Simple columnar epithelium of the small intestine mucosa (660×).

Microvilli (brush border)
Simple columnar epithelial cell
Goblet cell
Basement membrane
Connective tissue

(d) Pseudostratified columnar epithelium

Description: Single layer of cells of differing heights, some not reaching the free surface, but all touching the basement membrane; nuclei seen at different levels; may contain goblet cells and bear cilia.

Location: Nonciliated type in ducts of large glands, parts of male urethra; ciliated variety lines the trachea, most of the upper respiratory tract.

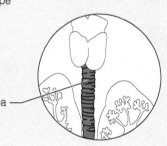

Trachea

Function: Secrete substances, particularly of mucus; propulsion of mucus by ciliary action.

Photomicrograph: Pseudostratified ciliated columnar epithelium lining the human trachea (530×).

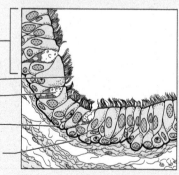

Pseudo-stratified epithelial layer
Cilia
Mucus of goblet cell
Basement membrane
Connective tissue

Figure 5.2 *(continued)* **Epithelial tissues.** Simple epithelia (**c** and **d**).
See also Plate 1 of the Histology Atlas to view simple columnar epithelium.

(e) Stratified squamous epithelium

Description: Thick membrane composed of several cell layers; basal cells are cuboidal or columnar; cells at the apical surface are flattened (squamous); in the keratinized type, the surface cells are full of keratin and dead; basal cells are active in mitosis and produce the cells of the more superficial layers.

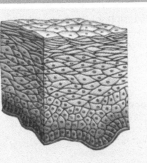

Location: Nonkeratinized type forms the moist linings of the esophagus, mouth, and vagina; keratinized variety forms the epidermis of the skin, a dry membrane.

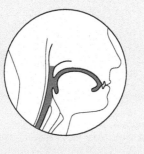

Function: Protects underlying tissues in areas subjected to abrasion.

Photomicrograph: Stratified squamous epithelium lining the esophagus (285×).

Nuclei

Basement membrane

Connective tissue

Stratified squamous epithelium

(f) Transitional epithelium

Description: Basal cells cuboidal or columnar; surface cells dome-shaped or squamouslike, depending on how much the organ is stretched.

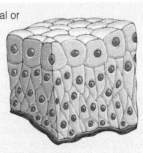

Location: Lines the ureters, urinary bladder, and part of the urethra.

Function: Stretches readily and permits distension of urinary organ by stored urine.

Photomicrograph: Transitional epithelium lining the bladder, relaxed state (360×); note the bulbous, or rounded, appearance of the cells at the surface; these cells flatten and become elongated when the bladder is filled with urine.

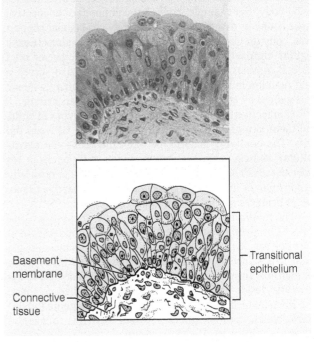

Basement membrane

Connective tissue

Transitional epithelium

Figure 5.2 *(continued)* Stratified epithelia **(e** and **f).**

5

Activity 1

Examining Epithelial Tissue Under the Microscope

Go to station 1 of the demonstration area to examine slides of simple squamous, simple cuboidal, simple columnar, stratified squamous (nonkeratinized), pseudostratified ciliated columnar, and transitional epithelia. Observe each carefully, and notice how the epithelial cells fit closely together to form intact sheets of cells, a necessity for a tissue that forms linings or covering membranes. Scan each epithelial type for modifications for specific functions, such as cilia (motile cell projections that help to move substances along the cell surface), microvilli, which increase the surface area for absorption, and goblet cells, which secrete lubricating mucus. Compare your observations with the photomicrographs in Figure 5.2.

While you work, check the questions in the laboratory Review Sheet section for this exercise. A number of the questions there refer to some of the observations you are asked to make during your microscopic study.

Connective Tissue

OBJECTIVE 2   List the general structural characteristics, functions, and locations of connective tissues in the body, and identify their subcategories when you are presented with a diagram or slide.

Connective tissue is found in all parts of the body. It is the most abundant and widely distributed of the tissue types.

The connective tissues perform a variety of functions, but they primarily protect, support, and bind together other tissues of the body. For example, bones are composed of connective tissue (**bone** or **osseous tissue**), and they protect and support other body tissues and organs. Ligaments and tendons (**dense regular connective tissue**) bind the bones together or bind skeletal muscles to bones. Connective tissue also serves a vital function in the repair of all body tissues: many wounds are repaired by connective tissue in the form of scar tissue.

Connective tissues are composed of many types of cells, and there is a great deal of nonliving material between the cells. The nonliving material between the cells—the **extracellular matrix**—distinguishes connective tissue from all other tissues. The matrix, secreted by the cells, is primarily responsible for the strength associated with connective tissue, but its firmness and relative amount vary.

The matrix has two components—ground substance and fibers. The **ground substance** is chiefly glycoproteins and large polysaccharide molecules. Depending on its makeup, the ground substance may be liquid, gel-like, or very hard. When the matrix is firm, as in cartilage and bone, the connective tissue cells reside in cavities in the matrix called *lacunae*. The fibers, which provide support, include **collagenic** (white) **fibers, elastic** (yellow) **fibers,** and **reticular** (fine collagenic) **fibers.**

Figure 5.3 lists the general characteristics, location, and function of some of the connective tissues found in the body. Blood, considered in detail in Exercise 19, is not covered here.

(a) Areolar connective tissue

Description: Gel-like matrix with all three fiber types; cells include fibroblasts (fiber-forming cells), phagocytes, some white blood cells, and others.

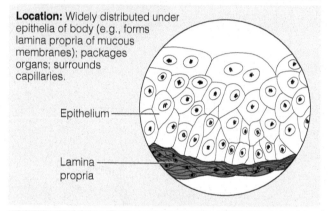

Location: Widely distributed under epithelia of body (e.g., forms lamina propria of mucous membranes); packages organs; surrounds capillaries.

Epithelium

Lamina propria

Function: Wraps and cushions organs; its phagocytes engulf bacteria; plays important role in inflammation; holds and conveys tissue fluid.

Photomicrograph: Areolar connective tissue from the lamina propria of a mucous membrane (340×).

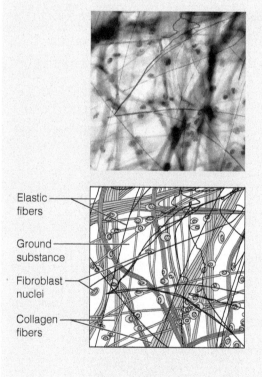

Elastic fibers

Ground substance

Fibroblast nuclei

Collagen fibers

Figure 5.3 Connective tissues. Loose connective tissue: areolar **(a)**.

Text continues on page 46. →

(b) Adipose tissue

Description: Matrix as in areolar, but very sparse; closely packed adipocytes, or fat cells, have nucleus pushed to the side by large fat droplet.

Location: Under skin; around kidneys and eyeballs; within abdomen; in breasts.

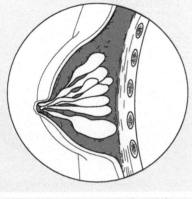

Function: Provides reserve food fuel; insulates against heat loss; supports and protects organs.

Photomicrograph: Adipose tissue from the subcutaneous layer under the skin (350×).

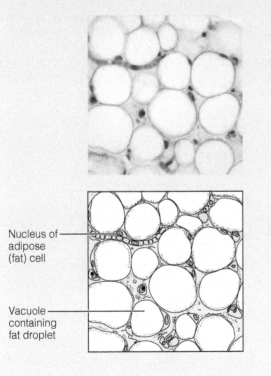

Nucleus of adipose (fat) cell

Vacuole containing fat droplet

(c) Reticular connective tissue

Description: Network of reticular fibers in a typical loose ground substance; reticular cells predominate.

Location: Lymphoid organs (lymph nodes, bone marrow, and spleen).

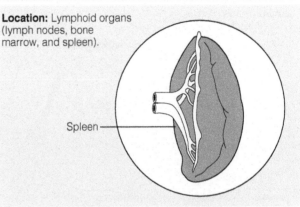

Spleen

Function: Fibers form a soft internal skeleton (stroma) that supports other cell types.

Photomicrograph: Dark-staining network of reticular connective tissue fibers forming the internal skeleton of the spleen (350×).

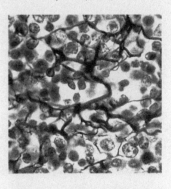

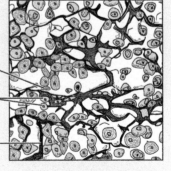

Reticular cell

White blood cells (lymphocytes)

Reticular fibers

Figure 5.3 *(continued)* Loose connective tissue: adipose **(b)** and reticular **(c)**.

Figure continues on next page. →

(d) Dense connective tissue

Description: Primarily parallel collagen fibers; a few elastin fibers; major cell type is the fibroblast.

Location: Tendons, most ligaments, aponeuroses.

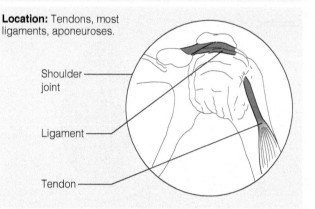

Shoulder joint

Ligament

Tendon

Function: Attaches muscles to bones or to muscles; attaches bones to bones; withstands great tensile stress when pulling force is applied in one direction.

Photomicrograph: Dense regular connective tissue from a tendon (430×).

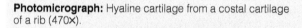

Collagen fibers

Nuclei of fibroblasts

(e) Hyaline cartilage

Description: Firm matrix; collagen fibers form an imperceptible network; chondroblasts (cartilage-forming cells) produce the matrix and when mature (chondrocytes) lie in lacunae.

Location: Forms most of the embryonic skeleton; covers the ends of long bones in joint cavities; forms costal cartilages of the ribs; cartilages of the nose, trachea, and larynx.

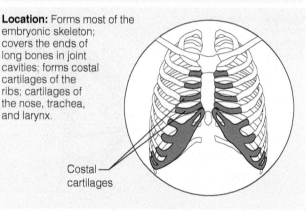

Costal cartilages

Function: Supports and reinforces; has cushioning properties; resists compression.

Photomicrograph: Hyaline cartilage from a costal cartilage of a rib (470×).

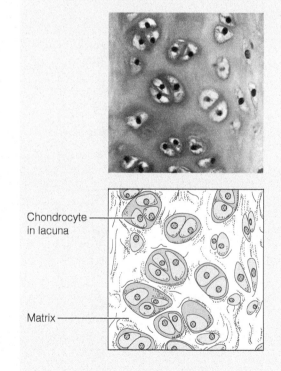

Chondrocyte in lacuna

Matrix

Figure 5.3 *(continued)* **Connective tissues.** Loose connective tissue: dense **(d)**. Hyaline cartilage **(e)**.

(f) Fibrocartilage

Description: Matrix similar but less firm than in hyaline cartilage; thick collagen fibers predominate.

Location: Intervertebral discs; pubic symphysis; discs of knee joint.

Intervertebral discs

Function: Tensile strength with the ability to absorb compressive shock.

Photomicrograph: Fibrocartilage of an intervertebral disc (125×). Special staining produced the blue color.

Chondrocytes in lacunae

Collagen fiber

(g) Bone (osseous tissue)

Description: Hard, calcified matrix containing many collagen fibers; osteocytes lie in lacunae. Very well vascularized.

Location: Bones

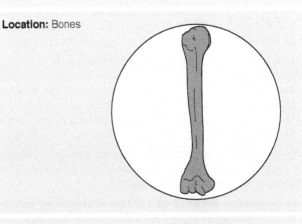

Function: Bone supports and protects (by enclosing); provides levers for the muscles to act on; stores calcium and other minerals and fat; marrow inside bones is the site for blood cell formation (hematopoiesis).

Photomicrograph: Cross-sectional view of bone (100×).

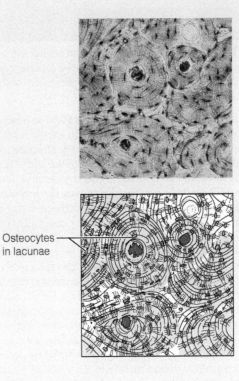

Osteocytes in lacunae

Figure 5.3 *(continued)* Fibrocartilage **(f)**. Bone (osseous tissue) **(g)**.

Activity 2

Examining Connective Tissue Under the Microscope

Go to station 2 at the demonstration area to examine prepared slides of adipose, areolar, reticular, and dense connective tissue; of fibrocartilage and hyaline cartilage; and of osseous connective tissue (bone). Compare your observations with the views illustrated in Figure 5.3.

• Distinguish the living cells from the matrix, and pay particular attention to the appearance of the matrix. For example, notice that the matrix of the dense fibrous connective tissue of tendons is packed with collagenic fibers and that the fibers are all running in the same direction.

• While examining the areolar connective tissue, a soft "packing tissue," notice how much empty space (*areol* = small empty space) there appears to be.

• In adipose tissue, locate a hollow-appearing cell in which the nucleus is pushed to one side by the large, fat-filled vacuole that appears to be a large empty space. Also notice how little matrix there is in fat or adipose tissue.

• Distinguish the living cells from the matrix in the dense fibrous, bone, and hyaline cartilage preparations.

Muscle Tissue

OBJECTIVE 3 List the general structural characteristics, functions, and locations of the three muscle types in the body, and identify subtypes when presented with a diagram or slide.

Muscle tissue is specialized to contract (shorten) to produce movement of some body parts. As you might expect, muscle cells are elongated to provide a long axis for contraction.

Skeletal muscle, the "meat," or flesh, of the body, is attached to the skeleton. It is under voluntary control (consciously controlled). As it contracts, it moves the limbs and other external body parts. Skeletal muscle cells are long, cylindrical, and multinucleate (several nuclei per cell); they have obvious *striations* (stripes).

Cardiac muscle is found only in the heart. As it contracts, the heart acts as a pump, propelling the blood into the blood vessels. Like skeletal muscle, it has striations, but cardiac cells are branching cells with one nucleus (or occasionally two) that fit together at junctions called **intercalated discs** that allow cardiac muscle to act as a unit. Cardiac muscle is under involuntary control, which means that we cannot voluntarily or consciously control the operation of the heart.

Smooth muscle is found mainly in the walls of all hollow organs (digestive and urinary tract organs, uterus, blood vessels) except the heart. Typically two layers run at right angles to each other, so the muscle can constrict or dilate the lumen (cavity) of an organ and also propel substances along existing pathways. No striations are visible, and the uninucleate smooth muscle cells are spindle-shaped. Smooth muscle is under involuntary control.

Activity 3

Examining Muscle Tissue Under the Microscope

Go to station 3 of the demonstration area to examine prepared slides of skeletal, cardiac, and smooth muscle. Notice their similarities and dissimilarities in your observations and in the illustrations in **Figure 5.4**. See also Plates 2 and 3 in the Histology Atlas.

Nervous Tissue

OBJECTIVE 4 List the general structural characteristics, functions, and locations of nervous tissue in the body. Identify neurons when presented with a diagram or slide.

Nervous tissue is composed of two major cell populations. **Neuroglia** are special supporting cells that protect, support, and insulate the more delicate neurons. The **neurons** are highly specialized to receive stimuli and to conduct impulses to all parts of the body. They are the cells that are most often associated with nervous system functioning.

Neurons all have a nucleus-containing cell body, and their cytoplasm is drawn out into long extensions (cell processes)—sometimes as long as 3 feet (about 1 m), a characteristic that allows a single neuron to conduct an impulse over relatively long distances. More detail about nervous tissue appears in Exercise 13.

Activity 4

Examining Nervous Tissue Under the Microscope

Go to station 4 at the demonstration area, and examine a prepared slide of a spinal cord smear. Locate a neuron, and compare it to **Figure 5.5** and Plate 5 of the Histology Atlas. Keep the light on the microscope dim—this will help you see the cellular extensions of the neurons.

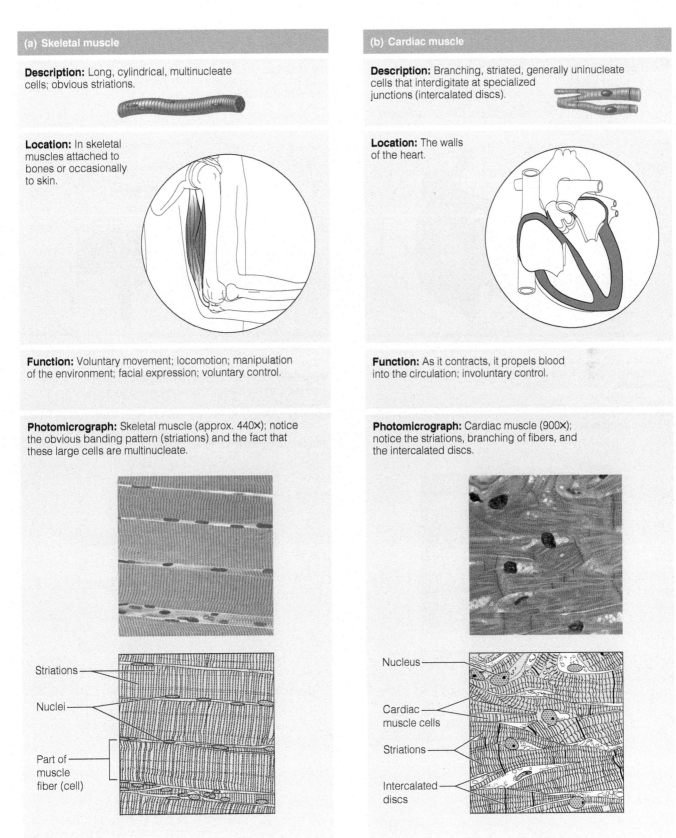

(a) Skeletal muscle

Description: Long, cylindrical, multinucleate cells; obvious striations.

Location: In skeletal muscles attached to bones or occasionally to skin.

Function: Voluntary movement; locomotion; manipulation of the environment; facial expression; voluntary control.

Photomicrograph: Skeletal muscle (approx. 440×); notice the obvious banding pattern (striations) and the fact that these large cells are multinucleate.

Striations

Nuclei

Part of muscle fiber (cell)

(b) Cardiac muscle

Description: Branching, striated, generally uninucleate cells that interdigitate at specialized junctions (intercalated discs).

Location: The walls of the heart.

Function: As it contracts, it propels blood into the circulation; involuntary control.

Photomicrograph: Cardiac muscle (900×); notice the striations, branching of fibers, and the intercalated discs.

Nucleus

Cardiac muscle cells

Striations

Intercalated discs

Figure 5.4 Muscle tissues. Skeletal muscle **(a)** and cardiac muscle **(b)**.

Figure continues on next page. →

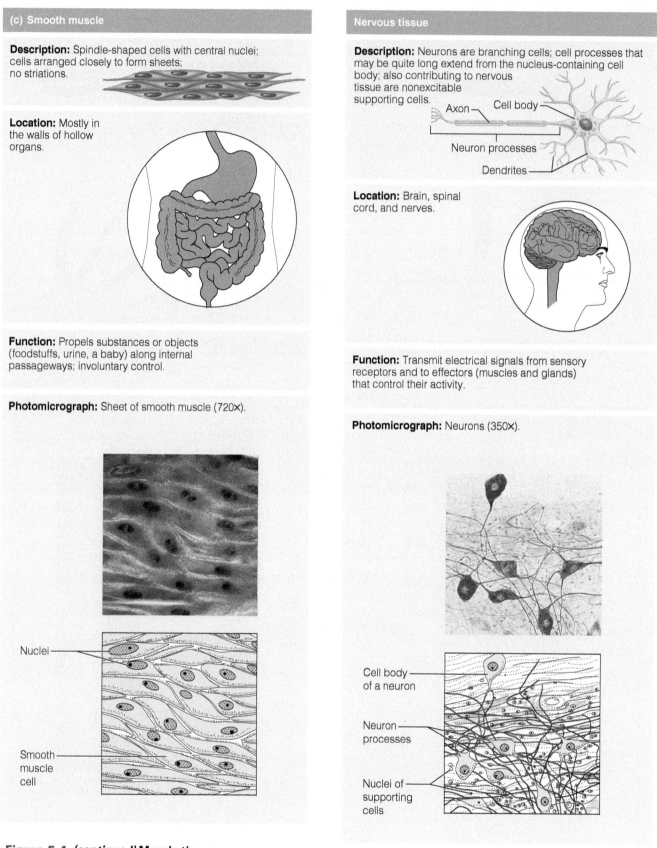

(c) Smooth muscle

Description: Spindle-shaped cells with central nuclei; cells arranged closely to form sheets; no striations.

Location: Mostly in the walls of hollow organs.

Function: Propels substances or objects (foodstuffs, urine, a baby) along internal passageways; involuntary control.

Photomicrograph: Sheet of smooth muscle (720×).

Nuclei

Smooth muscle cell

Figure 5.4 *(continued)* **Muscle tissues.** Smooth muscle **(c)**.

Nervous tissue

Description: Neurons are branching cells; cell processes that may be quite long extend from the nucleus-containing cell body; also contributing to nervous tissue are nonexcitable supporting cells.

Axon — Cell body

Neuron processes

Dendrites

Location: Brain, spinal cord, and nerves.

Function: Transmit electrical signals from sensory receptors and to effectors (muscles and glands) that control their activity.

Photomicrograph: Neurons (350×).

Cell body of a neuron

Neuron processes

Nuclei of supporting cells

Figure 5.5 Nervous tissue.

REVIEW SHEET
Classification of Tissues

Name _____ LabTime/Date _____

Tissue Structure and Function: General Review

1. Define *tissue*: _____

   _____

2. Use the key choices to identify the major tissue types described below. (Some choices may be used more than once.)

   Key: connective epithelium muscular nervous

   _____ 1. lines body cavities and covers the body's external surface

   _____ 2. pumps blood, flushes urine out of the body, allows one to swing a bat

   _____ 3. transmits waves of excitation

   _____ 4. anchors and packages body organs

   _____ 5. cells may absorb, protect, or form a filtering membrane

   _____ 6. most involved in regulating body functions quickly

   _____ 7. major function is to contract

   _____ 8. the most durable tissue type

   _____ 9. abundant nonliving extracellular matrix

   _____ 10. forms nerves

Epithelial Tissue

3. On what bases are epithelial tissues classified? _____

   _____

4. How is the function of an epithelium reflected in its arrangement? _____

   _____

   _____

5. Where is ciliated epithelium found? _____

   What role does it play? _____

6. Transitional epithelium is actually stratified squamous epithelium, but there is something special about it.

   How does it differ structurally from other stratified squamous epithelia? _____

   _____

How does this structural difference reflect its function in the body? _____

_____

_____

7. Use the key choices to respond to the following. (Some choices may be used more than once.)

Key: pseudostratified ciliated columnar   simple cuboidal   stratified squamous
        simple columnar   simple squamous   transitional

_____ 1. best suited for areas subject to friction

_____ 2. propels substances across its surface

_____ 3. most suited for rapid diffusion

_____ 4. tubules of the kidney

_____ 5. lines much of the respiratory tract

_____ 6. stretches

_____ 7. lines the small and large intestines

_____ 8. lining of the esophagus

_____ 9. lining of the bladder

_____ 10. alveolar sacs (air sacs) of the lungs

Connective Tissue

8. What are the components of the matrix in connective tissues? _____

_____

_____

9. How are the functions of connective tissue reflected in its structure? _____

_____

_____

10. Using the key, choose the best response to identify the connective tissues described below.

Key: adipose connective tissue   reticular connective tissue   fibrocartilage
        areolar connective tissue   hyaline cartilage   blood
        dense fibrous connective tissue   osseous tissue

_____ 1. attaches bones to bones and muscles to bones

_____ 2. forms your hip bone

_____ 3. composes basement membranes; a soft packaging tissue with a jellylike matrix

_____ 4. forms the larynx and the costal cartilages of the ribs

_____ 5. firm matrix heavily invaded with fibers; appears glassy and smooth

_____ 6. matrix hard; provides levers for muscles to act on

_____ 7. insulates against heat loss; provides reserve fuel

_____ 8. makes up the intervertebral discs

Muscle Tissue

11. The terms and phrases in the key relate to the muscle tissues. For each of the three muscle tissues, select the terms or phrases that characterize it, and write the corresponding letter of each term on the answer line.

Key: a. striated
      b. branching cells
      c. spindle-shaped cells
      d. cylindrical cells
      e. active during birth

      f. voluntary
      g. involuntary
      h. one nucleus
      i. many nuclei
      j. forms heart walls

      k. attached to bones
      l. intercalated discs
      m. in wall of bladder and stomach
      n. moves limbs, produces smiles
      o. arranged in sheets

Skeletal muscle: _____

Cardiac muscle: _____

Smooth muscle: _____

Nervous Tissue

12. In what ways are neurons similar to other cells?_____

How are they different? _____

How does the special structure of a neuron relate to its function? _____

_____

For Review

13. Write the name of each tissue type in illustrations (a) through (l), and label all major structures marked by leader lines and brackets.

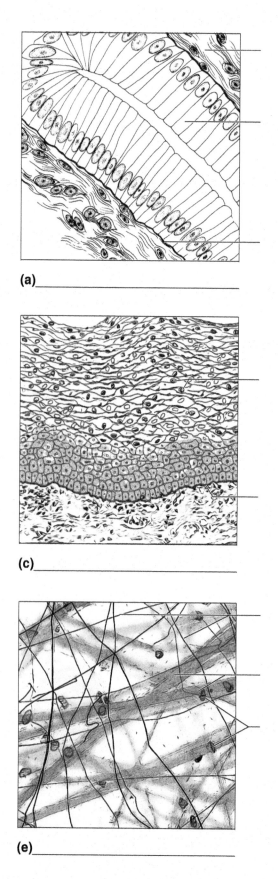

(a)_____

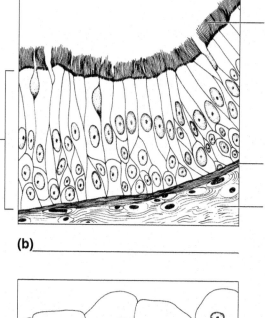

(b)_____

(c)_____

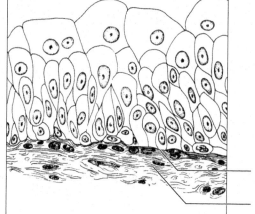

(d)_____

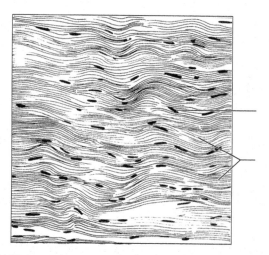

(e)_____

(f) _____

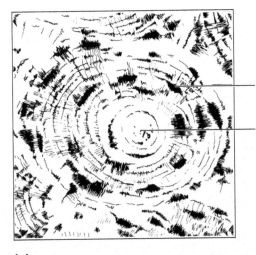

(g)_____

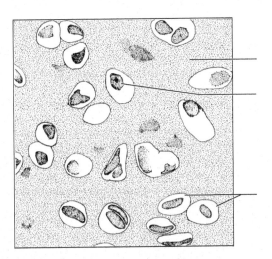

(h)_____

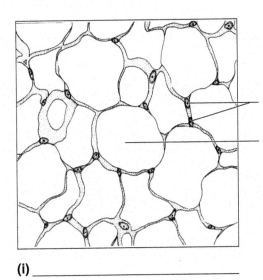

(i)_____

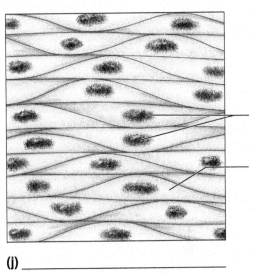

(j)_____

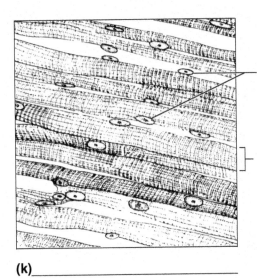

(k)_____

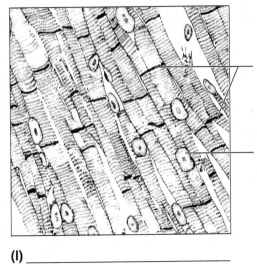

(l)_____

The Skin (Integumentary System)

Materials

- ☐ Skin model (three-dimensional, if available)
- ☐ Small metric ruler
- ☐ Four coins (nickels or quarters)
- ☐ Fine felt-tipped markers (2 different colors)
- ☐ Sheet of 20# bond paper ruled to mark off cm² areas
- ☐ Scissors
- ☐ Betadine swabs, or Lugol's iodine and cotton swabs
- ☐ Adhesive tape
- ☐ Small clear glass plates (5×5 inches or larger)
- ☐ Demonstration area:

  Station 1: Compound microscope set up to demonstrate human skin showing hair follicles (about 200×)

  Station 2: Prepared slide of skin; pointer on a Meissner's corpuscle

  Station 3: Prepared slide of skin; pointer on a Pacinian corpuscle

Pre-Lab Quiz

1. All the following are functions of the skin *except:*
   a. excretion of body wastes
   b. insulation
   c. protection from mechanical damage
   d. site of vitamin A synthesis

2. The skin has two distinct regions. The superficial layer is the _____, and the underlying connective tissue, the _____.

3. Circle True or False. Nails are hornlike derivatives of the epidermis.

4. The portion of a hair that you see that projects from the scalp surface is known as the:
   a. bulb   c. root
   b. matrix   d. shaft

5. Circle the correct term. The ducts of <u>sebaceous</u> / <u>sweat</u> glands usually empty into a hair follicle but may also open directly on the skin surface.

6. Circle the correct term. <u>Eccrine</u> / <u>Apocrine</u> glands are found primarily in the genital and axillary areas.

The **skin** is the major organ of the **integumentary system.** The skin does much more than just cover the body exterior. Architecturally the skin is a wonder. It is tough yet pliable, a characteristic that enables it to withstand constant insult from outside agents.

OBJECTIVE 1 List several important functions of the skin, or integumentary system.

The skin has several functions. It insulates and cushions the underlying body tissues and protects the entire body from mechanical damage (bumps and cuts), chemical damage (acids, alkalis, and the like), thermal damage (heat), and bacterial invasion. The hardened uppermost layer of the skin prevents water loss from the body.

Other skin functions include the following:

- Acting as a mini-excretory system; urea, salts, and water are lost when we sweat

- Performing important metabolic duties, such as producing proteins important to our immunity

- Synthesizing vitamin D for the body

- Containing the cutaneous sense organs (part of the nervous system that is in the dermis), which allow us to sense and enjoy the external environment

- Playing an important role in regulating heat loss from the body surface (a function of its abundant capillary network under the control of the nervous system)

Basic Structure of the Skin

The skin has two distinct regions—the superficial **epidermis** composed of epithelium, and an underlying connective tissue **dermis.** These layers are firmly "cemented" together along a wavy border. But friction, such as the rubbing of a poorly fitting shoe, may cause the layers to separate, resulting in a blister. Immediately deep to the dermis is the **hypodermis,** or **subcutaneous tissue** (primarily adipose tissue), which is not considered part of the skin. The main skin areas and structures are described below.

OBJECTIVE 2   Recognize and name during observation of a model, diagram, or slide, the following skin structures: epidermal and dermal layers, hair follicles and hairs, sebaceous and sweat glands.

Activity 1

Locating Structures on a Skin Model

As you read, locate the following structures in **Figure 6.1** and on a skin model.

Epidermis

Structurally, the avascular epidermis is a keratinized stratified squamous epithelium consisting of four distinct cell types and four or five distinct layers.

Most epidermal cells are **keratinocytes** (literally, "keratin cells"). These epithelial cells produce keratin, a tough, fibrous protein that gives the epidermis its durability and protective capabilities. Other cell types are described below.

Layers of the Epidermis

From deep to superficial, the layers of the epidermis are the stratum basale, stratum spinosum, stratum granulosum, stratum lucidum, and stratum corneum (Figure 6.1b).

• The **stratum basale (basal layer)** is a single row of cells that abuts the dermis. Its cells constantly undergo cell division to produce millions of new cells daily. About a quarter of the cells in this stratum are the spidery, brown-to-black pigment-producing cells called **melanocytes.** Melanocyte processes thread their way through this and the adjacent layers of keratinocytes. The melanocytes add color to the skin and provide protection from ultraviolet (UV) radiation. The skin tans because melanin production increases when the skin is exposed to sunlight.

• The **stratum spinosum (spiny layer)** is immediately superficial to the basal layer. Its cells appear spiky (hence their name) because as skin is prepared for histological examination, its cells shrink but their desmosomes hold tight. Cell division also occurs in this layer, but less often than in the basal layer. Cells in the basal and spiny layers are the only ones that receive adequate nourishment (via diffusion from the dermis). As their daughter cells are pushed away from the source of nutrition, they gradually die.

• The **stratum granulosum (granular layer)** is named for the abundant granules in its cells. Some of these granules contain a waterproofing glycolipid that is secreted into the extracellular space. Others contain the subunits of keratin. At the upper border of this layer, the cells are beginning to die.

• The **stratum lucidum (clear layer)** is a thin translucent band of flattened dead keratinocytes. This layer is present only in thick skin, such as the palms of the hands and soles of the feet.

• The **stratum corneum (horny layer),** the outermost epidermal layer, is 20 to 30 cell layers thick, and accounts for most of the epidermal thickness. Cells in this layer are dead, and their flattened scalelike remnants are full of keratin. They are constantly rubbing off and being replaced by division of the deeper cells.

Dermis

The dense fibrous connective tissue making up the bulk of the dermis has two principal regions—the papillary and reticular areas.

The more superficial **papillary layer** is very uneven and has fingerlike projections from its superior surface, called **dermal papillae,** which attach it to the epidermis above. In the palms of the hands and soles of the feet, the papillae produce the fingerprints, unique patterns of loops and ridges in the epidermis that remain unchanged throughout life. Capillaries in the papillary layer furnish nutrients for the epidermis and allow heat to radiate to the skin surface. The pain and touch receptors (Meissner's corpuscles) are also found here.

The **reticular layer** is the deepest skin layer. It contains blood vessels, sweat and sebaceous glands, and pressure receptors (Pacinian receptors).

Collagenic and elastic fibers are found throughout the dermis. Collagenic fibers make the dermis tough and attract and hold water, thus keeping the skin hydrated (moist). The elastic fibers give skin its exceptional elasticity in youth. Fibroblasts, adipose cells, various types of phagocytes (which are important in the body's defense), and other cell types are found throughout the dermis.

Dermal Blood Supply

The rich dermal blood supply allows the skin to play a role in regulating body temperature. When body temperature is high, the capillary network of the dermis becomes engorged with the heated blood, and body heat radiates from the skin surface. If the environment is cool and body heat must be conserved, the dermal blood vessels constrict so that blood bypasses the dermis temporarily.

Activity 2

Visualizing Changes in Skin Color Due to Continuous External Pressure

Go to the supply area and obtain a small glass plate. Press the heel of your hand firmly against the plate for a few seconds, and then observe and record the color of your skin in the compressed area by looking through the glass.

Color of compressed skin: _____

What is the reason for this color change? _____

_____

What would happen in this area if you continued the pressure for an extended period?

_____

_____

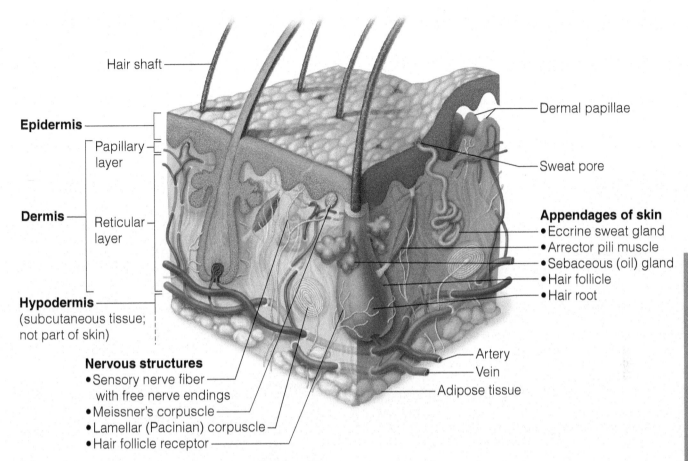

Hair shaft

Dermal papillae

Epidermis

Papillary layer

Sweat pore

Dermis

Reticular layer

Appendages of skin
- Eccrine sweat gland
- Arrector pili muscle
- Sebaceous (oil) gland
- Hair follicle
- Hair root

Hypodermis
(subcutaneous tissue; not part of skin)

Artery
Vein
Adipose tissue

Nervous structures
- Sensory nerve fiber with free nerve endings
- Meissner's corpuscle
- Lamellar (Pacinian) corpuscle
- Hair follicle receptor

(a)

6

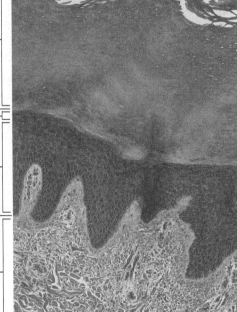

Epidermis
- Stratum corneum
- Stratum lucidum
- Stratum granulosum
- Stratum spinosum
- Stratum basale

Dermis

(b)

Figure 6.1 Skin structure. (a) Three-dimensional view of the skin and underlying subcutaneous tissue. **(b)** Photomicrograph showing layers of thick skin (75×).

Dermal Cutaneous Receptors

The dermis also has a rich nerve supply. Many of the nerve endings bear specialized receptor organs that respond to pain, pressure, or temperature extremes and transmit messages to the central nervous system for interpretation. Some of these receptors—free nerve endings (pain and temperature receptors), a lamellar (Pacinian) corpuscle, a Meissner's corpuscle, and a hair follicle receptor—are shown in Figure 6.1a. See also **Plates 11–13 in the Histology Atlas**.

Activity 3

Viewing Two Types of Pressure Receptors Microscopically

Go to the demonstration area where two types of dermal pressure receptors have been set up for viewing under the microscope.

- At station 2, examine the Meissner's corpuscle, which responds to touch or light pressure. Notice that its connective tissue capsule is located in a dermal papilla. It is typically found in hairless skin areas, where it responds to light touch. Compare your observations to **Plate 11 in the Histology Atlas**.

- At station 3, view the much larger lamellar (Pacinian) corpuscle, which responds to deep pressure as indicated by its location much deeper in the dermis. What vegetable does its structure remind you of? Compare your observations to **Plate 13 in the Histology Atlas**.

There are several simple experiments you can conduct to investigate the location and physiology of cutaneous receptors. In each of the following activities, work in pairs with one person as the subject and the other as the experimenter. After you have completed an experiment, switch roles and go through the procedures again so that all class members obtain individual results. Keep an accurate account of each test that you perform.

Activity 4

Determining the Two-Point Threshold

The density of the touch receptors varies significantly in different areas of the body. In general, areas that have the greatest density of tactile receptors have a heightened ability to "feel." These areas correspond to areas that receive the greatest motor innervation; thus, they are also typically areas of fine motor control. Let's check it out.

1. Using calipers or an esthesiometer and a metric ruler, test the ability of the subject to differentiate two distinct sensations when the skin is touched simultaneously at two points. The subject's eyes should be closed during testing. Beginning with the face, start with the caliper arms completely together. Gradually increase the distance between the points, testing the subject's skin after each adjustment. Continue with this testing procedure until the subject reports that *two points* of contact can be felt. This measurement, the smallest distance at which two points of contact can be felt, is the **two-point threshold.**

2. Repeat this procedure on the back and palm of the hand, fingertips, lips, back of the neck, and ventral forearm. Record your results in the **Activity 4 chart**.

3. Which area has the smallest two-point threshold?

Activity 4: Determining Two-Point Threshold	
Body area tested	**Two-point threshold (millimeters)**
Face	
Back of hand	
Palm of hand	
Fingertips	
Lips	
Back of neck	
Ventral forearm	

Activity 5

Testing Tactile Localization

The density of the touch receptors varies significantly in different areas of the body. In general, areas that have the greatest density of tactile receptors have a heightened ability to "feel." These areas correspond to areas that receive the greatest control of muscles from the nervous system; thus they are also typically areas of fine motor control. Let's check it out.

Tactile localization is the ability to determine which portion of the skin has been touched. The tactile receptor field of the body periphery has a corresponding "touch" field in the brain. Some body areas are well represented with touch receptors, and tactile stimuli can be localized with great accuracy, but density of touch receptors in other body areas allows only crude discrimination.

1. The subject's eyes should be closed during the testing. The experimenter touches the palm of the subject's hand with a pointed black felt-tipped marker. The subject should then try to touch the exact point with his or her own marker, which should be a different color. Measure the error of localization in millimeters.

2. Repeat the test in the same spot twice more, recording the error of localization for each test. Average the results of the three determinations and record it in the **Activity 5 chart**.

Activity 5: Testing Tactile Localization

Body area tested	Average error of localization (millimeters)
Palm of hand	
Fingertip	
Ventral forearm	
Back of hand	
Back of neck	

Does the ability to localize the stimulus improve the second time?

_____ The third time?_____ Explain. _____

_____

_____

3. Repeat the above procedure on a fingertip, the ventral forearm, the back of a hand, and the back of the neck. Record the averaged results in the Activity 5 chart.

4. Which area has the smallest error of localization (is most sensitive to touch)?

_____

_____

Activity 6

Demonstrating Adaptation of Touch Receptors

In many cases, when a stimulus is applied for a prolonged period the rate of receptor response slows, and our conscious awareness of the stimulus declines or is lost until some type of stimulus change occurs. This phenomenon is referred to as **adaptation.** The touch receptors adapt particularly rapidly, which is highly desirable. Who, for instance, would want to be continually aware of the pressure of clothing on skin? The simple experiment conducted next allows you to investigate the phenomenon of adaptation.

1. The subject's eyes should be closed. Place a coin on the anterior surface of the subject's forearm, and determine how long the sensation persists for the subject. Duration of the sensation: _____ sec

2. Repeat the test, placing the coin at a different forearm location. How long does the sensation persist at the second location? _____ sec

3. After awareness of the sensation has been lost at the second site, stack three more coins atop the first one.

Does the pressure sensation return? _____

If so, for how long is the subject aware of the pressure in

this instance? _____ sec

Are the same receptors being stimulated when the four

coins, rather than the one coin, are used?_____

Explain. _____

_____

Appendages of the Skin

The appendages of the skin—cutaneous glands, hair, and nails—all derive from the epidermis, but they reside in the dermis. They originate from the basal layer and grow downward into the deeper skin regions.

Cutaneous Glands

OBJECTIVE 3   Describe the distribution and function of eccrine and apocrine sweat glands and sebaceous glands.

The cutaneous glands fall primarily into two categories: the sebaceous glands and the sweat glands (Figure 6.1). The **sebaceous (oil) glands** are found nearly all over the skin,

except for the palms of the hands and the soles of the feet. Their ducts usually empty into a hair follicle, but some open directly onto the skin surface.

The product of the sebaceous glands, called **sebum,** is a mixture of oily substances and fragmented cells that acts as a natural skin cream or lubricant that keeps the skin soft and moist. *Blackheads* are accumulations of dried sebum and bacteria in the hair follicle. *Acne* is due to active infection of the sebaceous glands.

Epithelial openings, called *pores,* are the outlets for the **sweat (sudoriferous) glands.** These exocrine glands are widely distributed in the skin. There are two types of sweat glands. The **eccrine glands,** which are distributed all over the body, produce clear perspiration, consisting primarily of water, salts (mostly NaCl), and urea. The **apocrine glands,** found chiefly in the axillary and genital areas, secrete a milky protein- and fat-rich substance (also containing water, salts, and urea) that is an excellent source of nutrients for the bacteria typically found on the skin.

The sweat glands are controlled by the nervous system and are an important part of the body's heat-regulating apparatus. They secrete perspiration when the external temperature or body temperature is high. When this perspiration evaporates, it carries large amounts of body heat with it.

Activity 7

Plotting the Distribution of Sweat Glands

1. For this simple experiment, you will need two squares of bond paper (each 1 cm × 1 cm), adhesive tape, and a Betadine (povidone-iodine) swab *or* Lugol's iodine and a cotton-tipped swab. (The bond paper has been preruled in cm² — just cut along the lines to obtain the required squares.)

2. Using the iodine solution, paint an area of the medial aspect of your left palm (avoid the crease lines) and a region of your left forearm. Allow the iodine solution to dry thoroughly. The painted area in each case should be slightly larger than the paper squares to be used.

3. Mark one piece of ruled bond paper with an "H" (for hand) and the other "A" (for arm). Have your lab partner *securely* tape the appropriate square of bond paper letter side up over each iodine-painted area. Leave the squares in place for 10 minutes. (If it is very warm in

the laboratory, good results may be obtained within 5 minutes.) While waiting to determine the results, continue with the sections on hair and nails.

4. After 20 minutes, remove the paper squares, and count the number of blue-black dots on each square. The appearance of a blue-black dot on the paper indicates an active sweat gland. (The iodine in the pore dissolves in the sweat and reacts with the starch in the bond paper to produce the blue-black color.) Thus "sweat maps" have been produced for the two skin areas.

5. Which skin area tested has the most sweat glands?

_____

_____

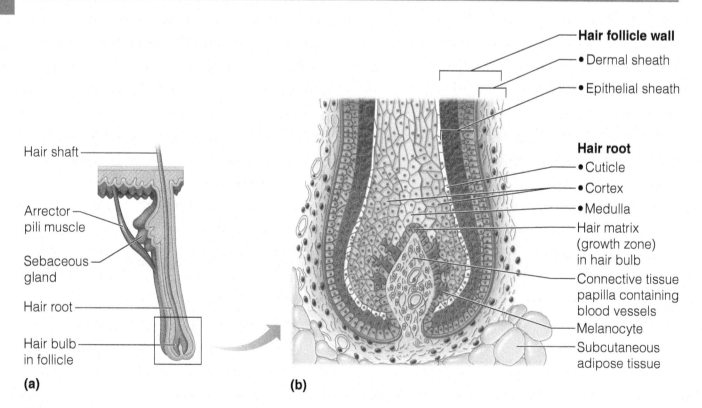

(a)

Hair shaft

Arrector pili muscle

Sebaceous gland

Hair root

Hair bulb in follicle

(b)

Hair follicle wall
• Dermal sheath
• Epithelial sheath

Hair root
• Cuticle
• Cortex
• Medulla
Hair matrix (growth zone) in hair bulb
Connective tissue papilla containing blood vessels
Melanocyte
Subcutaneous adipose tissue

Figure 6.2 Structure of a hair and hair follicle. (a) Longitudinal section of a hair within its follicle. **(b)** Enlarged longitudinal view of the expanded hair bulb in the follicle showing the matrix, the region of actively dividing epithelial cells that produces the hair.

Hair

OBJECTIVE 4 Identify the major regions of a hair and hair follicle.

Hairs are found over the entire body surface, except for the palms of the hands, the soles of the feet, parts of the external genitalia, the nipples, and the lips. A hair, enclosed in a hair **follicle,** is also an epithelial structure (**Figure 6.2**). The part of the hair enclosed within the follicle is called the **root;** the portion projecting from the skin is the **shaft.** The hair is formed by mitosis of the germinal epithelial cells at the base of the follicle (the **hair bulb**). As the daughter cells are pushed away from the growing region, they become keratinized and die; thus the bulk of the hair shaft, like the bulk of the epidermis, is dead material.

A hair (Figure 6.2b) consists of a central region (medulla) surrounded first by the cortex and then by a protective cuticle.

The hair follicle is structured from both epidermal and dermal cells (Figure 6.2b). Its inner *epithelial sheath* is enclosed by the *dermal sheath,* which is essentially connective tissue. A small nipple of dermal tissue, the *connective tissue papilla,* protrudes into the hair bulb from the dermal sheath and provides nutrition to the growing hair. If you look carefully at the structure of a hair follicle (**Figure 6.3**), you will see that it generally is in a slanted position. Small bands of smooth muscle cells—**arrector pili**—connect each hair follicle to the dermis. When these muscles contract (during cold or fright), the hair follicle is pulled upright, dimpling the skin surface with "goose bumps."

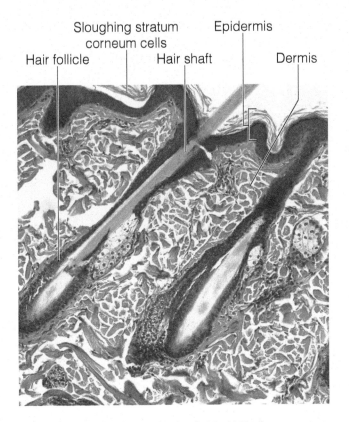

Sloughing stratum corneum cells
Epidermis
Hair follicle
Hair shaft
Dermis

Figure 6.3 Photomicrograph of skin (120×).

Microscopic Structure of Skin Appendages

Activity 8

Examining Hair Structures on a Skin Slide

Go to station 1 of the demonstration area to view a prepared slide of human skin. Study it carefully under the microscope. Identify hair shafts, roots, and hair follicles. Compare your tissue slide to the view shown in Figure 6.3, and identify as many of the other structures diagrammed in Figure 6.1 as possible.

How is this stratified squamous epithelium different from that observed in the lab on classification of tissues (Exercise 5)?

_____

_____

How does this difference relate to the functions of these two similar epithelia?

_____

_____

_____

_____

_____

Nails

OBJECTIVE 5 Identify the major regions of the nails.

Nails, the hornlike derivatives of the epidermis, are transparent and nearly colorless, but they appear pink because of the blood supply in the underlying dermis. The exception to this is the proximal region of the thickened nail matrix which appears as a white crescent called the *lunule* (**Figure 6.4**). When someone is cyanotic because of lack of oxygen in the blood, the nail beds take on a blue cast.

Nails consist of a *free edge,* a *body* (visible attached portion), and a *root* (embedded in the skin and adhering to an epithelial **nail bed**). The borders of the nail are overlapped by skin folds called **nail folds.** The thick proximal nail fold is commonly called the *cuticle* (Figure 6.4). The germinal cells in the **nail matrix,** the thickened proximal part of the nail bed, are responsible for nail growth. As new cells are produced by the matrix, they become heavily keratinized and die.

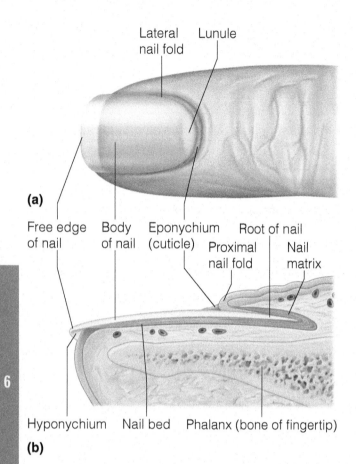

(a)

Lateral nail fold   Lunule

Free edge of nail   Body of nail   Eponychium (cuticle)   Root of nail
Proximal nail fold   Nail matrix

Hyponychium   Nail bed   Phalanx (bone of fingertip)

(b)

Figure 6.4 Structure of a nail. (a) Surface view of the distal part of a finger, showing nail parts. **(b)** Sagittal section of the fingertip.

6

Activity 9

Identifying Nail Structures

Identify the nail structures shown in Figure 6.4 on yourself or your lab partner.

REVIEW SHEET
The Skin (Integumentary System)

Name _____ Lab Time/Date _____

Basic Structure of the Skin

1. Complete the following statements by writing the appropriate word or phrase on the correspondingly numbered blank:

The two basic tissues of which the skin is composed are dense connective tissue, which makes up the dermis, and __1__, which forms the epidermis. Most cells of the epidermis are __2__. The protein __3__ makes the dermis tough and able to retain water. The specialized cells that produce the pigments that contribute to skin color are called __4__.

1. _____

2. _____

3. _____

4. _____

2. Name four protective functions of the skin: _____

_____

_____

_____

_____

3. Using the key choices, choose all responses that apply to the following descriptions. (Some choices may be used more than once.)

Key: stratum basale   stratum lucidum   reticular layer
      stratum corneum   stratum spinosum   epidermis (as a whole)
      stratum granulosum   papillary layer   dermis (as a whole)

_____ 1. layer containing sacs filled with fatty material or keratin subunits

_____ 2. dead cells

_____ 3. the more superficial dermis layer

_____ 4. avascular region

_____ 5. major skin area where derivatives (nails and hair) are located

_____ 6. epidermal region exhibiting the most mitoses

_____ 7. most superficial epidermal layer

_____ 8. has abundant elastic and collagenic fibers

_____ 9. region where melanocytes are most likely to be found

_____ 10. accounts for most of the epidermis

4. Label the skin structures and areas indicated in the accompanying diagram of skin.

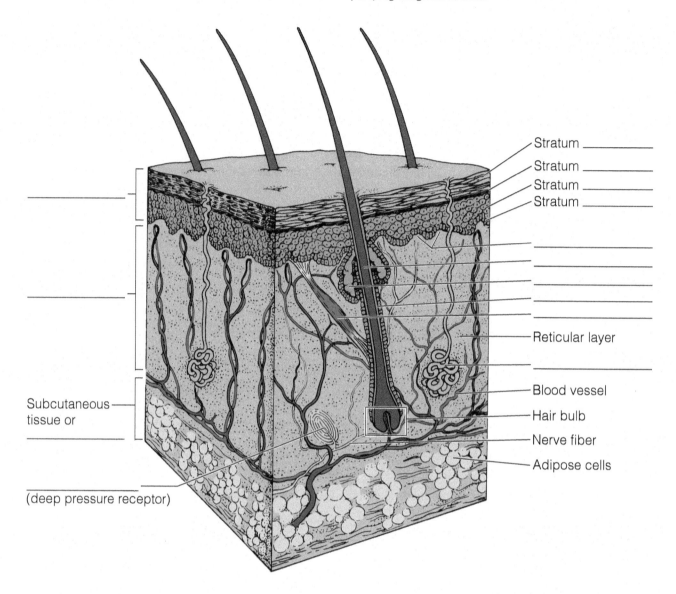

Stratum _____

Stratum _____

Stratum _____

Stratum _____

_____

_____

_____

_____

Reticular layer

_____

Blood vessel

Hair bulb

Nerve fiber

Adipose cells

Subcutaneous tissue or

_____

_____
(deep pressure receptor)

5. What substance is manufactured in the skin (but is not a secretion) to play a role in calcium absorption elsewhere in the body?

_____

6. How did the results you obtained in Activity 2, "Visualizing Changes in Skin Color Due to Continuous External Pressure," relate to formation of decubitus ulcers? (Use your textbook if necessary.)

_____

_____

7. Some injections hurt more than others. Based on what you have learned about skin structure, can you determine why

this is so? _____

_____

8. Two questions regarding general sensation are posed below. Answer each by placing your response in the appropriately numbered blanks to the right.

   1–2. Which two body areas tested were most sensitive to touch?   1–2. _____

   3–4. Which two body areas tested were the least sensitive to touch?   3–4. _____

9. Define *adaptation of sensory receptors:* _____

   _____

10. Why is it advantageous to have pain receptors that are sensitive to all vigorous stimuli, whether heat, cold, or pressure?

    _____

    Pain receptors do not adapt. Why is this important? _____

    _____

11. Imagine yourself without any cutaneous sense organs. Why might this be very dangerous? _____

    _____

Appendages of the Skin

12. Using the key choices, respond to the following descriptions. (Some choices may be used more than once.)

Key:	arrector pili muscle	hair follicle	sweat gland—apocrine
	cutaneous receptors	nail	sweat gland—eccrine
	hair	sebaceous glands	

    _____ 1. acne is an infection of this

    _____ 2. structure that houses a hair

    _____ 3. more numerous variety of perspiration gland that produces a secretion containing water, salts, and vitamin C; activated by rise in temperature

    _____ 4. sheath formed of both epithelial and connective tissues

    _____ 5. type of perspiration-producing gland that produces a secretion containing proteins and fats in addition to water and salts

    _____ 6. found everywhere on body except palms of hands and soles of feet

    _____ 7. primarily dead/keratinized cells

    _____ 8. specialized nerve endings that respond to temperature, touch, etc.

    _____ 9. its secretion contains cell fragments

    _____ 10. "sports" a lunule and a cuticle

13. How does the skin help to regulate body temperature? (Describe two different mechanisms.) _____

    _____

    _____

    _____

    _____

14. Several structures or skin regions are lettered in the photomicrograph below. Identify each by matching its letter with the appropriate term that follows.

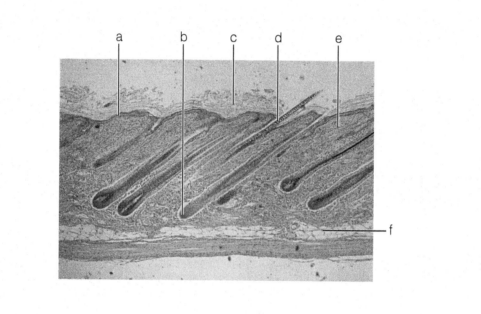

_____ adipose cells   _____ hair follicle

_____ dermis   _____ hair shaft

_____ epidermis   _____ sloughing stratum corneum cells

Plotting the Distribution of Sweat Glands

15. With what substance in the bond paper does the iodine painted on the skin react? _____

16. Which skin area—the forearm or palm of hand—has more sweat glands? _____

    Which other body areas would, if tested, prove to have a high density of sweat glands? _____

    _____

17. What organ system controls the activity of the eccrine sweat glands? _____

Overview of the Skeleton

Materials

Pre-Lab Quiz

1. All the following are functions of the skeleton *except:*
   a. attachment for muscles
   b. production of melanin
   c. site of red blood cell formation
   d. storage of lipids

2. Circle the correct term. <u>Compact</u> / <u>Spongy</u> bone looks smooth and homogeneous.

3. _____ bones are generally thin, with two waferlike layers of compact bone sandwiching a layer of spongy bone.
   a. Flat   c. Long
   b. Irregular   d. Short

4. Circle the correct term. The shaft of a long bone is known as the <u>epiphysis</u> / <u>diaphysis</u>.

5. A central canal and all the concentric lamellae surrounding it are referred to as: a. an osteon   b. canaliculi   c. lacunae

The **skeleton** is constructed of two of the most supportive tissues found in the human body—cartilage and bone. In embryos, the skeleton is composed mainly of hyaline cartilage, but in adults, most of the cartilage is replaced by more rigid bone.

OBJECTIVE 1   List three functions of the skeletal system.

Besides supporting the body as an internal framework and protecting many of its soft organs, the skeleton provides a system of levers the skeletal muscles use to move the body. In addition, the bones store lipids and many minerals (most importantly calcium). Finally, bones provide a site for blood cell formation in their red marrow cavities.

The skeleton is made up of bones that are connected at joints, or articulations. The skeleton is subdivided into two divisions: the **axial skeleton** (those bones that form the body's longitudinal axis) and the **appendicular skeleton** (bones of the girdles and limbs) (**Figure 7.1**).

Before beginning your study of the skeleton, imagine for a moment that your bones have turned to putty. What if you were running when this transformation took place? Now imagine your bones forming a continuous metal framework inside your body. What problems could you foresee with this arrangement? These images should help you understand how well the skeletal system provides support and protection while making movement possible.

Bone Markings

OBJECTIVE 2   Identify several surface bone markings and functions.

Bone surfaces are not featureless and smooth but have an array of bumps, holes, and ridges called **bone markings.** Bone markings fall into two categories: projections, or processes that grow out from the bone and serve as sites of muscle attachment or help form joints; and depressions or cavities, indentations or openings in the bone that sometimes serve as passageways for nerves and blood vessels. The bone markings are summarized in **Table 7.1**.

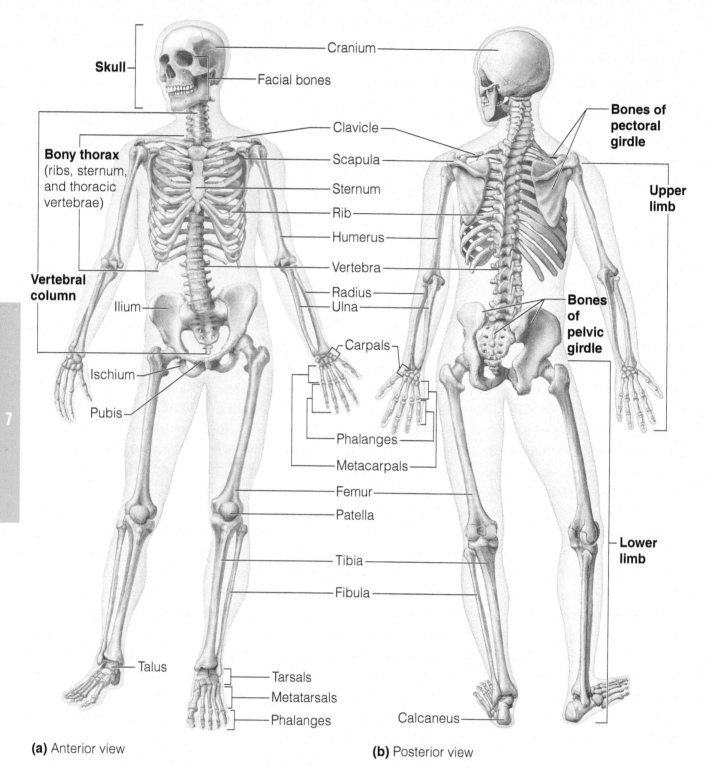

(a) Anterior view   **(b)** Posterior view

Figure 7.1 The human skeleton. The bones of the axial skeleton (colored green) are: the skull, the bony thorax, and the vertebral column. The bones of the appendicular skeleton make up the limbs and the girdles that the limbs attach to.

Classification of Bones

OBJECTIVE 3   Identify the four main kinds of bones.

The 206 bones of the adult skeleton are composed of two basic kinds of osseous tissue that differ in structure. **Compact bone** is dense and looks smooth and homogeneous. **Spongy bone** is composed of small *trabeculae* (needlelike bars) of bone and lots of open space.

Bones may be classified further on the basis of their gross anatomy into four groups: long, short, flat, and irregular bones.

Long bones, such as the femur (Figure 7.1) and phalanges (bones of the fingers), are much longer than they are wide and generally consist of a shaft with heads at either end. Long bones are mostly compact bone.

Short bones are typically cube-shaped, and they contain more spongy bone than compact bone. Notice the tarsals and carpals in Figure 7.1.

Flat bones are generally thin, with a layer of spongy bone sandwiched between two waferlike layers of compact bone. Bones of the skull are flat bones.

Irregular bones, such as the vertebrae, are bones that do not fall into one of the preceding categories (see Figure 7.1).

Table 7.1	Bone Markings	
Name of bone marking	Description	Illustrations

Projections That Are Sites of Muscle and Ligament Attachment

Tuberosity (too″bĕ-ros′ĭ-te)	Large rounded projection; may be roughened	
Crest	Narrow ridge of bone; usually prominent	
Trochanter (tro-kan′ter)	Very large, blunt, irregularly shaped process (the only examples are on the femur)	
Line	Narrow ridge of bone; less prominent than a crest	
Tubercle (too′ber-kl)	Small rounded projection or process	
Epicondyle (ep″ĭ-kon′dīl)	Raised area on or above a condyle	
Spine	Sharp, slender, often pointed projection	
Ramus (ra′mus)	Armlike bar of bone	
Process	Any bony prominence	

Projections That Help to Form Joints

Head	Bony expansion carried on a narrow neck	
Facet	Smooth, nearly flat articular surface	
Condyle (kon′dīl)	Rounded articular projection	

Depressions and Openings

For Passage of Blood Vessels and Nerves

Groove	Furrow	
Fissure	Narrow, slitlike opening	
Foramen (fo-ra′men)	Round or oval opening through a bone	
Notch	Indentation at the edge of a structure	

Others

Meatus (me-a′tus) Canal-like passageway

Sinus Cavity within a bone, filled with air and lined with mucous membrane

Fossa (fos′ah) Shallow, basinlike depression in a bone, often serving as an articular surface

7

Activity 1

Examining and Classifying Bones

Examine the isolated bones on display. See if you can find specific examples of the bone markings described in Table 7.1. Then classify each of the bones into one of the four anatomical groups: long, short, flat, irregular.

Gross Anatomy of the Typical Long Bone

OBJECTIVE 4 Identify the major anatomical areas of a longitudinally cut long bone.

Examining a Long Bone

1. Obtain a long bone that has been sawed lengthwise.

⚠️ *Note:* If the bone supplied is a fresh beef bone, put on plastic gloves before beginning your observations. If a cleaned dry bone is provided, you do not need to take any special precautions.

With the help of **Figure 7.2**, identify the shaft, or **diaphysis.** Observe its smooth surface composed of compact bone. If you are using a fresh specimen, look for its **periosteum,** a fibrous membrane that covers the bone surface. Notice that many fibers of the periosteum penetrate into the bone. These fibers are called **perforating fibers** or **Sharpey's fibers.**

2. Now inspect the **epiphysis,** the end of the long bone. Notice that it is composed of a thin layer of compact bone enclosing spongy bone.

3. Identify the **articular cartilage,** which covers the epiphyseal surface in place of the periosteum. Because it is composed of glassy hyaline cartilage, it provides a smooth surface to prevent friction at joint surfaces.

4. If the animal was still young and growing, you will be able to see the **epiphyseal plate,** a thin area of hyaline cartilage that provides for growth in bone length. When long bone growth ends, these areas are replaced with bone. Their barely discernible remnants are called **epiphyseal lines.**

5. In an adult animal, the *medullary cavity,* the central cavity of the shaft, is essentially a storage region for adipose tissue, or **yellow marrow.** In the infant, **red marrow,** involved in forming blood cells, is found in these central marrow cavities. In adult bones, red marrow is confined to the interior of the epiphyses.

6. If you are examining a fresh bone, look carefully to see if you can distinguish the delicate **endosteum** lining the medullary cavity.

⚠️ **7.** If you have been working with a fresh bone specimen, return it to the appropriate area, and properly dispose of your gloves, as designated by your instructor. Wash your hands before continuing on to the microscope study.

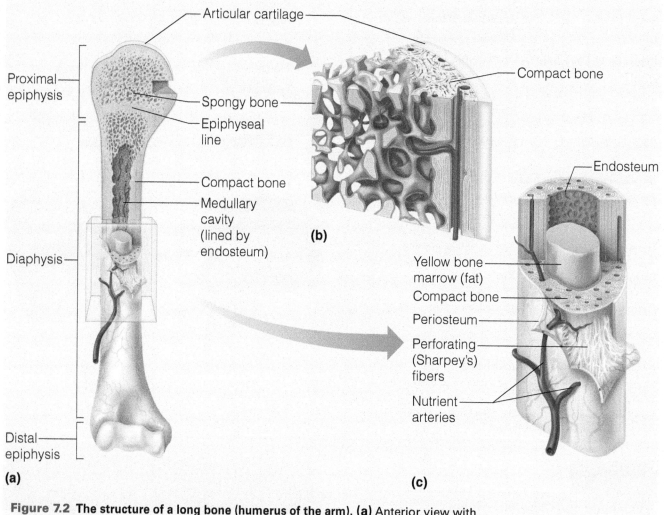

Figure 7.2 The structure of a long bone (humerus of the arm). (a) Anterior view with longitudinal section cut away at the proximal end. **(b)** Pie-shaped, three-dimensional view of spongy bone and compact bone of the epiphysis. **(c)** Cross section of the shaft (diaphysis). Note that the external surface of the diaphysis is covered by a periosteum, but the articular surface of the epiphysis is covered with hyaline cartilage.

Chemical Composition of Bone

Although it is relatively light, bone is one of the hardest materials in the body and it has a remarkable ability to resist tension and shear forces that continually act on it. Thus nature has given us an extremely strong, exceptionally simple (almost crude), and flexible supporting system without sacrificing mobility. The hardness of bone is due to the inorganic calcium salts in its ground substance. Its flexibility comes from the organic elements of the matrix, particularly the collagen fibers.

OBJECTIVE 5   Contrast the roles of inorganic salts and organic matrix in providing flexibility and hardness to bone.

Activity 3

Comparing the Relative Contributions of Bone Salts and Collagen Fibers in Bone Matrix

Go to the supply area and obtain a china cup, a leather belt or strap, and two or three large reference books. Carefully stack the books on the china cup to determine whether such a fragile-looking object can support the heavy books.

What happens? _____

Next, yank and pull on the leather belt (strap) a few times to see if you can break it.

What happens? _____

Which article—the cup or the belt—demonstrates the *compressional strength* provided by bone salts?

_____

Which item better illustrates the *tensile strength* (ability to resist stretch) provided by collagen fibers in bone?

_____

Activity 4

Examining the Effects of Heat and Hydrochloric Acid on Bones

Now, let's use another experimental approach to examine a bone's functional makeup. Obtain a bone sample that has been soaked in hydrochloric acid (or vinegar) and one that has been baked. Heating removes the organic part of bone, and acid dissolves out the minerals. Do the treated bones still have the shape of untreated specimens?

_____

Gently apply pressure to each bone sample. What happens to the heated bone?

_____

To the bone treated with acid?

_____

In rickets, the bones are not properly calcified. Which of the demonstration specimens more closely resembles the bones of a child with rickets?

_____

Microscopic Structure of Compact Bone

As you have seen, spongy bone has a spiky, open-work appearance due to the arrangement of the **trabeculae** that compose it, and compact bone appears dense and homogeneous. However, compact bone is riddled with passageways carrying blood vessels and nerves that provide the living bone cells with needed substances and a way to eliminate wastes.

OBJECTIVE 6   Identify the major elements of an osteon.

Activity 5

Examining the Microscopic Structure of Compact Bone

1. Go to the demonstration area to examine a prepared slide of ground bone under low power. Using **Figure 7.3** as a guide, focus on a **central (Haversian) canal** (one is indicated by the microscope pointer). The central canal

Text continues on next page. →

runs parallel to the long axis of the bone and carries blood vessels and nerves through the bony matrix. Identify the **lacunae** (chambers) where the **osteocytes** (mature bone cells) are found in living bone. These are arranged in concentric circles **(lamellae)** around the central canal. A central canal and all the lamellae surrounding it are referred to as an **osteon** or **Haversian system**. Also identify **canaliculi**, tiny canals running from a central canal to the lacunae of the first lamella and then from lamella to lamella. The canaliculi connect all the living cells of the osteon to the nutrient supply located in the central canal.

2. Also notice the **perforating (Volkmann's) canals** in Figure 7.3. These canals run into the compact bone and marrow cavity from the periosteum, at right angles to the shaft. With the central canals, the perforating canals complete the pathway between the bone interior and its external surface.

3. If a model of bone histology is available, identify the same structures on the model.

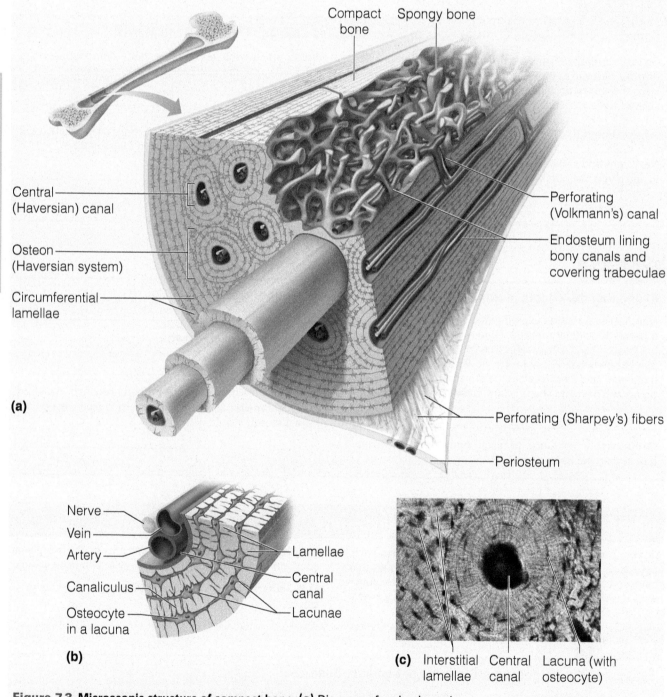

Figure 7.3 Microscopic structure of compact bone. (a) Diagram of a pie-shaped segment of compact bone. **(b)** Close-up of a portion of one osteon. Notice the position of osteocytes in lacunae (cavities in the matrix). **(c)** Photomicrograph of a cross-sectional view of an osteon (320×).

REVIEW SHEET
Overview of the Skeleton

Name _____   Lab Time/Date _____

Bone Markings

1. Match the terms in column B with the appropriate description in column A:

Column A	Column B
_____ 1. sharp, slender process	condyle
_____ 2. small rounded projection	foramen
_____ 3. large rounded projection	fossa
_____ 4. structure supported on neck	head
_____ 5. armlike projection	meatus
_____ 6. rounded, convex projection	ramus
_____ 7. canal-like structure	sinus
_____ 8. round or oval opening through a bone	spine
_____ 9. shallow depression	trochanter
_____ 10. air-filled cavity	tubercle
_____ 11. large, irregularly shaped projection	tuberosity

Classification of Bones

2. The four major anatomical classifications of bones are long, short, flat, and irregular. Which category has the least

   amount of spongy bone relative to its total volume? _____

3. Classify each of the bones in the following chart into one of the four major categories by checking the appropriate
   column. Use appropriate references as necessary.

	Long	Short	Flat	Irregular
Humerus				
Phalanx				
Parietal (skull bone)				
Calcaneus (tarsal bone)				
Rib				
Vertebra				

Gross Anatomy of the Typical Long Bone

4. Use the terms below to identify the structures marked by leader lines and brackets in the diagrams. (Some terms are used more than once.) After labeling the diagrams, use the listed terms to characterize the statements following the diagrams.

Key: articular cartilage   epiphyseal line   red marrow
          compact bone   epiphysis   spongy bone
          diaphysis   medullary cavity   trabeculae of spongy bone
          endosteum   periosteum   yellow marrow

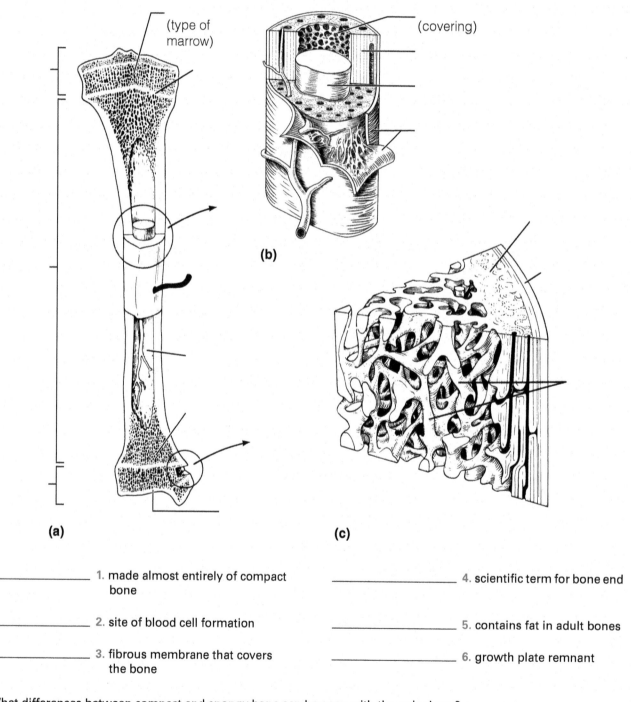

(type of marrow)

(covering)

(b)

(a)   (c)

_____ 1. made almost entirely of compact
                   bone

_____ 2. site of blood cell formation

_____ 3. fibrous membrane that covers
                   the bone

_____ 4. scientific term for bone end

_____ 5. contains fat in adult bones

_____ 6. growth plate remnant

5. What differences between compact and spongy bone can be seen with the naked eye?_____

_____

Chemical Composition of Bone

6. What is the function of the organic matrix in bone? _____

7. Name the important organic bone component. _____

8. Calcium salts form the bulk of the inorganic material in bone. What is the function of the calcium salts?

   _____

9. Which is responsible for bone structure? (circle the appropriate response)

   inorganic portion (bone salts)   organic portion   both contribute

Microscopic Structure of Compact Bone

10. Trace the route that nutrients take through a bone, starting with the periosteum and ending with an osteocyte in a lacuna.

   Periosteum ⟶ _____ ⟶ _____

   _____ ⟶ _____ ⟶ osteocyte

11. On the photomicrograph of bone below (480×), identify all structures listed in the key to the left.

   Key: canaliculi
           central canal
           lamellae
           lacuna
           bone matrix

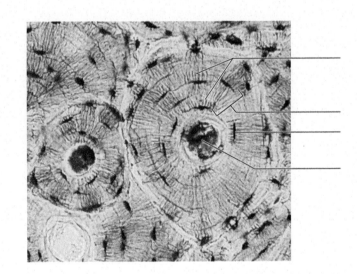

Materials

- [ ] Intact skull and Beauchene skull
- [ ] Isolated fetal skull
- [ ] X-ray films of individuals with scoliosis, lordosis, and kyphosis (if available)
- [ ] Articulated skeleton, articulated vertebral column
- [ ] Isolated cervical, thoracic, and lumbar vertebrae; sacrum, and coccyx

Pre-Lab Quiz

1. The axial skeleton is made up of the skull, the vertebral column, and the:
   a. bony thorax   c. hip bones
   b. femur   d. humerus

2. Eight bones make up the _____, which encloses and protects the brain.
   a. cranium   b. face   c. skull

3. Circle the correct term. The lower jawbone, or <u>maxilla</u> / <u>mandible</u>, articulates with the temporal bones in the only freely movable joint in the skull.

4. Circle the correct term. The <u>body</u> / <u>spinous process</u> of a typical vertebra forms the rounded, central portion that faces anteriorly in the human vertebral column.

5. The _____ vertebrae articulate with the corresponding ribs.
   a. cervical   c. spinal
   b. lumbar   d. thoracic

6. Circle True or False. The first seven pairs of ribs are called floating ribs because they have only indirect cartilage attachments to the sternum.

The **axial skeleton** (see Figure 7.1 on page 68) is made up of three parts: the skull, the vertebral column, and the bony thorax.

OBJECTIVE 1   Identify the bones of the axial skeleton either by examining isolated bones or by pointing them out on an articulated skeleton, and name the important markings on each. Be sure to observe how many cranial and facial bones contribute to the orbit (eye socket).

The Skull

The **skull** is composed of two sets of bones—the **cranial bones** and the **facial bones.** All but one of the bones of the skull are joined by interlocking joints called *sutures.* Only the mandible, or lower jawbone, is attached to the rest of the skull by a freely movable joint.

Activity 1

Identifying the Bones of the Adult Skull

The bones of the skull (**Figures 8.1–8.4**) are described in Tables 8.1 and 8.2 on pages 78–80. As you read through this material, identify each bone on a skull. The most important bone markings are listed in the tables for the bones on which they appear.

Text continues on page 81. →

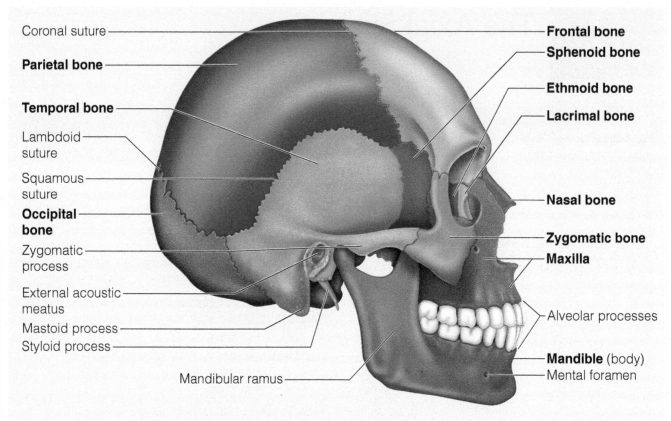

Figure 8.1 External anatomy of the right lateral aspect of the skull.

Table 8.1	The Axial Skeleton: Cranial Bones and Important Bone Markings
Cranial bone and important markings	**Description**
Frontal Figures 8.1–8.3	Anterior portion of cranium; forms the forehead, superior part of the orbit, and anterior part of cranial floor.
Parietal Bone Figures 8.1 and 8.4	Posterior and lateral to the frontal bone, forming sides of cranium.
Temporal Bone Figures 8.1–8.4	Inferior to parietal bone on lateral part of the skull.
• **Zygomatic process**	A bridgelike projection that joins the zygomatic bone (cheekbone) anteriorly. Together these two bones form the *zygomatic arch.*
• **External acoustic meatus**	Canal leading to eardrum.
• **Styloid process**	Needlelike projection inferior to external auditory meatus that serves as an attachment point for muscles and ligaments of the neck. This process is often broken off demonstration skulls.
• **Mastoid process**	Rough projection inferior and posterior to external auditory meatus; an attachment site for muscles.
Occipital Bone Figures 8.1–8.3	The most posterior bone of cranium: forms the floor and back wall. Joins the sphenoid bone anteriorly.
• **Foramen magnum**	Large opening in base of occipital that allows the spinal cord to join with the brain.
• **Occipital condyles**	Rounded projections lateral to the foramen magnum that articulate with the first cervical vertebra (atlas).

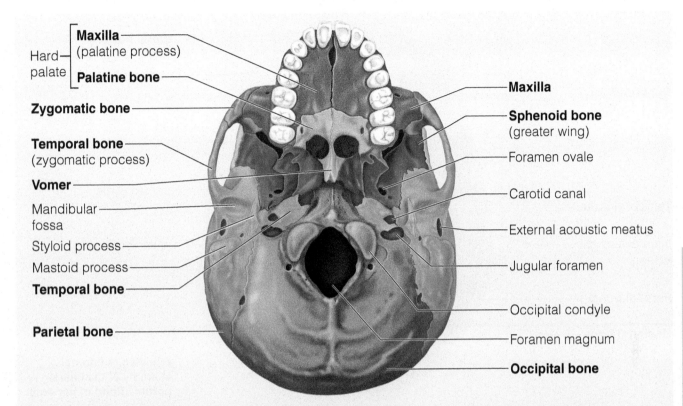

Figure 8.2 Inferior superficial view of the skull, mandible removed.

Table 8.1	(continued)
Cranial bone and important markings	**Description**
Sphenoid Bone Figures 8.1–8.4	Bat-shaped bone forming a plateau across the width of the skull. The sphenoid bone can be seen in its entire width if the top of the cranium is removed (Figure 8.3).
• **Greater wings**	Portions of the sphenoid seen exteriorly on the lateral aspect of the skull, anterior to the temporal bones. Form part of the orbits of the eyes.
• **Sella turcica**	A saddle-shaped region in the sphenoid midline that nearly encloses the pituitary gland.
• **Lesser wings**	Bat-shaped portions of the sphenoid anterior to the sella turcica.
• **Foramen ovale**	Opening posterior to the sella turcica that allows a branch of cranial nerve V to pass.
• **Optic canal**	Allows the optic nerve (cranial nerve II) to pass.
• **Superior orbital fissure**	Transmits cranial nerves III, IV, and VI to the eye.
Ethmoid Bone Figures 8.1, 8.3, and 8.4	Irregularly shaped bone anterior to the sphenoid. Forms the roof of the nasal cavity, upper nasal septum, and part of the medial orbit walls.
• **Crista galli**	Vertical projection to which the dura mater (outermost membrane covering of the brain) attaches.
• **Cribriform plates**	Bony plates lateral to the crista galli through which olfactory fibers pass to the brain from the nasal mucosa.
• **Superior and middle nasal conchae**	Thin, delicately coiled plates of bone extending medially from the ethmoid into the nasal cavity. The conchae increase the surface area of the mucosa that covers them, thus increasing the mucosa's ability to warm and humidify incoming air. Note that the superior nasal conchae are not visible in any of the figures in this exercise. They are located behind, and are obscured by, the nasal bones.

8

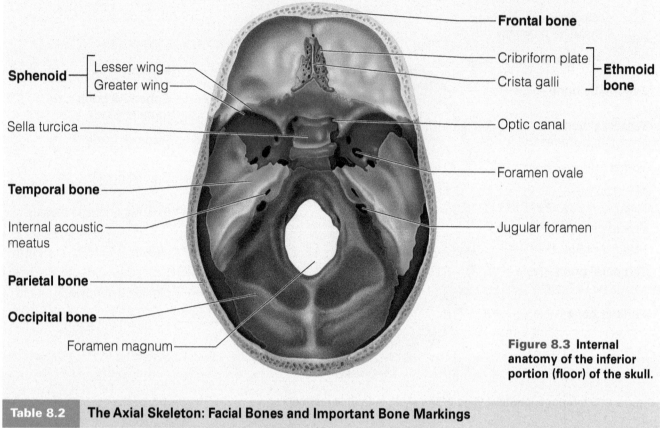

Figure 8.3 Internal anatomy of the inferior portion (floor) of the skull.

Table 8.2	The Axial Skeleton: Facial Bones and Important Bone Markings
Facial bone and important markings	**Description**
■ **Mandible** Figures 8.1 and 8.4	The lower jawbone; articulates with the temporal bones in the only freely movable joints of the skull.
• **Body**	Horizontal portion; forms the chin.
• **Ramus**	Vertical extension of the body on either side.
• **Alveolar process**	Superior margin of mandible; contains sockets for the lower teeth.
■ **Maxillae** Figures 8.1, 8.2, and 8.4	Two bones fused in a median suture; form the upper jawbone and part of the orbits. All facial bones, except the mandible, join the maxillae. Thus they are the main, or keystone, bones of the face.
• **Alveolar process**	Inferior margin containing sockets (alveoli) in which teeth lie.
• **Palatine processes**	Form the anterior hard palate.
▨ **Palatine Bone** Figure 8.2	Paired bones posterior to the palatine processes; form the posterior hard palate and part of the orbit.
■ **Zygomatic Bone** Figures 8.1, 8.2, and 8.4	Lateral to the maxilla; forms the part of the face commonly called the cheekbone, and part of the lateral orbit.
▨ **Lacrimal Bone** Figures 8.1 and 8.4	Fingernail-sized bones forming a part of the medial orbit walls between the maxilla and the ethmoid. Each lacrimal bone has an opening that serves as a passageway for tears (*lacrima* means "tear").
■ **Nasal Bone** Figures 8.1 and 8.4	Small rectangular bones forming the bridge of the nose.
▨ **Vomer** Figures 8.2 and 8.4	Blade-shaped bone in median plane of nasal cavity that forms most of the nasal septum.
■ **Inferior Nasal Conchae (Turbinates)** Figure 8.4	Thin curved bones protruding medially from the lateral walls of the nasal cavity; serve the same purpose as the nasal conchae of the ethmoid bone.

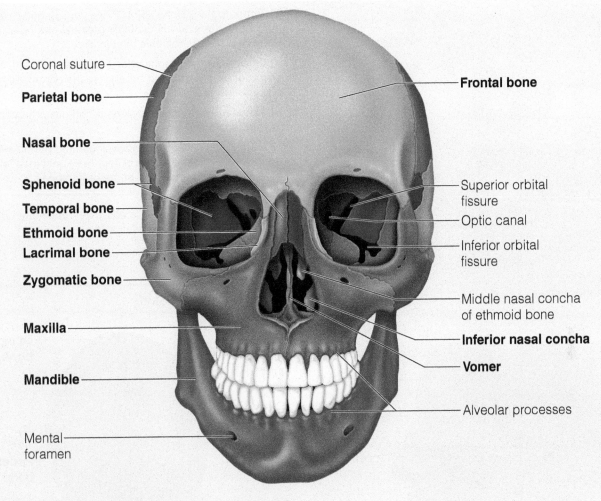

Figure 8.4 Anatomy of the anterior aspect of the skull.

The Cranium

Eight large flat bones construct the cranium, which encloses and protects the brain. *With the exception of two paired bones (the parietals and the temporals), all are single bones.*

Major Sutures

• **Sagittal suture:** Occurs where the left and right parietal bones meet superiorly.

• **Coronal suture:** Located where the parietal bones articulate with the frontal bone.

• **Squamous suture:** Occurs where each parietal bone meets each temporal bone, on each lateral aspect of the skull.

• **Lambdoid suture:** Occurs where the parietal bones meet the occipital bone posteriorly.

Hyoid Bone

The hyoid bone is not really considered or counted as a skull bone. Located in the throat above the larynx (**Figure 8.5**), it is the point of attachment for many tongue and neck muscles. It is horseshoe-shaped with a body and two pairs of **horns, or cornua.**

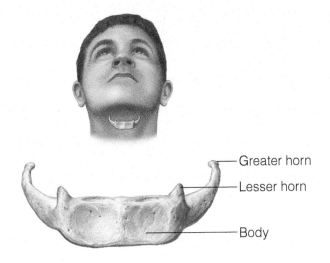

Figure 8.5 Hyoid bone.

Paranasal Sinuses

Four skull bones—maxillary, sphenoid, ethmoid, and frontal—contain sinuses (mucosa-lined air cavities), which lead into the nasal passages (**Figure 8.6**). These **paranasal sinuses** lighten facial bones and may act as resonance chambers for speech. The maxillary sinus is the largest of these sinuses.

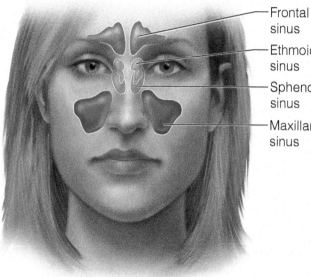

Frontal sinus

Ethmoid sinus

Sphenoidal sinus

Maxillary sinus

(a) Anterior view

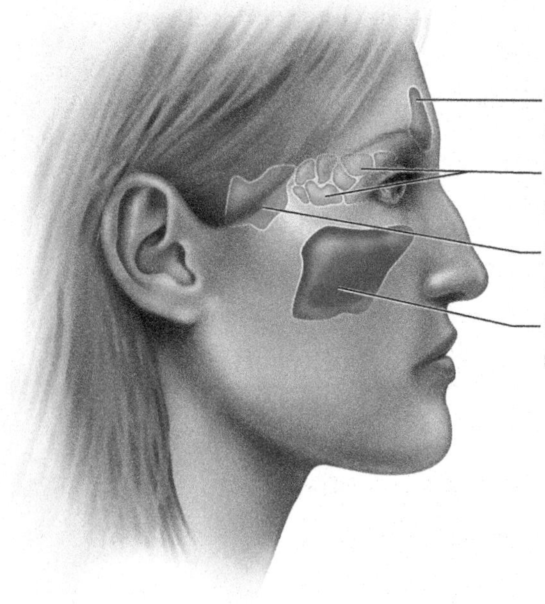

8

Frontal sinus

Ethmoid sinus

Sphenoidal sinus

Maxillary sinus

(b) Medial view

Figure 8.6 Paranasal sinuses.

Activity 2

Palpating Skull Markings

Palpate the following areas on yourself. (Place a check mark in the boxes as you locate the skull markings.)

☐ Zygomatic bone and arch. Run your hand anteriorly from your ear toward your eye and feel the zygomatic arch at the high point of your cheek just deep to the skin.

☐ Mastoid process (the rough area behind your ear).

☐ Temporomandibular joint. Place your finger directly in front of the external acoustic meatus, and open and close your jaws to feel this joint in action.

☐ Greater wing of sphenoid. Find the indented area posterior to the orbit and superior to the zygomatic arch on your lateral skull.

☐ Mandibular angle (most inferior and posterior aspect of your lower jaw).

☐ Nasal bones. Run your index finger and thumb along opposite sides of the bridge of your nose until they "slip" medially at the inferior end of the nasal bones.

OBJECTIVE 2 Demonstrate important differences between the fetal and adult skulls.

Activity 3

Examining a Fetal Skull

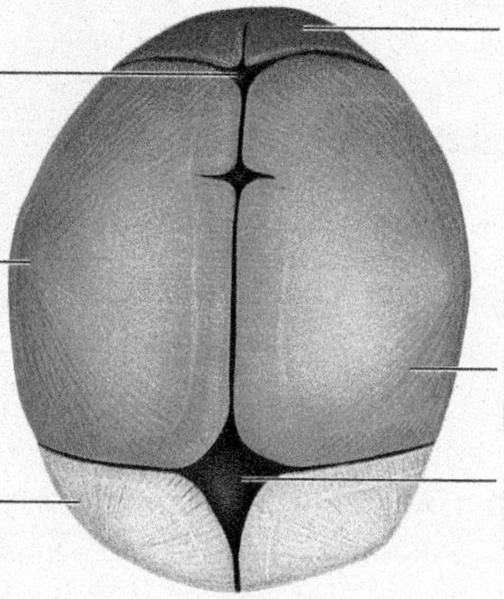

Posterior fontanel

Occipital bone

Ossification center

Parietal bone

Frontal bone

Anterior fontanel

Anterior

(a) Superior view

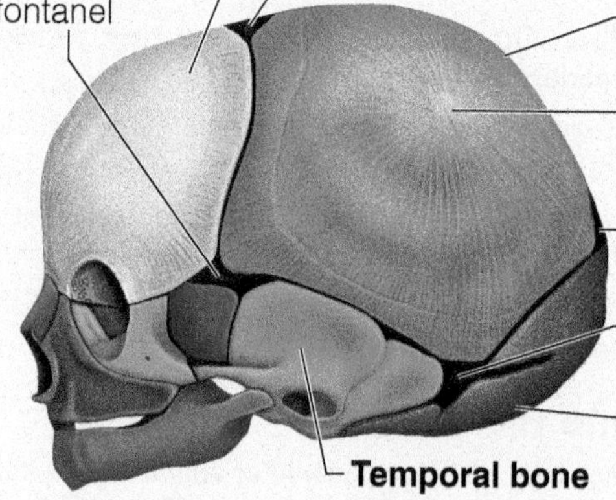

Frontal bone

Sphenoidal fontanel

Anterior fontanel

Parietal bone

Ossification center

Posterior fontanel

Mastoid fontanel

Occipital bone

Temporal bone (squamous part)

(b) Lateral view

Figure 8.7 The fetal skull.

1. Obtain a fetal skull, and study it carefully. Make observations as needed to answer the following questions.

- Does it have the same bones as the adult skull?

- How does the size of the fetal face relate to its cranium?

- How does this compare to what is seen in the adult?

2. **Fontanels,** fibrous membranes between the bones of the fetal skull, allow the fetal skull to be compressed slightly during birth and also allow for brain growth in the fetus and in an infant. These areas become bony (ossify) as the infant ages, completing the process by the age of 20 to 22 months. Locate the following fontanels on the fetal skull with the aid of **Figure 8.7**: anterior, mastoid, sphenoidal, and posterior.

3. Notice that some of the cranial bones have conical protrusions. These are growth (ossification) centers. Notice also that the frontal bone is still two bones and that the fetal temporal bone is little more than a ring of bone.

The Vertebral Column

The **vertebral column,** also called the *spine,* extends from the skull to the pelvis. It forms the body's major axial support and surrounds and protects the delicate spinal cord.

The vertebral column consists of 24 single bones called **vertebrae** and two bones that are formed of fused vertebrae (the sacrum and coccyx) that are connected in such a way as to provide a flexible curved structure (**Figure 8.8**). Of the 24 single vertebrae, the seven bones of the neck are called *cervical vertebrae;* the next 12 are *thoracic vertebrae;* and the 5 supporting the lower back are *lumbar vertebrae.* Remembering common mealtimes for breakfast, lunch, and dinner (7 A.M., 12 noon, and 5 P.M.) may help you to remember the number of bones in each region.

The individual vertebrae are separated by pads of fibrocartilage, **intervertebral discs,** that absorb shocks while providing the spine flexibility. Each disc has two major regions: a central gelatinous region that behaves like a fluid and an outer ring of tough collagen fibers that stabilizes the disc.

OBJECTIVE 3   Discuss the importance of the intervertebral discs and spinal curvatures.

The discs and the S-shaped or springlike construction of the vertebral column help prevent shock to the head in walking and running and make the body trunk flexible.

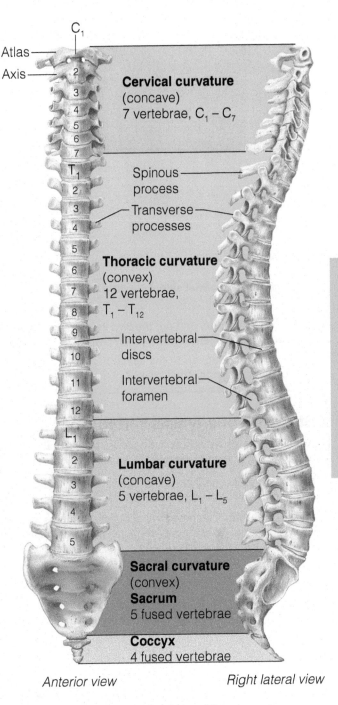

Figure 8.8 **The vertebral column.** (*Convex* and *concave* refer to the curvature of the posterior aspect of the vertebral column.)

Activity 4

Examining Spinal Curvatures

1. Observe the normal curves of the vertebral column in your laboratory specimen, and compare it to Figure 8.8. Then examine **Figure 8.9**, which depicts three abnormal spinal curvatures—*scoliosis, kyphosis,* and *lordosis.* These abnormalities may result from disease or poor posture. Also examine X-ray images, if they are available, showing these same conditions in a living person.

2. Next, using an articulated vertebral column (or an articulated skeleton), examine the freedom of movement between two lumbar vertebrae separated by an intervertebral disc.

- When the disc is properly positioned, are the spinal cord or peripheral nerves impaired in any way?

Text continues on next page. →

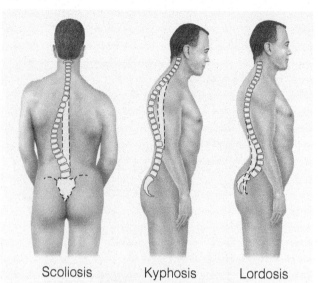

Scoliosis   Kyphosis   Lordosis

Figure 8.9 Abnormal spinal curvatures.

- Remove the disc, and put the two vertebrae back together. What happens to the nerve?
- What might happen to the spinal nerves in areas of malpositioned, or "slipped," discs?

Structure of a Typical Vertebra

Although they differ in size and specific features, all vertebrae have some common features (**Figure 8.10**).

Body: Rounded central portion of the vertebra; faces anteriorly in the human vertebral column.

Vertebral arch: Composed of pedicles, laminae, and a spinous process, it represents the junction of all posterior extensions from the vertebral body.

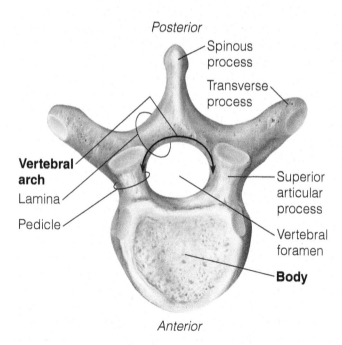

Posterior

Spinous process

Transverse process

Vertebral arch
Lamina
Pedicle

Superior articular process

Vertebral foramen

Body

Anterior

Figure 8.10 A typical vertebra, superior view. Inferior articulating surfaces are not shown.

Vertebral foramen: Opening enclosed by the body and vertebral arch through which the spinal cord passes.

Transverse processes: Two lateral projections from the vertebral arch.

Spinous process: Single posterior projection from the vertebral arch.

Superior and inferior articular processes: Paired projections lateral to the vertebral foramen that enable adjacent vertebrae to articulate with one another.

Figure 8.11 shows how specific vertebrae differ; refer to it as you read the sections that follow.

OBJECTIVE 4   Distinguish the different types of vertebrae.

Cervical Vertebrae

The seven cervical vertebrae (C_1 through C_7) form the neck portion of the vertebral column. The first two cervical vertebrae (atlas and axis) are modified to perform special functions. The **atlas** (C_1) lacks a body, and its lateral processes contain large depressions on their superior surfaces that receive the occipital condyles of the skull. This joint enables you to nod yes. The **axis** (C_2) acts as a pivot for rotation of the atlas (and skull) above. Its large vertical process, the **dens,** acts as the pivot point. The joint between C_1 and C_2 allows you to rotate your head from side to side to indicate "no."

The more typical cervical vertebrae (C_3 through C_7) are the smallest, lightest vertebrae (Figure 8.11a). The vertebral foramen is triangular and the spinous process is short and often bifid, or split into two branches. Transverse processes of the cervical vertebrae contain foramina through which the vertebral arteries pass superiorly to the brain. Any time you see these foramina in a vertebra, you can be sure that it is a cervical vertebra.

Activity 5

Palpating the Spinous Processes

Run your fingers inferiorly along the midline of the back of your neck to feel the *spinous processes* of the cervical vertebrae. The spine of C_7 is especially prominent, which is why this vertebra is sometimes called the *vertebra prominens.*

Thoracic Vertebrae

The 12 thoracic vertebrae (T_1 through T_{12}) have a larger body than the cervical vertebrae (Figure 8.11b). The body is somewhat heart-shaped, with two small articulating surfaces, or *costal facets,* on each side (one superior, the other inferior) that articulate with the heads of the corresponding ribs. The vertebral foramen is oval or round, and the spinous process is long, with a sharp downward hook. These vertebrae form the thoracic part of the spine and the posterior aspect of the bony thoracic cage (rib cage). They are the only vertebrae that articulate with the ribs.

Lumbar Vertebrae

The five lumbar vertebrae (L_1 through L_5) have massive blocklike bodies and short, thick, hatchet-shaped spinous processes extending directly backward (Figure 8.11c). Because the lumbar region is subjected to the most stress, these are also the sturdiest of the vertebrae.

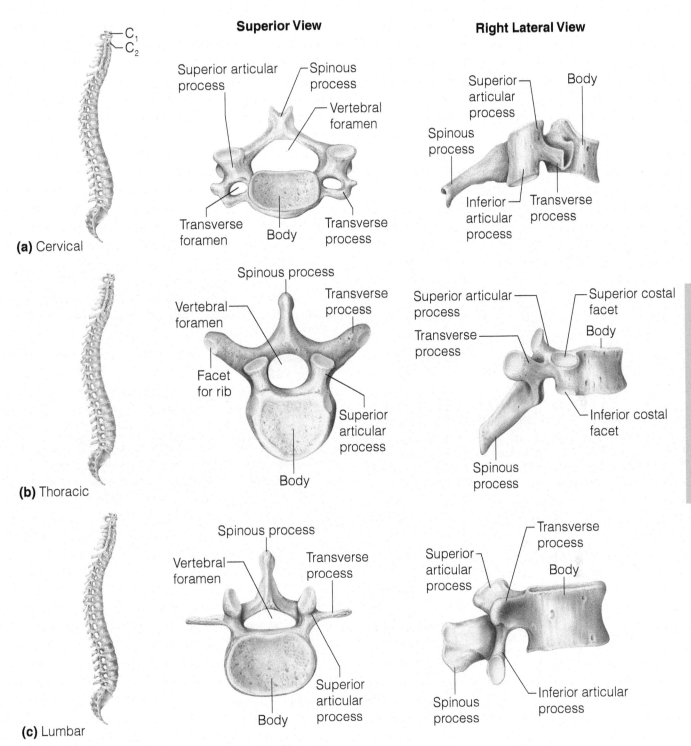

Superior View

(a) Cervical

C₁
C₂

Superior articular process

Spinous process

Vertebral foramen

Transverse foramen

Body

Transverse process

Right Lateral View

Superior articular process

Body

Spinous process

Inferior articular process

Transverse process

(b) Thoracic

Spinous process

Transverse process

Vertebral foramen

Facet for rib

Body

Superior articular process

Superior articular process

Transverse process

Superior costal facet

Body

Inferior costal facet

Spinous process

(c) Lumbar

Spinous process

Transverse process

Vertebral foramen

Body

Superior articular process

Superior articular process

Transverse process

Body

Spinous process

Inferior articular process

Figure 8.11 Regional characteristics of vertebrae.

8

Activity 6

Examining Vertebral Structure

Obtain examples of each type of vertebra and examine them carefully, comparing them to Figure 8.11 and to each other.

The Sacrum

The **sacrum** (**Figure 8.12**), formed from the fusion of five vertebrae, is the posterior border of the pelvis. Superiorly it articulates with L₅, and inferiorly it connects with the coccyx.

The **median sacral crest** is a remnant of the spinous processes of the fused vertebrae. The winglike **alae** articulate laterally with the hip bones, forming the sacroiliac joints. The paired **sacral foramina** are additional evidence that the sacrum is formed of separate fused vertebrae and serve as passageways for blood vessels and nerves. The vertebral canal continues inside the sacrum as the **sacral canal** and terminates near the coccyx in the **sacral hiatus.**

The Coccyx

The **coccyx** (see Figure 8.12) results from the fusion of three to five small, irregularly shaped vertebrae. Literally the human tailbone, it is a remnant of the tail that other vertebrates have.

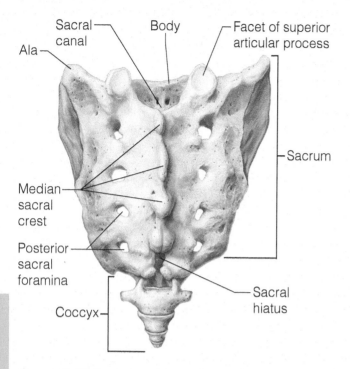

Figure 8.12 **Sacrum and coccyx, posterior view.**

Labels on figure:
Sacral canal
Ala
Body
Facet of superior articular process
Sacrum
Median sacral crest
Posterior sacral foramina
Coccyx
Sacral hiatus

The Bony Thorax

The **bony thorax** is composed of the sternum, ribs, and thoracic vertebrae (**Figure 8.13**). It is also referred to as the **thoracic cage** because it forms a protective cone-shaped enclosure around the organs of the thoracic cavity (heart and lungs, for example).

The Sternum

The **sternum** (breastbone), a typical flat bone, is a result of the fusion of three bones—from superior to inferior, the manubrium, body, and xiphoid process. It is attached to the first seven pairs of ribs. The **manubrium** looks like the knot of a tie; it articulates with the clavicle (collarbone) laterally. The **body** forms most of the sternum. The **xiphoid process,** at the inferior end of the sternum, lies at the level of the fifth intercostal space.

The Ribs

Twelve pairs of **ribs** form the walls of the thoracic cage (see Figure 8.13). All ribs articulate posteriorly with the vertebral column at two locations, the body and transverse processes of the thoracic vertebrae. They then curve downward and toward the anterior body surface. The first seven pairs, called the *true ribs,* attach directly to the sternum by their "own" costal cartilages. The next five pairs are called *false ribs.* Of these, rib pairs 8–10 have *indirect* cartilage attachments to the sternum. The last two pairs, also called *floating ribs,* have *no* sternal attachment.

Activity 7

Examining the Relationship Between Ribs and Vertebrae

First take a deep breath to expand your chest. Notice how your ribs seem to move outward and how your sternum rises. Then examine an articulated skeleton to observe the relationship between the ribs and the vertebrae.

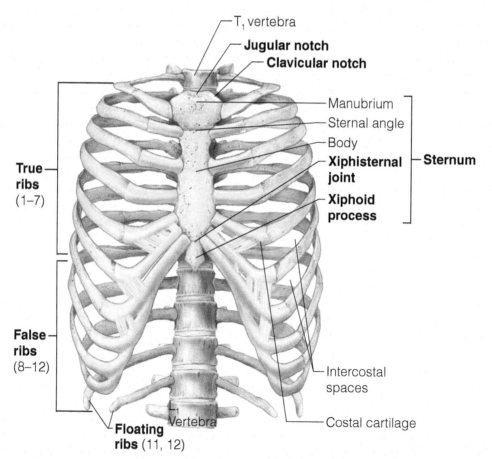

Labels on figure:
T₁ vertebra
Jugular notch
Clavicular notch
Manubrium
Sternal angle
Body
Xiphisternal joint
Xiphoid process
Sternum
True ribs (1–7)
False ribs (8–12)
Floating ribs (11, 12)
L₁ Vertebra
Intercostal spaces
Costal cartilage

Figure 8.13 **The bony thorax, anterior view.** (Costal cartilages are shown in light blue.)

REVIEW SHEET
The Axial Skeleton

Name _____ Lab Time/Date _____

The Skull

1. The skull is one of the major components of the axial skeleton. Name the other two.

   _____ and _____

   What structures does each of these three components of the axial skeleton protect? _____

   _____

   _____

2. Define *suture:* _____

3. With one exception, the skull bones are joined by sutures. Name the exception. _____

   _____

4. What are the four major sutures of the skull, and what bones do they connect?

   _____

   _____

   _____

   _____

5. Name the eight bones composing the cranium.

   _____ _____ _____ _____

   _____ _____ _____ _____

6. Give two possible functions of the sinuses. _____

   _____

7. What is the orbit? _____

8. Why can the sphenoid bone be called the keystone of the cranial floor? _____

   _____

   _____

9. Match the bone names in column B with the descriptions in column A. (Some choices may be used more than once.)

Column A		Column B

_____ 1. bone forming anterior cranium, or forehead   ethmoid

_____ 2. cheekbone   frontal

_____ 3. upper jaw   hyoid

_____ 4. bridge of nose   lacrimal

_____ 5. posterior roof of mouth   mandible

_____ 6. bone pair united by the sagittal suture   maxilla

_____ 7. site of jugular foramen and carotid canal   nasal

_____ 8. contains a "saddle" that houses the pituitary gland   occipital

_____ 9. has an opening that allows tears to pass   palatine

_____ 10. forms most of hard palate   parietal

_____ 11. superior and medial nasal conchae are part of this bone   sphenoid

_____ 12. site of external auditory meatus   temporal

_____ 13. has greater and lesser wings   vomer

_____ 14. its "holey" plate allows olfactory fibers to pass   zygomatic

_____ 15. facial bone that contains a sinus

_____, _____, and _____ 16. three cranial bones containing paranasal sinuses

_____ 17. its oval-shaped protrusions articulate with the atlas

_____ 18. spinal cord passes through a large opening in this bone

_____ 19. not really a skull bone

_____ 20. forms the chin

_____ 21. inferior part of nasal septum

_____, _____ 22. contain alveoli bearing teeth

_____ 23. bears an upward protrusion called the rooster's comb

10. Using choices from column B in question 9 and from the key to the right, identify all bones and bone markings provided with leader lines in the diagram below. (Some terms from the key may not be used.)

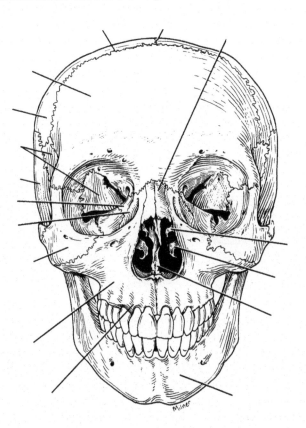

alveolar process

coronal suture

foramen magnum

greater wing of sphenoid

inferior nasal concha

middle nasal concha of ethmoid

sagittal suture

squamous suture

The Fetal Skull

11. Are the same skull bones present in the adult also found in the fetal skull? _____

12. How does the size of the fetal face compare to its cranium? _____

_____

How does this compare to the adult skull? _____

_____

_____

13. What are the outward conical projections in some of the fetal cranial bones? _____

_____

14. What is a fontanel? _____

What is its fate? _____

What is the function of the fontanels in the fetal skull? _____

_____

15. Using the terms listed, identify each of the fontanels shown on the fetal skull below.

anterior fontanel   mastoid fontanel   posterior fontanel   sphenoidal fontanel

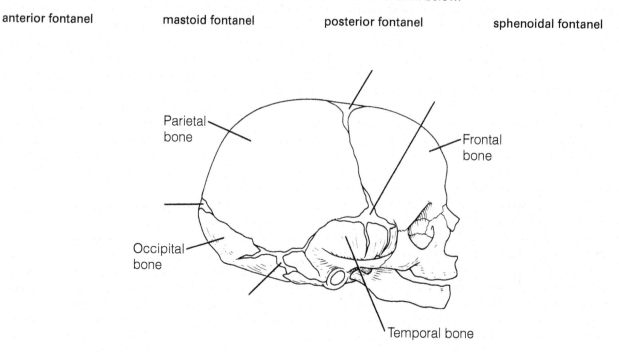

Parietal bone

Frontal bone

Occipital bone

Temporal bone

The Vertebral Column

16. Using the key, correctly identify the vertebral parts/areas described below. (More than one choice may apply in some cases.) Also use the key letters to correctly identify the vertebral areas in the diagram.

Key: a. body
       b. intervertebral foramina
       c. lamina

       d. pedicle
       e. spinous process
       f. superior articular facet

       g. transverse process
       h. vertebral arch
       i. vertebral foramen

_____ 1. cavity enclosing the nerve cord

_____ 2. weight-bearing portion of the vertebra

_____ , _____ 3. provide levers against which muscles pull

_____ , _____ 4. provide an articulation point for the ribs

_____ 5. opening providing for exit of spinal nerves

_____ , _____ 6. structures that form an enclosure for the spinal cord

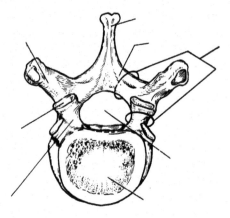

17. The distinguishing characteristics of the vertebrae composing the vertebral column are noted below. Correctly identify each described structure or region by choosing a response from the key. (Some choices may be used more than once.)

Key: atlas   coccyx   sacrum
        axis   lumbar vertebra   thoracic vertebra
        cervical vertebra—typical

_____ 1. vertebral type with a bifid (forked) spinous process

_____ 2. pivots on C_2; lacks a body

_____ 3. bear facets for articulation with ribs; form part of bony thoracic cage

_____ 4. forms a joint with the hip bone

_____ 5. vertebra with blocklike body and short, stout spinous process

_____ 6. "tailbone"

_____ 7. articulates with the occipital condyles

_____ 8. five components; unfused

_____ 9. twelve components; unfused

_____ 10. five components; fused

18. Identify as specifically as possible each of the vertebrae types shown in the diagrams below. Also identify and label the following markings on each: transverse processes, spinous process, body, superior articular processes, as well as the areas provided with leaders.

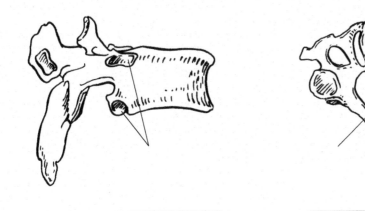

_____   _____

19. What kind of tissue makes up the intervertebral discs? _____

20. What is a herniated disc? _____

What problems might it cause? _____

_____

21. On this illustration of an articulated vertebral column, identify each structure provided with a leader line by using the key terms.

Key: atlas
axis
intervertebral disc
two thoracic vertebrae
two lumbar vertebrae
sacrum

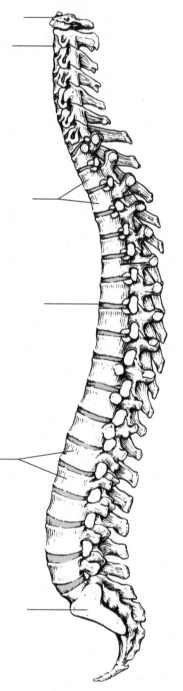

The Bony Thorax

22. The major components of the bony thorax (excluding the vertebral column) are the _____

and the _____.

23. What is the general shape of the thoracic cage? _____

_____

24. Using the terms at the right, identify the regions and landmarks of the bony thorax.

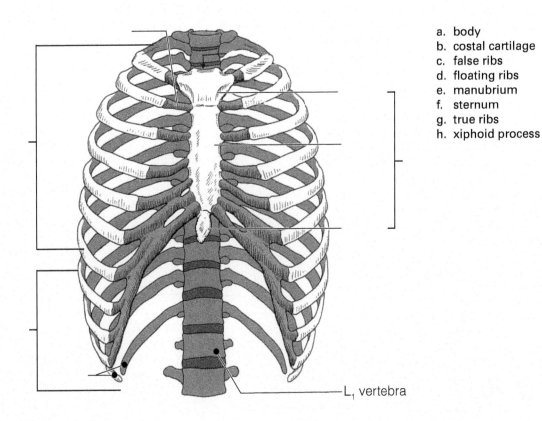

a. body
b. costal cartilage
c. false ribs
d. floating ribs
e. manubrium
f. sternum
g. true ribs
h. xiphoid process

L₁ vertebra

25. Differentiate a true rib from a false rib. _____

_____

26. What is a floating rib? _____

_____

The Appendicular Skeleton

Materials

☐ Articulated skeletons
☐ Disarticulated skeletons (complete)
☐ Articulated pelves (male and female for comparative study)
☐ X-ray images of bones of the appendicular skeleton
☐ Unknowns: six individual numbered bone specimens in kraft paper or muslin bags for identification by palpation

Pre-Lab Quiz

1. The _____ skeleton is composed of 126 bones of the appendages and pectoral and pelvic girdles.

2. The _____, or shoulder blades, are generally triangular in shape. They have no direct attachment to the axial skeleton but are held in place by trunk muscles.

3. The arm consists of one long bone, the:
   a. femur
   b. humerus
   c. tibia
   d. ulna

4. You are studying a pelvis that is wide and shallow. The acetabula are small and far apart. The pubic arch/angle is rounded and greater than 90°. It appears to be tilted forward, with a wide, short sacrum. Is this a male or a female pelvis? _____

5. The strongest, heaviest bone of the body is in the thigh. It is the:
   a. femur
   b. fibula
   c. tibia

6. Circle True or False. The fingers of the hand and the toes of the foot—with the exception of the great toe and the thumb—each have three phalanges.

The **appendicular skeleton** (see Figure 7.1 on page 68) is composed of the 126 bones of the appendages and the pectoral and pelvic girdles, which attach the limbs to the axial skeleton. The upper and lower limbs differ in their functions and mobility, but they have the same basic plan. Each limb is composed of three major segments connected by freely movable joints.

Activity 1

Examining and Identifying Bones of the Appendicular Skeleton

Examine each of the bones described in this exercise, and identify characteristic bone markings of each. The markings help you to determine whether a bone is the right or left member of its pair. *This is a very important instruction because before completing this laboratory exercise, you will be constructing your own skeleton.* When corresponding X-ray films are available, compare the actual bone specimen to its X-ray image.

Bones of the Pectoral Girdle and Upper Limb

OBJECTIVE 1 Identify the bones of the pectoral and pelvic girdles and their attached limbs.

OBJECTIVE 2 Compare and contrast the relative functions and stability of the two girdles.

The Pectoral (Shoulder) Girdle

The paired **pectoral,** or **shoulder, girdles** (**Figure 9.1**) each consist of two bones—a clavicle and a scapula. The shoulder girdles anchor the upper limbs to

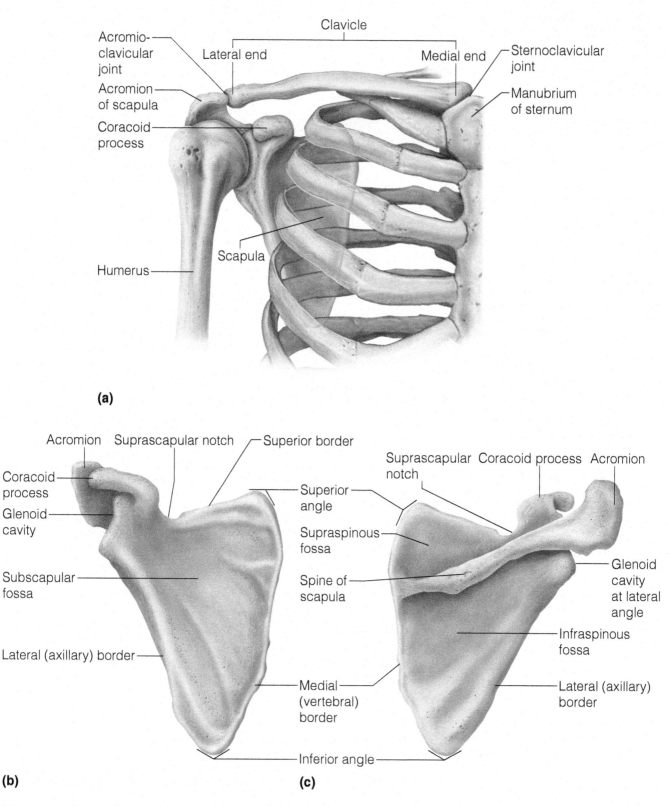

(a)

(b)   **(c)**

Figure 9.1 Bones of the right pectoral (shoulder) girdle. (a) Pectoral girdle articulated to show the relationship of the girdle to the bones of the thorax and arm. **(b)** Right scapula, anterior view. **(c)** Right scapula, posterior view.

the axial skeleton and provide attachment points for many trunk and neck muscles. The pectoral girdle allows for movement and flexibility, but it is not very stable.

The **clavicle,** or collarbone, is a slender, doubly curved bone—convex forward medially, and concave forward laterally.

Its medial end attaches to the sternal manubrium. This end projects above the manubrium and can be easily felt and (usually) seen. The lateral end of the clavicle is flattened where it articulates with the scapula to form part of the shoulder (acromioclavicular) joint. The clavicle serves as a brace, or strut, to hold the arm away from the top of the thorax.

The **scapulae** (Figure 9.1), or shoulder blades, are generally triangular. Each scapula has a flattened body and two important processes—the **acromion** (the enlarged end of the spine of the scapula) and the beaklike **coracoid process** (*corac* = crow, raven). The acromion connects with the clavicle; the coracoid process points anteriorly over the tip of the shoulder joint and anchors some of the upper limb muscles. The scapula has no direct attachment to the axial skeleton but is loosely held in place by trunk muscles.

The scapula has three angles (superior, inferior, and lateral) and three named borders (superior, medial [vertebral], and lateral [axillary]). Several shallow depressions (fossae) appear on both sides of the scapula and are named according to location. The **glenoid cavity,** a shallow socket that receives the head of the arm bone (humerus), is located in the lateral angle.

The Arm

The arm (**Figure 9.2**) consists of a single bone—the **humerus,** a typical long bone. Proximally its *head* fits into the shallow glenoid cavity of the scapula. Opposite the head

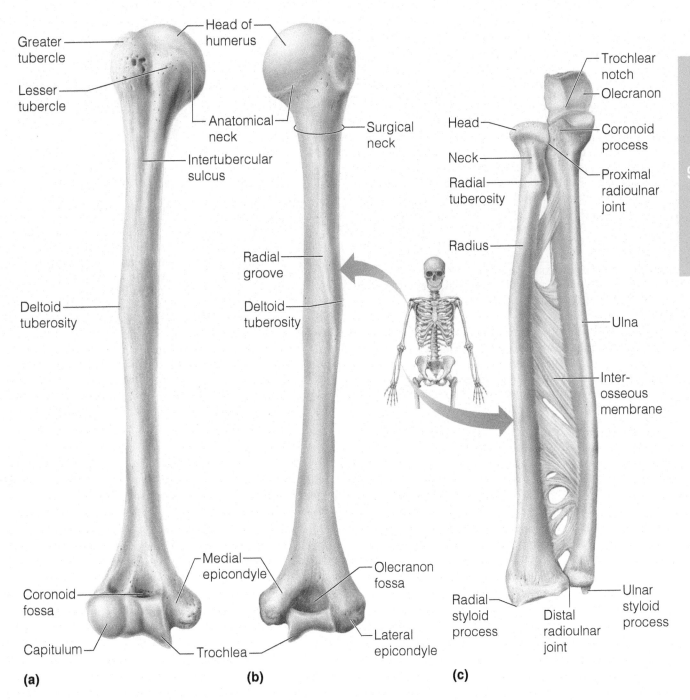

(a)   **(b)**   **(c)**

Figure 9.2 Bones of the right arm and forearm. (a) Humerus, anterior view.
(b) Humerus, posterior view. **(c)** Anterior view of bones of the forearm, the radius and the ulna.

are two prominences, the **greater** and **lesser tubercles** (from lateral to medial aspect), separated by a groove (the **intertubercular sulcus**) that guides the tendon of the biceps muscle to its point of attachment on the superior rim of the glenoid cavity. Midshaft is a roughened area, the **deltoid tuberosity,** where the large fleshy shoulder muscle, the deltoid, attaches.

At the distal end of the humerus are the medial **trochlea** (looking rather like a spool), which articulates with the ulna, and the lateral **capitulum,** which articulates with the radius of the forearm. These condyles are flanked medially and laterally by the **epicondyles.**

Above the trochlea is the **coronoid fossa;** on the posterior surface is the **olecranon.** These two depressions allow the corresponding processes of the ulna to move freely when the elbow is flexed and extended.

The Forearm

Two bones, the radius and the ulna, form the skeleton of the forearm (see Figure 9.2). In the anatomical position, the **radius** is in the lateral position, and the radius and ulna (joined along their length by an **interosseous membrane**) are parallel. Proximally, the disc-shaped head of the radius articulates with the capitulum of the humerus. Medially, just below the head is the **radial tuberosity,** where the tendon of the biceps muscle of the arm attaches. At the lateral aspect of its distal end is the expanded **radial styloid process.**

The **ulna** is the medial bone of the forearm. Its proximal end bears the anterior **coronoid process** and the posterior **olecranon process,** which are separated by the **trochlear notch.** Together these processes grip the trochlea of the humerus in a plierslike joint. The slimmer distal end, the ulnar *head,* bears a small medial **ulnar styloid process,** which anchors some ligaments of the wrist.

The Hand

The skeleton of the hand (**Figure 9.3**) includes three groups of bones: the carpals (wrist bones), metacarpals (bones of the palm), and phalanges (bones of the fingers).

The **carpus,** or wrist, is the proximal portion of the hand. (So you actually wear your wristwatch over the distal part of your forearm.) The eight bones composing the carpus, the **carpals,** are arranged in two irregular rows of four bones

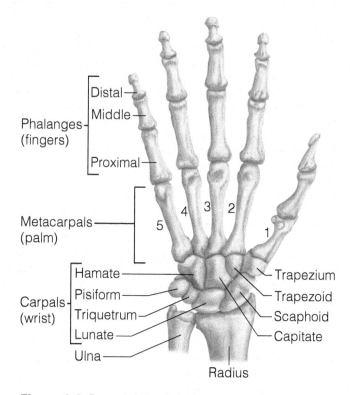

Figure 9.3 Bones of the right hand, anterior view.

each. These bones, named in Figure 9.3, are bound together by ligaments, which restrict movements between them.

The **metacarpals,** numbered 1 to 5 from the thumb side of the hand, radiate out from the wrist like spokes to form the palm of the hand. The *bases* of the metacarpals articulate with the carpals of the wrist; their *heads* articulate with the phalanges of the fingers distally.

Like the bones of the palm, the fingers are numbered from 1 to 5, beginning from the thumb side of the hand. The 14 bones of the fingers, or digits of each hand, are miniature long bones, called **phalanges** (singular: **phalanx**), as noted earlier. Each finger has three phalanges (proximal, middle, and distal), except the thumb, which has only two (proximal and distal).

Activity 2

Palpating the Surface Anatomy of the Pectoral Girdle and the Upper Limb

Before continuing on to study the bones of the pelvic girdle, identify the following bone markings on the skin surface of the upper limb. You will probably want to observe and palpate these bone markings on your lab partner, particularly since many can only be seen from the dorsal aspect.

Place a check mark in the boxes as you locate the bone markings.

☐ *Clavicle:* Palpate the clavicle along its entire length from sternum to shoulder. Where the clavicle joins the sternum, identify the rigid sternoclavicular joint.

☐ *Acromioclavicular joint:* At the high point of the shoulder, find the junction point between the clavicle and the acromion of the scapular spine.

☐ *Spine of the scapula:* Extend your arm at the shoulder so that your scapula moves posteriorly. As you do this, the spine of your scapula will be seen as a winglike protrusion on your dorsal thorax and can be easily palpated by your lab partner.

☐ *Olecranon process of the ulna:* Work your elbow— flexing and extending—as you palpate its dorsal aspect to feel the olecranon process of the ulna moving in and out of the olecranon fossa on the backside of the humerus.

☐ *Styloid process of the ulna:* With the hand in the anatomical position, feel out this small projection on the medial aspect at the distal end of the ulna.

☐ *Styloid process of the radius:* Find this projection at the distal end of the radius (lateral aspect). It is most easily located by moving the hand medially at the wrist. Once you have palpated the styloid process, move your fingers just medially onto the anterior wrist. Press firmly and then let up slightly on the pressure. You should be able to feel your pulse at this pressure point, which lies over the radial artery (radial pulse).

☐ *Metacarpophalangeal joints (knuckles):* Clench your fist and find the first set of flexed-joint protrusions beyond the wrist—these are your metacarpophalangeal joints.

Bones of the Pelvic Girdle and Lower Limb

The Pelvic (Hip) Girdle

As with the bones of the pectoral girdle and upper limb, pay particular attention to bone markings needed to identify right and left bones.

The **pelvic girdle,** or **hip girdle** (**Figure 9.4**), is formed by the two **coxal** (*coxa* = hip) **bones** (also called the **ossa coxae,** or hip bones). The two coxal bones together with the sacrum and coccyx form the **bony pelvis.** Unlike the bones of the shoulder girdle, those of the pelvic girdle are heavy and massive, and they attach securely to the axial skeleton. The sockets for the heads of the femurs (thigh bones) are deep and heavily reinforced by ligaments, ensuring a stable, strong limb attachment. The ability to bear weight is more important here than mobility and flexibility.

Each coxal bone is a result of the fusion of three bones—the ilium, ischium, and pubis. The **ilium,** a large flaring bone, forms most of the coxal bone. It connects posteriorly with the sacrum at the **sacroiliac joint.** The superior margin of the iliac bone, the **iliac crest,** terminates anteriorly in the **anterior superior iliac spine** and posteriorly in the **posterior superior iliac spine.** Two inferior spines are located below these.

The **ischium,** forming the inferior portion of the coxal bone, is the "sit-down" bone. Its rough **ischial tuberosity** receives the weight of the body when we sit. The **ischial spine,** superior to the ischial tuberosity, is an important anatomical landmark of the pelvic cavity. The **greater sciatic notch** allows the huge sciatic nerve to pass to and from the thigh.

The **pubis** is the most anterior part of the coxal bone. Fusion of the **rami** of the pubic bone anteriorly and the ischium posteriorly forms a bar of bone enclosing the **obturator foramen,** through which a small number of blood vessels and nerves run from the pelvic cavity into the thigh. The two pubic bones meet anteriorly at a joint called the **pubic symphysis.**

The ilium, ischium, and pubis unite at the deep hemispherical socket called the **acetabulum** (literally, "vinegar cup"), which receives the head of the thigh bone.

Activity 3

Palpating the Surface Anatomy of the Pelvic Girdle

Locate and palpate the following bone markings on yourself and/or your lab partner.

Place a check mark in the boxes as you locate the bone markings.

☐ *Iliac crest:* Rest your hands on your hips—they will be overlying the iliac crests.

☐ *Anterior superior iliac spine:* Trace the crest anteriorly to the anterior superior iliac spine. This bone marking is easily felt in almost everyone and is clearly visible through the skin (and perhaps the clothing) of very slim people. (The posterior superior iliac spine is much less obvious and is usually indicated only by a dimple in the overlying skin. Check it out in the mirror tonight.)

OBJECTIVE 3   Differentiate a male from a female pelvis.

Comparison of the Male and Female Pelves

Although bones of males are usually larger and heavier, the male and female skeletons are very similar. The outstanding exception to this generalization is pelvic structure. The female pelvis is modified for childbearing. Generally speaking, the female pelvis is wider, shallower, lighter, and rounder than that of the male. (See **Table 9.1.**)

To describe pelvic sex differences, we need to introduce a few more anatomical terms. The **false pelvis** is the superior portion bounded by the ilia laterally and the sacrum and lumbar vertebrae posteriorly (Figure 9.4). The false pelvis supports the abdominal viscera, but it does not restrict childbirth in any way. The **true pelvis** is the inferior region that is almost entirely surrounded by bone. Its posterior boundary is the sacrum. The ilia, ischia, and pubic bones define its limits laterally and anteriorly.

The dimensions of the true pelvis, particularly its inlet and outlet, are critical if delivery of a baby is to be uncomplicated; and they are carefully measured by the obstetrician. The **pelvic inlet,** or **pelvic brim,** is the superiormost margin of the true pelvis. It is widest from left to right, that is, along the frontal plane. The **pelvic outlet** (Table 9.1) is the inferior margin of the true pelvis. It is bounded anteriorly by the pubic bones, laterally by the ischia, and posteriorly by the sacrum and coccyx. Because both the coccyx and the ischial spines protrude into the outlet opening, a sharply angled coccyx or large, sharp ischial spines can dramatically narrow the outlet. The largest dimension of the outlet is the anterior-posterior diameter.

Activity 4

Comparing Male and Female Pelves

Examine Figure 9.4, Table 9.1, and if possible both a male and a female pelvis. Pay particular attention to differences in the relative size and shape of the inlet, ischial spines, and sacrum, and to the angle of the pubic arch.

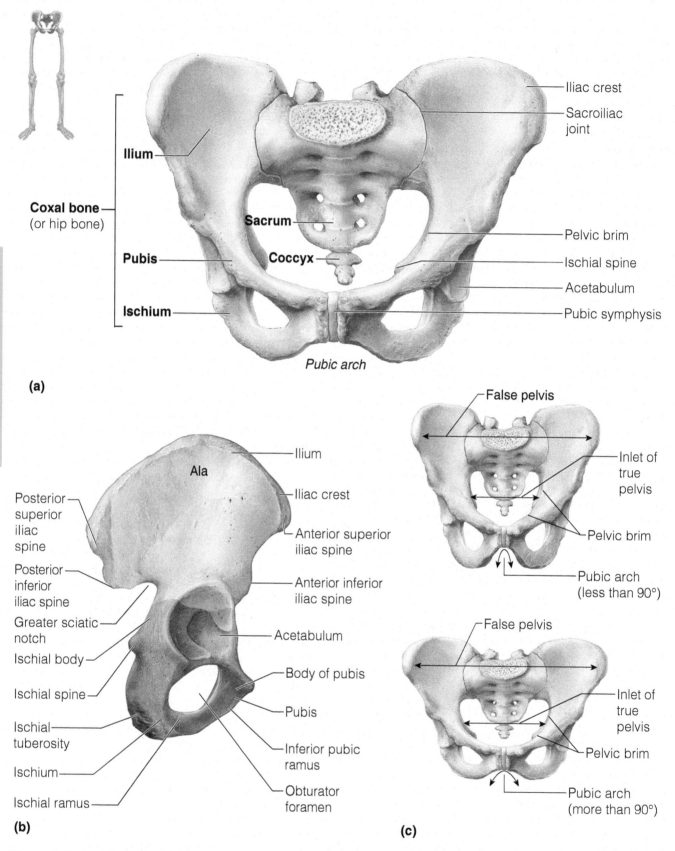

(a)

(b)

(c)

Figure 9.4 The bony pelvis. (a) Articulated male pelvis. **(b)** Right coxal bone, showing the point of fusion of the ilium, ischium, and pubic bones. **(c)** Comparison of the pelves of the male (above) and female (below).

Table 9.1	Comparison of the Male and Female Pelves	
Characteristic	**Female**	**Male**
General structure and functional modifications	Tilted forward; adapted for childbearing; true pelvis defines the birth canal; cavity of the true pelvis is broad, shallow, and has a greater capacity	Tilted less far forward; adapted for support of a male's heavier build and stronger muscles; cavity of the true pelvis is narrow and deep
Bone thickness	Less; bones lighter, thinner, and smoother	Greater; bones heavier and thicker, and markings are more prominent
Acetabula	Smaller; farther apart	Larger; closer together
Pubic angle/arch	Broader (80°–90°); more rounded	More acute (50°–60°)
Anterior view		

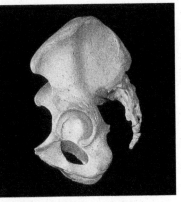 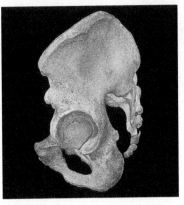

Pelvic brim

Pubic arch

Sacrum	Wider; shorter; sacrum is less curved	Narrower; longer; sacral promontory projects anteriorly
Coccyx	More movable; straighter	Less movable; sharply angled anteriorly
Left lateral view		

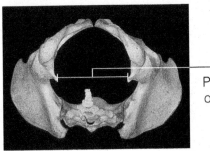 *(Note: left lateral view images shown for Female and Male)*

Pelvic inlet (brim)	Wider; oval from side to side	Narrower; basically heart shaped
Pelvic outlet	Wider; ischial spines shorter, farther apart, and everted	Narrower; ischial spines longer, sharper, and point more medially
Posteroinferior view		

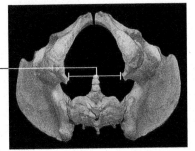

Pelvic outlet

9

The Thigh

The **femur,** or thigh bone (**Figure 9.5**), is the only bone of the thigh. It is the heaviest, strongest bone in the body. Its ball-like head articulates with the hip bone via the deep, secure socket of the acetabulum. The head of the femur is carried on a short, constricted *neck,* which angles laterally to join the shaft, and which is the weakest part of the femur. At the junction of the shaft and neck are the **greater** and **lesser trochanters** (separated posteriorly by the **intertrochanteric crest**). The trochanters and trochanteric crest, as well as the **gluteal tuberosity** located on the shaft, are sites of muscle attachment.

Distally, the femur terminates in the **lateral** and **medial condyles,** which articulate with the tibia below. There, the femur's anterior surface, which forms a joint with the patella (kneecap) anteriorly, is called the patellar surface. Posteriorly, the deep groove between the condyles is called the *intercondylar notch* or *fossa.*

The Leg

Two bones, the tibia and the fibula, form the skeleton of the leg (see Figure 9.5c). Joined along its length to the fibula by the *interosseous membrane,* the **tibia,** or *shinbone,* is the larger and more medial bone. At the proximal end, its **medial** and **lateral condyles** (separated by the **intercondylar eminence**) receive the distal end of the femur to form the knee joint. The **tibial tuberosity,** a roughened protrusion on the anterior tibial surface, is the attachment site of the patellar ligament. Distally, the tibia articulates with the talus bone of the foot, and a process called the **medial malleolus** forms the inner (medial) bulge of the ankle. The **anterior border** of the tibia is a sharpened crest relatively unprotected by muscles; it is easily felt beneath the skin.

The sticklike **fibula,** which lies parallel to the tibia, takes no part in forming the knee joint. Its proximal head articulates with the lateral condyle of the tibia. It terminates distally in the **lateral malleolus,** which forms the lateral bulge of the ankle.

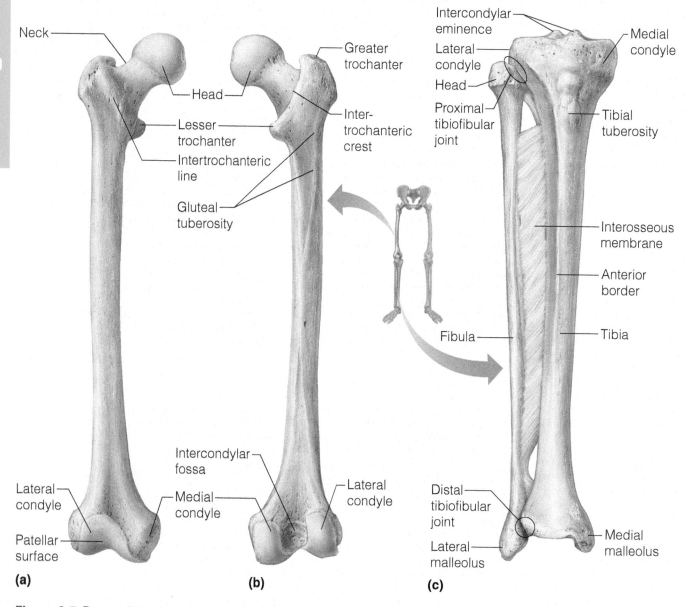

Figure 9.5 Bones of the right thigh and leg. (a) Femur (thigh bone), anterior view.
(b) Femur, posterior view. **(c)** Tibia and fibula of the leg, anterior view.

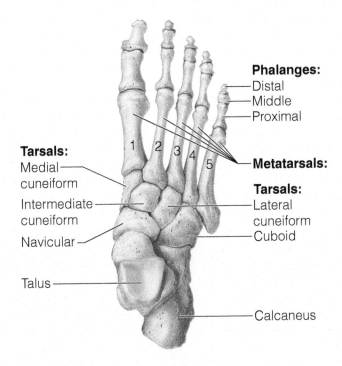

Figure 9.6 Bones of the right foot, superior view.

Phalanges:
— Distal
— Middle
— Proximal

Tarsals:
Medial cuneiform

Intermediate cuneiform

Navicular

Talus

Metatarsals:

Tarsals:
Lateral cuneiform

Cuboid

Calcaneus

The Foot

The bones of the foot include the 7 **tarsal** bones forming the ankle, 5 **metatarsals,** which form the sole, and 14 **phalanges,** which form the toes (**Figure 9.6**). Body weight is concentrated on the two largest tarsals—the *calcaneus* (heel bone) and the *talus,* which lies between the tibia and the calcaneus. Like the fingers of the hand, each toe has three phalanges except the great toe, which has two.

Activity 5

Palpating the Surface Anatomy of the Lower Limb

Locate and palpate the following bone markings on yourself and/or your lab partner. Place a check mark in the boxes as you locate the bone markings.

☐ *Greater trochanter of the femur:* This is easier to locate in women than in men because of the wider female pelvis. Also it is more likely to be covered by bulky muscles in men. Try to locate it on yourself—it is the most lateral point of the proximal femur and it typically lies 6–8 inches below the iliac crest.

☐ *Patella and tibial tuberosity:* Feel your kneecap (patella) and palpate the ligaments attached to its borders. Follow the inferior ligament to the tibial tuberosity where it attaches.

☐ *Medial malleolus:* Feel the medial protrusion of your ankle, the medial malleolus of the distal tibia.

☐ *Lateral malleolus:* Feel the bulge of the lateral aspect of your ankle, the lateral malleolus of the fibula.

☐ *Calcaneus:* Attempt to follow the extent of your calcaneus or heel bone.

Activity 6

Identifying Bone Unknowns

Go to the demonstration area, and identify by touch the six numbered bones that are concealed in bags. As you identify each bone, record its name below. Verify your identifications with your instructor before leaving the lab.

1. _____   4. _____

2. _____   5. _____

3. _____   6. _____

OBJECTIVE 4 Arrange unmarked, disarticulated bones in proper relative position to form a skeleton.

Activity 7

Constructing a Skeleton

1. When you finish examining the disarticulated bones of the appendicular skeleton and yourself, work with your lab partner to arrange the disarticulated bones on the laboratory bench in their proper relative positions to form an entire skeleton. Remember—the bone markings should help you distinguish between right and left members of bone pairs.

2. When you believe that you have accomplished this task correctly, ask the instructor to check your arrangement. If it is not correct, go to the articulated skeleton and check your bone arrangements. Also review the descriptions of the bone markings to help you make the necessary changes.

9

REVIEW SHEET
The Appendicular Skeleton

Name _____   Lab Time/Date _____

Bones of the Pectoral Girdle and Upper Limb

1. Match the bone names or markings in the key with the leader lines in the figure. The bones are numbered 1–8. (Some terms may be used more than once.)

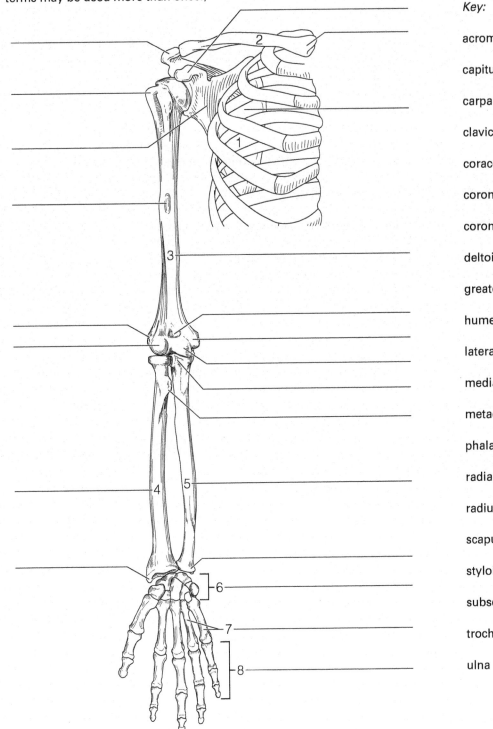

Key:

acromion

capitulum

carpals

clavicle

coracoid process

coronoid fossa

coronoid process of ulna

deltoid tuberosity

greater tubercle

humerus

lateral epicondyle

medial epicondyle

metacarpals

phalanges

radial tuberosity

radius

scapula

styloid process

subscapular fossa

trochlea

ulna

2. Match the bone names or markings in column B with the descriptions in column A. (Some terms may be used more than once, and some terms may not be used.)

Column A   **Column B**

_____ 1. raised area on lateral surface of humerus to which deltoid muscle   acromion
                                attaches
                                                                                capitulum
_____ 2. arm bone
                                                                                carpals
_____ , _____ 3. bones of the shoulder girdle
                                                                                clavicle
_____ , _____ 4. forearm bones
                                                                                coracoid process
_____ 5. scapular region to which the clavicle connects
                                                                                coronoid fossa
_____ 6. shoulder girdle bone that is unattached to the axial skeleton
                                                                                deltoid tuberosity
_____ 7. shoulder girdle bone that articulates with and transmits forces to
                                the bony thorax   glenoid cavity

_____ 8. depression in the scapula that articulates with the humerus   humerus

_____ 9. process above the glenoid cavity that permits muscle attachment   metacarpals

_____ 10. the "collarbone"   olecranon fossa

_____ 11. distal condyle of the humerus that articulates with the ulna   olecranon process

_____ 12. medial bone of forearm in anatomical position   phalanges

_____ 13. rounded knob on the humerus; articulates with the radius   radial tuberosity

_____ 14. anterior depression, superior to the trochlea, that receives part of   radius
                                the ulna when the forearm is flexed
                                                                                scapula
_____ 15. forearm bone involved in formation of the elbow joint
                                                                                sternum
_____ 16. wrist bones
                                                                                styloid process
_____ 17. finger bones
                                                                                trochlea
_____ 18. heads of these bones form the knuckles
                                                                                ulna
_____ , _____ 19. bones that articulate with the clavicle

3. Why is the clavicle at risk to fracture when a person falls on his or her shoulder? _____

_____

4. The scapula has no direct attachment to the axial skeleton. How does this affect the movement of the shoulder?

_____

_____

5. What is the total number of phalanges in the hand? _____

6. What is the total number of carpals in the wrist? _____

Bones of the Pelvic Girdle and Lower Limb

7. Compare the pectoral and pelvic girdles in terms of flexibility (range of motion) allowed, security, and ability to bear weight.

Flexibility: _____

Security: _____

Weight-bearing ability: _____

8. What organs are protected, at least in part, by the pelvic girdle? _____

_____

9. Distinguish the true pelvis from the false pelvis. _____

_____

_____

10. Use terms from the key to identify the bones and bone markings on this illustration of a coxal bone. The bones are numbered 1–3.

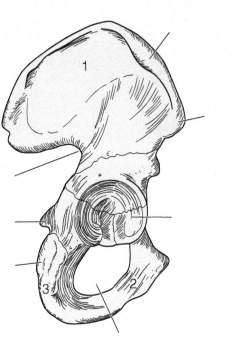

Key:

acetabulum

anterior superior iliac spine

greater sciatic notch

iliac crest

ilium

ischial spine

ischial tuberosity

ischium

obturator foramen

pubis

11. The pelvic bones of a four-legged animal, such as the cat or pig, are much less massive than those of the human. Make an educated guess as to why this is so.

_____

_____

12. A person instinctively curls over the abdominal area in times of danger. Why? _____

_____

13. Match the terms in the key with the appropriate leader lines on the diagram of the femur. Also decide whether this bone is a right or left bone.

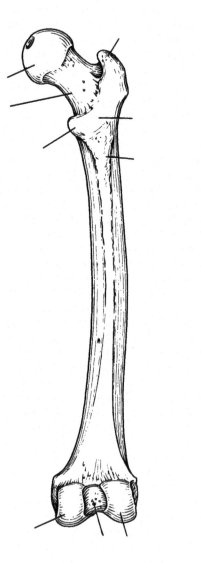

Key:

gluteal tuberosity

greater trochanter

head of femur

intercondylar fossa

intertrochanteric crest

lateral condyle

lesser trochanter

medial condyle

neck of femur

The femur shown is the _____ member of the two femurs.

14. Match the bone names and markings in the key with the leader lines in the figure. The bones are numbered 1–11.

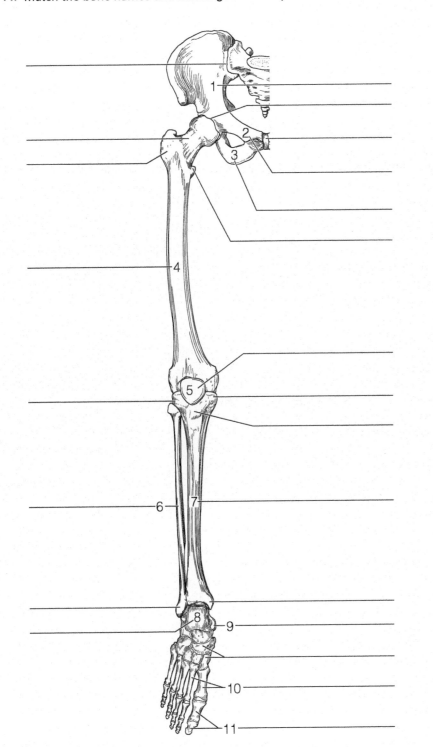

Key:

acetabulum (rim)

calcaneus

femur

fibula

greater trochanter

ilium

ischium

lateral condyle

lateral malleolus

lesser trochanter

medial condyle

medial malleolus

metatarsals

neck of femur

patella

phalanges

pubic symphysis

pubis

sacroiliac joint

talus

tarsals

tibia

tibial tuberosity

15. Match the bone names or markings in column B with the descriptions in column A. (Some terms may be used more than once, and some terms may not be used.)

Column A   **Column B**

_____, _____, and   acetabulum

_____ 1. fuse to form the coxal bone   calcaneus

_____ 2. "sit-down" bone of the coxal bone   femur

_____ 3. point where the coxal bones join anteriorly   fibula

_____ 4. superiormost margin of the coxal bone   gluteal tuberosity

_____ 5. deep socket in the coxal bone that receives the head of the   greater and lesser
                    thigh bone   trochanters

_____ 6. joint between axial skeleton and pelvic girdle   greater sciatic
                                                                             notch

_____ 7. longest, strongest bone in body   iliac crest

_____ 8. thin lateral leg bone   ilium

_____ 9. heavy medial leg bone   ischial tuberosity

_____, _____ 10. bones forming knee joint   ischium

_____ 11. point where the patellar ligament attaches   lateral malleolus

_____ 12. kneecap   medial malleolus

_____ 13. shinbone   metatarsals

_____ 14. medial ankle projection   obturator foramen

_____ 15. lateral ankle projection   patella

_____, _____ 16. the two largest tarsal bones   pubic symphysis

_____ 17. ankle bones   pubis

_____ 18. bones forming the instep of the foot   sacroiliac joint

_____ 19. opening in hip bone formed by the pubic and ischial rami   talus

_____, _____ 20. sites of muscle attachment on the   tarsals
                                       proximal femur

_____ 21. tarsal bone that "sits" on the calcaneus   tibia

_____ 22. weight-bearing bone of the leg   tibial tuberosity

_____ 23. tarsal bone that articulates with the tibia

10 Joints and Body Movements

Materials

- ☐ Articulated skeleton
- ☐ Skull
- ☐ Diarthrotic beef joint (fresh or preserved), preferably a knee joint sectioned sagittally
- ☐ Disposable gloves
- ☐ Water balloons and clamps
- ☐ Anatomical chart of joint types (if available)
- ☐ X-ray images of normal and arthritic joints (if available)

Pre-Lab Quiz

1. Name one of the two functions of an articulation, or joint. _____

   _____

2. Structural classification of joints includes fibrous, cartilaginous, and _____, which have a fluid-filled cavity between articulating bones.

3. Circle True or False. All synovial joints are diarthroses, or freely movable joints.

4. Circle the correct term. Every muscle of the body is attached to a bone or other connective tissue structure at two points. The origin / insertion is the more movable attachment.

5. Movement of a limb *away* from the midline or median plane of the body in the frontal plane is known as:
   a. abduction   c. extension
   b. eversion   d. rotation

6. Circle the correct term. This type of movement is common in ball-and-socket joints and can be described as the movement of a bone around its longitudinal axis. It is rotation / flexion.

Nearly every bone in the body is connected to, or forms a joint with, at least one other bone. **Joints,** or **articulations,** perform two functions for the body. They (1) hold bones together and (2) allow the rigid skeleton some flexibility so that gross body movements can occur.

Joints may be classified by structure or by function. The *structural classification* is based on what separates the articulating bones—fibers, cartilage, or a joint cavity. Structurally, there are *fibrous, cartilaginous,* and *synovial joints.*

The functional classification focuses on the amount of movement the joint allows. On this basis, there are **synarthroses,** or immovable joints; **amphiarthroses,** or slightly movable joints; and **diarthroses,** or freely movable joints. Freely movable joints predominate in the limbs, whereas immovable and slightly movable joints are largely restricted to the axial skeleton.

The structural categories are more clear-cut, so we will use that classification here and indicate functional properties as appropriate. See **Figure 10.1**.

OBJECTIVE 1   Name the three structural categories of joints and compare their structure and mobility.

Fibrous Joints

In **fibrous joints,** the bones are joined by fibrous tissue. Some fibrous joints are slightly movable, but most are synarthrotic and permit virtually no movement.

The two major types of fibrous joints are sutures and syndesmoses. In **sutures** (Figure 10.1a), the irregular edges of the bones interlock and are united by very short connective tissue fibers, as in most joints of the skull. In **syndesmoses,** the articulating bones are connected by short ligaments of dense fibrous tissue; the bones do not interlock. The joint at the distal end of the tibia and fibula is an example of a syndesmosis (Figure 10.1b). Although this syndesmosis allows some give, it is classified functionally as a synarthrosis.

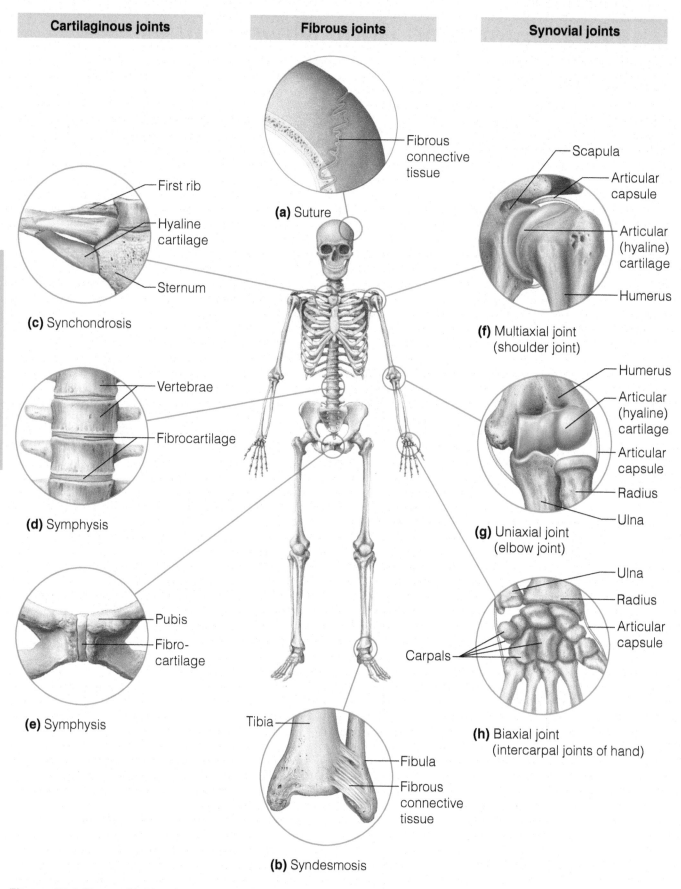

Cartilaginous joints

Fibrous joints

Synovial joints

Fibrous connective tissue

(a) Suture

First rib

Hyaline cartilage

Sternum

(c) Synchondrosis

Scapula

Articular capsule

Articular (hyaline) cartilage

Humerus

(f) Multiaxial joint (shoulder joint)

Vertebrae

Fibrocartilage

(d) Symphysis

Humerus

Articular (hyaline) cartilage

Articular capsule

Radius

Ulna

(g) Uniaxial joint (elbow joint)

Pubis

Fibro-cartilage

(e) Symphysis

Ulna

Radius

Articular capsule

Carpals

(h) Biaxial joint (intercarpal joints of hand)

Tibia

Fibula

Fibrous connective tissue

(b) Syndesmosis

Figure 10.1 Types of joints. Joints to the left of the skeleton are cartilaginous joints; joints above and below the skeleton are fibrous joints; joints to the right of the skeleton are synovial joints.

Activity 1

Identifying Fibrous Joints

Examine a human skull. Notice that adjacent bone surfaces do not actually touch but are separated by a wavy seam of ossified fibrous connective tissue. Also examine a skeleton and an anatomical chart of joint types for examples of fibrous joints.

Cartilaginous Joints

In **cartilaginous joints,** the articulating bone ends are connected by cartilage. Although there is variation, most cartilaginous joints are *slightly movable* (amphiarthrotic) functionally. An important type of cartilaginous joint is the symphysis. In a **symphysis** (*symphysis* means "a growth together"), the bones are connected by a broad, flat disc of **fibrocartilage.** The intervertebral joints and the pubic symphysis of the pelvis are symphyses (see Figure 10.1d and e). **Synchondrosis** is a cartilaginous joint that is held together by hyaline cartilage. This can be found between rib 1 and the sternum (see Figure 10.1c).

Activity 2

Identifying Cartilaginous Joints

Identify the cartilaginous joints on a human skeleton and on an anatomical chart of joint types.

Synovial Joints

In **synovial joints,** the articulating bone ends are separated by a joint cavity containing synovial fluid (see Figure 10.1f–h). All synovial joints are diarthroses, or freely movable joints. Their mobility varies, however; some can move in only one plane, and others can move in several directions (multiaxial movement). Most joints in the body are synovial joints.

All synovial joints have the following structural characteristics (**Figure 10.2**):

• The joint surfaces are enclosed by a two-layered *articular capsule* (a sleeve of connective tissue) creating a joint cavity.

• The outer part of this capsule is dense fibrous connective tissue. It is lined inside with a smooth connective tissue membrane, called *synovial membrane,* which produces a lubricating fluid (synovial fluid) that reduces friction.

• Articulating surfaces of the bones forming the joint are covered with *articular* (hyaline) *cartilage.*

• The articular capsule is typically reinforced with ligaments and may contain bursae, or tendon sheaths that reduce friction where muscles, tendons, or ligaments cross bone.

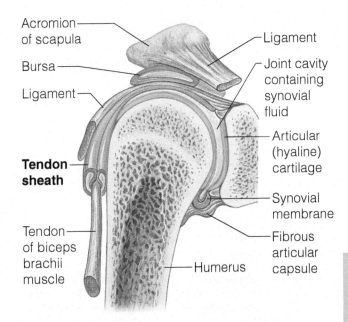

Figure 10.2 Major structural features of the shoulder joint, a synovial joint.

Activity 3

Examining Synovial Joint Structure

Examine a beef joint to identify the general structural features of diarthrotic joints.

⚠️ Put on disposable gloves before beginning your observations.

OBJECTIVE 2   Identify the types of synovial joints.

Activity 4

Demonstrating the Importance of Friction-Reducing Structures

1. Obtain a small water balloon and clamp. Partially fill the balloon with water (it should still be flaccid), and clamp it closed.

2. Position the balloon atop one of your fists and press down on its top surface with the other fist. Push on the balloon until your two fists touch, and move your fists back and forth over one another. Assess the amount of friction generated.

3. Unclamp the balloon and add more water. The goal is to get just enough water in the balloon so that your fists cannot come into contact with one another but remain separated by a thin water layer when pressure is applied to the balloon.

4. Once again, perform the same movements to assess the amount of friction generated.

Text continues on next page. →

How does the presence of a sac containing fluid influence the amount of friction generated?

_____

_____

What anatomical structure(s) does the water-containing balloon mimic?

_____

_____

What anatomical structures might be represented by your fists?

_____

_____

Activity 5

Identifying Types of Synovial Joints

Synovial joints are divided into the following subcategories on the basis of the movements they allow. As you read through the description of each joint type, manipulate the joints identified as examples on yourself and on an articulated skeleton to observe its possible movements. Range of motion allowed by synovial joints varies from **uniaxial movement** (movement in one plane) to **biaxial movement** (movement in two planes) to **multiaxial movement** (movement in or around all three planes of space and axes).

- _Plane:_ Articulating surfaces are flat or slightly curved, allowing sliding movements in one or two planes. Examples are the intercarpal and intertarsal joints.

- _Hinge:_ The rounded process of one bone fits into the concave surface of another to allow movement in one plane (uniaxial), usually flexion and extension. Examples are the elbow and interphalangeal joints.

- _Pivot:_ The rounded or conical surface of one bone articulates with a shallow depression or foramen in another bone. Pivot joints allow uniaxial rotation, as in the joint between the atlas and axis (C$_1$ and C$_2$).

- _Condylar:_ The oval condyle of one bone fits into an oval depression in another bone, allowing biaxial (two-way) movement. The wrist joint and the metacarpophalangeal joints (knuckles) are examples.

- _Saddle:_ Articulating surfaces are saddle shaped. The articulating surface of one bone is convex, and the abutting surface is concave. Saddle joints, which are biaxial, include the joint between the thumb metacarpal and the trapezium (a carpal) of the wrist.

- _Ball-and-socket:_ The ball-shaped head of one bone fits into a cuplike depression of another. These multiaxial joints allow movement in all directions. Examples are the shoulder and hip joints.

Movements Allowed by Synovial Joints

OBJECTIVE 3 Define _origin_ and _insertion_ in relation to skeletal muscles.

Every muscle of the body is attached to bone (or other connective tissue structures) by at least two points—the **origin** (the stationary, immovable, or less movable attachment) and the **insertion** (the movable attachment). Body movement occurs when muscles contract across diarthrotic synovial

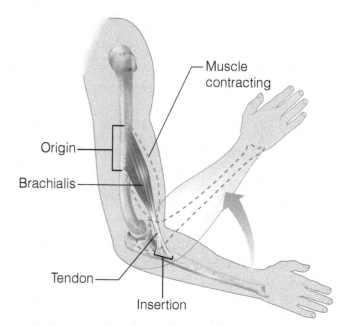

Figure 10.3 Muscle attachments (origin and insertion). When a skeletal muscle contracts, its insertion moves toward its origin.

joints (**Figure 10.3**). When the muscle contracts and its fibers shorten, the insertion moves toward the origin. The type of movement depends on the construction of the joint (uniaxial, biaxial, or multiaxial) and on the position of the muscle relative to the joint. The most common types of body movements are described below and shown in **Figure 10.4**.

OBJECTIVE 4 Demonstrate or identify the various body movements.

Activity 6

Demonstrating Movements of Synovial Joints

Attempt to demonstrate each movement on a skeleton or on yourself as you read through the following material:

Flexion (Figure 10.4a and b): A movement, generally in the sagittal plane, that decreases the angle of the joint and reduces the distance between the two bones. Flexion is typical of hinge joints (bending the knee or elbow), but it is also common at ball-and-socket joints (bending forward at the hip).

Extension (Figure 10.4a and b): A movement that increases the angle of a joint and the distance between two bones (straightening the knee or elbow). Extension is the opposite of flexion. If extension proceeds beyond anatomical position (for example, bending the trunk or head backward), it is termed _hyperextension_ (Figure 10.4b).

Rotation (Figure 10.4c): Movement of a bone around its longitudinal axis. Rotation, a common movement of ball-and-socket joints, also describes the movement of the atlas around the odontoid process of the axis.

Abduction (Figure 10.4d): Movement of a limb away from the midline or median plane of the body, generally on the frontal plane, or the fanning movement of fingers or toes when they are spread apart.

Adduction (Figure 10.4d): Movement of a limb toward the midline of the body. Adduction is the opposite of abduction.

Text continues on page 116. →

10

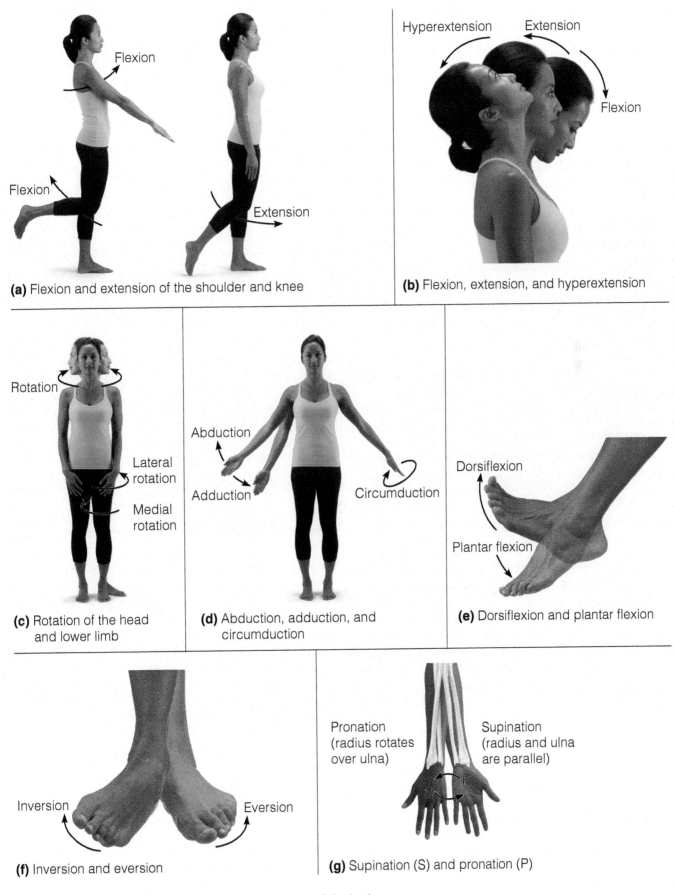

(a) Flexion and extension of the shoulder and knee

(b) Flexion, extension, and hyperextension

(c) Rotation of the head and lower limb

(d) Abduction, adduction, and circumduction

(e) Dorsiflexion and plantar flexion

(f) Inversion and eversion

(g) Supination (S) and pronation (P)

Figure 10.4 Movements occurring at synovial joints of the body.

Circumduction (Figure 10.4d): A combination of flexion, extension, abduction, and adduction commonly observed in ball-and-socket joints, such as the shoulder. The proximal end of the limb remains stationary, and the distal end moves in a circle. The limb as a whole outlines a cone.

The next six movements are special movements that occur at only a few joints.

Dorsiflexion (Figure 10.4e): A movement of the ankle joint in a dorsal direction (standing on one's heels).

Plantar flexion (Figure 10.4e): A movement of the ankle joint in which the foot is flexed downward (standing on one's toes or pointing the toes).

Inversion (Figure 10.4f): A movement that results in the medial turning of the sole of the foot.

Eversion (Figure 10.4f): A movement that results in the lateral turning of the sole of the foot; the opposite of inversion.

Pronation (Figure 10.4g): Movement of the palm of the hand from an anterior or upward-facing position to a posterior or downward-facing position. This action moves the distal end of the radius across the ulna so that the two bones form an X.

Supination (Figure 10.4g): Movement of the palm from a posterior position to an anterior position (the anatomical position). Supination is the opposite of pronation. During supination, the radius and ulna are parallel.

Activity 7

Demonstrating Uniaxial, Biaxial, and Multiaxial Movements

Using the information in the previous activity, perform the following demonstrations and complete the Activity 7 charts.

1. Demonstrate movement at two joints that are uniaxial.

Activity 7: Uniaxial Joints	
Name of joint	Movement allowed

2. Demonstrate movement at two joints that are biaxial.

Activity 7: Biaxial Joints		
Name of joint	Movement allowed	Movement allowed

3. Demonstrate movement at two joints that are multiaxial.

Activity 7: Multiaxial Joints			
Name of joint	Movement allowed	Movement allowed	Movement allowed

Joint Disorders

Most of us don't think about our joints until something goes wrong with them. Joint pains and malfunctions can be due to a variety of causes. For example, a hard blow to the knee can cause a painful bursitis, known as "water on the knee," due to damage to the patellar bursa. Tearing a ligament may result in a painful condition that persists over a long period because these poorly vascularized structures heal so slowly.

Sprains and dislocations are other types of joint problems. In a **sprain,** the ligaments reinforcing a joint are damaged by excessive stretching or are torn away from the bony attachment. Because both ligaments and tendons are cords of dense connective tissue with a poor blood supply, sprains heal slowly and are quite painful.

Dislocations occur when bones are forced out of their normal position in the joint cavity. They are normally accompanied by torn or stressed ligaments and considerable inflammation. The process of returning the bone to its proper position, called reduction, should be done only by a physician. Attempts by the untrained person to "snap the bone back into its socket" are often more harmful than helpful.

Age also takes its toll on joints. Weight-bearing joints in particular eventually begin to degenerate. *Adhesions* (fibrous bands) may form between the surfaces where bones join, and excess bone tissue (*spurs*) may grow along the joint edges.

☐ If possible, compare an X-ray image of an arthritic joint to one of a normal joint.

Place a check mark in the box after you have completed this task.

REVIEW SHEET
Joints and Body Movements

Name _____ Lab Time/Date _____

Types of Joints

1. Use the key terms to identify the joint types described below.

   Key: cartilaginous   fibrous   synovial

   _____ 1. typically allow a slight degree of movement

   _____ 2. include joints between the vertebral bodies and the pubic symphysis

   _____ 3. essentially immovable joints

   _____ 4. sutures are the most remembered examples

   _____ 5. cartilage connects the bony portions

   _____ 6. have a fibrous articular capsule lined with a synovial membrane surrounding a joint cavity

   _____ 7. all are freely movable or diarthrotic

   _____ 8. bone regions are united by fibrous connective tissue

   _____ 9. include the hip, knee, and elbow joints

2. Match the joint subcategories in column B with their descriptions in column A, and place an asterisk (*) beside all choices that are examples of synovial joints. (Some terms may be used more than once.)

Column A	Column B
_____ 1. joint between most skull bones	ball-and-socket
_____ 2. joint between the axis and atlas	condylar
_____ 3. hip joint	plane
_____ 4. joint between forearm bones and wrist	hinge
_____ 5. elbow	pivot
_____ 6. interphalangeal joints	saddle
_____ 7. intercarpal joints	suture
_____ 8. joint between the skull and vertebral column	symphysis
_____ 9. joints between proximal phalanges and metacarpal bones	syndesmosis
_____ 10. multiaxial joint	

3. What characteristics do all joints have in common? _____

_____

4. Describe the structure and function of the following structures or tissues in relation to a synovial joint, and label the structures indicated by leader lines in the diagram.

ligament _____

_____

articular cartilage _____

_____

synovial membrane _____

_____

_____

bursa _____

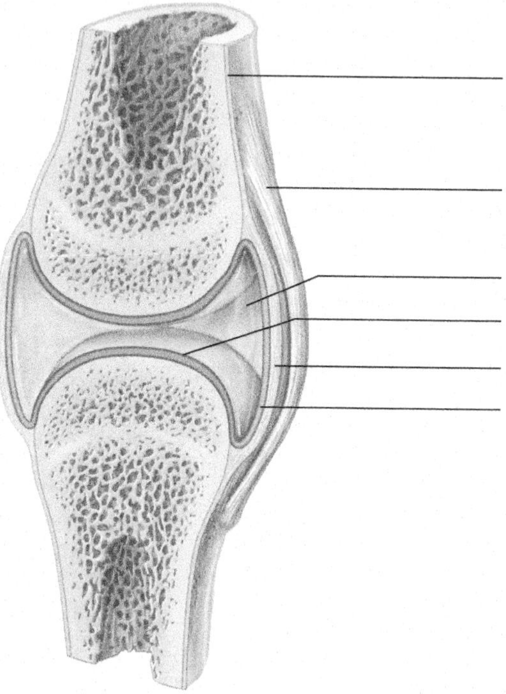

5. Which joint, the hip or the knee, is more stable? _____

Name two important factors that contribute to the stability of the hip joint.

_____ and _____

Movements Allowed by Synovial Joints

6. Label the *origin* and *insertion* points on the diagram below, and complete the following statement:

During muscle contraction, the _____

moves toward the _____.

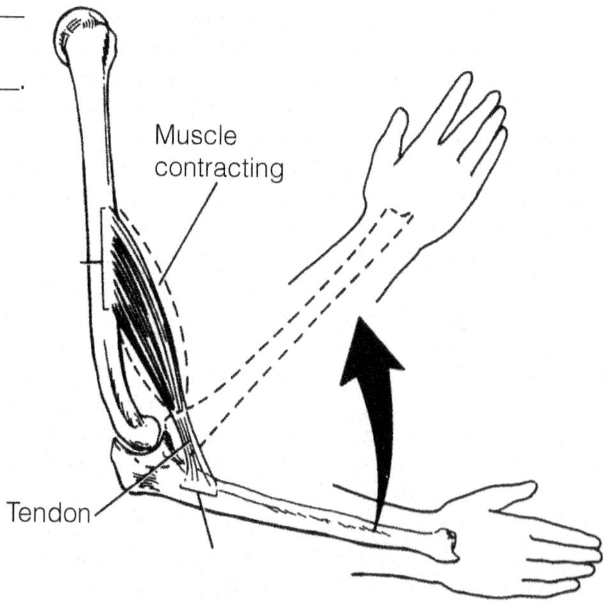

Muscle contracting

Tendon

7. Complete the descriptions below the diagrams by inserting the type of movement in each answer blank.

 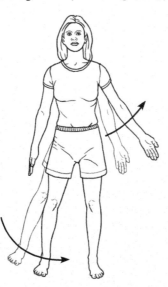 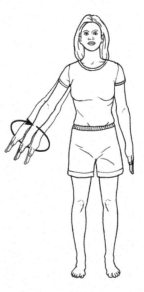

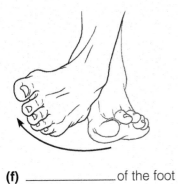 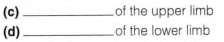

(a) _____ at the elbow

(b) _____ at the knee

(c) _____ of the upper limb

(d) _____ of the lower limb

(e) _____ of the upper limb

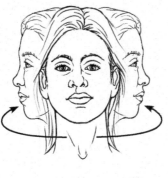 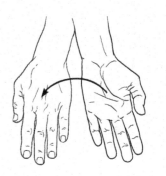

(f) _____ of the foot

(g) _____ of the head

(h) _____ of the forearm

Joint Disorders

8. What structural joint changes are common in older people? _____

_____

9. Define *dislocation:* _____

_____

Microscopic Anatomy and Organization of Skeletal Muscle

Materials

☐ Three-dimensional model of skeletal muscle cells (if available)

☐ Three-dimensional model of skeletal muscle showing neuromuscular junction (if available)

☐ Demonstration area: Prepared slides of skeletal muscle (longitudinal and cross-sectional views) and skeletal muscle showing neuromuscular junctions set up for student viewing

Pre-Lab Quiz

1. Circle True or False. Skeletal muscle cells have more than one nucleus.

2. The two contractile proteins that make up the myofilaments of skeletal muscle are _____ and _____.

3. Each muscle cell is surrounded by thin connective tissue called the:
   a. aponeurosis   c. epimysium
   b. endomysium   d. perimysium

4. The junction between a nerve fiber and a muscle cell is called a(n) _____.

5. Circle True or False. The neuron and muscle fiber membranes do not actually touch but are separated by a fluid-filled gap.

The bulk of the body's muscle is called **skeletal muscle** because it is attached to the skeleton. Skeletal muscle influences body shape, allows you to grin and frown, provides a means of getting around, and enables you to manipulate the environment. Smooth muscle and cardiac muscle make up the remainder of the body's muscle. Smooth muscle is the major component of the walls of hollow organs. Cardiac muscle forms the walls of the heart. Smooth and cardiac muscle are involved with the transport of materials within the body.

Each of the three muscle types has a structure and function uniquely suited to its task in the body. However, the term *muscular system* applies specifically to skeletal muscle, and our objective here is to investigate the structure and function of skeletal muscle.

The Cells of Skeletal Muscle

OBJECTIVE 1 Describe the microscopic structure of skeletal muscle, and explain the role of myofibrils and myofilaments.

Skeletal muscle is composed of relatively large, cylindrical cells, some ranging up to 25 or 30 cm in length (10–12 in.), that can be seen with the naked eye.

Skeletal muscle cells (**Figure 11.1a**) are multinucleate. The multiple oval nuclei can be seen just beneath the plasma membrane (called the *sarcolemma* in these cells). The nuclei are pushed aside by longitudinally arranged **myofibrils,** which nearly fill the cell interior (Figure 11.1b). Alternating light (I) and dark (A) bands along the length of the perfectly aligned myofibrils give the muscle fiber as a whole its striped appearance.

The myofibrils are made up of even smaller threadlike structures called **myofilaments** (Figure 11.1c). The myofilaments are composed largely of two varieties of contractile proteins—**actin** and **myosin**—which slide past each other during muscle activity to bring about shortening or contraction. The precise arrangement of the myofilaments within the myofibrils is responsible for the banding pattern in skeletal muscle. The actual contractile units of muscle, called **sarcomeres,** extend from the middle of one I band (its Z disc, or Z line) to the middle of the next along the length of the myofibrils. (See Figure 11.1c.)

11

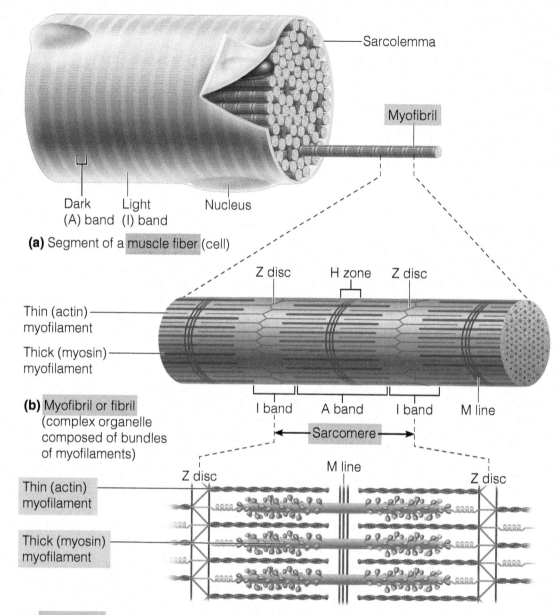

Sarcolemma

Myofibril

Dark   Light   Nucleus
(A) band (I) band

(a) Segment of a muscle fiber (cell)

Z disc   H zone   Z disc

Thin (actin)
myofilament

Thick (myosin)
myofilament

(b) Myofibril or fibril
(complex organelle
composed of bundles
of myofilaments)

I band   A band   I band   M line

Sarcomere

Thin (actin)
myofilament

M line

Z disc   Z disc

Thick (myosin)
myofilament

(c) Sarcomere (segment of a myofibril, sectioned lengthwise)

Figure 11.1 Anatomy of a skeletal muscle cell (fiber). (a) A muscle fiber. One myofibril has been extended. **(b)** Enlarged view of a myofibril showing its banding pattern. **(c)** Enlarged view of one sarcomere (contractile unit) of a myofibril showing its banding pattern.

Activity 1

Examining Skeletal Muscle Cell Anatomy

1. Look at the three-dimensional model of skeletal muscle cells, paying attention to the relative shape and size of the cells. Identify the nuclei, myofibrils, and light and dark bands.

2. Now go to the demonstration area and view professionally prepared skeletal muscle (longitudinal section) under the microscope. Identify nuclei and A and I bands. Compare your observations with **Figure 11.2** and Plate 2 in the Histology Atlas.

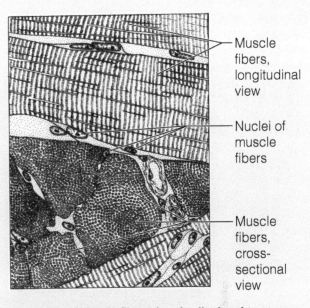

Muscle fibers, longitudinal view

Nuclei of muscle fibers

Muscle fibers, cross-sectional view

Figure 11.2 Muscle fibers, longitudinal and transverse views. See also Plate 2 in the Histology Atlas.

11

Organization of Skeletal Muscle Cells into Muscles

OBJECTIVE 2   Describe gross muscle structure, and indicate the names of its connective tissue coverings.

Muscle fibers, which are soft and fragile, are bundled together with connective tissue to form skeletal muscles (**Figure 11.3**). Each muscle fiber is enclosed in a delicate connective tissue sheath called **endomysium.** Several sheathed muscle fibers are wrapped by a collagenic membrane called **perimysium,** forming a fiber bundle called a **fascicle.** Large numbers of fascicles are bound together by a substantially coarser "overcoat" of dense connective tissue called an **epimysium,** which encloses the entire muscle. These epimysia blend into strong cordlike **tendons** or sheetlike **aponeuroses,** which attach muscles to each other or indirectly to bones. A muscle's more movable attachment is called its *insertion,* whereas its fixed (or immovable) attachment is the *origin* (see Exercise 10).

In addition to supporting and binding the muscle fibers—and strengthening the muscle as a whole and its attachment to the tendon—the connective tissue wrappings provide a route for the entry and exit of nerves and blood vessels that serve the muscle fibers.

Activity 2

Observing the Structure of a Skeletal Muscle

Go to the appropriate microscope at the demonstration area, and examine a slide showing a cross section of a skeletal muscle. Using Figure 11.3 as a reference, identify the muscle fibers, endomysium, perimysium, and epimysium (if visible).

The Neuromuscular Junction

OBJECTIVE 3   Describe the structure and function of the neuromuscular junction.

Skeletal muscle cells are always stimulated by motor neurons via nerve impulses. The junction between a nerve fiber (axon) and a muscle cell is called a **neuromuscular,** or **myoneural, junction** (**Figure 11.4**).

Each motor axon breaks up into many branches called *axon terminals* as it nears the muscle, and each branch forms

a neuromuscular junction with a single muscle cell. Thus a single neuron may stimulate many muscle fibers. Together, a neuron and all the muscle cells it stimulates make up the functional structure called the **motor unit (Figure 11.5).**

The neuron and muscle fiber membranes, close as they are, do not actually touch. They are separated by a small fluid-filled gap called the **synaptic cleft** (see Figure 11.4).

Within the axon terminals are mitochondria and vesicles containing a neurotransmitter chemical called acetylcholine

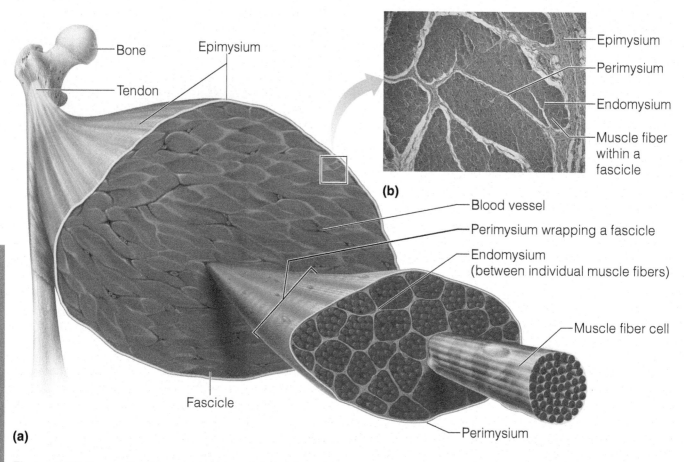

Figure 11.3 Connective tissue coverings of skeletal muscle.

(ACh). When a nerve impulse reaches the axon endings, some of the vesicles release their contents into the synaptic cleft. The ACh rapidly diffuses across the junction and combines with the receptors on the sarcolemma. If sufficient ACh is released, the permeability of the sarcolemma changes briefly, allowing more sodium ions to diffuse into the muscle fiber. If enough sodium enters the fiber, an action potential is generated along its length.

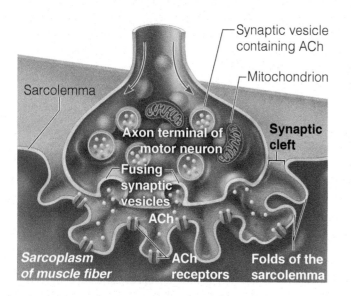

Figure 11.4 The neuromuscular junction.

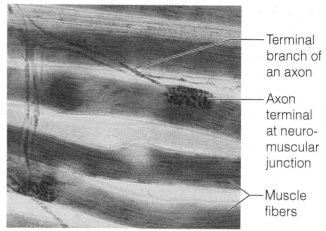

Figure 11.5 Photomicrograph of neuromuscular junctions (750×).

Studying the Structure of a Neuromuscular Junction

1. If possible, examine a three-dimensional model of skeletal muscle cells that illustrates the neuromuscular junction. Identify the structures just described.

2. Go to the demonstration area to examine a slide of skeletal muscle stained to show a portion of a motor unit. Identify the axonal fibers extending leashlike to the muscle cells. Follow one of the axonal fibers to its terminus to identify the oval-shaped axon terminal. Compare your observations to Figure 11.5 and Plate 4 in the Histology Atlas.

Classification of Skeletal Muscles

OBJECTIVE 4   List the criteria used in naming muscles.

Naming Skeletal Muscles

Remembering the names of the skeletal muscles is a monumental task, but certain clues help. Muscles are named on the basis of the following criteria:

- **Direction of muscle fibers.** Some muscles are named relative to some imaginary line, usually the midline of the body or the longitudinal axis of a limb bone. For example, the rectus abdominis is the straight muscle of the abdomen. The terms *rectus, transverse,* and *oblique* indicate that the muscle fibers run with, at right angles, or obliquely (respectively) to the imaginary line. **Figure 11.6** shows how muscle structure is determined by fascicle arrangement.

- **Relative size of the muscle.** When size is the criterion, terms such as *maximus* (largest), *minimus* (smallest), *longus* (long), and *brevis* (short) are often used—as in gluteus maximus and gluteus minimus.

- **Location of the muscle.** Some muscles are named for the bone with which they are associated. For example, the temporalis muscle overlies the temporal bone.

- **Number of origins.** When the term *biceps, triceps,* or *quadriceps* forms part of a muscle name, you can assume that the muscle has two, three, or four origins (respectively). For example, the biceps brachii muscle of the arm has two origins.

- **Location of the muscle's origin and insertion.** For example, the sternocleidomastoid muscle has its origin on the sternum (*sterno*) and clavicle (*cleido*), and it inserts on the mastoid process of the temporal bone.

- **Shape of the muscle.** For example, the deltoid muscle is roughly triangular (*deltoid* = triangle), and the trapezius muscle resembles a trapezoid.

- **Action of the muscle.** For example, all the adductor muscles of the anterior thigh bring about its adduction.

Types of Muscles

OBJECTIVE 5   Define terms used to describe muscle actions in the body.

Most often, body movements involve the coordinated action of several muscles acting together. Muscles that are primarily responsible for producing a particular movement are called **prime movers,** or **agonists.**

Muscles that oppose or reverse a movement are called **antagonists.** When a prime mover is active, the fibers of the antagonist are stretched and relaxed.

Synergists aid the action of prime movers by reducing undesirable or unnecessary movement. For example, you can make a fist without bending your wrist only because synergist muscles stabilize the wrist joint and allow the prime mover to exert its force at the finger joints.

Fixators, or fixation muscles, are specialized synergists. They immobilize the origin of a prime mover so that all the tension is exerted at the insertion. Muscles that help maintain posture and those that "fix" the scapula during arm movements are fixators.

11

11

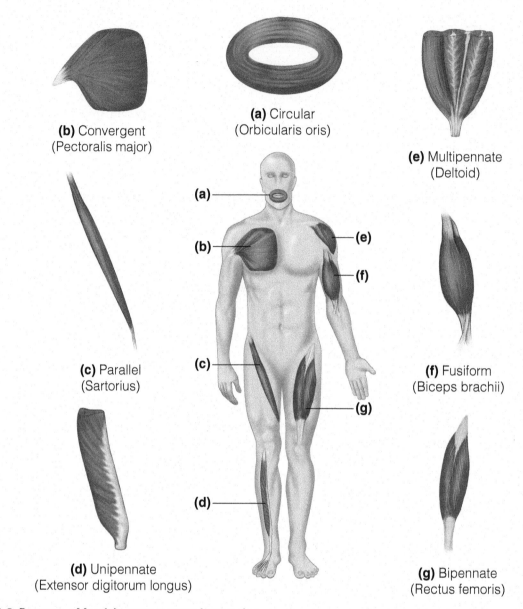

(b) Convergent
(Pectoralis major)

(a) Circular
(Orbicularis oris)

(e) Multipennate
(Deltoid)

(c) Parallel
(Sartorius)

(f) Fusiform
(Biceps brachii)

(d) Unipennate
(Extensor digitorum longus)

(g) Bipennate
(Rectus femoris)

Figure 11.6 Patterns of fascicle arrangement in muscles.

REVIEW SHEET
Microscopic Anatomy and Organization of Skeletal Muscle

Name _____ Lab Time/Date _____

Skeletal Muscle Cells and Their Packaging into Muscles

1. From the inside out, name the three types of connective tissue wrappings of a skeletal muscle.

   a. _____ b. _____ c. _____

   Why are the connective tissue wrappings of skeletal muscle important? (Give at least three reasons.)

   _____

   _____

   _____

2. On the following figure, label endomysium, perimysium, epimysium, and fascicle.

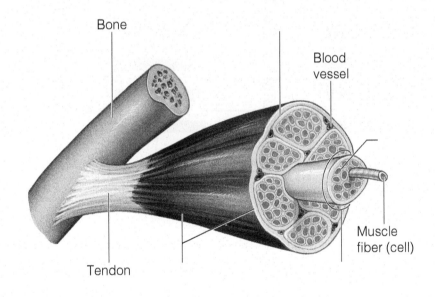

Bone

Blood vessel

Tendon

Muscle fiber (cell)

3. Use the items in the key to correctly identify the structures described below.

Key: fiber   sarcolemma   sarcoplasm
        myofibril   sarcomere   tendon
        myofilament

_____ 1. contractile unit of muscle

_____ 2. a muscle cell

_____ 3. plasma membrane of the muscle fiber

_____ 4. a long filamentous organelle with a banded appearance found within muscle cells

_____ 5. actin- or myosin-containing structure

_____ 6. cord of collagen fibers that attaches a muscle to a bone

4. The diagram illustrates a small portion of a muscle myofibril in a highly simplified way. Using terms from the key, correctly identify each structure indicated by a leader line or a bracket.

Key: actin filament   I band   sarcomere
        A band   myosin filament   Z disc

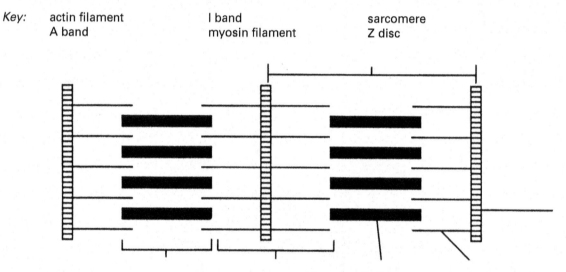

The Neuromuscular Junction

5. For skeletal muscle cells to contract, they must be excited by motor neurons. However, the electrical impulse cannot pass directly from a nerve cell to the skeletal muscle cells to excite them. Just what *does* pass from the neuron to the muscle cells, and what effect does it produce?

_____

_____

_____

6. Why is it that the electrical impulse cannot pass from neuron to muscle cell? _____

_____

7. The events that occur at a neuromuscular junction are depicted below. Identify by labeling every structure provided with a leader line.

Key: axon terminal   myelinated axon   synaptic cleft
           muscle fiber (cell)   sarcolemma   vesicle containing ACh

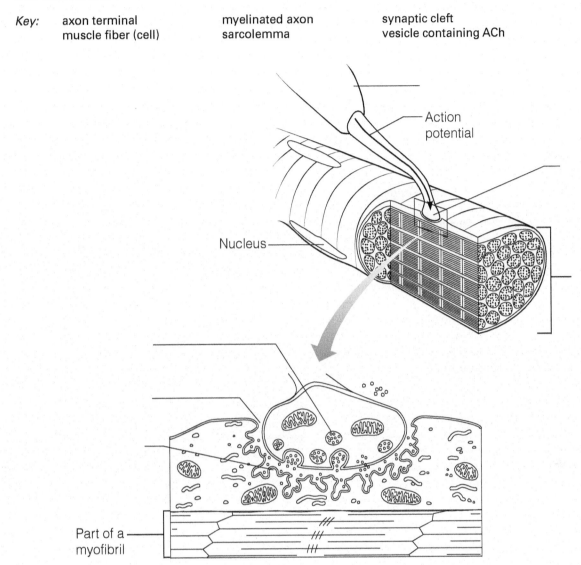

Action
potential

Nucleus

Part of a
myofibril

Classification of Skeletal Muscles

8. Several criteria were given for the naming of muscles. Match the muscle names (column B) to the criteria (column A). Note that more than one muscle may fit the criterion in some cases.

Column A	Column B
_____ 1. action of the muscle	abdominis transversus
_____ 2. shape of the muscle	biceps brachii
_____ 3. location of the origin and/or insertion of the muscle	deltoid
_____ 4. number of origins	erector spinae
_____ 5. location of the muscle relative to a bone or body region	external intercostals
	flexor digitorum superficialis
_____ 6. direction in which the muscle fibers run relative to some imaginary line	pectoralis major
_____ 7. relative size of the muscle	rectus abdominis

9. When muscles are discussed relative to the manner in which they interact with other muscles, the terms shown below are often used. Define each term.

   Antagonist: _____

   Fixator: _____

   Prime mover (agonist): _____

   Synergist: _____

Materials

☐ Human torso model or large anatomical chart showing human musculature
☐ Tubes of body (or face) paint
☐ 1-inch-wide artist's bristle brushes

Pre-Lab Quiz

1. Circle True or False. Muscles of facial expression differ from most skeletal muscles because they insert into the skin or other muscles rather than into bone.

2. The _____ musculature includes muscles that move the vertebral column and muscles that move the ribs.
   a. head and neck   b. lower limb   c. trunk

3. Muscles that act on the _____ cause movement at the hip, knee, and foot joints.
   a. lower limb   b. trunk   c. upper limb

4. Circle the correct term. This lower limb muscle, which attaches to the calcaneus via the calcaneal tendon and plantar flexes the foot when the knee is extended, is the sartorius / gastrocnemius.

Identification of Human Muscles

Muscles of the Head and Neck

OBJECTIVE 1   Name and locate the major muscles of the head and neck, and state their actions.

The muscles of the head serve many functions. For instance, the muscles of facial expression differ from most skeletal muscles because they insert into the skin (or other muscles) rather than into bone. As a result, they move the facial skin, allowing a wide range of emotions to be shown on the face. Other head muscles are the muscles of mastication, which are active during chewing, and the six extrinsic eye muscles located within the orbit, which aim the eye. (Orbital muscles are studied in Exercise 17.)

Neck muscles primarily move the head and shoulder girdle.

Activity 1

Identifying Head and Neck Muscles

Figure 12.1 and Figure 12.2 are summary figures illustrating the superficial muscles of the body. Head and neck muscles are discussed in Table 12.1, on p. 135, and shown in Figure 12.3, on p. 134.

While reading the tables and identifying the head and neck muscles in the figures, try to visualize what happens when the muscle contracts. Then, use a torso model or an anatomical chart to again identify as many of these muscles as possible. Also carry out the following palpation on yourself:

☐ To demonstrate the temporalis, clench your teeth. The masseter can also be palpated now at the angle of the jaw.

☐ Smile. You are using your zygomaticus.

☐ Close your lips and pucker up. The orbicularis oris muscle does this.

As you complete each task, place a check mark in the corresponding box.

Text continues on next page. →

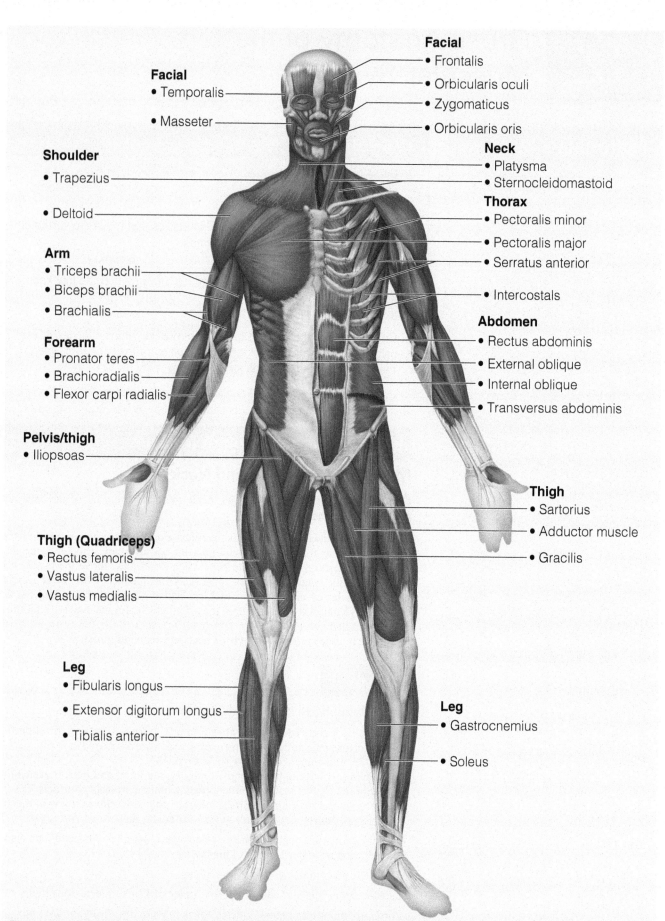

Facial
- Frontalis
- Orbicularis oculi
- Zygomaticus
- Orbicularis oris

Facial
- Temporalis
- Masseter

Neck
- Platysma
- Sternocleidomastoid

Shoulder
- Trapezius
- Deltoid

Thorax
- Pectoralis minor
- Pectoralis major
- Serratus anterior
- Intercostals

Arm
- Triceps brachii
- Biceps brachii
- Brachialis

Forearm
- Pronator teres
- Brachioradialis
- Flexor carpi radialis

Abdomen
- Rectus abdominis
- External oblique
- Internal oblique
- Transversus abdominis

Pelvis/thigh
- Iliopsoas

Thigh
- Sartorius
- Adductor muscle
- Gracilis

Thigh (Quadriceps)
- Rectus femoris
- Vastus lateralis
- Vastus medialis

Leg
- Fibularis longus
- Extensor digitorum longus
- Tibialis anterior

Leg
- Gastrocnemius
- Soleus

12

Figure 12.1 Anterior view of superficial muscles of the body. The abdominal surface has been partially dissected on the left side of the body to show somewhat deeper muscles.

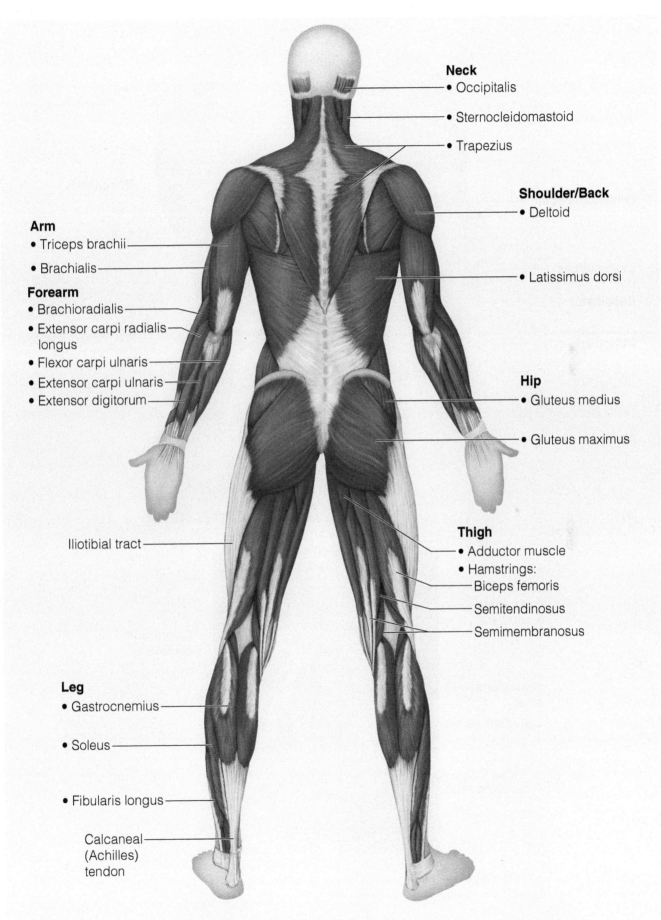

Neck
- Occipitalis
- Sternocleidomastoid
- Trapezius

Shoulder/Back
- Deltoid
- Latissimus dorsi

Arm
- Triceps brachii
- Brachialis

Forearm
- Brachioradialis
- Extensor carpi radialis longus
- Flexor carpi ulnaris
- Extensor carpi ulnaris
- Extensor digitorum

Hip
- Gluteus medius
- Gluteus maximus

Iliotibial tract

Thigh
- Adductor muscle
- Hamstrings:
  - Biceps femoris
  - Semitendinosus
  - Semimembranosus

Leg
- Gastrocnemius
- Soleus
- Fibularis longus

Calcaneal (Achilles) tendon

12

Figure 12.2 Posterior view of superficial muscles of the body.

Text continues on next page. →

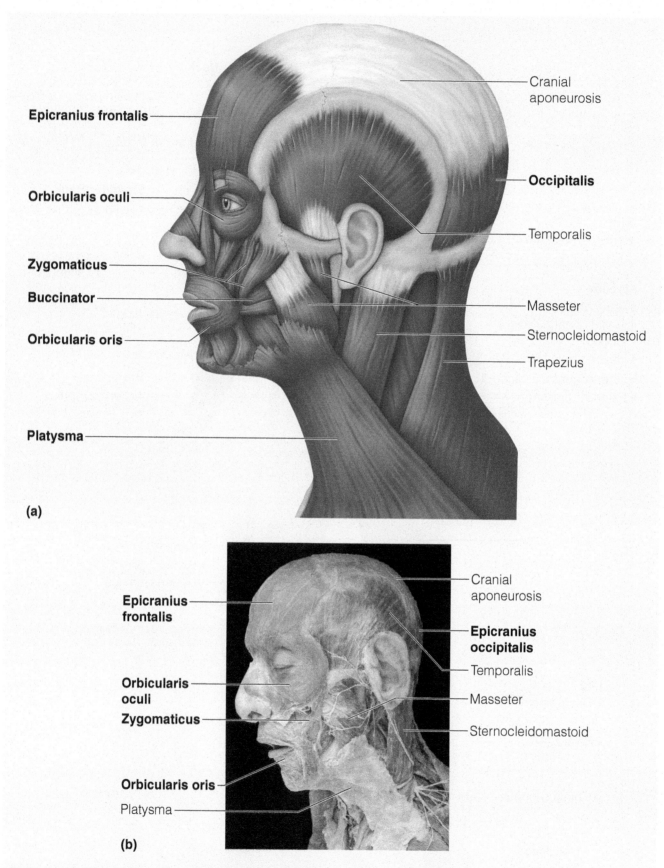

Figure 12.3 Muscles of the scalp, face, and neck; left lateral view. (a) Superficial muscles. **(b)** Photo of superficial structures of head and neck.

Table 12.1	Major Muscles of Human Head and Neck (see Figure 12.3)			
Muscle	**Comments**	**Origin**	**Insertion**	**Action**
Facial Expression				
Epicranius frontalis and occipitalis	Two-part muscle consisting of frontalis and occipitalis that covers dome of skull	Frontalis: cranial aponeurosis Occipitalis: occipital and temporal bones	Frontalis: skin of eyebrows and root of nose Occipitalis: cranial aponeurosis	With aponeurosis fixed, frontalis raises eyebrows; occipitalis pulls scalp posteriorly
Orbicularis oculi	Sphincter muscle of eyelids	Frontal and maxillary bones	Encircles orbit and inserts into tissue of eyelids	Various parts can be activated individually; closes eyes, produces blinking and squinting
Zygomaticus	Extends diagonally from corner of mouth to cheekbone	Zygomatic bone	Skin and muscle at corner of mouth	Raises lateral corners of mouth upward (smiling muscle)
Orbicularis oris	Encircles mouth; sphincter muscle of lips with fibers that run in many different directions	Maxilla and mandible; fibers blended with fibers of other muscles associated with lips	Muscle and skin at angles of mouth	Closes lips; purses and protrudes lips (kissing muscle)
Mastication				
Masseter	Extends across jawbone	Zygomatic process and arch	Mandible	Closes jaws and elevates mandible
Temporalis	Fan-shaped muscle over temporal bone	Temporal bone	Mandible	Closes jaw and elevates mandible
Buccinator	Principal muscle of cheek; runs horizontally, deep to the masseter	Maxilla and mandible near molars	Orbicularis oris	Compresses cheek (as in whistling); holds food between teeth during chewing
Neck				
Platysma	Thin, sheetlike superficial neck muscle, plays role in facial expression	Fascia of chest (over pectoral muscles) and deltoid	Lower margin of mandible and muscle at corner of mouth	Tenses skin of neck; depresses mandible; pulls lower lip back and down (produces downward sag of the mouth)
Sternocleidomastoid	Two-headed muscle located deep to platysma on anterolateral surface of neck	Sternum and clavicle	Mastoid process of temporal bone	Simultaneous contraction of both muscles of pair causes flexion of neck forward; acting independently, rotate head toward opposite shoulder

12

Muscles of the Trunk

OBJECTIVE 2 Name and locate the major muscles of the trunk.

The trunk musculature includes muscles that move the vertebral column; anterior thorax muscles, which move the ribs, head, and arms; and abdominal muscles, which help move the vertebral column, and—an even more important function—form the "natural girdle," or the major portion of the abdominal body wall.

Activity 2

Identifying Muscles of the Trunk

The trunk muscles are described in Table 12.2, on p. 136 and Table 12.3, on p. 138 and are also shown in Figure 12.4, on p. 137 and Figure 12.5, on p. 137. As before, identify the muscles in the figure as you read the tabular descriptions, and then identify them on the torso or laboratory chart.

Text continues on next page. →

12

Table 12.2	Anterior Muscles of Trunk and Upper Limb (see Figure 12.4)			
Muscle	**Comments**	**Origin**	**Insertion**	**Action**
Thorax and Shoulder, Superficial				
Pectoralis major	Large fan-shaped muscle covering upper portion of chest	Clavicle, sternum, and cartilage of first 6 ribs	Fibers insert by short tendon into greater tubercle of humerus	Prime mover of arm flexion; adducts, medially rotates arm
Deltoid	Fleshy triangular muscle forming shoulder muscle mass	Lateral third of clavicle; acromion and spine of scapula	Deltoid tuberosity of humerus	Acting as a whole, prime mover of arm abduction; when only specific fibers are active, can aid in flexion, extension, and rotation of humerus
Abdominal Wall				
Rectus abdominis	Medial superficial muscle, extends from pubis to rib cage; segmented	Pubis	Sternum and costal cartilages of ribs 5–7	Flexes and rotates vertebral column; increases abdominal pressure
External oblique	Most superficial lateral muscle; fibers run downward and medially	Anterior surface of last 8 ribs	Iliac crest	See rectus abdominis, above; also aids muscles of back to rotate and laterally flex the trunk
Internal oblique	Fibers run at right angles to those of external oblique, which it underlies	Iliac crest	Costal cartilages of last 3 ribs	As for external oblique
Transversus abdominis	Deepest muscle of abdominal wall; fibers run horizontally	Iliac crest and cartilages of last 5 or 6 ribs	Pubis	Compresses abdominal contents
Arm/Forearm				
Biceps brachii	Two-headed muscle of anterior arm	Coracoid process of scapula	Proximal radius	Flexes elbow and supinates forearm
Brachialis	Immediately deep to the biceps brachii	Anterior surface of distal humerus	Coronoid process of ulna	A major arm flexor
Brachioradialis (see Figure 12.1)	Superficial muscle of lateral forearm	Distal humerus	Base of styloid process of radius	Synergist of brachialis in forearm flexion
Pronator teres (see Figure 12.1)	Anterior forearm; superficial to brachialis	Distal humerus and coronoid process of ulna	Radius, midshaft	Pronates forearm
Flexor carpi radialis (see Figure 12.1)	Superficial; runs diagonally across forearm	Medial epicondyle of humerus	Second and third metacarpals	Powerful wrist flexor; abducts hand
Flexor carpi ulnaris (see Figure 12.2)	Superficial; medial to flexor carpi radialis	Distal humerus and posterior ulna	Fifth metacarpal and carpals	Powerful flexor of wrist; adducts hand
Flexor digitorum superficialis (not illustrated)	Deeper muscle; overlain by muscles named above; visible at distal end of forearm	Distal humerus, ulna, and radius	Middle phalanges of second through fifth fingers	Flexes wrist and middle phalanges of fingers 2–5

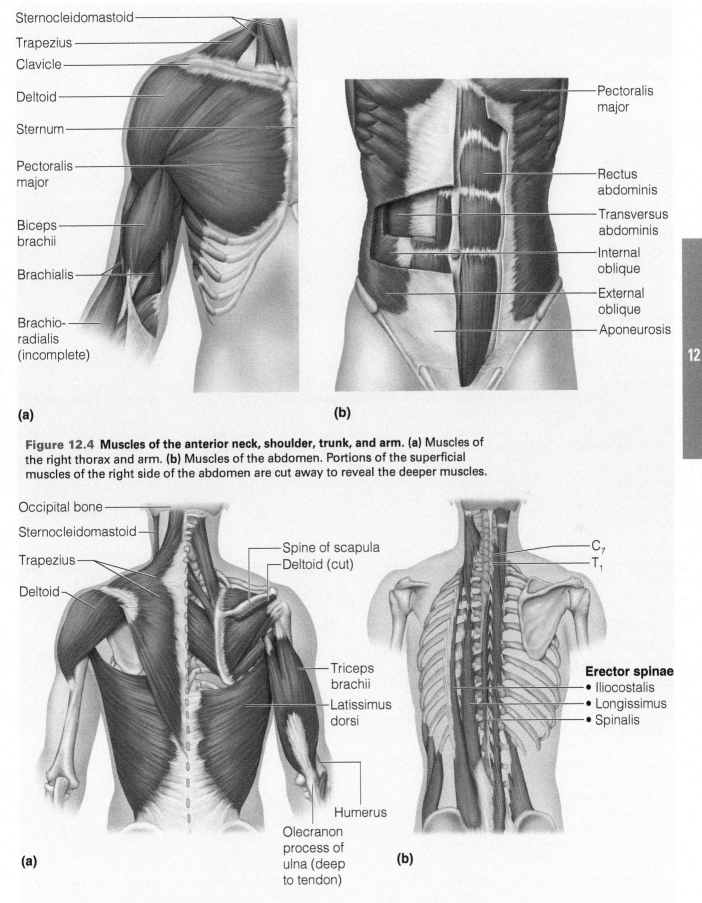

Figure 12.4 Muscles of the anterior neck, shoulder, trunk, and arm. (a) Muscles of the right thorax and arm. **(b)** Muscles of the abdomen. Portions of the superficial muscles of the right side of the abdomen are cut away to reveal the deeper muscles.

Figure 12.5 Muscles of the posterior neck, trunk, and arm. (a) Superficial muscles. **(b)** The erector spinae muscles, deep muscles of the back.

Text continues on next page. →

Table 12.3   Posterior Muscles of Human Neck, Trunk, and Upper Limb (see Figure 12.5)

Muscle	Comments	Origin	Insertion	Action
Muscles of the Neck, Shoulder, and Thorax				
Trapezius	Most superficial muscle of posterior neck and thorax; broad origin and insertion	Occipital bone and all cervical and thoracic vertebrae	Acromion and spinous process of scapula; clavicle	Extends neck, raises, rotates, and retracts (adducts) scapula and stabilizes it
Latissimus dorsi	Broad flat muscle of lower back (lumbar region); extensive superficial origins	Lower 3 to 4 ribs, inferior spine, and iliac crest	Proximal humerus	Prime mover of arm extension; adducts and medially rotates arm; brings arm down in power stroke, as in striking a blow
Erector spinae	A long three-part muscle composed of iliocostalis (lateral), longissimus, and spinalis (medial) muscle columns; extends from pelvis to head	Sacrum, iliac crest, lumbar, thoracic, and cervical vertebrae, and/or ribs 3–12 depending on specific part	Ribs and thoracic and cervical vertebrae	All act to extend and bend the vertebral column laterally; longissimus also extends the head
Deltoid	(see Table 12.2)			
Arm/Forearm Muscles				
Triceps brachii	Sole, large fleshy muscle of posterior humerus; three-headed origin	Glenoid cavity of scapula, posterior humerus	Olecranon process of ulna	Powerful forearm extensor; antagonist of biceps brachii
Extensor carpi radialis longus (see Figure 12.2)	Superficial; parallels brachioradialis on lateral forearm	Lateral humerus	Second and third metacarpal	Extends and abducts wrist
Extensor digitorum (see Figure 12.2)	Superficial; between extensor carpi ulnaris and extensor carpi radialis	Lateral epicondyle of humerus	Distal phalanges of second through fifth fingers	Prime mover of finger extension; extends wrist; can flare (adduct) fingers
Extensor carpi ulnaris (see Figure 12.2)	Superficial; medial posterior forearm	Lateral epicondyle of humerus	Fifth metacarpal	Extends and adducts wrist

Activity 3

Demonstrating Operation of Trunk Muscles

Now work with a partner to demonstrate the operation of the following muscles. One of you can demonstrate the movement (in which case the following steps are addressed to the partner doing the demonstration). The other can supply resistance and palpate the muscle being tested.

1. Fully abduct the arm and extend the elbow. Now abduct the arm against resistance. You are using the *latissimus dorsi* and *pectoralis major* muscles.

2. To observe the action of the *deltoid,* abduct your arm against resistance. Now attempt to elevate your shoulder against resistance; you are contracting the upper portion of the *trapezius.*

3. The *pectoralis major* is used when you press your hands together at chest level with your elbows widely abducted.

Muscles of the Upper Limb

OBJECTIVE 3   Name and locate the major muscles of the upper limb.

The muscles that act on the upper limb fall into three groups: those that move the arm, those causing movement at the elbow, and those moving the wrist and hand.

The muscles that cross the shoulder joint to insert on the humerus and move the arm are primarily trunk muscles that originate on the axial skeleton or shoulder girdle. These muscles are included with the trunk muscles.

The second group of muscles forms the musculature of the humerus and crosses the elbow joint. They flex and extend the forearm.

The third group forms the musculature of the forearm. Most of these muscles insert on the digits and produce movements at the wrist and fingers.

The origins, insertions, and actions of these last two groups of muscles are summarized in Tables 12.2 and 12.3 and are shown in Figures 12.1, 12.2, 12.4, and 12.5.

Activity 4

Identifying Muscles of the Upper Limb

First study the tables and figures, and then see whether you can identify these muscles on a torso model or anatomical chart. Complete this portion of the exercise by palpating upper limb muscles, as outlined next. (As you complete each task, place a check mark in the corresponding box.)

☐ To observe the *biceps brachii* in action, attempt to flex your forearm (hand supinated) against resistance.

☐ Acutely flex your elbow, and then try to extend it against resistance to demonstrate the action of your *triceps brachii*.

☐ Strongly flex your wrist, and make a fist. Palpate your contracting wrist flexor muscles (which originate from the medial epicondyle of the humerus) and their insertion tendons, which can be easily felt at the anterior aspect of the wrist.

☐ Flare your fingers to identify the tendons of the *extensor digitorum* muscle on the dorsum of your hand.

Muscles of the Hip and Lower Limb

OBJECTIVE 4   Name and locate the major muscles of the hip and lower limb.

Muscles that act on the lower limb cause movement at the hip, knee, and foot joints. Muscles acting on the thigh (femur) cause various movements at the multiaxial hip joint (flexion, extension, rotation, abduction, and adduction). These include the iliopsoas, the adductor group, and various other muscles.

Muscles acting on the leg form the musculature of the thigh. (Anatomically, the term *leg* refers only to that portion between the knee and the ankle.) The thigh muscles cross the knee to allow its flexion and extension. They include the hamstrings and the quadriceps. Some of these muscles also attach on the pelvic girdle, so they can cause movement at the hip joint.

Muscles originating on the leg act on the foot and toes. These lower limb muscles are described in **Table 12.4**, on p. 139–140 and **Table 12.5**, on p. 140 and are shown in **Figure 12.6**, on p. 141 and **Figure 12.7**, on p. 142.

12

Table 12.4	Anteromedial Muscles of the Hip and Lower Limb (see Figure 12.6)			
Muscle	**Comments**	**Origin**	**Insertion**	**Action**
Origin on the Pelvis				
Iliopsoas—iliacus and psoas major	Two closely related muscles; fibers pass under inguinal ligament to insert into femur via a common tendon	Iliacus: iliac fossa; psoas major: transverse processes, bodies, and discs of T_{12} and lumbar vertebrae	Lessor trochanter of femur	Flex trunk on thigh; major flexor of hip (or thigh on pelvis when pelvis is fixed)
Sartorius	Straplike superficial muscle running obliquely across anterior surface of thigh to knee	Anterior superior iliac spine	By an aponeurosis into medial aspect of proximal tibia	Flexes, abducts, and laterally rotates thigh; flexes knee
Thigh				
Adductors (magnus, longus, and brevis)	Large muscle mass forming medial aspect of thigh; arise from front of pelvis and insert at various levels on femur	Magnus: ischial and pubic rami; longus: pubis near pubic symphysis; brevis: body and inferior ramus of pubis	Magnus: linea aspera and adductor tubercle of femur; longus and brevis: linea aspera	Adduct and medially rotate and flex thigh; posterior part of magnus is also a synergist in thigh extension
Quadriceps				
• Rectus femoris	Superficial muscle of thigh; runs straight down thigh; only muscle of group to cross hip joint; arises from two heads	Anterior inferior iliac spine and superior margin of acetabulum	Tibial tuberosity via patellar ligament	Extends knee and flexes thigh at hip
• Vastus lateralis	Forms lateral aspect of thigh	Greater trochanter of femur	Tibial tuberosity	Extends and stabilizes knee
• Vastus medialis	Forms medial aspect of thigh	Linea aspera and intertrochanteric line of femur	Tibial tuberosity	Extends knee
• Vastus intermedius	Obscured by rectus femoris; lies between vastus lateralis and vastus medialis	Femur (not shown in figure)	Tibial tuberosity	Extends knee

→

Table 12.4	Anteromedial Muscles of the Hip and Lower Limb (see Figure 12.6) *(continued)*			
Muscle	**Comments**	**Origin**	**Insertion**	**Action**
Leg				
Tibialis anterior	Superficial muscle of anterior leg; parallels sharp anterior margin of tibia	Lateral condyle and upper two-thirds of tibia; interosseous membrane	By tendon into inferior surface of first cuneiform and metatarsal 1	Prime mover of dorsiflexion; inverts foot
Extensor digitorum longus	Lateral to tibialis anterior	Lateral condyle and upper two-thirds of tibia; proximal fibula; interosseous membrane	By tendons (4) into middle and distal phalanges of toes 2–5	Prime mover of toe extension; dorsiflexes foot
Fibularis (peroneus) muscles	Superficial lateral muscle; overlies fibula	Upper portion of fibula	By long tendon under foot to metatarsals	Plantar flexes and everts foot; helps keep foot flat on ground

Table 12.5	Muscles of the Hip and Lower Limb, Posterior Aspect (see Figure 12.7)			
Muscle	**Comments**	**Origin**	**Insertion**	**Action**
Origin on the Pelvis				
Gluteus maximus	Largest and most superficial of gluteal muscles (which form buttock mass)	Ilium, sacrum, and coccyx	Gluteal tuberosity of femur	Powerful hip extensor (most effective when hip is flexed, as in climbing stairs—but not as in walking)
Gluteus medius	Partially covered by gluteus maximus	Lateral surface of ilium	Greater trochanter of femur	Abducts and medially rotates thigh; steadies pelvis during walking
Thigh				
Hamstrings*				
• Biceps femoris	Most lateral muscle of group; arises from two heads	Ischial tuberosity and distal femur	Tendon passes laterally to insert into head of fibula	Extends thigh; laterally flexes knee
• Semitendinosus	Medial to biceps femoris	Ischial tuberosity	Proximal tibia	Extends thigh; flexes knee; medially rotates leg
• Semimembranosus	Deep to semitendinosus	Ischial tuberosity	Proximal tibia	Extends thigh; flexes knee; medially rotates leg
Leg				
Gastrocnemius	Superficial muscle with two prominent bellies	By two heads from medial and lateral condyles of the femur	Calcaneus via calcaneal tendon	Plantar flexes foot; crosses knee joint; flexes knee when foot is dorsiflexed
Soleus	Deep to gastrocnemius	Proximal tibia and fibula	Calcaneus via calcaneal tendon	Plantar flexes foot

*The hamstrings are the fleshy muscles of the posterior thigh. The name comes from the butchers' practice of using the tendons of these muscles to hang hams for smoking. As a group, they are strong extensors of the hip; they counteract the powerful quadriceps by stabilizing the knee joint when standing.

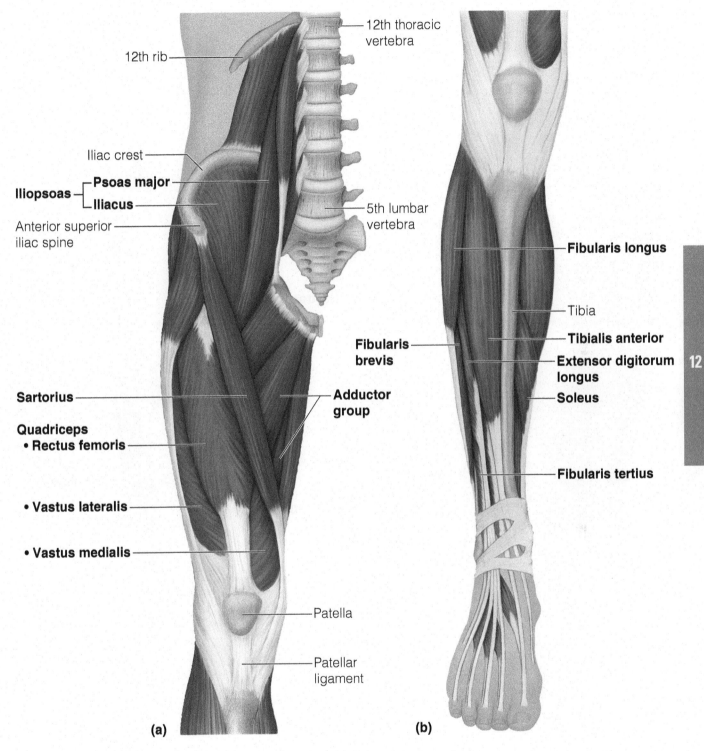

12

Figure 12.6 **Pelvic, thigh, and leg muscles of the right side of the body, anterior view. (a)** Pelvic and thigh muscles. **(b)** Leg muscles.

12

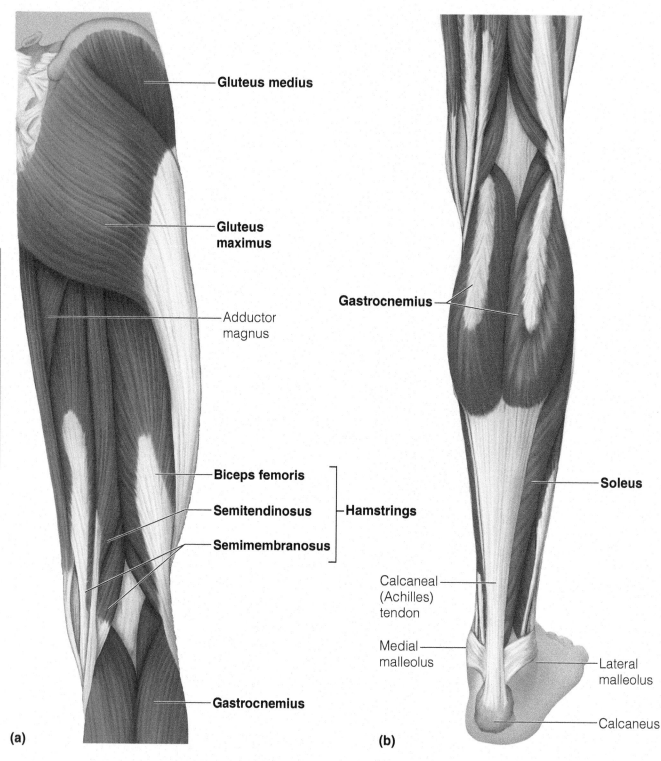

Gluteus medius

Gluteus maximus

Adductor magnus

Gastrocnemius

Biceps femoris

Semitendinosus — **Hamstrings**

Semimembranosus

Gastrocnemius

Soleus

Calcaneal (Achilles) tendon

Medial malleolus

Lateral malleolus

Calcaneus

(a)   (b)

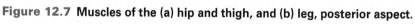

Figure 12.7 Muscles of the (a) hip and thigh, and (b) leg, posterior aspect.

Activity 5

Identifying Muscles of the Hip and Lower Limb

Identify the muscles acting on the thigh, leg, foot, and toes as instructed previously.

Activity 6

Palpating Muscles of the Hip and Lower Limb

Complete this exercise by performing the following palpation demonstrations with your lab partner. (As you complete each task, place a check mark in the corresponding box.)

☐ Go into a deep knee bend, and palpate your own *gluteus maximus* muscle as you extend your hip to return to the upright posture.

☐ Demonstrate the contraction of the anterior *quadriceps femoris* by trying to extend your knee against resistance. Do this while seated, and notice how the patellar tendon reacts. The hamstrings of the posterior thigh come into play when you flex your knee against resistance.

☐ Now stand on your toes. Have your partner palpate the lateral and medial heads of the *gastrocnemius* and follow it to its insertion in the calcaneal tendon.

☐ Dorsiflex and invert your foot while palpating your *tibialis anterior* muscle (which parallels the sharp anterior crest of the tibia laterally).

Activity 7

Making a Muscle Painting

1. Choose a male student to be "muscle painted."

2. Obtain brushes and water-based paints from the supply area while the "volunteer" removes his shirt and rolls up his pant legs (if necessary).

3. Using different colored paints, identify the muscles listed here by painting his skin. If a muscle covers a large body area, you can opt to paint only its borders.

- Biceps brachii
- Deltoid
- Erector spinae
- Pectoralis major
- Rectus femoris
- Tibialis anterior
- Triceps brachii
- Vastus lateralis
- Biceps femoris
- Extensor carpi radialis longus
- Latissimus dorsi
- Rectus abdominis
- Sternocleidomastoid
- Trapezius
- Vastrocnemius
- Vastus medialis

4. Check your "human painting" with your instructor before cleaning your bench and leaving the laboratory.

12

REVIEW SHEET
Gross Anatomy of the Muscular System

Name _____   LabTime/Date _____

Muscles of the Head and Neck

1. Using choices from the list at the right, correctly identify the muscles provided with leader lines on the diagram.

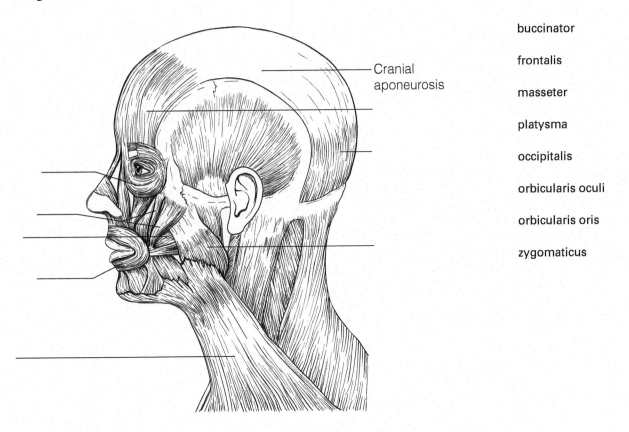

Cranial
aponeurosis

buccinator

frontalis

masseter

platysma

occipitalis

orbicularis oculi

orbicularis oris

zygomaticus

2. Using the terms provided above, identify the muscles described next.

_____ 1. used to grin

_____ 2. muscle used during whistling

_____ 3. used in blinking and squinting

_____ 4. its contraction makes the "sad clown" face (pulls the corners of the mouth downward)

_____ 5. raises your eyebrows for a questioning expression

_____ 6. your "kisser"

_____ 7. allows you to "bite" that carrot stick

_____ 8. tenses skin of the neck during shaving

Muscles of the Trunk and Upper Limb

3. Using choices from the key, identify the major muscles described next:

_____ 1. a major spine flexor

_____ 2. prime mover for pulling the arm posteriorly

_____ 3. elbow extender

_____, _____. 4. help form the
_____, _____.   abdominal girdle
(four pairs of muscles)

_____ 5. extends and adducts wrist

_____ 6. allows you to raise your arm laterally

_____, _____. 7. shoulder adductors
(two muscles)

_____ 8. flexes elbow; supinates the forearm

_____ 9. small muscles between the ribs

_____ 10. extends the head

_____ 11. extends the spine

_____ 12. extends and abducts the wrist

Key:

biceps brachii

deltoid

erector spinae

extensor carpi radialis

extensor carpi ulnaris

extensor digitorum superficialis

intercostals

external oblique

flexor carpi radialis

internal oblique

latissimus dorsi

pectoralis major

rectus abdominis

transversus abdominis

trapezius

triceps brachii

Muscles of the Lower Limb

4. Use the key terms to respond to the descriptions below. (Some terms may be used more than once.)

_____ 1. lateral compartment muscle that plantar flexes
and everts the ankle

_____ 2. forms the buttock

_____ 3. a prime mover of ankle plantar flexion

_____ 4. a prime mover of ankle dorsiflexion

_____ 5. allow you to grip a horse's back with your thighs

_____, _____. 6. muscles that insert
into the tibial tuber-
osity (two choices)

_____, _____, _____ 7. muscles that extend
thigh and flex knee

_____ 8. prime mover of inversion of the foot

_____ 9. prime mover of dorsiflexion of the foot

Key:

adductor group

biceps femoris

extensor digitorum longus

fibularis (peroneus) muscles

gastrocnemius

gluteus maximus

rectus femoris

semimembranosus

semitendinosus

tibialis anterior

tibialis posterior

vastus muscles

_____ 10. adduct the thigh, as when standing at attention

_____ 11. extends the toes

_____ 12. extends knee and flexes thigh

_____ 13. used to extend the hip when climbing stairs

_____ 14. prime movers of plantar flexion (two muscles) of the foot

General Review: Muscle Descriptions

5. Complete the following statements (use your textbook, as necessary):

   1. _____, _____, and _____ are commonly used for intramuscular injections (three muscles).

   2. The insertion tendon of the _____ group contains a large sesamoid bone, the patella.

   3. The gastrocnemius and soleus muscles insert in common into the _____ tendon.

   4. The bulk of the tissue of a muscle tends to lie _____ to the part of the body it causes to move.

   5. The extrinsic muscles of the hand originate on the _____.

   6. Most flexor muscles are located on the _____ aspect of the body; most extensors are located _____. An exception to this generalization is the extensor-flexor musculature of the _____.

General Review: Muscle Recognition

6. Identify the lettered muscles in the diagram of the human anterior superficial musculature by matching each letter with one of the following muscle names:

_____ 1. orbicularis oris

_____ 2. pectoralis major

_____ 3. external oblique

_____ 4. sternocleidomastoid

_____ 5. biceps brachii

_____ 6. deltoid

_____ 7. vastus lateralis

_____ 8. frontalis

_____ 9. rectus femoris

_____ 10. rectus abdominis

_____ 11. sartorius

_____ 12. platysma

_____ 13. flexor carpi radialis

_____ 14. orbicularis oculi

_____ 15. gastrocnemius

_____ 16. masseter

_____ 17. trapezius

_____ 18. tibialis anterior

_____ 19. adductors

_____ 20. vastus medialis

_____ 21. transversus abdominis

_____ 22. fibularis longus

_____ 23. iliopsoas

_____ 24. temporalis

_____ 25. zygomaticus

_____ 26. triceps brachii

_____ 27. brachialis

_____ 28. extensor digitorum longus

_____ 29. internal oblique

_____ 30. soleus

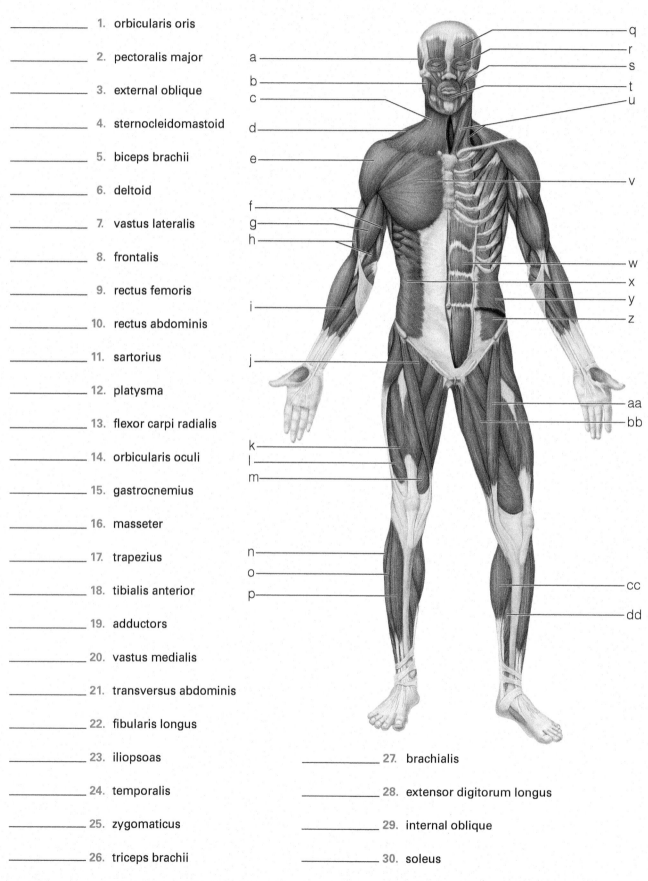

7. Identify each of the lettered muscles in this diagram of the human posterior superficial musculature by matching the letter to one of the following muscle names:

_____ 1. gluteus maximus

_____ 2. semimembranosus

_____ 3. gastrocnemius

_____ 4. latissimus dorsi

_____ 5. deltoid

_____ 6. semitendinosus

_____ 7. trapezius

_____ 8. biceps femoris

_____ 9. triceps brachii

_____ 10. external oblique

_____ 11. gluteus medius

_____ 12. flexor carpi ulnaris

_____ 13. extensor carpi ulnaris

_____ 14. extensor digitorium

_____ 15. extensor carpi radialis

_____ 16. sternocleidomastoid

_____ 17. adductor magnus

_____ 18. soleus

Neuron Anatomy and Physiology

Materials

☐ Model of a "typical" (motor) neuron (if available)

☐ Demonstration area: Microscopes set up with the following prepared slides for student examination:

Station 1: Ox spinal cord smear (under oil)

Station 2: Teased myelinated nerve fibers

Station 3: Nerve (cross section)

Pre-Lab Quiz

1. Circle the correct term. Nervous tissue is made up of <u>two</u> / <u>three</u> principal cell populations.

2. These branching neuron processes serve as receptive regions and transmit electrical signals toward the cell body. They are:
   a. axons   c. dendrites
   b. collaterals   d. neuroglia

3. Circle True or False. Axons are the neuron processes that generate and conduct nerve impulses.

4. Most axons are covered with a fatty material called _____, which insulates the fibers and increases the speed of neurotransmission.

5. Circle the correct term. Neurons can be classified according to function. <u>Afferent</u> / <u>Efferent</u> or motor neurons carry activating impulses from the central nervous system primarily to body muscles or glands.

6. Within a nerve, each fiber is surrounded by a delicate connective tissue sheath called the:
   a. endoneurium   b. epineurium   c. perineurium

The nervous system is the master control system of the body. Every thought, action, and sensation is a reflection of its activity.

OBJECTIVE 1   Distinguish the functions of neurons and neuroglia.

Despite its complexity, nervous tissue is made up of just two principal cell populations: **neurons** and **supporting cells,** also called **neuroglia** or **glial cells.** The supporting cells in the CNS (central nervous system: brain and spinal cord) include several cell types that serve the needs of the neurons by acting as phagocytes and by protecting and myelinating the delicate neurons. In addition, they act as a selective barrier between the capillary blood supply and the neurons. The most important neuroglia in the peripheral nervous system (PNS: neural structures outside the CNS) are *Schwann cells.* Schwann cells insulate nerve fibers. In this exercise, we focus on the highly excitable (irritable) neurons.

Neuron Anatomy

OBJECTIVE 2   Identify the important anatomical characteristics of a neuron.

Neurons are specialized to transmit messages (nerve impulses) from one part of the body to another. Neurons differ structurally, but they have many features in common (**Figure 13.1a**). All have a **cell body** from which slender **processes** or **fibers** extend. Clusters of neuron cell bodies that are located in the CNS are called **nuclei,** and clusters of neuron cell bodies located in the PNS are called **ganglia.** Nuclei of the CNS make up the gray matter of the nervous system. Neuron fibers running through the CNS form **tracts** of white matter. In the PNS, they form the peripheral **nerves.**

The neuron cell body contains a large round nucleus, with a prominent nucleolus, surrounded by cytoplasm. The cytoplasm is riddled with *neurofibrils,* cytoskeletal

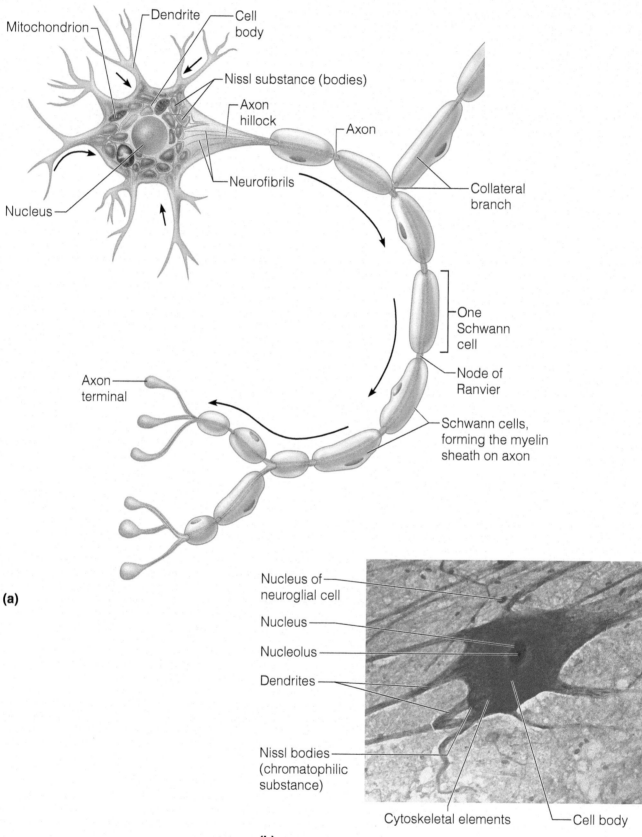

(a)

(b)

Figure 13.1 Structure of a typical motor neuron. (a) Diagrammatic view.
The arrows indicate directions in which signals travel along the neuron.
(b) Photomicrograph of a motor neuron (450×). See also Plate 5 in the
Histology Atlas.

elements of the neuron, which have a support and intracellular transport function, and an elaborate rough endoplasmic reticulum called *Nissl bodies* or *chromatophilic substance.*

Generally speaking, neuron processes that conduct electrical currents *toward* the cell body are called **dendrites,** and those that carry impulses *away from* the nerve cell body are called **axons.** Neurons have only one axon (which may branch into *collaterals*) but may have many dendrites, depending on the neuron type.

OBJECTIVE 3 Explain how a nerve impulse is transmitted from one neuron to another.

A neuron is excited by other neurons when their axons release neurotransmitters close to its dendrites or cell body that bind to receptors and create an electrical current that travels down its axon. As Figure 13.1a shows, the axon ends in many small structures called **axon terminals,** which store the neurotransmitter chemical in tiny vesicles. Each axon terminal is separated from the cell body or dendrites of the next (postsynaptic)

neuron by a tiny gap called the **synaptic cleft.** Thus, although they are close, there is no actual physical contact between neurons. When an impulse reaches the axon terminals, some of the synaptic vesicles fuse with the plasma membrane and then rupture and release neurotransmitter into the synaptic cleft. The neurotransmitter then diffuses across the synaptic cleft to bind to membrane receptors on the next neuron, initiating the action potential. Specialized synapses in skeletal muscle are called *neuromuscular junctions* (discussed in Exercise 11).

OBJECTIVE 4 Describe the functional importance of myelin sheaths, and describe how those sheaths are formed by Schwann cells.

Most long nerve fibers are covered with a fatty material called *myelin,* and such fibers are referred to as **myelinated fibers.** Axons in the peripheral nervous system are myelinated by special supporting cells called **Schwann cells.** Schwann cells create the myelination by wrapping tightly around the axon in a jelly-roll fashion. When the wrapping process is completed, a tight core of plasma membrane material called the **myelin sheath** encompasses the axon (**Figure 13.2**). The Schwann cell nucleus and the bulk of its cytoplasm end up just beneath the outermost portion of its plasma membrane. This part of the Schwann cell external to the myelin sheath is referred to as the **neurilemma.** Because the myelin sheath is formed by many individual Schwann cells, it has gaps or indentations called **nodes of Ranvier** (see Figure 13.1). (Within the CNS, myelination is accomplished by glial cells called *oligodendrocytes.*) Myelin insulates the fibers and greatly increases the speed of neurotransmission by neuron fibers.

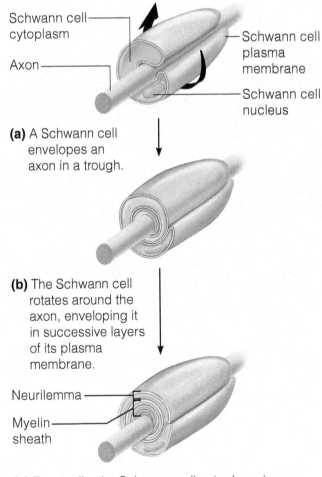

(a) A Schwann cell envelopes an axon in a trough.

(b) The Schwann cell rotates around the axon, enveloping it in successive layers of its plasma membrane.

(c) Eventually, the Schwann cell cytoplasm is squeezed from between the membranes and comes to lie just beneath the exposed portion of the Schwann cell membrane.

Figure 13.2 Relationship of Schwann cells to axons in the peripheral nervous system. The tight Schwann cell membrane wrappings surrounding the axon form the myelin sheath; the area of Schwann cell cytoplasm and its exposed membrane is referred to as the neurilemma.

Activity 1

Identifying Parts of a Neuron

1. Study the typical motor neuron shown in Figure 13.1, noting the structural details described above, and then identify these structures on a neuron model.

2. Go to station 1 of the demonstration area, where the microscopes are set up, and view a prepared slide of the ox spinal cord smear, which has large, easily identifiable neurons. Study one representative neuron, and identify the cell body, the nucleus, and the large, "owl's eye" nucleolus. If possible, distinguish the axon from the many dendrites. Sketch the cell in the space provided here, and label the important anatomical details you observe. Compare your sketch to Figure 13.1b and Plate 5 in the Histology Atlas. Also reexamine Figure 13.1a, which differentiates the neuronal processes more clearly in conjunction with your observation of Plate 6 in the Histology Atlas.

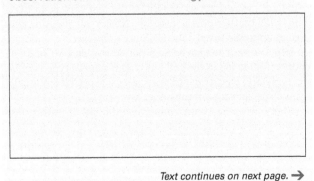

Text continues on next page. →

3. At station 2, view a prepared slide of teased myelinated nerve fibers. Using Figures 13.1 and 13.2 and Plate 8 in the Histology Atlas as guides, identify the following: nodes of Ranvier, neurilemma, axis cylinder (the axon itself), Schwann cell nuclei, and myelin sheath.

Sketch a portion of a myelinated nerve fiber in the space below, illustrating two or three nodes of Ranvier. Label the axon, myelin sheath, nodes, and neurilemma.

Do the nodes seem to occur at consistent intervals, or are they distributed irregularly?

_____

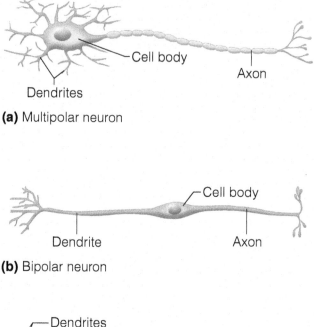

(a) Multipolar neuron

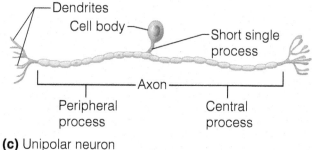

(b) Bipolar neuron

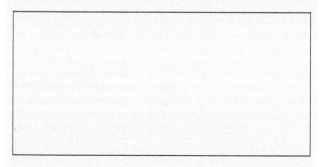

(c) Unipolar neuron

Figure 13.3 Classification of neurons based on structure (number of processes extending from the cell body). See also Plates 6 and 7 in the Histology Atlas.

13 Neuron Classification

OBJECTIVE 5 Classify neurons according to structure and function.

On the Basis of Structure

The number of processes attached to the cell body determines the structural class of a neuron (**Figure 13.3**). In **unipolar neurons,** one very short process, which divides into *distal (peripheral)* and *proximal (central) processes,* extends from the cell body. Functionally, only the most distal portions of the central process act as dendrites; the rest acts as an axon along with the peripheral process. Nearly all neurons that conduct impulses toward the CNS are unipolar.

Bipolar neurons have two processes—one axon and one dendrite—attached to the cell body. This neuron type is quite rare; typically, bipolar neurons serve as sensory receptor cells in some special sense organs (e.g., eye, ear).

Many processes issue from the cell body of **multipolar neurons,** and all are dendrites except for a single axon. Most neurons in the brain and spinal cord (CNS neurons) and those

whose axons carry impulses away from the CNS fall into this last category.

On the Basis of Function

Neurons carrying impulses from the sensory receptors in the internal organs or in the skin are called **sensory,** or **afferent, neurons** (**Figure 13.4**). The dendritic endings of sensory neurons often bear specialized receptors that are stimulated by specific changes in their immediate environment. The cell bodies of sensory neurons are always found in a ganglion outside the CNS, and these neurons are typically unipolar.

Neurons carrying activating impulses from the CNS to the viscera and/or body muscles and glands are **motor,** or **efferent, neurons.** Motor neurons are most often multipolar, and their cell bodies are almost always located in the CNS.

The third functional category of neurons is the **interneurons,** or **association neurons,** which are situated in pathways that connect sensory and motor neurons. Their cell bodies are always located within the CNS, and they are multipolar.

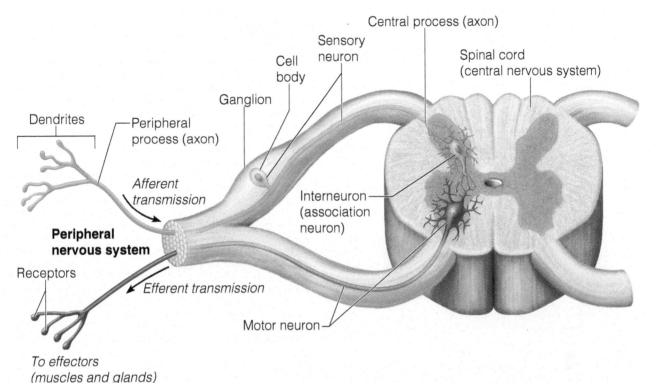

Figure 13.4 Classification of neurons on the basis of function. Sensory (afferent) neurons conduct impulses from the body's sensory receptors to the central nervous system; most are unipolar neurons with their nerve cell bodies in ganglia in the peripheral nervous system (PNS). Motor (efferent) neurons transmit impulses from the CNS to effectors such as muscles and glands. Association neurons (interneurons) complete the communication line between sensory and motor neurons. They are typically multipolar and their cell bodies reside in the CNS.

Structure of a Nerve

OBJECTIVE 6   Describe the structure of a nerve, identifying the connective tissue coverings.

As illustrated in **Figure 13.5**, a nerve is a bundle of neuron fibers or processes that extends to and/or from the CNS and visceral organs or structures of the body periphery (such as skeletal muscles, glands, and skin).

Within a nerve, each fiber is surrounded by a delicate connective tissue sheath called an **endoneurium,** which insulates it from the other neuron processes adjacent to it. Groups of fibers are bound by a coarser connective tissue, called the **perineurium,** to form bundles of fibers called **fascicles.** Finally, all the fascicles are bound together by a tough, white, fibrous connective tissue sheath called the **epineurium,** forming the cordlike nerve (Figure 13.5).

Like neurons, nerves are classified according to the direction in which they transmit impulses. Nerves carrying both sensory (afferent) and motor (efferent) fibers are **mixed nerves;** all spinal nerves are mixed nerves. Nerves that carry only sensory processes and conduct impulses only toward the CNS are **sensory,** or **afferent, nerves.** A few of the cranial nerves are pure sensory nerves, but the majority are mixed nerves. The ventral roots of the spinal cord, which carry only motor fibers, are **motor,** or **efferent, nerves.**

13

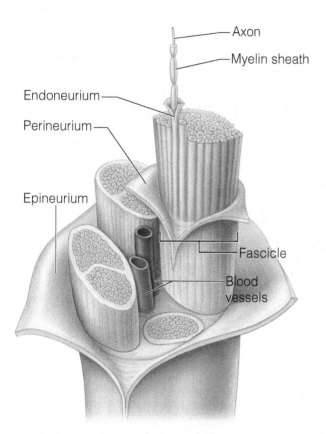

Axon
Myelin sheath
Endoneurium
Perineurium
Epineurium
Fascicle
Blood vessels

Figure 13.5 Three-dimensional view of a portion of a nerve showing connective tissue wrappings.

Activity 2

Examining the Microscopic Structure of a Nerve

Go to station 3 of the demonstration area, and examine under the compound microscope a prepared cross section of a peripheral nerve. Identify nerve fibers, myelin sheaths, fascicles, and endoneurium, perineurium, and epineurium sheaths. If desired, sketch the nerve in the space below. Compare your sketch to Figure 13.5 and Plate 10 in the Histology Atlas.

Neuron Physiology: The Nerve Impulse

13

OBJECTIVE 7 Describe briefly how a nerve impulse is generated.

Neurons have two major physiological properties: (1) the ability to respond to stimuli and convert them into nerve impulses, and (2) the ability to transmit the impulse to other neurons, muscles, or glands. In a resting neuron, the outside surface of the membrane is slightly more positively charged than the inside surface, as shown in **Figure 13.6a**. This difference in electrical charge on the two sides of the membrane is called the **resting membrane potential,** and a neuron in this state is said to be **polarized.** In a resting neuron, the main intracellular cation is potassium (K^+); sodium ions (Na^+) are found in greater concentration in the extracellular fluids. The resting potential is maintained by a very active sodium-potassium pump, which transports Na^+ out of the cell and K^+ into the cell.

When the neuron is activated by a threshold stimulus, the membrane briefly becomes more permeable to sodium (sodium gates are opened), and sodium ions rush into the cell (Figure 13.6b). Thus the inside of the membrane becomes less negative at that point, and the outside surface becomes less positive—a phenomenon called **depolarization.** When depolarization reaches the point when local membrane polarity changes (momentarily the external face becomes negative, and the internal face becomes positive), it initiates an **action potential**[*] (Figure 13.6c).

Within a millisecond after the inward rush of sodium, the membrane permeability again changes. As a result, Na^+ permeability decreases, K^+ permeability increases, and K^+ rushes out of the cell. Because K^+ ions are positively charged, their movement out of the cell reverses the membrane potential again, so that the external membrane surface is again positive relative to the internal membrane face (Figure 13.6d). This event, called **repolarization,** reestablishes the resting membrane potential.

Once started, the action potential spreads rapidly along the entire length of the neuron. It is never partially transmitted; that is, it is an all-or-none response. This propagation of the action potential in neurons is also called the **nerve impulse.** When the nerve impulse reaches the axon terminals, they release a neurotransmitter that acts either to stimulate or to inhibit the next neuron in the transmission chain.

Because only tiny amounts of sodium and potassium ions change places, once repolarization has been completed, the neuron can quickly respond again to a stimulus. Eventually, however, the original ionic concentrations must be restored on the two sides of the membrane. This is accomplished by enhanced activity of the Na^+-K^+ pump (Figure 13.6e).

[*] If the stimulus is of less than threshold intensity, depolarization is limited to a small area of the membrane, and no action potential is generated.

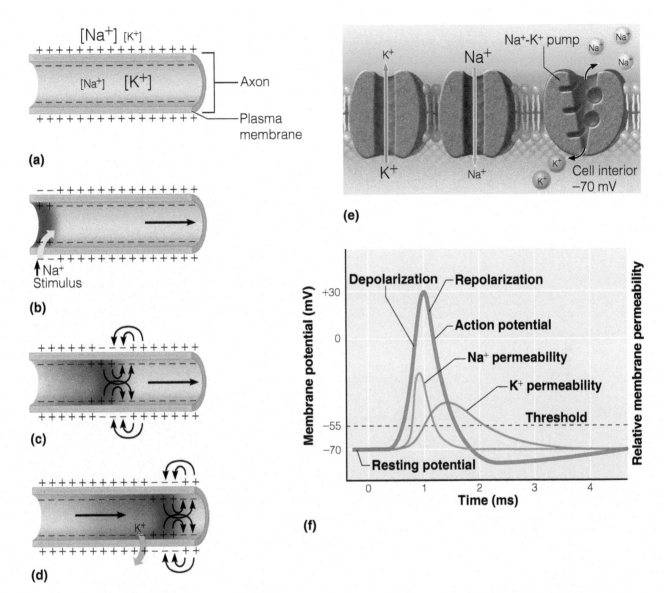

Figure 13.6 The nerve impulse.
(a) In a resting neuron, there is an excess of positive ions outside the cell, with Na⁺ as the main extracellular fluid ion and K⁺ as the predominant intracellular ion. The plasma membrane has a low permeability to Na⁺.
(b) Depolarization—local reversal of the resting membrane potential. Application of a stimulus changes the membrane permeability, and Na⁺ ions are allowed to diffuse rapidly into the cell. The interior face of the membrane becomes less negative (moves toward positive).
(c) Generation of the action potential or nerve impulse. If the stimulus is strong enough, the depolarization wave spreads rapidly along the entire length of the membrane.
(d) Repolarization—reestablishment of the resting membrane potential. The negative charge on the internal plasma membrane surface and the positive charge on its external surface are reestablished by diffusion of K⁺ ions out of the cell, proceeding in the same direction as in depolarization.
(e) The original ionic concentrations of the resting state are restored by the Na⁺-K⁺ pump. (f) A tracing of an action potential.

13

REVIEW SHEET
Neuron Anatomy and Physiology

Name _____ Lab Time/Date _____

1. The cellular unit of the nervous system is the neuron. What is the major function of this cell type?

   _____

   _____

2. The supporting cells, or neuroglia, have numerous functions. Name three.

   _____

   _____

3. Match each statement with a response chosen from the key.

   Key: afferent neuron   interneuron   nuclei
              central nervous system   neurotransmitters   peripheral nervous system
              efferent neuron   nerve   synaptic cleft
              ganglion   neuroglia   tract

   _____ 1. the brain and spinal cord collectively

   _____ 2. a tiny gap that separates two neurons

   _____ 3. a collection of nerve cell bodies found outside the central nervous system

   _____ 4. neuron connecting sensory and motor neurons

   _____ 5. neuron processes running through the CNS

   _____ 6. collections of nerve cell bodies inside the CNS

   _____ 7. neuron that conducts impulses away from the CNS to muscles and glands

   _____ 8. neuron that conducts impulses toward the CNS from the body periphery

   _____ 9. chemicals released by axon terminals

   _____ 10. specialized supporting cells of the nervous system

Neuron Anatomy

4. Draw a "typical" neuron in the space below. Include and label the following structures on your diagram: cell body, nucleus, dendrites, axon, axon terminals, myelin sheath, and nodes of Ranvier.

5. How is one-way conduction at synapses ensured? _____

   _____

6. What anatomical characteristic determines whether a particular neuron is classified as unipolar, bipolar, or multipolar?

   _____

   Make a simple line drawing of each type here.

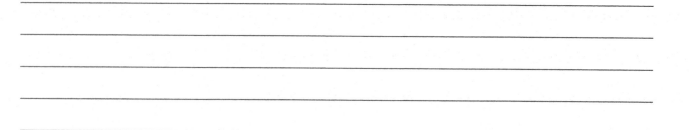

| Unipolar neuron | Bipolar neuron | Multipolar neuron |

7. Describe how the Schwann cells form the myelin sheath and the neurilemma encasing an axon. (You may want to diagram the process.)

   _____

   _____

   _____

   _____

   _____

8. Correctly identify the sensory (afferent) neuron, interneuron, and motor (efferent) neuron in the figure below.

Which of these neuron types is/are unipolar? _____

Which is/are most likely multipolar? _____

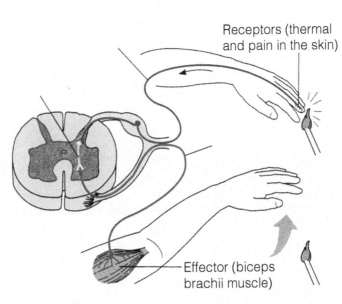

Receptors (thermal and pain in the skin)

Effector (biceps brachii muscle)

Structure of a Nerve

9. What is a nerve? _____

_____

10. State the location of each of the following connective tissue coverings:

endoneurium _____

perineurium _____

epineurium _____

11. What is the value of the connective tissue wrappings found in a nerve? _____

_____

12. Define *mixed nerve:* _____

_____

The Nerve Impulse

13. Match each of the terms in column B to the appropriate definition in column A.

Column A

_____ 1. reversal of the resting potential resulting from an influx of sodium ions

_____ 2. period during which potassium ions are diffusing out of the neuron

_____ 3. transmission of the depolarization wave along the neuronal membrane

_____ 4. mechanism that restores the resting membrane voltage and intracellular ionic concentrations

Column B

action potential

depolarization

repolarization

sodium-potassium pump

14. Would a substance that decreases membrane permeability to sodium increase _or_ decrease the probability of generating a nerve impulse? _____

_____

15. Why don't the terms _depolarization_ and _action potential_ mean the same thing? (_Hint:_ Under what conditions will a local depolarization _not_ lead to the action potential?) _____

_____

_____

Gross Anatomy of the Brain and Cranial Nerves

Materials

☐ Human brain model (dissectible)
☐ Three-dimensional model of ventricles
☐ Preserved human brain (if available)
☐ Coronally sectioned human brain slice (if available)
☐ Materials as needed for cranial nerve testing (see Table 14.1)
☐ Preserved sheep brain (meninges and cranial nerves intact)
☐ Dissecting tray and instruments
☐ Disposable gloves

Pre-Lab Quiz

1. Circle the correct term. The <u>central nervous system</u> / <u>peripheral nervous system</u> consists of the brain and spinal cord.

2. On the ventral surface of the brain, you can observe the optic nerves and chiasma, the pituitary gland, and the mammillary bodies. These externally visible structures form the floor of the:
   a. brain stem
   b. diencephalon
   c. frontal lobe
   d. occipital lobe

3. Circle the correct term. The lowest region of the brain stem, the <u>medulla oblongata</u> / <u>cerebellum</u> houses many vital autonomic centers involved in the control of heart rate, respiratory rhythm, and blood pressure.

4. Directly under the occipital lobes of the cerebrum is a large cauliflower-like structure known as the:
   a. brain stem
   b. cerebellum
   c. diencephalon

5. The brain and spinal cord are covered and protected by three connective tissue layers called:
   a. lobes
   b. meninges
   c. sulci
   d. ventricles

6. How many pairs of cranial nerves are there?

Because the nervous system is so complex, its structures are usually considered in terms of two principal divisions: the **central nervous system (CNS)** and the **peripheral nervous system (PNS)**. The central nervous system consists of the brain and spinal cord, which interpret incoming sensory information and issue instructions based on past experience. The peripheral nervous system consists of the cranial and spinal nerves, ganglia, and sensory receptors. These structures serve as communication lines as they carry impulses—from the sensory receptors to the CNS and from the CNS to the appropriate glands or muscles.

In this exercise both CNS (brain) and PNS (cranial nerves) structures are studied because of their close anatomical relationship.

The Human Brain

OBJECTIVE 1 Identify externally visible regions of the cerebral hemispheres, diencephalon, brain stem, and cerebellum, and generally locate the well-recognized functional areas of the cerebral hemispheres.

Activity 1

Identifying External Brain Structures

Generally, the brain is studied in terms of four major regions: the cerebral hemispheres, diencephalon, brain stem, and cerebellum. Identify external brain structures using a model of the human brain and the figures cited in the following sections. *Text continues on page 165.* →

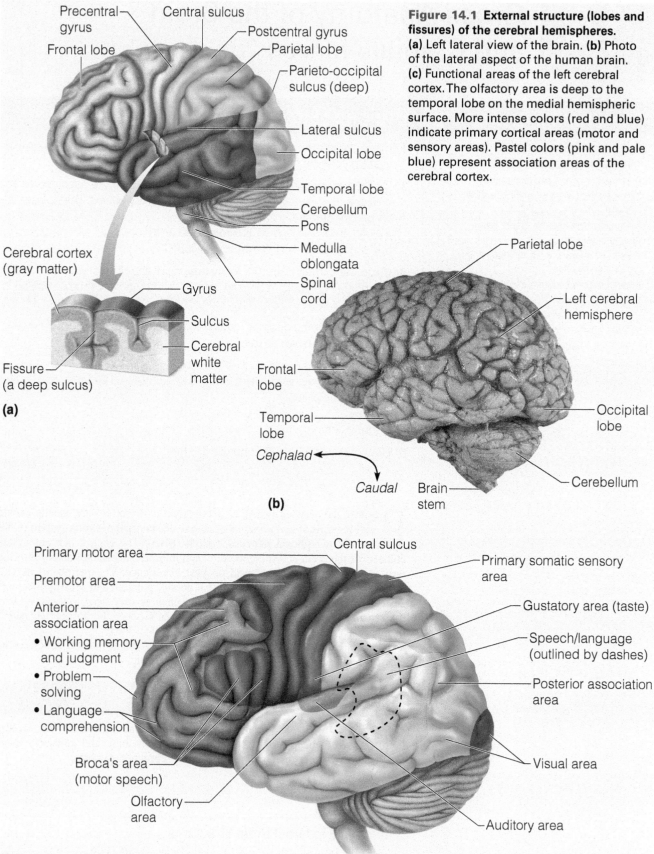

Precentral gyrus
Central sulcus
Frontal lobe
Postcentral gyrus
Parietal lobe
Parieto-occipital sulcus (deep)
Lateral sulcus
Occipital lobe
Temporal lobe
Cerebellum
Pons
Medulla oblongata
Spinal cord

Cerebral cortex (gray matter)
Gyrus
Sulcus
Cerebral white matter
Fissure (a deep sulcus)

(a)

Figure 14.1 External structure (lobes and fissures) of the cerebral hemispheres. (a) Left lateral view of the brain. **(b)** Photo of the lateral aspect of the human brain. **(c)** Functional areas of the left cerebral cortex. The olfactory area is deep to the temporal lobe on the medial hemispheric surface. More intense colors (red and blue) indicate primary cortical areas (motor and sensory areas). Pastel colors (pink and pale blue) represent association areas of the cerebral cortex.

Parietal lobe
Left cerebral hemisphere
Frontal lobe
Temporal lobe
Occipital lobe
Cerebellum
Cephalad
Caudal
Brain stem

(b)

Primary motor area
Premotor area
Anterior association area
• Working memory and judgment
• Problem solving
• Language comprehension
Broca's area (motor speech)
Olfactory area

Central sulcus
Primary somatic sensory area
Gustatory area (taste)
Speech/language (outlined by dashes)
Posterior association area
Visual area
Auditory area

(c)

Cerebral Hemispheres

The **cerebral hemispheres** are the most superior part of the brain (**Figure 14.1**). Their entire surface is thrown into elevated ridges called **gyri** that are separated by depressed areas called **fissures** or **sulci.** Many of the fissures and gyri are important anatomical landmarks.

The cerebral hemispheres are divided by the deep **longitudinal fissure.** The **central sulcus** divides the **frontal lobe** from the **parietal lobe,** and the **lateral sulcus** separates the **temporal lobe** from the parietal lobe. The **parieto-occipital sulcus,** which divides the **occipital lobe** from the parietal lobe, is not visible externally. Notice that the cerebral hemisphere lobes are named for the cranial bones that lie over them.

Some important functional areas of the cerebral hemispheres have also been located (Figure 14.1c). The **primary somatic sensory area** is located in the parietal lobe just posterior to the central fissure. Impulses traveling from the body's sensory receptors (such as those for pressure, pain, and temperature) are localized and interpreted in this area of the brain.

Impulses from the special sense organs are interpreted in other areas also noted in Figure 14.1c. For example, the visual areas are in the posterior part of the occipital lobe, and the auditory area borders the lateral sulcus in the temporal lobe. The olfactory area is deep within the temporal lobe along its medial surface.

The **primary motor area,** which allows us to consciously move our skeletal muscles, is located anterior to the central fissure in the frontal lobe, and just anterior to

that is the **premotor area,** a region that stores the instructions for sequences of motor activity (e.g., playing a piano). A specialized motor speech area called **Broca's area** is found at the base of the primary motor area just above the lateral sulcus. Areas involved in complex reasoning and personality lie in the anterior portions of the frontal lobes.

A rather poorly defined region at the junction of the parietal and temporal lobes is the speech / language area in which unfamiliar words are sounded out. Like Broca's area, this area is located in only one cerebral hemisphere, typically the left.

The cell bodies of neurons involved in these functions are found only in the outermost gray matter of the cerebrum, the area called the **cerebral cortex.** Most of the balance of cerebral tissue—the deeper **cerebral white matter**—consists of fiber tracts carrying impulses to or from the cortex.

☐ Using a preserved human brain and/or brain slices if available, identify the areas and structures of the cerebral hemispheres that have been described above.

Place a check mark in the box when you have completed this task. Then continue using the preserved brain along with the model and figures as you read about other structures.

Diencephalon

The **diencephalon** is sometimes considered the most superior portion of the brain stem.

Turn the brain model to view the ventral surface of the brain. Using **Figure 14.2** as a guide, start superiorly and identify the visible external structures that mark the

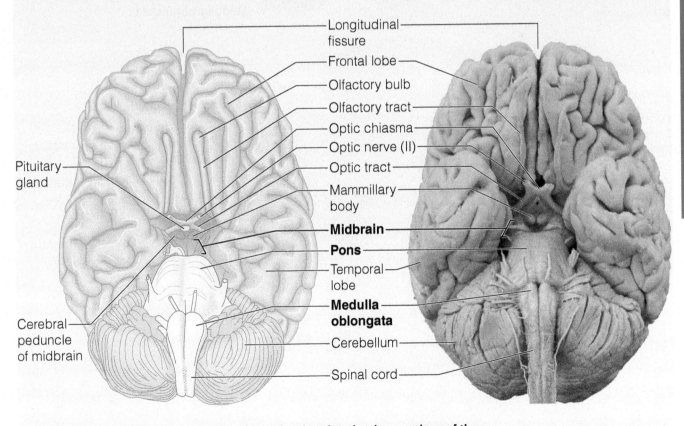

- Longitudinal fissure
- Frontal lobe
- Olfactory bulb
- Olfactory tract
- Optic chiasma
- Optic nerve (II)
- Optic tract
- Mammillary body
- **Midbrain**
- **Pons**
- Temporal lobe
- **Medulla oblongata**
- Cerebellum
- Spinal cord

Pituitary gland

Cerebral peduncle of midbrain

Figure 14.2 Ventral aspect of the human brain, showing the three regions of the brain stem. Only a small portion of the midbrain can be seen; the rest is surrounded by other brain regions.

Text continues on next page. →

14

position of the floor of the diencephalon. These are the **olfactory bulbs** and **tracts, optic nerves, optic chiasma, optic tracts, pituitary gland,** and **mammillary bodies.**

Brain Stem

Continue inferiorly to identify **brain stem** structures—the **cerebral peduncles** (fiber tracts in the **midbrain** connecting the pons below with cerebrum above), the pons, and the medulla oblongata. *Pons* means "bridge," and the **pons** consists primarily of motor and sensory fiber tracts connecting the brain with lower CNS centers. The lowest brain stem region, the **medulla oblongata,** is also composed primarily of fiber tracts. The medulla also houses many vital autonomic centers involved in the control of visceral activities, such as heart rate, respiratory rhythm, and blood pressure.

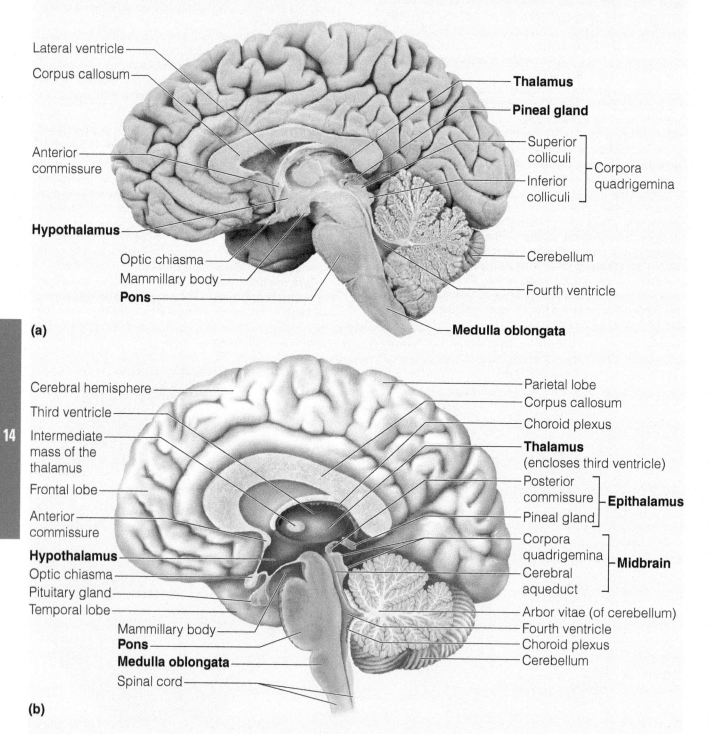

Figure 14.3 Diencephalon and brain stem structures as seen in a midsagittal section of the brain. (a) Photograph. **(b)** Diagrammatic view.

Cerebellum

1. Turn the brain model so you can see the dorsal aspect. Identify the large cauliflowerlike **cerebellum,** which projects dorsally from under the occipital lobe of the cerebrum. Notice that, like the cerebrum, the cerebellum has two major hemispheres and a convoluted surface.

2. Remove the cerebellum to view the **corpora quadrigemina,** located on the posterior aspect of the midbrain. The two superior prominences are visual reflex centers. The two smaller inferior prominences are auditory reflex centers (**Figure 14.3**).

OBJECTIVE 2 Identify important internal areas of the cerebral hemispheres, diencephalon, brain stem, and cerebellum.

Activity 2

Identifying Internal Brain Structures

The deeper structures of the brain have also been well mapped. Like the external structures, these can be studied in terms of the four major regions. As the internal brain areas are described, identify them on the figures cited. Also use the brain model, and preserved human brains if available, to help you in this study.

Cerebral Hemispheres

1. Take the brain model apart to see a median sagittal view of the internal brain structures (Figure 14.3). Examine the model closely to see the extent of the outer cortex (gray matter), which contains the cell bodies of cerebral neurons.

2. Observe the deeper area of white matter, which is composed of fiber tracts. Identify the large **corpus callosum,** the major fiber tract connecting the cerebral hemispheres. The corpus callosum arches above the structures of the diencephalon.

3. Buried deep within the white matter of the cerebral hemispheres are several "islands" of gray matter (clusters of neuron cell bodies) called **nuclei.** One important group of cerebral nuclei, called the **basal nuclei** (or **basal ganglia**), flank the lateral and third ventricles. The basal nuclei help regulate voluntary motor activities. If you have an appropriate dissectible model or a coronally or cross-sectioned human brain slice, identify the basal nuclei.

Diencephalon

1. The major internal structures of the diencephalon are the thalamus, hypothalamus, and epithalamus (see Figure 14.3). The **thalamus** consists of two large lobes of gray matter that laterally enclose the shallow third ventricle of the brain. A stalk of thalamic tissue, the **intermediate mass,** connects the two lobes and spans the ventricle. The thalamus is a major relay station for sensory impulses passing upward to the cortical sensory areas.

2. The **hypothalamus** makes up the floor of the third ventricle. It is an important autonomic center involved in body temperature regulation and water balance, as well as in many other activities and drives. Locate again the **pituitary gland,** which hangs from the floor of the hypothalamus by a slender stalk. (The pituitary gland is usually not present in preserved brain specimens and is not shown in Figure 14.3a.) In life, the pituitary rests in the sella turcica of the sphenoid bone.

Anterior to the pituitary, identify the optic chiasma portion of the optic pathway to the brain. The **mammillary bodies,** relay stations for olfaction, bulge exteriorly from the floor of the hypothalamus just posterior to the pituitary gland.

3. The **epithalamus** forms the roof of the third ventricle. Important structures in the epithalamus are the **pineal gland** (part of the endocrine system) and the **choroid plexus** of the third ventricle. The choroid plexuses, capillary knots within each ventricle, form cerebrospinal fluid.

Brain Stem

1. Now trace the short midbrain from the mammillary bodies to the rounded pons below. Refer to Figure 14.3. The **cerebral aqueduct** is a slender canal traveling through the midbrain; it connects the third ventricle to the fourth ventricle in the pons and medulla below. The cerebral peduncles and the rounded corpora quadrigemina lie anterior and posterior (respectively) to the cerebral aqueduct.

2. Trace the rounded pons to the medulla oblongata below, and identify the fourth ventricle posterior to these structures. Attempt to identify the three orifices in the walls of the fourth ventricle, which allow cerebrospinal fluid to circulate into the subarachnoid space from the fourth ventricle.

Cerebellum

Examine the internal structure of the cerebellum. The cerebellum has an outer cortical area of gray matter and an inner area of branching white matter. The treelike branching of the cerebellar white matter is referred to as the **arbor vitae,** or "tree of life." Like an automatic pilot that continually compares the plane's motion with its preset course, the cerebellum is concerned with unconscious coordination of skeletal muscle activity and control of balance and equilibrium.

14

Meninges of the Brain

OBJECTIVE 3 Identify the three meningeal layers, and state the function of each.

The brain is covered and protected by three connective tissue membranes called **meninges.** The outermost membrane is the leathery double-layered **dura mater** (**Figure 14.4a**).

One of its layers (the *periosteal layer*) is attached to the inner surface of the skull, forming the periosteum. The other (the *meningeal layer*) forms the outermost brain covering and continues as the dura mater of the spinal cord.

The dural layers are fused together except in three places where the inner membrane extends inward to form a fold that

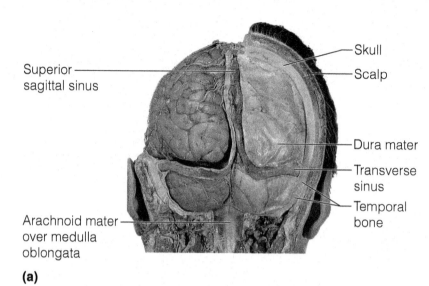

Superior sagittal sinus

Skull

Scalp

Dura mater

Transverse sinus

Temporal bone

Arachnoid mater over medulla oblongata

(a)

Figure 14.4 Meninges of the brain.
(a) Posterior view of the brain in place, surrounded by the dura mater. **(b)** Three-dimensional frontal section showing the relationship of the dura mater, arachnoid mater, and pia mater. The meningeal dura forms the falx cerebri fold, which extends into the longitudinal fissure and attaches the brain to the ethmoid bone of the skull. A dural sinus, the superior sagittal sinus, is enclosed by the dural membranes superiorly. Arachnoid villi, which return cerebrospinal fluid to the dural sinus, are also shown.

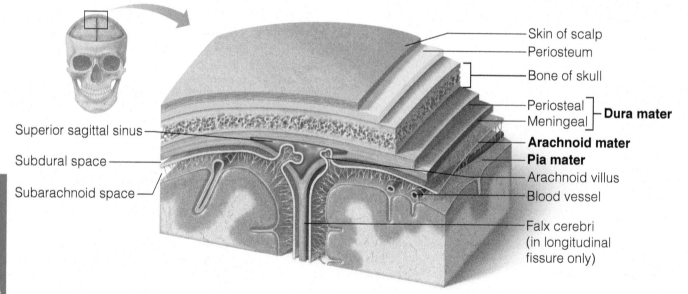

Skin of scalp

Periosteum

Bone of skull

Periosteal
Meningeal — **Dura mater**

Arachnoid mater

Pia mater

Arachnoid villus

Blood vessel

Falx cerebri (in longitudinal fissure only)

Superior sagittal sinus

Subdural space

Subarachnoid space

(b)

secures the brain in the cranial cavity. One such extension, the **falx cerebri** (Figure 14.4b), dips into the longitudinal fissure to attach to the crista galli of the ethmoid bone of the skull. The cavity created at this point is the large **superior sagittal sinus,** which collects blood draining from the brain tissue.

The middle layer, the weblike **arachnoid mater,** underlies the dura mater and is partially separated from it by the **subdural space.** Its threadlike projections bridge the

subarachnoid space and attach to the innermost membrane, the **pia mater.** The delicate pia mater is highly vascular and clings to the surface of the brain.

In life, the subarachnoid space is filled with cerebrospinal fluid. Specialized projections of the arachnoid tissue called **arachnoid villi** protrude through the dura mater to allow the cerebrospinal fluid to drain back into the venous blood via the superior sagittal sinus and other dural sinuses.

Cerebrospinal Fluid

OBJECTIVE 4   Discuss the formation, circulation, and drainage of cerebrospinal fluid.

The cerebrospinal fluid is continually formed by the **choroid plexuses,** small capillary knots hanging from the roof of the ventricles of the brain. Cerebrospinal fluid forms a watery cushion that protects the delicate brain tissue against blows to the head.

Within the brain, the cerebrospinal fluid circulates from the two lateral ventricles (in the cerebral hemispheres) via the interventricular foreman into the third ventricle and then through the cerebral aqueduct of the midbrain into the fourth ventricle (**Figure 14.5**). From the fourth ventricle,

14

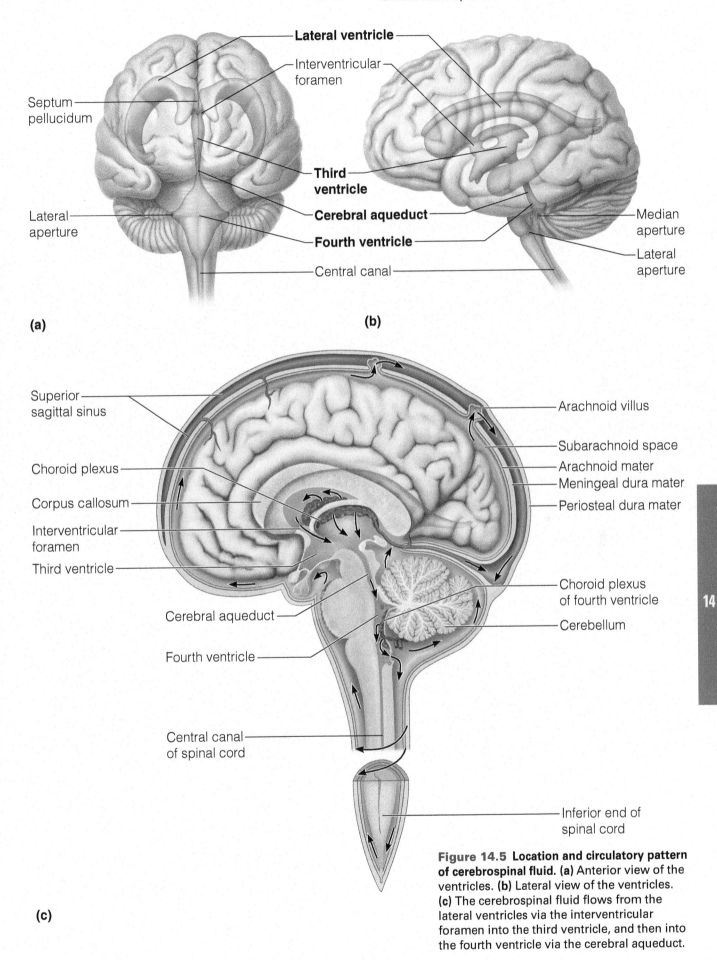

(a)

(b)

Lateral ventricle

Interventricular foramen

Septum pellucidum

Third ventricle

Cerebral aqueduct

Fourth ventricle

Lateral aperture

Central canal

Median aperture

Lateral aperture

Superior sagittal sinus

Choroid plexus

Corpus callosum

Interventricular foramen

Third ventricle

Cerebral aqueduct

Fourth ventricle

Central canal of spinal cord

Arachnoid villus

Subarachnoid space

Arachnoid mater

Meningeal dura mater

Periosteal dura mater

Choroid plexus of fourth ventricle

Cerebellum

Inferior end of spinal cord

(c)

14

Figure 14.5 Location and circulatory pattern of cerebrospinal fluid. (a) Anterior view of the ventricles. **(b)** Lateral view of the ventricles. **(c)** The cerebrospinal fluid flows from the lateral ventricles via the interventricular foramen into the third ventricle, and then into the fourth ventricle via the cerebral aqueduct.

some fluid continues down the central canal of the spinal cord, but the bulk of it circulates into the subarachnoid space via three openings in the walls of the fourth ventricle. The fluid returns to the blood in the dural sinuses via the arachnoid villi.

Tracing the Pathway of Cerebrospinal Fluid in the Brain

Obtain a three-dimensional model of the ventricles, and trace the path of cerebrospinal fluid circulation through the internal brain cavities from the lateral ventricles to the subarachnoid space.

Table 14.1	The Cranial Nerves (see Figure 14.6)	
Number and name	**Function**	**Testing methods**
I. Olfactory	Purely sensory—carries impulses for sense of smell.	Person is asked to sniff and identify aromatic substances, such as oil of cloves and vanilla.
II. Optic	Purely sensory—carries impulses for vision.	Vision and visual field are determined with eye chart and by testing the point at which the person first sees an object (finger) moving into the visual field. Eye interior viewed with ophthalmoscope to detect swelling of optic disc (point at which optic nerve leaves the eye) and to observe blood vessels.
III. Oculomotor	Mixed—motor fibers to inferior oblique and superior, inferior, and medial rectus muscles, which direct eyeball; to levator palpebrae muscles of eyelid; to iris and smooth muscle controlling lens shape and pupil size.	Pupils are examined for size, shape, and equality. Pupillary reflex is tested with penlight (pupils should constrict when illuminated). Convergence for near vision is tested, as is subject's ability to follow objects up, down, side to side, and diagonally with eyes.
IV. Trochlear	Mixed—provides motor fibers to superior oblique muscle (an extrinsic eye muscle).	Tested in common with cranial nerve III.
V. Trigeminal	Mixed—conducts sensory impulses from skin of face and anterior scalp, from mucosae of mouth and nose. Also contains motor fibers that activate the chewing muscles.	Sensations of pain, touch, and temperature are tested with safety pin and hot and cold objects. Corneal reflex tested with wisp of cotton. Motor branch assessed by asking person to clench the teeth, open the mouth against resistance, and move the jaw side to side.
VI. Abducens	Carries motor fibers to lateral rectus muscle of eye.	Tested in common with cranial nerve III.
VII. Facial	Mixed—supplies motor fibers to muscles of facial expression and to lacrimal and salivary glands; carries sensory fibers from taste receptors of anterior tongue.	Anterior two-thirds of tongue is tested for ability to taste sweet (sugar), salty, sour (vinegar), and bitter (quinine) substances. Symmetry of face is checked. Subject is asked to close eyes, smile, whistle, and so on. Tearing is assessed with ammonia fumes.
VIII. Vestibulocochlear	Purely sensory—transmits impulses for senses of equilibrum and hearing.	Hearing is checked by air and bone conduction using tuning fork.
IX. Glossopharyngeal	Mixed—motor fibers serve pharyngeal muscles and salivary glands; sensory fibers carry impulses from pharynx, posterior tongue (taste buds), and pressure receptors of carotid artery.	Gag and swallowing reflexes are checked. Subject is asked to speak and cough. Posterior third of tongue may be tested for taste.
X. Vagus	Mixed—Motor fibers to pharynx and larynx and sensory fibers from same structures; a very large portion is composed of parasympathetic motor fibers, which supply heart and smooth muscles of abdominal visceral organs; transmits sensory impulses from viscera.	As for cranial nerve IX (IX and X are tested in common, because they both serve muscles of throat and mouth).
XI. Accessory	Mixed—provides motor fibers to sternocleidomastoid and trapezius muscles.	Sternocleidomastoid and trapezius muscles are checked for strength by asking person to rotate head and elevate shoulders against resistance.
XII. Hypoglossal	Mixed—motor fibers serve muscles of tongue and sensory fibers carry impulses from tongue.	Person is asked to protrude and retract tongue. Any deviations in position are noted.

Cranial Nerves

OBJECTIVE 5 Identify the cranial nerves by number and name on an appropriate model or diagram, stating the function of each.

The **cranial nerves** are part of the peripheral nervous system, but they are best identified during the study of the brain. The 12 pairs of cranial nerves primarily serve the head and neck. Only one pair, the vagus nerves, extends into the thoracic and abdominal cavities.

The cranial nerves are numbered in order, and in most cases their names reflect the major structures they control. **Table 14.1** describes the cranial nerves by number (Roman numeral), name, function, and testing methods. This information should be committed to memory. A catchy saying that might help you to remember the cranial nerves in order is "*O*n *o*ccasion *o*ur *t*rusty *t*ruck *a*cts *f*unny—*v*ery *g*ood *v*ehicle *a*ny*h*ow." The first letter of each word and the "a" and "h" of the final word "anyhow" will remind you of the first letter of the cranial nerve name.

Most cranial nerves are mixed nerves (containing both motor and sensory fibers), but three pairs—optic, olfactory, and vestibulocochlear—are purely sensory. Neuron cell bodies of the sensory cranial nerves are located in ganglia. Those of the mixed cranial nerves are found both in the brain and in peripheral ganglia.

Activity 4

Identifying and Testing the Cranial Nerves

1. Using **Figure 14.6** as a guide, identify the cranial nerves on the anterior surface of the brain model. Notice that the first (olfactory) cranial nerves are not visible on the model because they consist only of short axons that run from the nasal mucosa through the cribriform plate of the ethmoid bone. However, the synapse points of the first cranial nerves, the *olfactory bulbs,* are visible on the model, so identify these.

2. The last column of Table 14.1 describes techniques for testing cranial nerves, which is an important part of any neurological examination. Conduct tests of cranial nerve function following these directions.

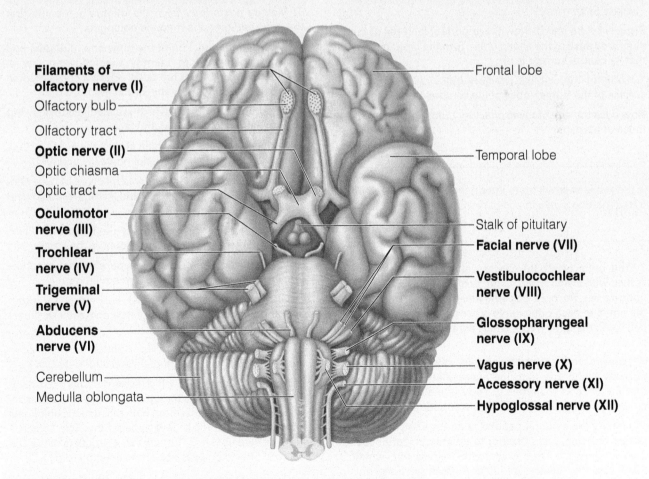

Figure 14.6 Ventral aspect of the human brain, showing the cranial nerves.

✂ **DISSECTION**

The Sheep Brain

Obtain a sheep brain, dissecting tray, and instruments, and bring them to your laboratory bench. Obtain and put on disposable gloves.

1. Turn your sheep brain so that you are viewing its left lateral aspect. Compare the various areas of the sheep brain (cerebrum, brain stem, cerebellum) to the photo of the human brain in **Figure 14.7**. Relatively speaking, which of these structures is obviously much larger in humans?

2. Place the ventral surface of the sheep brain down on the dissecting tray and observe the fragments of the dura mater. Feel its consistency and notice its toughness. Cut through the dura mater along the line of the longitudinal fissure. Gently force the cerebral hemispheres apart laterally to expose the corpus callosum, the huge fiber tract deep to the longitudinal fissure.

3. Examine the superior surface of the brain. Notice that like the human brain, its surface is thrown into convolutions (fissures and gyri). Identify the arachnoid mater, which appears on the brain surface as a delicate "cottony" material spanning the fissures. In contrast, the innermost pia mater follows the cerebral contours.

Ventral Structures

Figure 14.8a and **b** show the important features of the ventral surface of the sheep brain. Turn the brain over so that its ventral surface is up.

1. Look for the clublike olfactory bulbs on the inferior surface of the frontal lobes of the cerebral hemispheres.

How does the size of these olfactory bulbs compare with those of humans?

_____

Is the sense of smell more important as a protective and a food-getting sense in sheep *or* in humans?

_____

2. The optic nerve (II) carries sensory impulses concerned with vision from the retina of the eye. Identify the optic nerves, the optic chiasma (the point where some of the fibers of each optic nerve cross over to the opposite side), and the optic tracts, which continue from the optic chiasma.

3. Posterior to the optic chiasma, identify the stalk of the pituitary gland and then the mammillary body. Notice that the sheep's mammillary body is a single rounded eminence. In humans it is a double structure.

4. Identify the cerebral peduncles on the ventral aspect of the midbrain, just posterior to the mammillary body. Also identify the large oculomotor nerves (III), which arise from the ventral midbrain surface, and the tiny trochlear nerves (IV), seen at the midbrain-pons junction.

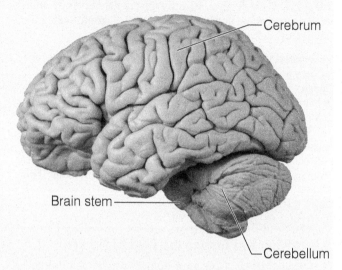

Cerebrum

Brain stem

Cerebellum

Figure 14.7 Photo of lateral aspect of the human brain.

These cranial nerves provide motor fibers to extrinsic muscles of the eyeball.

5. Moving posteriorly from the midbrain, identify first the pons and then the medulla oblongata.

6. Return to the junction of the pons and midbrain, and proceed posteriorly to identify the following cranial nerves, all arising from the pons. (Place a check mark in the boxes as you identify the structures.)

☐ Trigeminal nerves (V), which are involved in chewing and sensations of the head and face

☐ Abducens nerves (VI), which abduct the eye (and thus work in conjunction with cranial nerves III and IV)

☐ Facial nerves (VII), large nerves involved in taste sensation, gland function (salivary and lacrimal glands), and facial expressions

7. Continue posteriorly to identify the following. (Place a check mark in the boxes as you identify the structures.)

☐ Vestibulocochlear nerves (VIII), purely sensory nerves that are involved with hearing and equilibrium

☐ Glossopharyngeal nerves (IX), which contain motor fibers innervating throat structures and sensory fibers transmitting taste stimuli

☐ Vagus nerves (X), often called "wanderers," which serve many organs of the head, thorax, and abdominal cavity

☐ Accessory nerves (XI), which serve muscles of the neck, larynx, and shoulder. Although historically the accessory nerves were said to arise from both the medulla oblongata and the spinal cord, it now appears that this "cranial" nerve really arises only from the C_1–C_5 rootlets of the spinal cord. They then pass upward to enter the skull.

☐ Hypoglossal nerves (XII), which stimulate tongue and neck muscles

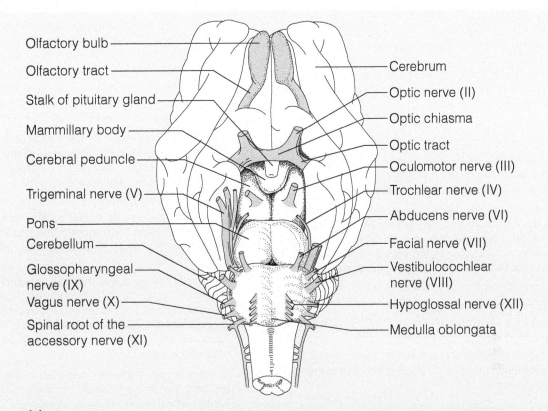

(a)

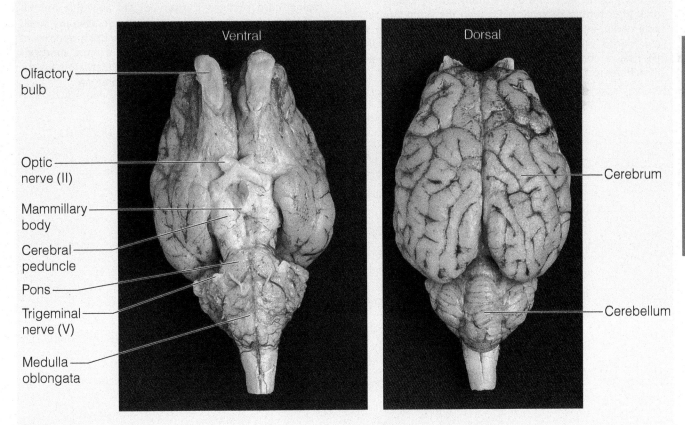

(b)

Figure 14.8 Intact sheep brain. (a) Diagrammatic ventral view. **(b)** Photographs showing ventral and dorsal views.

Text continues on next page. →

Dorsal Structures

1. Refer to Figure 14.8b as a guide in identifying the following structures. Reidentify the cerebral hemispheres. How does the depth of the fissures in the sheep's cerebral hemispheres compare to that in the human brain?

_____

2. Examine the cerebellum. Notice that, in contrast to the human cerebellum, it is not divided longitudinally and that its fissures are oriented differently.

3. To expose the dorsal surface of the midbrain, gently force the cerebrum and cerebellum apart, as shown in **Figure 14.9**. Identify the corpora quadrigemina, four rounded prominences on the dorsal midbrain surface. What is the function of the corpora quadrigemina?

_____

Also locate the pineal gland, which appears as a small oval protrusion in the midline just anterior to the corpora quadrigemina.

Internal Structures

1. The internal structure of the brain can be examined only after further dissection. Position the brain ventral side down, and make a cut completely through it in a superior to inferior direction. Cut through the longitudinal fissure, corpus callosum, and midline of the cerebellum. Refer to **Figure 14.10** as you work.

2. A thin nervous tissue membrane immediately ventral to the corpus callosum separates the lateral ventricles from each other. Pierce this membrane, and probe the cavity of the lateral ventricle.

3. Identify the thalamus, which forms the walls of the third ventricle. The intermediate mass spanning the ventricular cavity appears as a round protrusion of the thalamus wall.

4. The hypothalamus forms the floor of the third ventricle. Identify the optic chiasma, stalk of the pituitary, and mammillary body on its exterior surface. You can see the pineal gland at the posterior end of the third ventricle.

5. Locate the midbrain by identifying the corpora quadrigemina that form its dorsal roof. Follow the cerebral aqueduct through the midbrain tissue to the fourth ventricle. Identify the cerebral peduncles, which form its anterior walls.

6. Identify the pons and medulla oblongata, anterior to the fourth ventricle. The medulla oblongata continues into the spinal cord without any obvious anatomical change, but the point at which the fourth ventricle narrows to a small canal is generally accepted as the beginning of the spinal cord.

7. Identify the cerebellum posterior to the fourth ventricle, and notice the internal treelike arrangement of its white matter, called the _arbor vitae_.

8. Check with your instructor to determine whether cow spinal cord sections (preserved) are available for the spinal cord studies in Exercise 15. If not, save the small portion of the spinal cord from your brain specimen. Otherwise, dispose of all organic debris in the appropriate laboratory container, and clean the dissecting instruments and tray before leaving the laboratory.

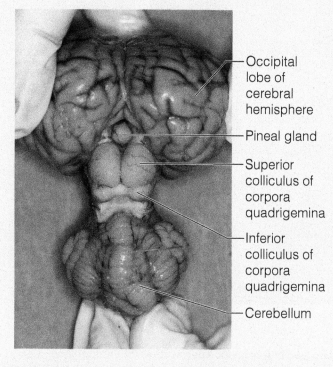

Occipital lobe of cerebral hemisphere

Pineal gland

Superior colliculus of corpora quadrigemina

Inferior colliculus of corpora quadrigemina

Cerebellum

Figure 14.9 Means of exposing the dorsal midbrain structures of the sheep brain.

14

Cerebral hemisphere

Corpus callosum

Cerebral peduncle

Optic chiasma

Parietal lobe

Cerebellum

Pineal gland

Arbor vitae

Corpora quadrigemina

Medulla oblongata

Pons

Figure 14.10 **Sagittal section of the sheep brain showing internal structures.**

14

REVIEW SHEET
Gross Anatomy of the Brain and Cranial Nerves

Name _____ Lab Time/Date _____

The Human Brain

1. In which of the cerebral lobes (frontal, parietal, occipital, or temporal) would the following functional areas be found?

auditory area _____ olfactory area _____

primary motor area _____ visual area _____

somatic sensory area _____ Broca's area _____

2. Match the letters on the diagram of the human brain (right lateral view) to the appropriate terms listed at the left:

_____ 1. frontal lobe

_____ 2. parietal lobe

_____ 3. temporal lobe

_____ 4. precentral gyrus

_____ 5. parieto-occipital sulcus

_____ 6. postcentral gyrus

_____ 7. lateral sulcus   _____ 10. medulla oblongata

_____ 8. central sulcus   _____ 11. occipital lobe

_____ 9. cerebellum   _____ 12. pons

a —
b —
c —
d —
e —

f
g
h
i
j
k
l

3. Which of the following structures are *not* part of the brain stem? (Circle the appropriate response or responses.)

cerebral hemispheres   pons   midbrain   cerebellum   medulla

4. Complete the following statements by writing the proper word or phrase in the corresponding blank at the right.

1. _____

2. _____

3. _____

4. _____

5. _____   7. _____

6. _____   8. _____

A(n) _1_ is an elevated ridge of cerebral tissue. Inward folds of cerebral tissue are called _2_ or _3_. Gray matter is composed of _4_. White matter is composed of _5_. A bundle of fibers that provides for communication between different parts of the CNS is called a(n) _6_, whereas one that carries impulses between the periphery and CNS areas is called a(n) _7_. Nuclei deep within the cerebral hemisphere white matter are collectively called the _8_.

5. Identify the structures on the following sagittal view of the human brain by matching the lettered areas to the proper terms at the left:

_____   1. cerebellum

_____   2. cerebral aqueduct

_____   3. cerebral hemisphere

_____   4. cerebral peduncle

_____   5. choroid plexus

_____   6. corpora quadrigemina

_____   7. corpus callosum

_____   8. fourth ventricle

_____   9. hypothalamus

_____ 10. mammillary bodies

_____ 11. intermediate mass

_____ 12. medulla oblongata

_____ 13. optic chiasma

_____ 14. pineal gland

_____ 15. pituitary gland

_____ 16. pons

_____ 17. thalamus

6. Using the anatomical terms from item 5, match the appropriate structures with the following descriptions:

_____   1. site of regulation of body temperature and water balance; most important autonomic center of brain

_____   2. located in the midbrain; contains reflex centers for vision and hearing

_____   3. coordinates complex muscular movements

_____   4. contains autonomic centers regulating heart rate, respiration, and other visceral activities

_____   5. large fiber tract connecting the cerebral hemispheres

_____   6. part of the endocrine system

_____   7. canal that connects the third and fourth ventricles

_____   8. the intermediate mass is part of it

7. Explain why trauma to the base of the brain is often much more dangerous than trauma to the frontal lobes. (*Hint:* Think about the relative function of the cerebral hemispheres and the brain stem structures. Which contain centers more vital to life?)

_____

_____

Meninges of the Brain

8. Identify the meningeal (or associated) structures described below:

_____ 1. outermost layer; tough fibrous connective tissue

_____ 2. innermost vascular layer covering the brain; follows every convolution

_____ 3. drains cerebrospinal fluid into the venous blood in the dural venous sinuses

_____ 4. structure that forms the cerebrospinal fluid

_____ 5. middle layer; delicate with cottony fibers

_____ 6. a dural fold that attaches the cerebrum to the crista galli of the skull

Cerebrospinal Fluid

9. Fill in the following flowchart to indicate the path of cerebrospinal fluid from its formation site (assume that this is one of the lateral ventricles) to where it is reabsorbed into the venous blood:

Lateral ventricle $\rightarrow$ _____ $\rightarrow$ _____

$\rightarrow$ _____ $\rightarrow$ _____ $\rightarrow$

via openings in the
wall of the 4th ventricle

_____ surrounding the brain and cord (and central canal of the cord) → arachnoid villi →

_____ containing venous blood

10. On the accompanying diagram, label correctly the structures involved with circulation of cerebrospinal fluid. (These structures are identified by leader lines.)

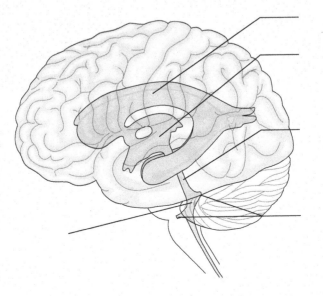

Cranial Nerves

11. Using the following terms, correctly identify all structures indicated by leader lines on the diagram.

abducens nerve (VI)

accessory nerve (XI)

cerebellum

cerebral peduncle

facial nerve (VII)

frontal lobe of cerebral hemisphere

glossopharyngeal nerve (IX)

hypoglossal nerve (XII)

longitudinal fissure

mammillary body

medulla oblongata

oculomotor nerve (III)

olfactory bulb

optic chiasma

optic nerve (II)

optic tract

pituitary gland

pons

spinal cord

temporal lobe of cerebral hemisphere

trigeminal nerve (V)

trochlear nerve (IV)

vagus nerve (X)

vestibulocochlear nerve (VIII)

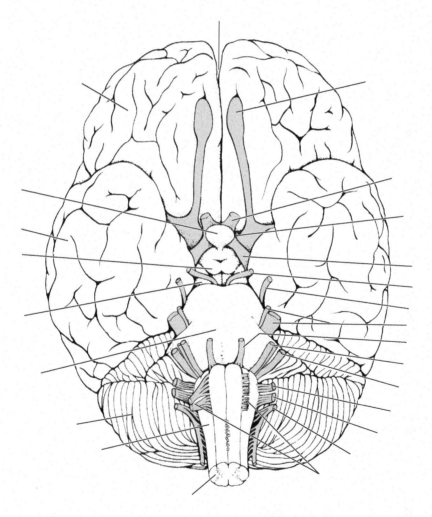

12. Using choices from the key, provide the name and number of the cranial nerves involved in each of the following activities, sensations, or disorders.

_____ 1. smelling a flower

_____ 2. slowing the heart

_____ 3. chewing food

_____ 4. reading the newspaper

_____ 5. feeling a toothache

_____ 6. tasting well-seasoned food

_____ 7. listening to music

_____ 8. rotating the head

_____ 9. raising the eyelids

Key:

abducens

accessory

facial

glossopharyngeal

hypoglossal

oculomotor

olfactory

optic

trigeminal

trochlear

vagus

vestibulocochlear

Dissection of Sheep Brain

13. In your own words, describe the relative hardness of the sheep brain tissue that you noticed when cutting into it.

_____

Given that formalin hardens all tissue, what conclusions might you draw about the relative hardness and texture of

living brain tissue? _____

14. How does the relative size of the cerebral hemispheres compare in sheep and human brains? _____

_____

What is the significance of this difference? _____

_____

15. What is the significance of the fact that the olfactory bulbs are much larger in the sheep brain than in the human brain?

_____

_____

Materials

- ☐ Spinal cord model (cross section)
- ☐ Laboratory charts of the spinal cord and spinal nerves
- ☐ Colored pencils
- ☐ Preserved cow spinal cord sections with meninges and nerve roots intact (or spinal cord segment saved from the brain dissection in Exercise 14)
- ☐ Petri dishes
- ☐ Dissecting tray and single-edge razor blades
- ☐ Dissecting microscope or magnifying glass
- ☐ Disposable gloves

Pre-Lab Quiz

1. How many pairs of spinal nerves do humans have?
   - a. 10
   - b. 12
   - c. 31
   - d. 47

2. Circle the correct term. In cross section, the gray / white matter of the spinal cord looks like a butterfly or the letter H.

3. Circle the correct term. Fiber tracts conducting impulses to the brain are called ascending or sensory / motor tracts.

4. The ventral rami of all spinal nerves except for T_2 through T_{12} form complex networks of nerves known as:
   - a. fissures
   - b. ganglia
   - c. plexuses
   - d. sulci

5. Severe injuries to the _____ plexus cause weakness or paralysis of the entire upper limb.
   - a. brachial
   - b. cervical
   - c. lumbar
   - d. sacral

Anatomy of the Spinal Cord

The cylindrical **spinal cord,** a continuation of the brain, is an association and communication center. It plays a major role in spinal reflex activity and provides neural pathways to and from the brain. Enclosed within the vertebral column, the spinal cord extends from the foramen magnum of the skull to the first or second lumbar vertebra (**Figure 15.1**).

Like the brain, the spinal cord is cushioned and protected by meninges. The dura mater and arachnoid meningeal coverings extend beyond L_2 and the spinal cord, approximately to the level of S_2, and a fibrous extension of the pia mater extends even farther to attach to the posterior coccyx.

In humans, 31 pairs of spinal nerves arise from the spinal cord and serve the body area at their approximate level of emergence. Most of the spinal cord is about the diameter of a thumb, but it is obviously enlarged in the cervical and lumbar areas, where the nerves serving the upper and lower limbs leave the cord.

Because the spinal cord does not extend to the end of the vertebral column, spinal nerves emerging from the inferior end of the cord travel through the vertebral canal for some distance before exiting. This collection of spinal nerves at the inferior end of the vertebral canal is called the **cauda equina** ("horse's tail").

OBJECTIVE 1 Identify important anatomical areas on a model or appropriate diagram of the spinal cord.

Activity 1

Identifying Structures of the Spinal Cord

Obtain a model of a cross section of a spinal cord, and identify its structures as they are described next.

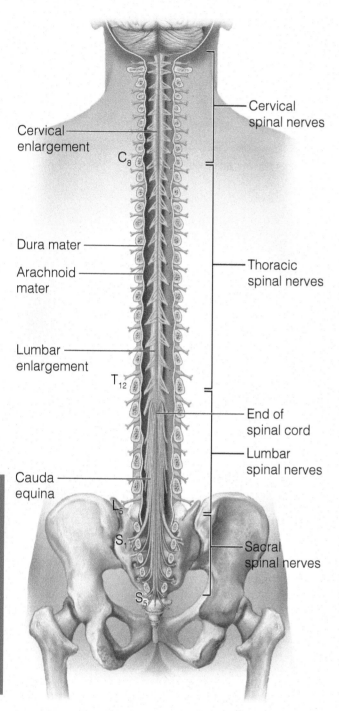

The dorsal horns contain association neurons and sensory fibers that enter the cord via the **dorsal root.** The cell bodies of these sensory neurons are found in an enlarged area of the dorsal root called the **dorsal root ganglion.** The ventral horns contain cell bodies of motor neurons of the somatic nervous system, which send their axons out via the **ventral root** of the cord to enter the adjacent spinal nerve. The dorsal and ventral roots fuse to form the **spinal nerves.** The lateral horns, where present, contain nerve cell bodies of motor neurons of the autonomic nervous system (sympathetic division).

White Matter

The **white matter** of the spinal cord is composed of myelinated fibers—most running to or from higher centers. Because of the irregular shape of the gray matter, the white matter on each side of the cord is divided into three regions: the **posterior, lateral,** and **anterior columns.** Each white column contains a number of fiber **tracts** composed of axons with the same origin, destination, and function. *Ascending (sensory) tracts* conduct sensory impulses to the brain. *Descending (motor) tracts* carry impulses from the brain to skeletal muscles.

DISSECTION

Spinal Cord

1. Obtain a dissecting tray and razor blade, Petri dish, and disposable gloves. Place a segment of preserved spinal cord (from a cow or saved from the brain specimen used in Exercise 14) on the Petri dish, and bring it to your laboratory bench. Identify the tough outer dura mater and the weblike arachnoid mater.

What name is given to the third meningeal layer, and where is it found?

_____

Peel back the dura mater, and observe the fibers making up the dorsal and ventral roots. If possible, identify a dorsal root ganglion.

2. Using the razor blade, cut a thin cross section of the cord and identify the ventral and dorsal horns of the gray matter with the naked eye or with a dissecting microscope or magnifying glass.

How can you be certain that you are correctly identifying the ventral and dorsal horns?

_____

_____

Also identify the central canal and the general location of the posterior, anterior, and lateral columns of white matter.

3. Refer to **Figure 15.3** and Plate 9 of the Histology Atlas as you examine the section carefully. Using colored pencils, color Figure 15.3 to match the spinal cord tissue you are viewing.

Observe the shape of the central canal. Is it basically

circular or oval? _____

Figure 15.1 Anatomy of the spinal cord, posterior view.

Gray Matter

In cross section, the **gray matter** of the spinal cord looks like a butterfly or the letter H (**Figure 15.2**). The two posterior projections are the **dorsal (posterior) horns.** The two broader anterior projections are the **ventral (anterior) horns.** In the thoracic and lumbar regions of the cord, there is also a lateral outpocketing of gray matter on each side referred to as the **lateral horn.** The central area of gray matter surrounds the **central canal** of the cord, which contains cerebrospinal fluid.

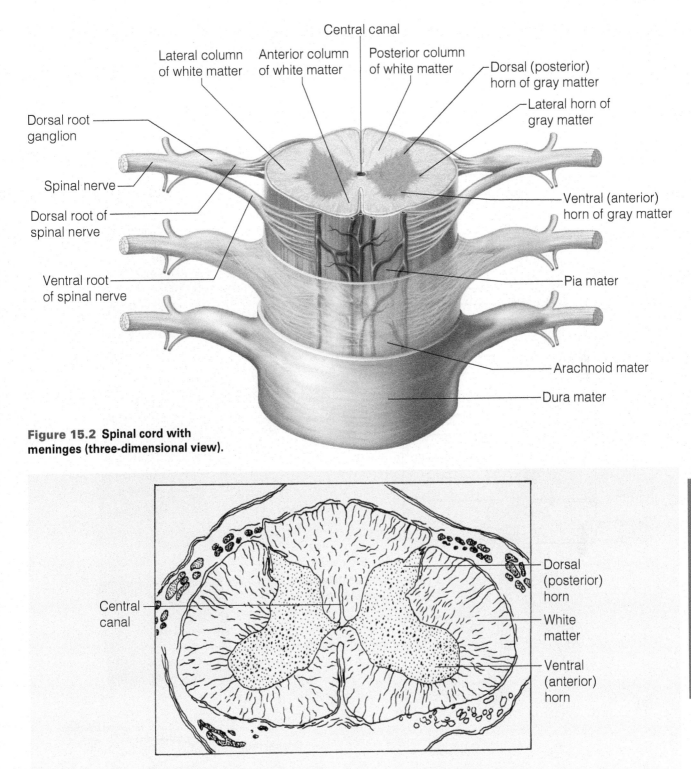

Central canal

Lateral column
of white matter

Anterior column
of white matter

Posterior column
of white matter

Dorsal (posterior)
horn of gray matter

Lateral horn of
gray matter

Dorsal root
ganglion

Spinal nerve

Dorsal root of
spinal nerve

Ventral root
of spinal nerve

Ventral (anterior)
horn of gray matter

Pia mater

Arachnoid mater

Dura mater

Figure 15.2 Spinal cord with meninges (three-dimensional view).

Central
canal

Dorsal
(posterior)
horn

White
matter

Ventral
(anterior)
horn

Figure 15.3 Cross section of the spinal cord. See also Plate 9 in the Histology Atlas.

What fills this canal in the living animal?

_____

What makes up the gray matter in the butterfly-shaped

structure? _____

What type of neurons would you expect to find in the
ventral horns—motor, association, or sensory?

_____

What type of neurons would you expect to find in the
dorsal horns—motor, association, or sensory? _____

_____

15

Spinal Nerves and Nerve Plexuses

OBJECTIVE 2   Describe the origin, fiber composition, and distribution of the spinal nerves, differentiating between roots, the spinal nerve proper, and rami.

Figure 15.4 shows how the nerves are named according to their point of origin. The first pair of spinal nerves leaves the

vertebral canal between the base of the occipital bone and the atlas. All other spinal nerves exit via the intervertebral foramina. The first through seventh pairs of cervical nerves emerge *above* the vertebra for which they are named. C_8 emerges between C_7 and T_1. (Notice that there are seven cervical

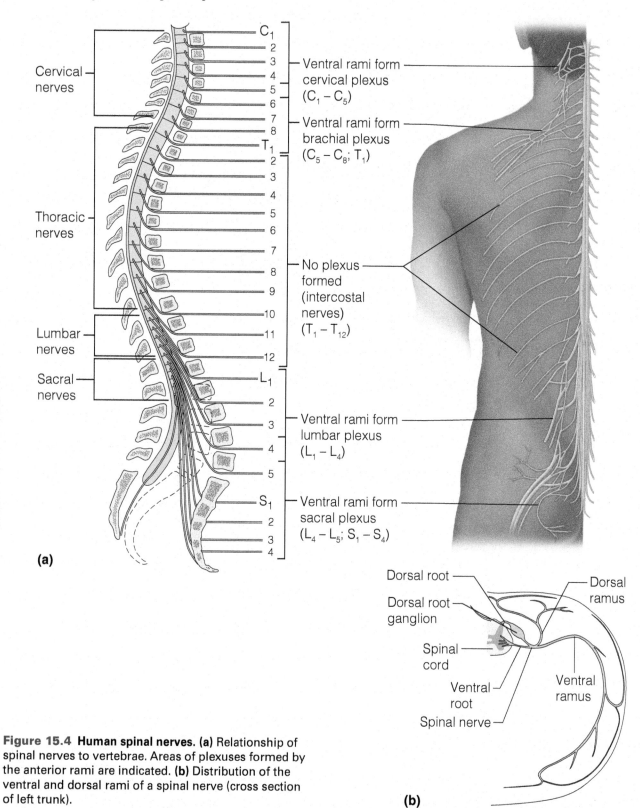

(a)

(b)

Figure 15.4 Human spinal nerves. (a) Relationship of spinal nerves to vertebrae. Areas of plexuses formed by the anterior rami are indicated. **(b)** Distribution of the ventral and dorsal rami of a spinal nerve (cross section of left trunk).

vertebrae, but eight pairs of cervical nerves.) The remaining spinal nerve pairs emerge from the spinal cord *below* the same-numbered vertebra.

Almost immediately after emerging, each nerve divides into **dorsal** and **ventral rami.** (Thus each spinal nerve is only about 1 cm [1/2 in.] long.) The rami, like the spinal nerves, contain both motor and sensory fibers. The smaller dorsal rami serve the skin and muscles of the posterior body trunk. The ventral rami of spinal nerves T_2–T_{12} pass anteriorly as the **intercostal nerves** to supply the muscles of intercostal spaces, and the skin and muscles of the anterior and lateral trunk. The ventral rami of all other spinal nerves form complex nerve networks called **plexuses,** which serve the motor and sensory needs of the limbs. From the plexuses the fibers diverge again to form peripheral nerves. Next we describe the four major nerve plexuses and their chief peripheral nerves. See also Table 15.1.

Cervical Plexus and the Neck

OBJECTIVE 3   Identify the four major nerve plexuses, the major nerves of each, and their distribution.

The **cervical plexus** (see Figure 15.4 and Table 15.1) arises from the ventral rami of C_1 through C_5 and supplies muscles of the shoulder and neck. The major motor branch of this plexus is the **phrenic nerve,** which arises from C_3–C_5 and passes into the thoracic cavity in front of the first rib to innervate the diaphragm. The primary danger of a broken neck is that the phrenic nerve may be severed, paralyzing the diaphragm and stopping breathing. A jingle to help you remember the rami (roots) forming the phrenic nerves is "C_3, C_4, C_5 keep the diaphragm alive."

Table 15.1	**Spinal Nerve Plexuses**			
Plexus	**Origin (from ventral rami)**	**Important nerves**	**Body areas served**	**Result of damage to plexus or its nerves**
Cervical	C_1–C_5	Phrenic	Diaphragm and muscles of shoulder and neck; skin of shoulder and neck	Respiratory paralysis (and death if not treated promptly)
Brachial	C_5–C_8 and T_1	Axillary	Deltoid muscle of shoulder	Paralysis and atrophy of deltoid muscle
		Radial	Triceps and extensor muscles of the forearm	Wristdrop—inability to extend hand at wrist
		Median	Flexor muscles of forearm and some muscles of hand	Decreased ability to flex and abduct hand and flex and abduct thumb and index finger—therefore, inability to pick up small objects
		Musculocutaneous	Flexor muscles of arm	Decreased ability to flex forearm on arm
		Ulnar	Wrist and many hand muscles	Clawhand—inability to spread fingers apart
Lumbar	L_1–L_4 and sometimes T_{12}	Femoral (including lateral and anterior cutaneous branches)	Lower abdomen, buttocks, anterior thighs and skin of anteromedial leg and thigh	Inability to extend leg and flex hip; loss of cutaneous sensation
		Obturator	Adductor muscles of medial thigh and small hip muscles; skin of medial thigh and hip joint	Inability to adduct thigh
Sacral	L_4–L_5 and S_1–S_4	Sciatic (largest nerve in body; splits to common fibular and tibial nerves)	Lower trunk and posterior surface of thigh (and leg)	Inability to extend hip and flex knee; sciatica
		• Common fibular (superficial, and deep branches)	Lateral aspect of leg and foot	Footdrop—inability to dorsiflex foot
		• Tibial (including sural and plantar branches)	Posterior aspect of leg and foot	Inability to plantar flex and invert foot; shuffling gait
		Superior and inferior gluteal	Gluteus muscles of hip	Inability to extend hip (maximus) or abduct and medially rotate thigh (medius)

15

Brachial Plexus and the Upper Limb

The **brachial plexus,** arising from the ventral rami of C_5 through C_8, and T_1 (**Figure 15.5** and Table 15.1), is finally subdivided into five major *peripheral nerves.*

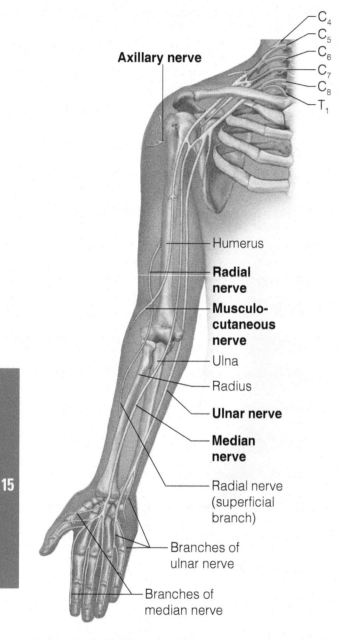

Axillary nerve

C_4
C_5
C_6
C_7
C_8
T_1

Humerus

Radial nerve

Musculo-cutaneous nerve

Ulna

Radius

Ulnar nerve

Median nerve

Radial nerve (superficial branch)

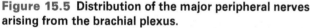

Branches of ulnar nerve

Branches of median nerve

Figure 15.5 Distribution of the major peripheral nerves arising from the brachial plexus.

The **axillary nerve,** serving the muscles and skin of the shoulder, has the most limited distribution. The large **radial nerve** passes down the posterolateral surface of the limb, supplying all the extensor muscles of the arm, forearm, and hand and the skin along its course. The **median nerve** passes down the anterior surface of the arm to supply most of the flexor muscles in the forearm and several muscles in the lateral part of the hand.

☐ Hyperextend your wrist to identify the long, obvious tendon of your palmaris longus muscle, which crosses the exact midline of the anterior wrist. Your median nerve lies immediately deep to that tendon, and the radial nerve lies just *lateral* to it.

Check the box when you have completed this task.

The **musculocutaneous nerve** supplies the arm muscles that flex the forearm and the skin of the lateral surface of the forearm. The **ulnar nerve,** which travels down the posteromedial surface of the arm, supplies the flexor carpi ulnaris and all intrinsic muscles of the hand not served by the median nerve.

Lumbar Plexus and the Lower Limb

The **lumbar plexus** arises from ventral rami of L_1 through L_4 (**Figure 15.6a**). Its nerves serve the lower abdominal region and the anteromedial thigh (Table 15.1). The largest nerve of this plexus is the **femoral nerve,** which innervates the anterior thigh muscles.

Sacral Plexus and the Lower Limb

Arising from L_4 through S_4, the nerves of the **sacral plexus** (Figure 15.6b) supply the buttock, the posterior thigh, and virtually all of the leg and foot (Table 15.1). The major peripheral nerve of this plexus is the **sciatic nerve,** the largest nerve in the body. The sciatic nerve travels through the greater sciatic notch and down the posterior thigh, serving its flexor muscles and skin. In the popliteal region, the sciatic nerve divides into the **common fibular nerve** and the **tibial nerve,** which together supply the balance of the leg and foot, both directly and via several branches.

Activity 2

Identifying the Major Nerve Plexuses and Peripheral Nerves

Identify each of the four major nerve plexuses (and its major nerves) on a large laboratory chart or model. Trace the courses of the nerves, and relate your observations to the information in Table 15.1.

15

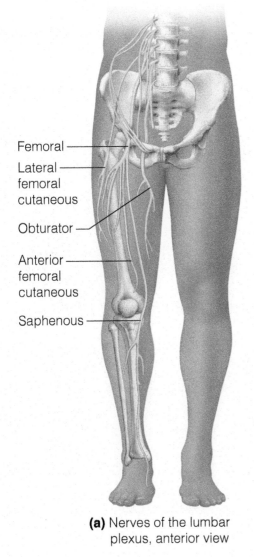

Femoral

Lateral femoral cutaneous

Obturator

Anterior femoral cutaneous

Saphenous

(a) Nerves of the lumbar plexus, anterior view

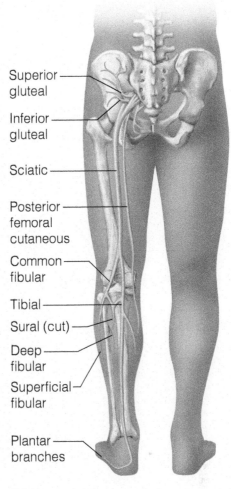

Superior gluteal

Inferior gluteal

Sciatic

Posterior femoral cutaneous

Common fibular

Tibial

Sural (cut)

Deep fibular

Superficial fibular

Plantar branches

(b) Nerves of the sacral plexus, posterior view

Figure 15.6 Distribution of the major peripheral nerves of the lower limb.
(a) Lumbar plexus. **(b)** Sacral plexus.

15

REVIEW SHEET
Spinal Cord and Spinal Nerves

Name _____ Lab Time/Date _____

Anatomy of the Spinal Cord

1. Complete the following statements by inserting the proper anatomical terms in the answer blanks.

   The superior boundary of the spinal cord is at the level of the foramen magnum of the skull, and its inferior boundary

   is at the level of vertebra _____. The collection of spinal nerves traveling in the vertebral canal below

   the terminus of the spinal cord is called the _____.

2. Using the terms below, correctly identify on the diagram all structures provided with leader lines.

ventral (anterior) horn	dorsal root of spinal nerve	spinal nerve
arachnoid mater	dura mater	ventral ramus of spinal nerve
central canal	lateral horn	ventral root of spinal nerve
dorsal ramus of spinal nerve	pia mater	white matter
dorsal root ganglion	dorsal (posterior) horn	

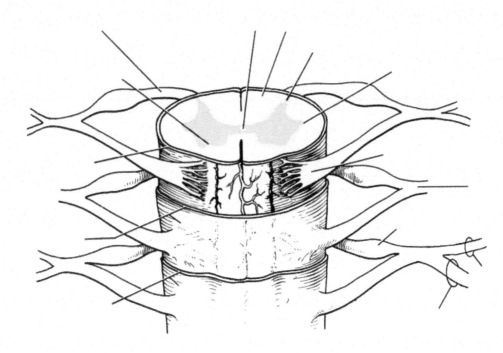

3. The spinal cord is enlarged in two regions, the _____ and the _____ regions.

   What is the significance of these enlargements? _____

   _____

Spinal Nerves and Nerve Plexuses

4. In the human, there are 31 pairs of spinal nerves named according to the region of the vertebral column where they originate. The spinal nerves are named below. Note, by number, the vertebral level at which they emerge:

   cervical nerves _____   sacral nerves _____

   lumbar nerves _____   thoracic nerves _____

5. The ventral rami of spinal nerves C_1 through T_1 and T_{12} through S_4 form _____,

   which serve the _____ of the body. The ventral rami of T_2 through T_{12} run between the ribs to serve

   the _____.

   The dorsal rami of the spinal nerves serve _____.

6. What would happen (i.e., loss of sensory or motor function or both) if the following structures were damaged or transected?

   1. dorsal root of a spinal nerve _____

   2. ventral root of a spinal nerve _____

   3. ventral ramus of a spinal nerve _____

7. Define *plexus:* _____

   _____

8. Name the major nerves that serve the following body areas:

   _____   1. deltoid muscle

   _____   2. diaphragm

   _____   3. posterior thigh

   _____   4. lateral leg and foot

   _____   5. flexor muscles of forearm and some hand muscles

   _____   6. flexor muscles of arm

   _____   7. lower abdomen and anterior thigh

   _____   8. triceps muscle

   _____   9. posterior leg and foot

Human Reflex Physiology

Materials

- ☐ Reflex hammer
- ☐ Cot (if available)
- ☐ Absorbent cotton (sterile)
- ☐ Metric and 12-inch rulers
- ☐ Flashlight
- ☐ Disposable autoclave bag
- ☐ Wash bottle containing 10% bleach solution

Pre-Lab Quiz

1. List the components of a human reflex arc. _____

    _____

2. Circle the correct term. <u>Autonomic</u> / <u>Somatic</u> reflexes include all those reflexes that involve stimulation of skeletal muscles.

3. In a reflex arc, the _____ transmits afferent impulses to the central nervous system.
    - a. integration center
    - b. motor neuron
    - c. receptor
    - d. sensory neuron

4. Circle True or False. Most reflexes are simple, two-neuron, monosynaptic reflex arcs.

5. Stretch reflexes are initiated by tapping a _____ that stretches the associated muscle.
    - a. bone
    - b. ligament
    - c. tendon

6. Which reflex can be tested to determine whether damage has occurred to the corticospinal tract?

    _____

The Reflex Arc

OBJECTIVE 1   Define *reflex* and *reflex arc*.

Neurons communicate in many ways, but much of what the body *must* do every day is programmed as reflexes. **Reflexes** are rapid, predictable, involuntary motor responses to stimuli and they occur over neural pathways called **reflex arcs.**

Reflexes can be classed as either autonomic or somatic reflexes. **Autonomic** (or visceral) **reflexes** are not subject to conscious control. These reflexes activate smooth muscles, cardiac muscle, and the glands of the body and they regulate body functions such as digestion and blood pressure. **Somatic reflexes** include all reflexes that stimulate skeletal muscles. For example, a somatic reflex causes you to withdraw your foot rapidly from a piece of glass you have just stepped on.

Components of a Reflex Arc

OBJECTIVE 2   Identify and describe the function of each element of a reflex arc.

All reflex arcs have at least five functional elements (**Figure 16.1**):

1. The *receptor* is the site that receives the stimulus.

2. The *sensory neuron* conducts the afferent impulses to the CNS.

3. The *integration center* consists of one or more synapses in the CNS.

4. The *motor neuron* conducts the efferent impulses from the integration center to an effector.

5. The *effector,* muscle fibers or glands, responds to the efferent impulses by contracting or secreting a product, respectively.

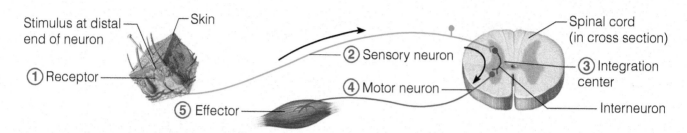

Figure 16.1 **Five basic components of a reflex arc.**

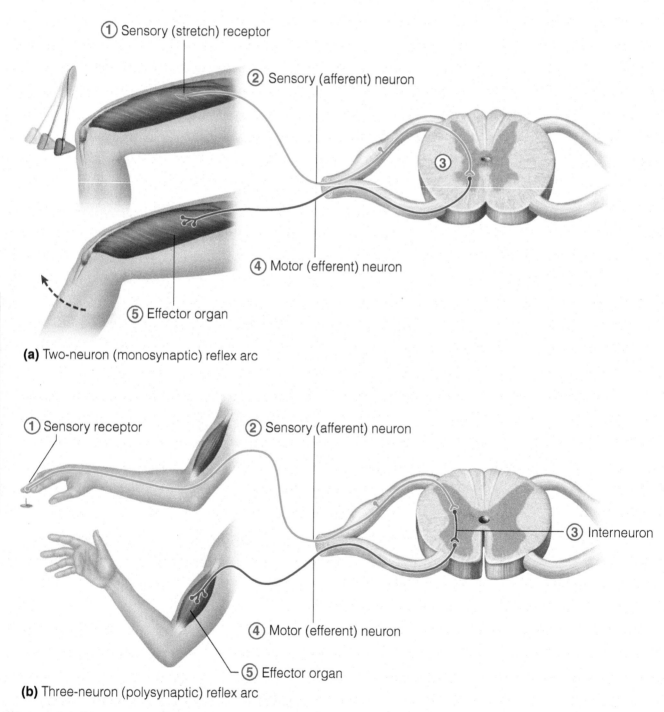

(a) Two-neuron (monosynaptic) reflex arc

(b) Three-neuron (polysynaptic) reflex arc

Figure 16.2 **Two-neuron and three-neuron reflex arcs.** The integration center is in the spinal cord, and in each example the receptor and effector are in the same limb. **(a)** The patellar reflex, a two-neuron monosynaptic reflex. **(b)** A flexor reflex, an example of a polysynaptic reflex.

16

The simple patellar, or knee-jerk, reflex shown in **Figure 16.2a** is an example of a simple, two-neuron, *monosynaptic* (literally, "one synapse") reflex arc. (It will be demonstrated in the laboratory.) However, most reflexes are more complex and *polysynaptic,* involving one or more association neurons in the reflex arc pathway. Figure 16.2b shows a three-neuron polysynaptic reflex arc (flexor reflex). **Note:** The term **synapse** is used to describe the point of close contact between the neurons or a neuron and an effector cell.

Somatic Reflexes

OBJECTIVE 3   Describe several types of reflex activity as observed in the laboratory.

There are many types of somatic reflexes, including several that you will be inducing during this laboratory session—the stretch, superficial cord, and corneal reflexes. Some require only spinal cord activity; others require brain involvement as well.

Spinal Reflexes

Stretch Reflexes

Stretch reflexes are important postural reflexes that maintain posture, balance, and locomotion. Stretch reflexes are produced by tapping a tendon, which stretches the attached muscle. This stimulates muscle spindles (specialized sensory receptors in the muscle) and causes reflex contraction of the stretched muscle, which resists further stretching. Even as the primary stretch reflex is occurring, impulses are relayed to higher brain centers to advise of muscle length and speed of shortening—information needed to maintain muscle tone and posture.

Activity 1

Initiating Stretch Reflexes

1. To test the **patellar,** or knee-jerk, **reflex,** seat a subject on the laboratory bench with legs hanging free (or with knees crossed). Tap the patellar ligament sharply with the reflex hammer just below the knee to elicit the response. The knee-jerk reflex assesses the L_2–L_4 level of the spinal cord (**Figure 16.3**). Test both knees, and record your observations.

_____

_____

Which muscles contracted? _____

_____

What nerve is carrying the afferent and efferent impulses?

_____

2. Fatigue influences the stretch reflex response. To demonstrate its effect, the subject should jog in position until she or he is very fatigued (*really fatigued*—no slackers). Test the patellar reflex again, and record whether it is more *or* less vigorous than the first response.

_____

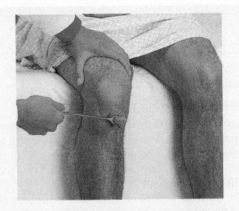

Figure 16.3 Testing the patellar reflex. The examiner supports the subject's knee so that the subject's muscles are relaxed and then strikes the patellar ligament with the reflex hammer. The proper location may be ascertained by palpating the patella.

Would you say that nervous system activity *or* muscle function is responsible for the changes you have just observed?

_____

3. The **calcaneal tendon reflex** (*Achilles, or ankle-jerk, reflex*) assesses the first two sacral segments of the spinal cord. Remove your shoe. Have your partner use one hand to dorsiflex your foot to increase the tension of the gastrocnemius (calf) muscle, and sharply tap your calcaneal (Achilles) tendon with the reflex hammer (**Figure 16.4**).

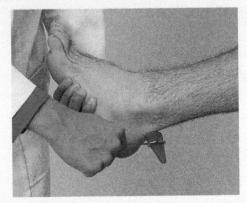

Figure 16.4 Testing the calcaneal tendon reflex. The examiner slightly dorsiflexes the subject's ankle by supporting the foot lightly in the hand and then taps the calcaneal (Achilles) tendon just above the ankle.

Text continues on next page. ➔

16

What is the result? _____

_____

Does the contraction of the gastrocnemius normally result in the activity you have observed?

_____

_____

The stretch reflexes that have been demonstrated so far are examples of reflexes in which the reflex pathway is initiated and completed at the spinal cord level.

Superficial Cord Reflexes

The **superficial cord reflexes** (abdominal and plantar reflexes) are initiated by stimulating receptors in the skin and mucosae. The superficial cord reflexes depend *both* on brain participation and on the cord-level reflex arc. We will use the plantar reflex as our example.

The **plantar reflex,** an important neurological test, is elicited by stimulating the cutaneous receptors in the sole of the foot. In adults, stimulation of these receptors causes the toes to flex and move closer together. Damage to the corticospinal tract (the major voluntary motor tract), however, produces *Babinski's sign,* an abnormal response in which the toes flare and the great toe moves upward. (In newborn infants, it is normal to see Babinski's sign because the nervous system is still incompletely myelinated.)

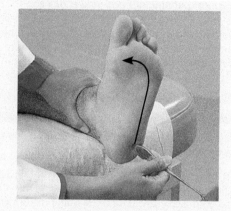

Figure 16.5 Testing the plantar reflex. Using a moderately sharp object, the examiner strokes the lateral border of the subject's sole, starting at the heel and continuing upward across the ball of the foot toward the big toe.

Cranial Nerve Reflex Test

For the cranial nerve reflex test, you will be working with your lab partner to illustrate a somatic reflex mediated by cranial nerves, the **corneal reflex.** This reflex is mediated through the trigeminal nerve (cranial nerve V). The absence of this reflex is an ominous sign because it often indicates damage to the brain stem.

Activity 2

Initiating the Plantar Reflex

Have the subject remove a shoe and lie on the cot or laboratory bench with knees slightly bent and thighs rotated so that the lateral side of the foot rests on the cot. Alternatively, the subject may sit up and rest the lateral surface of the foot on a chair. Draw the handle of the reflex hammer (or other moderately pointed object) firmly up the lateral side of the exposed sole from the heel to the base of the great toe (**Figure 16.5**).

What is the response?

_____

Is this a normal plantar reflex or Babinski's sign?

_____

_____

Activity 3

Initiating the Corneal Reflex

Stand to one side of the subject; the subject should look away from you toward the opposite wall. Wait a few seconds and then quickly, *but gently,* touch the subject's cornea (on the side toward you) with a wisp of absorbent cotton. What is the reaction?

_____

What is the function of this reflex? _____

_____

Was the sensation that of touch *or* of pain? _____

Autonomic Reflexes

The autonomic reflexes include the pupillary reflexes as well as many others. Work with your partner to demonstrate the pupillary reflexes described next.

Pupillary Reflexes

There are several types of pupillary reflexes. Here we will examine the **pupillary light reflex** and the **consensual reflex.** In both of these reflexes, the retina of the eye is the receptor, the optic nerve (cranial nerve II) contains the afferent fibers, the oculomotor nerve (cranial nerve III) conducts efferent impulses to the eye, and the smooth muscle of the iris is the effector. Many CNS centers are involved in the integration of these responses. Absence of the normal pupillary reflexes is generally an indication of severe trauma or deterioration of the vital brain stem tissue.

Activity 4

Initiating Pupillary Reflexes

1. Conduct the reflex testing in an area where the lighting is relatively dim. Before beginning, obtain a flashlight and a metric ruler.

2. Measure and record the size of the subject's pupils as best you can. **Note:** It may be easier to measure the size of the pupil in an individual with light-colored eyes.

Right pupil: _____ mm   Left pupil: _____ mm

3. Stand to the left of the subject to conduct the testing. The subject should shield his or her right eye by holding a hand vertically between the eye and the right side of the nose.

4. Using a quick right-to-left motion, shine a flashlight into the subject's left eye. What is the pupillary response?

_____

Measure the size of the left pupil: _____ mm

5. Observe the right pupil. Has the same type of change (called a *consensual reflex*) occurred in the right eye?

_____

Measure the size of the right pupil: _____ mm

The consensual reflex, or any reflex observed on one side of the body when the *other* side has been stimulated, is called a **contralateral response.** The pupillary light reflex, or any reflex occurring on the same side stimulated, is referred to as an **ipsilateral response.**

What is the function of these pupillary reflexes?

_____

_____

_____

16

REVIEW SHEET
Human Reflex Physiology

Name _____   Lab Time/Date _____

The Reflex Arc

1. Define *reflex:*

   _____

2. Name five essential components of a reflex arc: _____, _____,

   _____, _____, and _____.

3. In general, what is the importance of reflex testing in a routine physical examination? _____

   _____

   _____

Somatic and Autonomic Reflexes

4. Use the key terms to complete the statements given below. (Some responses may be used more than once.)

   Key: calcaneal tendon reflex   patellar reflex   pupillary light reflex
               corneal reflex   plantar reflex

   Reflexes classified as somatic reflexes include _____, _____, _____,

   and _____.

   Of these, the simple stretch reflexes are _____ and _____, and the superficial cord reflex is _____.

   A reflex classified as an autonomic reflex is the _____.

5. Name two cord-mediated reflexes: _____ and _____

   _____

   Name one somatic reflex in which the higher brain centers participate: _____

6. Trace the reflex arc, naming efferent and afferent nerves, receptors, effectors, and integration centers, for the following reflexes:

   patellar reflex _____

   _____

   _____

calcaneal tendon reflex _____

_____

_____

7. What was the effect of muscle fatigue on your ability to produce the patellar reflex?

_____

8. The pupillary light reflex and the corneal reflex illustrate the purposeful nature of reflex activity. Describe the protective aspect of each:

pupillary light reflex _____

corneal reflex _____

9. Was the pupillary consensual reflex a contralateral or an ipsilateral response? _____

Why would such a response be of significant value in this particular reflex? _____

_____

10. Differentiate between the types of effectors used by the somatic and autonomic reflexes, and the types of activities accomplished by somatic and autonomic reflexes.

_____

_____

_____

The Special Senses

Materials

For Vision
- ☐ Dissectible eye model
- ☐ Chart of eye anatomy
- ☐ Preserved cow or sheep eye
- ☐ Dissecting tray and instruments
- ☐ Disposable gloves
- ☐ Metric ruler
- ☐ Common straight pins
- ☐ Snellen eye chart (floor marked with chalk to indicate 20-ft distance from posted Snellen chart)
- ☐ Ishihara's color plates

For Hearing and Equilibrium
- ☐ Three-dimensional dissectible ear model and/or chart of ear anatomy
- ☐ Otoscope (if available)
- ☐ Alcohol swabs
- ☐ Absorbent cotton
- ☐ Watch or clock that ticks
- ☐ 12-inch ruler
- ☐ Tuning forks (range of frequencies)
- ☐ Rubber mallet
- ☐ *Demonstration area:*
  Cochlea slide set up under a compound microscope for student observation

For Smell and Taste
- ☐ Small mirror
- ☐ Paper towels
- ☐ Granulated sugar
- ☐ Cotton-tipped swabs
- ☐ Disposable autoclave bag
- ☐ Paper cups; paper plates
- ☐ Beaker containing 10% bleach solution
- ☐ Prepared dropper bottles of oil of cloves, oil of peppermint, and oil of wintergreen or corresponding flavorings found in the condiment section of a supermarket
- ☐ Equal-sized food cubes of cheese, apple, dried prunes, banana, and hard-cooked egg white (These prepared foods should be in an opaque container; a foil-lined egg carton would work well.)
- ☐ Chipped ice
- ☐ Absorbent cotton

Pre-Lab Quiz

1. Name the mucous membrane that lines the internal surface of the eyelids and continues over the anterior surface of the eyeball. _____

2. Circle the correct term. The <u>aqueous humor</u> / <u>vitreous humor</u> is a clear, watery fluid that helps to maintain the intraocular pressure of the eye and provides nutrients for the avascular lens and cornea.

3. Circle the correct term. Sound waves that enter the external acoustic meatus eventually encounter the <u>tympanic membrane</u> / <u>oval window</u>, which then vibrates at the same frequency as the sound waves hitting it.

4. Three small bones found within the middle ear are the malleus, incus, and:
   a. auricle   b. cochlea   c. eardrum   d. stapes

5. Circle the correct term. Olfactory receptor cells are <u>bipolar</u> / <u>unipolar</u> neurons whose olfactory cilia extend outward from the epithelium.

I n contrast to the small and widely distributed general receptors (touch, temperature, pressure, and pain), the **special sense receptors** are large, complex sensory organs (eyes and ears) or localized clusters of receptors (taste buds and olfactory epithelium). This chapter focuses on the functional anatomy of each of the special sense organs individually, but keep in mind that sensory inputs are overlapping.

Anatomy of the Eye

OBJECTIVE 1   Describe the structure and function of the accessory visual structures.

External Anatomy and Accessory Structures

The adult human eye is a sphere some 2.5 cm (1 inch) in diameter. Only about one-sixth of the eye's anterior surface is observable (**Figure 17.1**); the remainder is protected by a cushion of fat and the walls of the bony orbit. The accessory structures of the eye include the eyebrows, eyelids, conjunctivae, lacrimal apparatus, and extrinsic eye muscles (**Table 17.1**, Figure 17.1, and **Figure 17.2**).

Six **extrinsic eye muscles** attached to the exterior surface of each eyeball control eye movements. Figure 17.2 notes the names, positioning, and actions of these extrinsic muscles.

Activity 1

Identifying Accessory Eye Structures

Observe the eyes of another student, and identify as many accessory structures as possible. Ask your partner to look to the left. What extrinsic eye muscles produce this action?

Right eye _____   Left eye _____

Ask your partner to look superiorly. What *two* extrinsic muscles of each eye can bring about this motion?

Right eye _____   Left eye _____

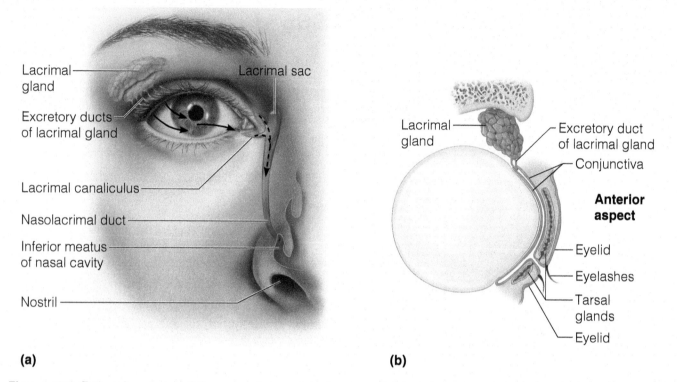

Figure 17.1 External anatomy of the eye and accessory structures. (a) Anterior view. **(b)** Sagittal section.

Table 17.1	Accessory Structures of the Eye (Figures 17.1 and 17.2)	
Structure	**Description**	**Function**
Eyebrows	Short hairs located on the supraorbital margins	Shade and prevent sweat from entering the eyes.
Eyelids	Skin-covered upper and lower lids, with eyelashes projecting from their free margin	Protect the eyes and spread lacrimal fluid (tears) with blinking.
Tarsal glands	Modified sebaceous glands embedded in the tarsal plate of the eyelid	Secrete an oily secretion that lubricates the surface of the eye.
Ciliary glands	Typical sebaceous and modified sweat glands that lie between the eyelash follicles	Secrete an oily secretion that lubricates the surface of the eye and the eyelashes. An infection of a ciliary gland is called a sty.
Conjunctivae	A clear mucous membrane that lines the eyelids and the anterior white of the eye	Secrete mucus to lubricate the eye. Inflammation of the conjunctiva results in conjunctivitis (commonly called "pinkeye").
Medial and lateral commissures	Junctions where the eyelids meet medially and laterally	Form the corners of the eyes. The medial commissure contains the lacrimal caruncle.
Lacrimal apparatus	Includes the lacrimal gland and a series of ducts that drain the lacrimal fluid into the nasal cavity	Protects the eye by keeping it moist. Blinking spreads the lacrimal fluid.
Lacrimal gland	Located in the superior and lateral aspect of the orbit of the eye	Secretes lacrimal fluid, which contains mucus, antibodies, and lysozyme.
Lacrimal canaliculi	Two tiny canals that are located in the eyelids	Allow lacrimal fluid to drain into the lacrimal sac.
Lacrimal sac	A single pouch located in the medial orbital wall	Allows lacrimal fluid to drain into the nasolacrimal duct.
Nasolacrimal duct	A single tube that empties into the nasal cavity	Allows lacrimal fluid to flow into the nasal cavity.
Extrinsic eye muscles	Six muscles for each eye; four recti and two oblique muscles (see Figure 17.2)	Control the movement of each eyeball and hold the eyes in the orbits.

17

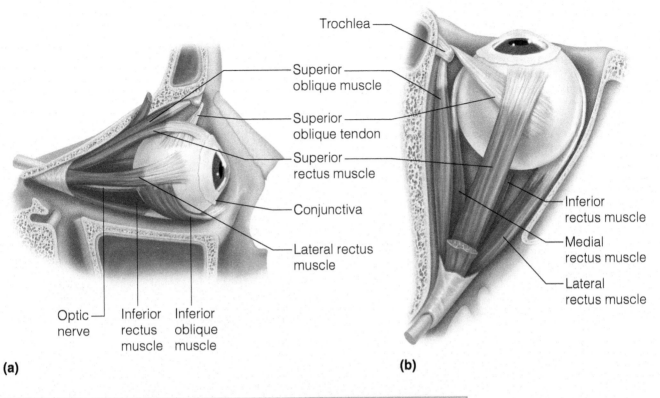

Figure 17.2 labels (part a): Superior oblique muscle, Superior oblique tendon, Superior rectus muscle, Conjunctiva, Lateral rectus muscle, Optic nerve, Inferior rectus muscle, Inferior oblique muscle

(part b): Trochlea, Inferior rectus muscle, Medial rectus muscle, Lateral rectus muscle

(a)   **(b)**

Name	Action	Controlling cranial nerve
Lateral rectus	Moves eye laterally	VI (abducens)
Medial rectus	Moves eye medially	III (oculomotor)
Superior rectus	Elevates eye and turns it medially	III (oculomotor)
Inferior rectus	Depresses eye and turns it medially	III (oculomotor)
Inferior oblique	Elevates eye and turns it laterally	III (oculomotor)
Superior oblique	Depresses eye and turns it laterally	IV (trochlear)

(c)

Figure 17.2 Extrinsic muscles of the eye. (a) Lateral view of the right eye. **(b)** Superior view of right eye. **(c)** Summary of actions of the extrinsic eye muscles and cranial nerves that control them.

17

Internal Anatomy of the Eye

OBJECTIVE 2 Identify the internal structures of the eye when provided with a model, diagram, or preserved animal eye, and list the functions of each.

The eye itself is a hollow sphere. Its wall is constructed of three layers: the **fibrous layer,** the **vascular layer,** and the **sensory layer.**

Distribution of Photoreceptors

The inner sensory layer is composed of three major populations of neurons. From outer to inner aspect, they are **photoreceptors** (rods and cones), **bipolar cells,** and **ganglion cells** (**Figure 17.3**). The rods are specialized for dim light, whereas cones are color photoreceptors that permit sharp vision in good light. The rods and cones begin the electrical events that pass from the photoreceptors to the bipolar cells and then to the ganglion cells. When stimulated, the ganglion cells generate nerve impulses that are ultimately transmitted to the brain. Vision is the result. The photoreceptor cells are distributed over the entire retina, except where the optic nerve (the bundled axons of the ganglion cells) leaves the eyeball. This site is called the **optic disc,** or **blind spot** (**Figure 17.4**). Lateral to each blind spot is an area of high cone density. In its center is the **fovea centralis,** a minute pit about 0.4 mm in diameter, which contains only cones and is the area of greatest visual acuity. Focusing for discriminative vision occurs in the fovea centralis.

Internal Chambers and Fluids

The **lens** divides the eye into two segments. The **anterior segment** anterior to the lens contains a clear watery fluid called the **aqueous humor.** The **posterior segment** behind the lens is filled with the gel-like **vitreous humor.** The aqueous humor is continually formed by the capillaries of the ciliary body. It helps to maintain the intraocular pressure of the eye and provides nutrients for the avascular lens and cornea. Aqueous humor is reabsorbed into the **scleral venous sinus (canal of Schlemm),** a drainage duct located at the junction of the sclera and cornea. The vitreous humor reinforces the posterior part of the eyeball, and helps to keep the retina pressed firmly against the wall of the eyeball.

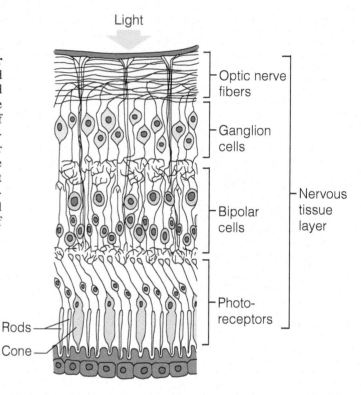

Figure 17.3 Microscopic anatomy of the retina. See also Plate 15 in the Histology Atlas.

Activity 2

Identifying Internal Structures of the Eye

Obtain a dissectible eye model or observe a chart of eye anatomy to identify the structures shown in Figure 17.4 and described in Table 17.2.

Table 17.2	Layers of the Eye (Figure 17.4)	
Structure	**Description**	**Function**
Fibrous Layer (External Layer)		
Sclera	Opaque white connective tissue that forms the "white of the eye."	Helps to maintain the shape of the eyeball and provides an attachment point for the extrinsic eye muscles.
Cornea	Structurally continuous with the sclera; modified to form a transparent layer that bulges anteriorly.	Forms a clear window that is the major light bending (refracting) medium of the eye.
Vascular Layer (Middle Layer)		
Choroid	A blood vessel–rich, dark membrane.	The blood vessels nourish the other layers of the eye, and the melanin helps to absorb excess light.
Ciliary body	Modification of the choroid that encircles the lens.	Contains the ciliary muscle and the ciliary body.
Ciliary muscle	Smooth muscle found within the ciliary body.	Alters the shape of the lens with contraction and relaxation.
Ciliary zonule (suspensory ligament)	A halo of fine fibers that extends from the ciliary body around the lens.	Attaches the lens to the ciliary body.
Iris	The anterior portion of the vascular layer that is pigmented. It contains two layers of smooth muscle (sphincter pupillae and dilator pupillae).	Controls the amount of light entering the eye by changing the size of the pupil diameter.
Pupil	The round central opening of the iris.	Allows light to enter the eye.

Table 17.2	*(continued)*	
Structure	**Description**	**Function**
Sensory Layer (Retina)		
Pigmented layer of the retina	The outer layer that is composed of only a single layer of pigment cells.	Absorbs light and prevents it from scattering in the eye. Pigment cells act as phagocytes for cleaning up cell debris.
Neural layer of the retina	The thicker inner layer composed of three main types of neurons: photoreceptors (rods and cones), bipolar cells, and ganglion cells.	Photoreceptors respond to light and convert the light energy into action potentials that travel to the brain.

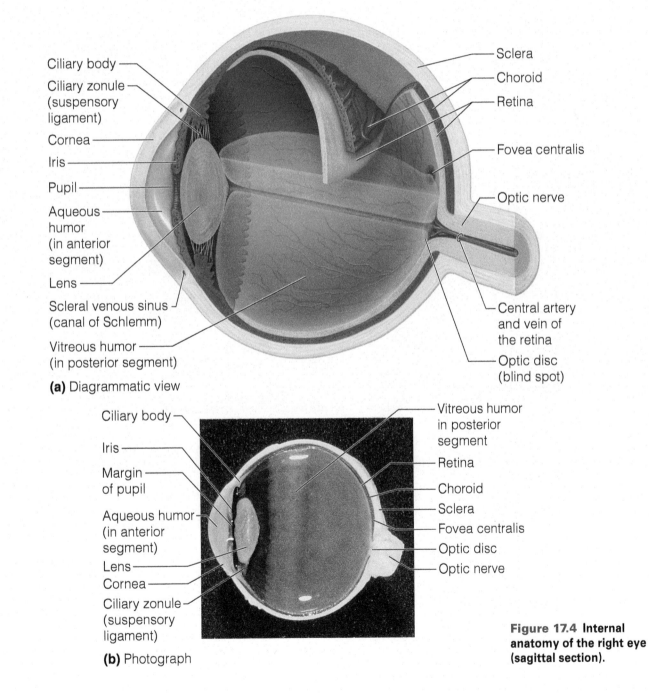

(a) Diagrammatic view

Ciliary body
Ciliary zonule (suspensory ligament)
Cornea
Iris
Pupil
Aqueous humor (in anterior segment)
Lens
Scleral venous sinus (canal of Schlemm)
Vitreous humor (in posterior segment)

Sclera
Choroid
Retina
Fovea centralis
Optic nerve
Central artery and vein of the retina
Optic disc (blind spot)

(b) Photograph

Ciliary body
Iris
Margin of pupil
Aqueous humor (in anterior segment)
Lens
Cornea
Ciliary zonule (suspensory ligament)

Vitreous humor in posterior segment
Retina
Choroid
Sclera
Fovea centralis
Optic disc
Optic nerve

Figure 17.4 Internal anatomy of the right eye (sagittal section).

17

DISSECTION

The Cow (Sheep) Eye

1. Obtain a preserved cow or sheep eye, dissecting instruments, and a dissecting tray. Put on disposable gloves if desired.

2. Examine the external surface of the eye, noticing the thick cushion of adipose tissue. Identify the optic nerve (cranial nerve II) as it leaves the eyeball, the cut remnants of the extrinsic eye muscles, the conjunctiva, the sclera, and the cornea. The normally transparent cornea is opalescent or opaque if the eye has been preserved. Refer to **Figure 17.5** as you work.

3. Trim away most of the fat and connective tissue, but leave the optic nerve intact. Holding the eye with the cornea facing downward, carefully make an incision with a sharp scalpel into the sclera about ¼ inch above the cornea. Then, using scissors, cut carefully around the circumference of the eyeball paralleling the corneal edge.

4. Carefully lift the anterior part of the eyeball away from the posterior portion. Conditions being proper, the vitreous humor should remain with the posterior part of the eyeball.

5. Examine the anterior part of the eye, and identify the following structures.

Ciliary body: Black pigmented body that appears in a halo encircling the lens.

Lens: Biconvex structure that is opaque in preserved specimens. **Ciliary zonule (suspensory ligaments):** A halo of delicate fibers attaching the lens to the ciliary body.

Carefully remove the lens, and identify the adjacent structures:

Iris: Anterior continuation of the ciliary body penetrated by the pupil. **Cornea:** More convex anteriormost portion of the sclera; normally transparent but cloudy in preserved specimens.

6. Examine the posterior portion of the eyeball. Remove the vitreous humor, and identify the following structures:

Retina: The neural layer of the retina appears as a delicate white, probably crumpled membrane that separates easily from the pigmented choroid.

Notice its point of attachment. What is this point called?

_____

Pigmented choroid coat: Appears iridescent in the cow or sheep eye because of a special reflecting surface called the **tapetum lucidum**. This specialized surface reflects the light within the eye and is found in the eyes of animals that live under conditions of low-intensity light. It is not found in humans.

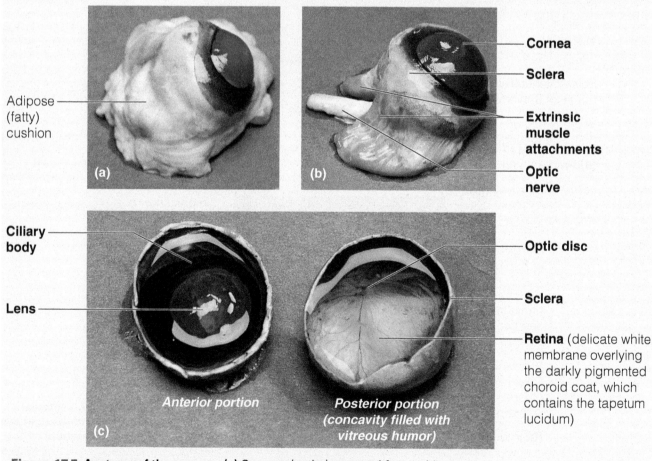

Figure 17.5 Anatomy of the cow eye. (a) Cow eye (entire) removed from orbit. **(b)** Cow eye (entire) with fat removed to show the extrinsic muscle attachments and optic nerve. **(c)** Cow eye cut along the frontal plane to reveal internal structures.

Visual Tests and Experiments

OBJECTIVE 3 Define *blind spot, refraction, hyperopia, myopia,* and *astigmatism,* and discuss image formation on the retina.

Activity 3

Demonstrating the Blind Spot

1. Hold **Figure 17.6** about 18 inches from your eyes. Close your left eye, and focus your right eye on the X, which should be positioned so that it is directly in line with your right eye. Move the figure slowly toward your face, keeping your right eye focused on the X. When the dot focuses on the blind spot, which lacks photoreceptors, it will disappear.

2. Have your laboratory partner record in metric units the distance at which this occurs. The dot will reappear as the figure is moved closer. Distance at which the dot disappears:

Right eye _____

Repeat the test for the left eye. This time close the right eye, and focus the left eye on the dot. Record the distance at which the X disappears:

Left eye _____

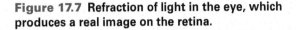

Figure 17.6 Blind spot test figure.

Refraction, Visual Acuity, and Astigmatism

When light passes from one substance to another with a different density, its velocity, or speed of transmission, changes, and the rays are bent, or **refracted.** Thus light rays are refracted as they encounter the cornea, lens, and vitreous humor of the eye.

The bending power of the cornea and vitreous humor are constant. But the lens's refractive strength can be varied by changing its shape—that is, by making it more or less convex so that the light is properly converged and focused on the retina. The greater the lens convexity, or bulge, the more the light will be bent and the stronger the lens.

In general, light from a distant source (over 20 feet) approaches the eye as parallel rays, and no change in lens shape is necessary for it to focus properly on the retina. However, light from a close source tends to diverge, and the lens must bulge more to make close vision possible. To achieve this, the ciliary muscle contracts, decreasing the tension of the suspensory ligament attached to the lens and allowing the elastic lens to "round up." The ability of the eye to focus specifically for close objects (less than 20 feet) is called **accommodation.** It should be noted that the image formed on the retina as a result of the light-bending activity

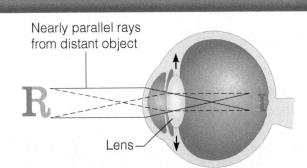

Nearly parallel rays from distant object

Lens—

Figure 17.7 Refraction of light in the eye, which produces a real image on the retina.

of the lens (**Figure 17.7**) is a **real image** (reversed from left to right, inverted, and smaller than the object).

The normal eye, or **emmetropic eye,** is able to accommodate properly. However, visual problems may result from (1) lenses that are too strong or too "lazy" (overconverging and underconverging, respectively); (2) structural problems, such as an eyeball that is too long or too short; or (3) a cornea or lens with improper curvatures.

Individuals in whom the image focuses in front of the retina have **myopia,** or "nearsightedness"; they can see close objects without difficulty, but distant objects are blurred or indistinct. Correction requires a concave lens, which causes the light reaching the eye to diverge.

If the image focuses behind the retina, the individual has **hyperopia,** or farsightedness. Such persons have no problems with distant vision but need glasses with convex lenses to boost the converging power of the lens for close vision.

Irregularities in the curvatures of the lens and/or the cornea lead to a blurred vision problem called **astigmatism.** Cylindrically ground lenses, which compensate for inequalities in the curvatures of the refracting surfaces, are prescribed to correct the condition.

The elasticity of our natural lens decreases with age, making it difficult to focus for close vision. This condition is called **presbyopia**—literally, "old vision." Lens elasticity can be tested by measuring the **near point of accommodation,** which is about 10 cm from the eye in young adults. It is closer in children and farther in old age.

17

Activity 4

Determining Near Point of Accommodation

To determine your near point of accommodation, hold a common straight pin at arm's length in front of one eye. Slowly move the pin toward that eye until the pin image becomes distorted. Have your lab partner use the metric ruler to measure the distance from your eye to the pin at this point, and record the distance below. Repeat the procedure for the other eye.

Near point for right eye _____

Near point for left eye _____

Visual acuity, or sharpness of vision, is generally tested with a Snellen eye chart, which consists of letters of various sizes printed on a white card. The distance at which the normal eye can read a line of letters is printed at the end of that line.

Activity 5

Testing Visual Acuity

1. Have your partner stand 20 feet from the posted Snellen eye chart and cover one eye with a card or hand. As he or she reads each consecutive line aloud, check for accuracy. If this individual wears glasses, give the test twice—first with glasses off and then with glasses on.

2. Record the number of the line with the smallest-sized letters read. If it is 20/20, the person's vision for that eye is normal. If it is 20/40, or any ratio with a value less than one, he or she has less than the normal visual acuity. (Such an individual is myopic, so a person with 20/40 vision is seeing objects clearly at 20 feet that a person with normal vision sees clearly at 40 feet.) If the visual acuity ratio is greater than 1, vision is better than normal. Give your partner the number of the line corresponding to the smallest letters read, to record in step 4.

3. Repeat the process for the other eye.

4. Have your partner test and record your visual acuity. If you wear glasses, record your test results *without glasses* first.

Visual acuity, right eye _____

Visual acuity, left eye _____

Activity 6

Testing for Astigmatism

The astigmatism chart (**Figure 17.8**) tests for defects in the refracting surface of the lens and/or cornea.

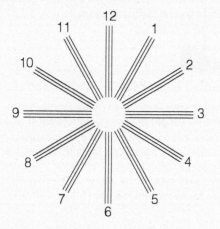

Figure 17.8 Astigmatism testing chart.

View the chart first with one eye and then with the other, focusing on the center of the chart. If all the radiating lines appear equally dark and distinct, your refracting surfaces are not distorted. If some of the lines are blurred or appear less dark than others, you have at least some degree of astigmatism.

Is astigmatism present in your left eye? _____

Right eye? _____

Color Blindness

Ishihara's color plates are designed to test for deficiencies in the cones or color photoreceptor cells. There are three cone types—one type primarily absorbs the red wavelengths of visible light, another the blue wavelengths, and a third the green wavelengths. Nerve impulses reaching the brain from these different photoreceptor types are then interpreted (seen) as red, blue, and green, respectively. Interpretation of the intermediate colors of the visible light spectrum is a result of overlapping input from more than one cone type.

Activity 7

Testing for Color Blindness

1. View the color plates in bright light or sunlight while holding them about 30 inches away and at right angles to your line of vision. Report to your laboratory partner what you see in each plate. Take no more than 3 seconds for each decision.

2. Your partner is to write down your responses and then check their accuracy with the correct answers provided in the color plate book. Is there any indication that you have some degree of color blindness?

_____ If so, what type? _____

Repeat the procedure to test your partner's color vision.

Eye Reflexes

OBJECTIVE 4   Discuss the importance of the accommodation pupillary reflex and the convergence reflex.

Both intrinsic (internal) and extrinsic (external) muscles are necessary for proper eye function. The *intrinsic muscles,* controlled by the autonomic nervous system, are those of the ciliary body (which alters the lens curvature) and the radial and circular muscles of the iris (which control pupil size and thus regulate the amount of light entering the eye). The *extrinsic muscles* are the rectus and oblique muscles, which are attached to the outside of the eyeball (see Figure 17.2). These muscles control eye movement and make it possible to keep moving objects focused on the fovea centralis. They are also responsible for **convergence,** or medial eye movement, which is essential for near vision. When convergence occurs, both eyes are aimed at the near object viewed. The somatic nervous system controls the extrinsic eye muscles.

Demonstrating Reflex Activity of Intrinsic and Extrinsic Eye Muscles

Activity of both the intrinsic and extrinsic muscle types is brought about by reflex actions that can be observed by conducting simple experiments. The *convergence reflex* mediated by the extrinsic eye muscles and the *accommodation reflex* mediated by the intrinsic eye muscles are described here. (The photopupillary reflex, which protects the delicate photoreceptor cells from damage due to excessive light, also involves the intrinsic muscles. See page 197 in Exercise 16.)

Accommodation Pupillary Reflex

Have your partner gaze for approximately 1 minute at a distant object in the lab—*not* toward the windows or another light source. Observe your partner's pupils. Then hold some printed material 6 to 10 inches from his or her face, and direct him or her to focus on it.

How does pupil size change as your partner focuses on the printed material?

_____

_____

Explain the value of this reflex.

_____

_____

Convergence Reflex

Repeat the previous experiment, this time noting the position of your partner's eyeballs both while he or she is gazing at the distant and at the close object (a pen or pencil). Do they change position as the object of focus is changed?

_____

_____ In what way? _____

_____

Explain the importance of the convergence reflex.

_____

_____

_____

The Ear and Hearing and Balance

OBJECTIVE 5 Identify the structures of the external, middle, and internal ear by correctly labeling a diagram.

Gross Anatomy of the Ear

The ear, which contains sensory receptors for hearing and equilibrium, is a complex structure. It is divided into three major areas: the *external ear,* the *middle ear,* and the *internal ear* (**Figure 17.9**). The external and middle ear structures serve the needs of the sense of hearing *only,* whereas internal ear structures function both in equilibrium and hearing.

Identifying Structures of the Ear

Obtain a dissectible ear model and identify the structures described below. Refer to Figure 17.9 as you work.

The **external,** or **outer, ear** is composed of the **auricle,** or **pinna,** and the **external acoustic meatus.** The auricle is the skin-covered cartilage encircling the acoustic meatus opening. The external acoustic meatus, also called the *auditory canal,* is a short, narrow chamber carved into the temporal bone. In its skin-lined walls are wax-secreting glands called **ceruminous glands.** The sound waves that enter the external acoustic meatus eventually hit the **tympanic membrane,** or **eardrum,** causing it to vibrate. The eardrum separates the outer from the middle ear.

The **middle ear** is a small air-filled chamber—the **tympanic cavity**—within the temporal bone. The cavity is spanned by three small bones, collectively called the **auditory ossicles** (hammer, anvil, and stirrup),* which transmit the vibratory motion of the eardrum to the fluids of the inner ear via the **oval window.**

Connecting the middle ear chamber with the nasopharynx is the **pharyngotympanic (auditory) tube,** which can be opened temporarily to equalize the pressure of the middle ear cavity with external air pressure. This is an important function because the eardrum does not vibrate properly unless the pressure on both of its surfaces is the same.

The **internal,** or **inner, ear** is a system of bony and rather tortuous chambers called the **osseous,** or **bony, labyrinth,** which is filled with a watery fluid called **perilymph.** Floating in the perilymph is the **membranous labyrinth** ("maze"), a system filled with a more viscous fluid called **endolymph.** The three subdivisions of the bony labyrinth are the **cochlea,** the **vestibule,** and the **semicircular canals,** with the vestibule situated between the cochlea and semicircular canals.

Examining the Ear with an Otoscope (Optional)

1. Obtain an otoscope and two alcohol swabs. Inspect your partner's ear canal and then select the speculum with the largest *diameter* (not length!) that will fit comfortably

Text continues on next page. →

*The ossicles are often referred to by their Latin names, that is, **malleus, incus,** and **stapes,** respectively.

17

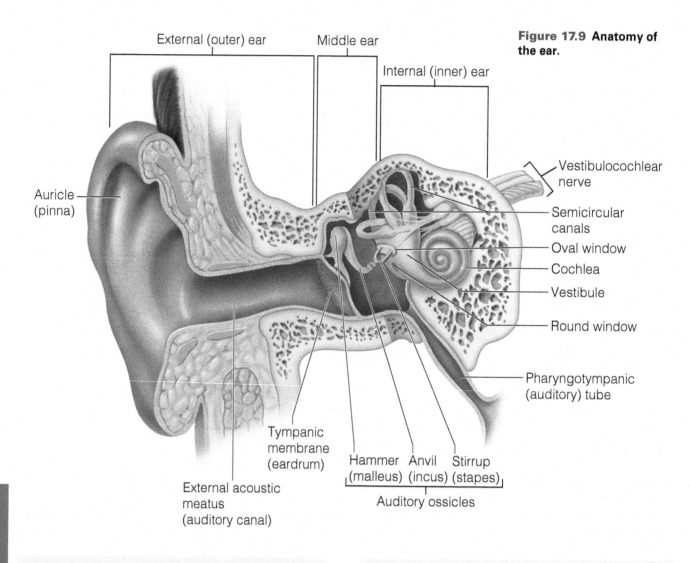

External (outer) ear   Middle ear

Figure 17.9 Anatomy of the ear.

Internal (inner) ear

Vestibulocochlear nerve

Auricle (pinna)

Semicircular canals

Oval window

Cochlea

Vestibule

Round window

Pharyngotympanic (auditory) tube

Tympanic membrane (eardrum)

Hammer (malleus)   Anvil (incus)   Stirrup (stapes)

Auditory ossicles

External acoustic meatus (auditory canal)

into his or her ear and permit good visibility. Clean the speculum thoroughly with an alcohol swab, and then attach it to the battery-containing otoscope handle. Before beginning, check that the otoscope light beam is strong. (If not, obtain another otoscope or new batteries.)

⚠ 2. When you are ready to begin the examination, hold the lighted otoscope securely between your thumb and forefinger (like a pencil), and rest the little finger of your otoscope-holding hand against your partner's head. This maneuver forms a brace that allows the speculum to move as your partner moves and prevents it from penetrating too deeply into the ear canal during the unexpected movements.

3. Grasp the auricle firmly and pull it up, back, and slightly laterally. If this causes your partner pain or discomfort, the external ear may be inflamed or infected. If this occurs, do not attempt to examine the ear canal.

4. Carefully insert the speculum of the otoscope into the external acoustic meatus in a downward and forward direction just far enough to permit examination of the tympanic membrane or eardrum. Note its shape, color, and vascular network. The healthy tympanic membrane is pearly white. During the examination, notice whether there is any discharge or redness in the canal, and identify earwax.

5. After the examination, thoroughly clean the speculum with the second alcohol swab before returning the otoscope to the supply area.

Microscopic Anatomy of the Spiral Organ of Corti and the Mechanism of Hearing

OBJECTIVE 6   Describe the anatomy of the spiral organ of Corti, and explain its role in hearing.

The snail-like cochlea (see Figure 17.9 and **Figure 17.10**) contains the receptors for hearing. The cochlear membranous labyrinth, the **cochlear duct,** is a soft wormlike tube about 1½ inches long that winds through the turns of the cochlea and separates the perilymph-containing cochlear cavity into upper and lower chambers. The upper chamber, the scala vestibuli, abuts the oval window, which "seats" the foot plate of the stirrup located laterally in the tympanic cavity. The lower chamber, the scala tympani, is bounded by a membranous area called the **round window.** The cochlear duct, itself filled with endolymph, supports the **spiral organ of Corti,** which contains the receptors for hearing and nerve endings of the cochlear division of the vestibulocochlear nerve (VIII).

Figure 17.10b shows the structure of the spiral organ of Corti. The hair (auditory receptor) cells rest on the **basilar**

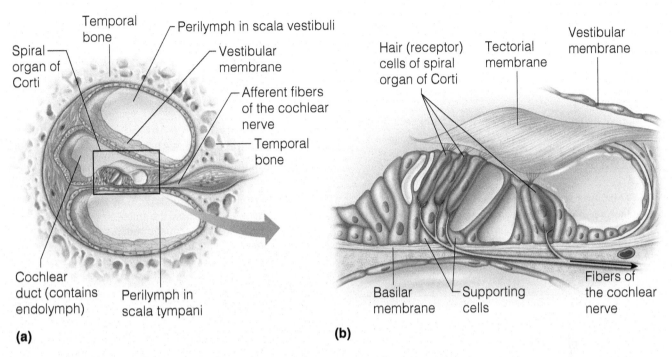

Figure 17.10 Anatomy of the cochlea. (a) A cross-sectional view of one turn of the cochlea, showing the position of the spiral organ of Corti in the cochlear duct. The cavities of the bony labyrinth contain perilymph. The cochlear duct contains endolymph. **(b)** Detailed structure of the spiral organ of Corti. The receptor cells (hair cells) rest on the basilar membrane.

membrane, which forms the floor of the cochlear duct, and their "hairs" (stereocilia) project into the gel-like **tectorial membrane** that overlies them. The roof of the cochlear duct is called the **vestibular membrane.**

Activity 11

Examining the Microscopic Structure of the Cochlea

Go to the demonstration area, and view the prepared microscope slide of the cochlea. Identify the areas described above and shown in Figure 17.10. Compare your observations to the view shown in Plate 16 in the Histology Atlas.

The mechanism of hearing begins as sound waves pass through the external acoustic meatus and through the middle ear into the inner ear, where the vibration eventually reaches the spiral organ of Corti, which contains the receptors for hearing.

The traveling sound waves stimulate the hair cells of the spiral organ of Corti where they peak. High-frequency waves (high-pitched sounds) peak close to the oval window and low-frequency waves (low-pitched sounds) peak farther up the basilar membrane near the apex of the cochlea. Once stimulated, the hair cells depolarize and begin the chain of nervous impulses to the auditory centers of the temporal lobe cortex. This series of events results in the phenomenon we call hearing.

OBJECTIVE 7   Describe how we are able to localize sounds and to differentiate sensorineural from conduction deafness.

Activity 12

Conducting Laboratory Tests of Hearing

Perform the following hearing tests in a quiet area.

Acuity Test

Have your lab partner pack one ear with cotton and sit quietly with eyes closed. Obtain a ticking clock or watch, and hold it very close to his or her *unpacked* ear. Then slowly move it away from the ear until your partner signals that the ticking is no longer audible. Record the distance in inches at which ticking is inaudible.

Right ear _____ Left ear _____

Is the threshold of audibility sharp or indefinite?

_____

Sound Localization

Ask your partner to close both eyes. Hold the watch at an audible distance (about 6 inches) from his or her ear, and move it to various locations (front, back, sides, and

Text continues on next page. →

17

above his or her head). Have your partner locate the position by pointing in each instance. Can the sound be localized equally well at all positions?

_____

If not, at what position(s) was the sound less easily located?

_____

The ability to localize the source of a sound depends on two factors—the difference in the loudness of the sound reaching each ear and the time of arrival of the sound at each ear. How does this information help to explain your findings?

_____

Weber Test to Determine Conductive and Sensorineural Deafness

Obtain a tuning fork and a rubber mallet. Strike the tuning fork with the rubber mallet, and place the handle of the tuning fork medially on your partner's head (**Figure 17.11a**). Is the tone equally loud in both ears, or is it louder in one ear?

_____

If it is equally loud in both ears, you have equal hearing or equal loss of hearing in both ears. If sensorineural deafness is present in one ear, the tone will be heard in the unaffected ear, but not in the ear with sensorineural deafness. If conduction deafness is present, the sound will be heard more strongly in the ear in which there is a hearing loss. Conduction deafness can be simulated by plugging one ear with cotton to interfere with the conduction of sound to the inner ear.

Rinne Test for Comparing Bone- and Air-Conduction Hearing

1. Strike the tuning fork, and place its handle on your partner's mastoid process (Figure 17.11b).

2. When your partner indicates that he or she can no longer hear the sound, hold the still-vibrating prongs close to his or her external acoustic meatus (Figure 17.11c). If your partner hears the fork again (by air conduction) when it is moved to that position, hearing is not impaired. Record the test result as positive (+). (Record in step 4.)

3. Repeat the test, but this time test air-conduction hearing first. After the tone is no longer heard by air conduction, hold the handle of the tuning fork on the bony mastoid process. If the subject hears the tone again by bone conduction after hearing by air conduction is lost, there is some conductive deafness, and the result is recorded as negative (−).

4. Repeat the sequence for the opposite ear.

Right ear _____ Left ear _____

Does the subject hear better by bone or by air conduction?

_____

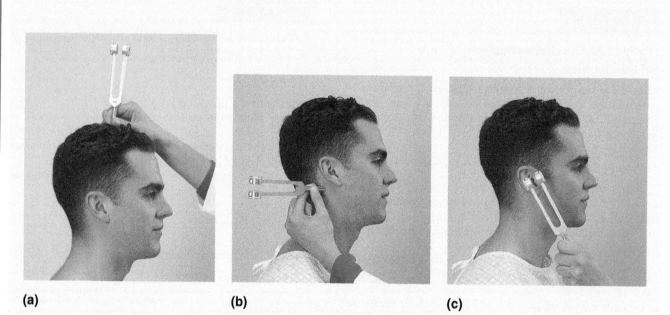

(a)   **(b)**   **(c)**

Figure 17.11 The Weber and Rinne tuning fork tests. (a) The Weber test to evaluate whether the sound remains centralized (normal) or lateralizes to one side or the other (indicative of some degree of conductive or sensorineural deafness). **(b)** and **(c)** The Rinne test to compare bone conduction and air conduction.

Anatomy of the Equilibrium Apparatus and Mechanisms of Equilibrium

OBJECTIVE 8   Describe the anatomy of the equilibrium organs of the inner ear, and explain their relative roles in maintaining balance.

The equilibrium apparatus of the inner ear is in the vestibular and semicircular canal portions of the bony labyrinth (**Figure 17.12**). The vestibule contains the saclike **utricle** and **saccule,** and the semicircular chambers contain membranous **semicircular ducts.** Like the cochlear duct, these membranes (1) are suspended in perilymph within the bony chambers, (2) are filled with endolymph, and (3) contain receptor cells that are activated by the disturbance of their cilia.

The semicircular canals house *dynamic equilibrium* receptors. The canals are about ½ inch in circumference and are oriented in the three planes of space. At the base of each semicircular duct is an enlarged region, the **ampulla,** which contains a receptor region called a **crista ampullaris.** This receptor consists of a tuft of hair cells covered with a gelatinous cap, or **cupula** (**Figure 17.13**). These dynamic equilibrium receptors react to *changes* in angular motion, as described and illustrated in Figure 17.13b and c.

The membrane sacs within the vestibule contain **maculae,** *static equilibrium* receptors that respond to gravitational pull (thus providing information on which way is up or down) and to linear or straightforward changes in speed. The **otolithic membrane,** a gelatinous material containing small grains of calcium carbonate (**otoliths**), overrides the hair cells in each macula. As the head moves, the otoliths roll in response to changes in gravitational pull (**Figure 17.14** on page 215). As they bend different hair cells, they modify the rate of impulse transmission along the vestibular nerve.

The receptors of the semicircular canals and the vestibule rarely act independently. Also, the information these balance senses provide is enhanced by the proprioceptors

and sight, as some of the following laboratory experiments demonstrate.

OBJECTIVE 9   State the purpose of the Romberg test, and describe the role of vision in maintaining equilibrium.

Activity 13

Conducting Laboratory Tests on Equilibrium

The functions of the semicircular canals and vestibule are not routinely tested in the laboratory, but the following simple tests should serve to illustrate normal equilibrium apparatus functioning.

Balance Test

Have your partner walk a straight line, placing one foot directly in front of the other.

Is he or she able to walk without noticeable wobbling from side to side?

_____

Did he or she experience any dizziness? _____

The ability to walk with balance and without dizziness, unless subject to rotational forces, indicates normal function of the equilibrium apparatus.

Was nystagmus* present? _____

*__Nystagmus__ is the involuntary rolling of the eyes in any direction or the trailing of the eyes slowly in one direction, followed by their rapid movement in the opposite direction. It is normal after rotation; abnormal otherwise. The direction of nystagmus is that of its quick phase on acceleration.

Text continues on next page. →

17

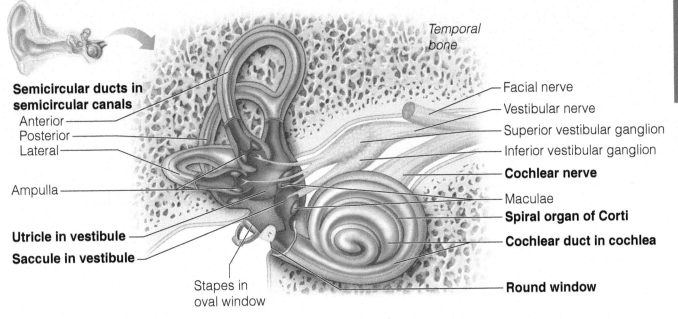

Semicircular ducts in semicircular canals
- Anterior
- Posterior
- Lateral

Ampulla

Utricle in vestibule
Saccule in vestibule

Stapes in oval window

Temporal bone

- Facial nerve
- Vestibular nerve
- Superior vestibular ganglion
- Inferior vestibular ganglion
- **Cochlear nerve**
- Maculae
- **Spiral organ of Corti**
- **Cochlear duct in cochlea**
- **Round window**

Figure 17.12 Internal ear. Right membranous labyrinth shown within the bony labyrinth. The locations of sensory organs for hearing and equilibrium are shown as well.

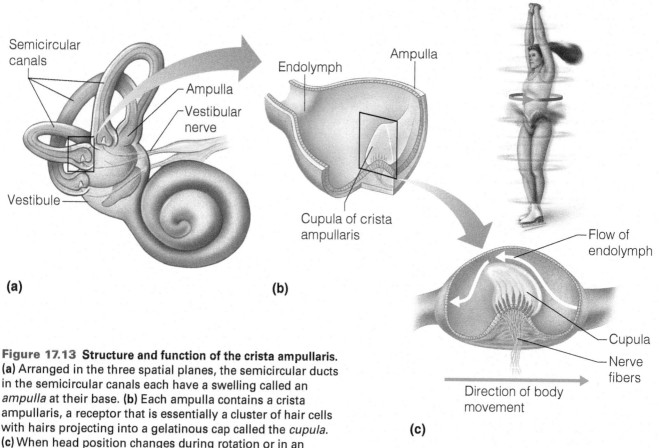

Figure 17.13 Structure and function of the crista ampullaris.
(a) Arranged in the three spatial planes, the semicircular ducts in the semicircular canals each have a swelling called an *ampulla* at their base. **(b)** Each ampulla contains a crista ampullaris, a receptor that is essentially a cluster of hair cells with hairs projecting into a gelatinous cap called the *cupula*. **(c)** When head position changes during rotation or in an angular direction, the endolymph in the semicircular canals lags behind, pushing the cupula and bending the hair cells in the opposite direction. The bending results in increased impulse transmission in the sensory neurons. The mechanism adjusts quickly if rotation continues at a constant speed.

Romberg Test

The Romberg test determines the soundness of the dorsal white column of the spinal cord, which transmits impulses to the brain from the proprioceptors involved with posture.

1. Have your partner stand with his or her back to the blackboard.

2. Draw one line parallel to each side of your partner's body. He or she should stand erect, with feet together, eyes open and staring straight ahead for 2 minutes while you observe any movements. Did you see any gross swaying movements?

_____

3. Repeat the test. This time the subject's eyes should be closed. Note and record the degree of side-to-side movement.

_____

4. Repeat the test with the subject's eyes first open and then closed. This time, however, the subject should be positioned with his or her left shoulder toward, but not touching, the board so that you may observe and record the degree of front-to-back swaying.

_____

Do you think the equilibrium apparatus of the inner ear was operating equally well in all these tests? _____

The proprioceptors? _____

Why was the observed degree of swaying greater when the eyes were closed?

_____

What conclusions can you draw regarding the factors necessary for maintaining body equilibrium and balance?

_____

Role of Vision in Maintaining Equilibrium

To further demonstrate the role of vision in maintaining equilibrium, perform the following experiment. (Ask your lab partner to record observations and act as a "spotter.") Stand erect, with your eyes open. Raise your left foot approximately 1 foot off the floor, and hold it there for 1 minute.

Record the observations: _____

Rest for 1 or 2 minutes; and then repeat the experiment with the same foot raised, but with your eyes closed.

Record the observations: _____

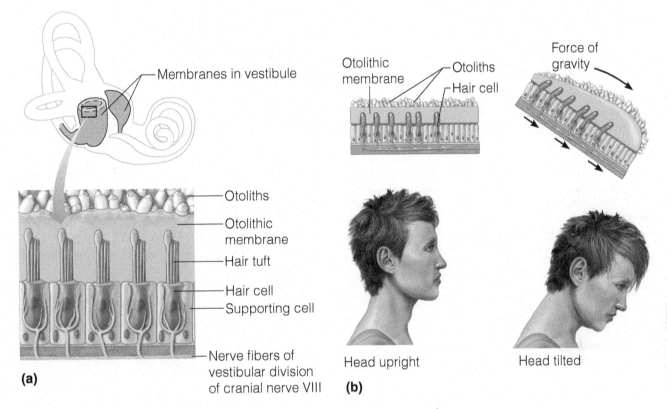

(a) Membranes in vestibule — Otoliths — Otolithic membrane — Hair tuft — Hair cell — Supporting cell — Nerve fibers of vestibular division of cranial nerve VIII

(b) Otolithic membrane — Otoliths — Hair cell — Force of gravity — Head upright — Head tilted

Figure 17.14 Structure and function of maculae (static equilibrium receptors). **(a)** Diagrammatic view of part of a macula. **(b)** When the head is tipped, the otoliths in the gelatinous otolithic membrane move in the direction of gravitational pull, stimulating the maculae. This creates a pull on the hair cells.

The Chemical Senses: Smell and Taste

The receptors for smell (olfaction) and taste (gustation) are classified as **chemoreceptors** because they respond to chemicals in solution.

Location and Anatomy of the Olfactory and Taste Receptors

OBJECTIVE 10   Describe the location, structure, and function of the olfactory and taste receptors.

The **olfactory epithelium** (organ for the sense of smell) occupies an area of about 0.5 cm^2 in the roof of each nasal cavity (**Figure 17.15** and Plate 18 in the Histology Atlas). The **olfactory receptor cells** are bipolar neurons whose **olfactory hairs (cilia)** protrude from the epithelium. Axons emerging from their basal ends are gathered into small fascicles called **olfactory filaments.** These penetrate the cribriform plate of the ethmoid bone and proceed as the *olfactory nerves* (cranial nerve I) to synapse in the *olfactory bulbs* lying on either side of the crista galli of the ethmoid bone. Impulses from neurons of the olfactory bulbs are then conveyed to the olfactory portion of the cortex.

The **taste buds,** specific receptors for the sense of taste, are widely distributed in the oral cavity. Most are located on the tongue (as described next). A few are found on the soft palate, pharynx, and inner surface of the cheeks.

The superior tongue surface is covered with small peglike projections, or **papillae,** of three major types: sharp *filiform papillae* and the rounded *fungiform* and *vallate (circumvallate) papillae.* The taste buds are located primarily on the sides of the vallate papillae (arranged in a V-formation on the posterior surface of the tongue) and on the more numerous

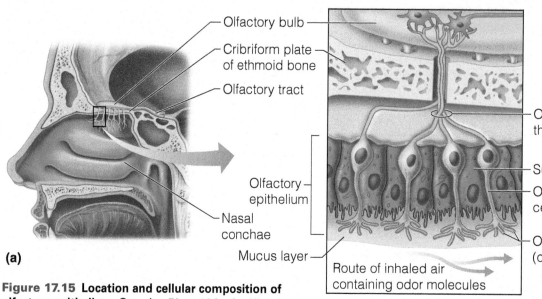

Figure 17.15 Location and cellular composition of olfactory epithelium. See also Plate 18 in the Histology Atlas.

fungiform papillae. The latter look rather like minute mushrooms and are widely distributed on the tongue. See **Figure 17.16**.

When taste is tested with pure chemical compounds, most taste sensations can be grouped into one of five basic qualities—sweet, salty, sour, bitter, and umami (u-mam′e; "delicious"), the last responsible for the savory and monosodium glutamate tastes.

Activity 14

Identifying Papillae on the Tongue

Use a mirror to examine your tongue. Can you identify the various papillae types?

_____ If so, which? _____

_____

_____

Each taste bud consists of a globular arrangement of two types of epithelial cells: the **gustatory,** or **taste, cells,** which are the actual receptor cells, and **supporting cells.** Basal cells at the bottom of each taste bud provide for new receptor cells. Several nerve fibers enter each taste bud and supply sensory nerve endings to each of the taste cells. The long microvilli of the receptor cells penetrate through an opening called the **taste pore.** When these microvilli, called **gustatory hairs,** are stimulated by specific chemicals in the solution, the taste cells depolarize. The afferent fibers from the taste buds to the gustatory cortex of the brain are carried in three cranial nerves: the *facial (VII),* glossopharyngeal (IX), and *vagus (X) nerves.*

Laboratory Experiments

Notify instructor of any food or scent allergies or restrictions before beginning experiments.

Activity 15

Stimulating Taste Buds

1. Obtain several paper towels and a disposable autoclave bag, and bring them to your bench.

2. With a paper towel, dry the superior surface of your tongue.

⚠ Immediately dispose of the paper towel in the autoclave bag.

3. Place a few sugar crystals on your dried tongue. Do *not* close your mouth. Time how long it takes to taste the sugar.

_____ sec.

Why couldn't you taste the sugar immediately?

_____

_____

OBJECTIVE 11 List several factors that influence taste.

Activity 16

Examining the Combined Effects of Smell, Texture, and Temperature on Taste

Effects of Smell and Texture

1. Ask the subject to sit with eyes closed and to pinch his or her nostrils shut.

2. Using a paper plate, obtain samples of the food items listed in the Activity 16 chart. At no time should the subject be allowed to see the foods being tested.

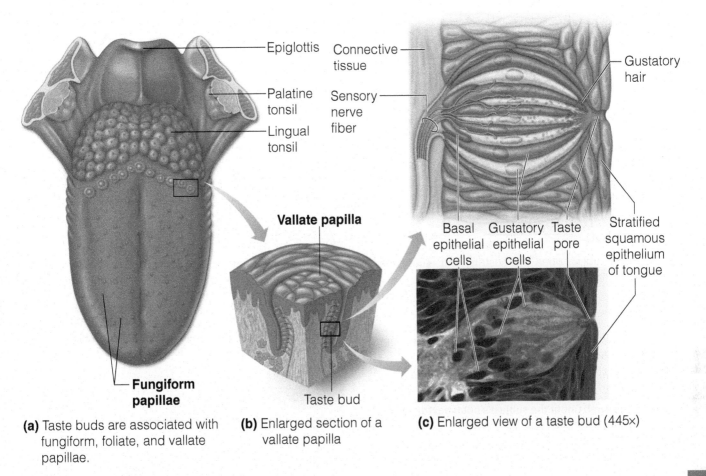

(a) Taste buds are associated with fungiform, foliate, and vallate papillae.

(b) Enlarged section of a vallate papilla

(c) Enlarged view of a taste bud (445×)

Figure 17.16 Location and structure of taste buds. See also Plate 17 in the Histology Atlas.

3. Use an out-of-sequence order of food testing. For each test, place a cube of food in the subject's mouth, and ask him or her to identify the food by using the following sequence of activities:

• First, move the food around in the mouth with the tongue.

• Second, chew the food.

• Third, if the first two techniques and the taste sense do not yield a positive identification, ask the subject to release the pinched nostrils and to continue chewing with the nostrils open to see whether he or she can identify the food.

Record the results in the Activity 16 chart by checking the appropriate column.

Was the sense of smell equally important in all cases?

_____

Where did it seem to be important, and why?

_____

_____

17

Activity 16: Method of Identification				
Food	Texture only	Chewing with nostrils pinched	Chewing with nostrils open	Identification not made
Cheese				
Apple				
Banana				
Dried prunes				
Hard-cooked egg white				

Text continues on next page. →

Effect of Olfactory Stimulation

There is no question that what is commonly called taste depends heavily on the sense of smell, particularly for strongly scented substances. The following experiments should illustrate this fact.

1. Obtain paper cups; vials of oil of wintergreen, peppermint, and cloves; and some fresh cotton-tipped swabs. Ask the subject to sit so that he or she cannot see which vial is being used and to dry the tongue and close the nostrils.

2. Apply a drop of one of the oils to the subject's tongue. Can he or she distinguish the flavor?

_____

3. Have the subject open the nostrils, and record the change in sensation he or she reports.

_____

4. Have the subject rinse the mouth well with water and dry the tongue.

5. Prepare two swabs, each with one of the two remaining oils.

6. Hold one swab under the subject's open nostrils while touching the second swab to the tongue.

Record the reported sensations. _____

_____

_____

_____

7. Dispose of the used swabs and paper towels in the autoclave bag before continuing.

Which sense, taste or smell, appears to be more important for identifying a strongly flavored volatile substance?

_____

Effect of Temperature

In addition to the roles that olfaction and food texture play in determining our taste sensations, the temperature of foods also helps determine whether we appreciate or even taste the food. To illustrate this, have your partner hold some chipped ice on the tongue for approximately a minute and then close his or her eyes. Immediately place any of the foods previously identified in his or her mouth, and ask for an identification.

Results? _____

_____

_____

REVIEW SHEET
The Special Senses

Name _____ Lab Time/Date _____

The Eye and Vision: Anatomy

1. Several accessory eye structures contribute to the formation of tears and/or help lubricate the eyeball. Match the described accessory structures with their secretion by choosing answers from the key.

   Key: conjunctiva   lacrimal glands   tarsal glands

   _____ 1. mucus

   _____ 2. oil

   _____ 3. salt solution

2. The eyeball is wrapped in adipose tissue within the orbit. What is the function of the adipose tissue?

   _____

3. Why may it be necessary to blow one's nose after crying? _____

   _____

4. What is a sty? _____

   _____

   What is conjunctivitis? _____

   _____

5. Which seven bones form the bony orbit? (If you can't remember, check a skull or your textbook.)

   _____   _____   _____

   _____   _____   _____

   _____

6. Identify the lettered structures on the diagram by matching each letter with one of the terms listed below.

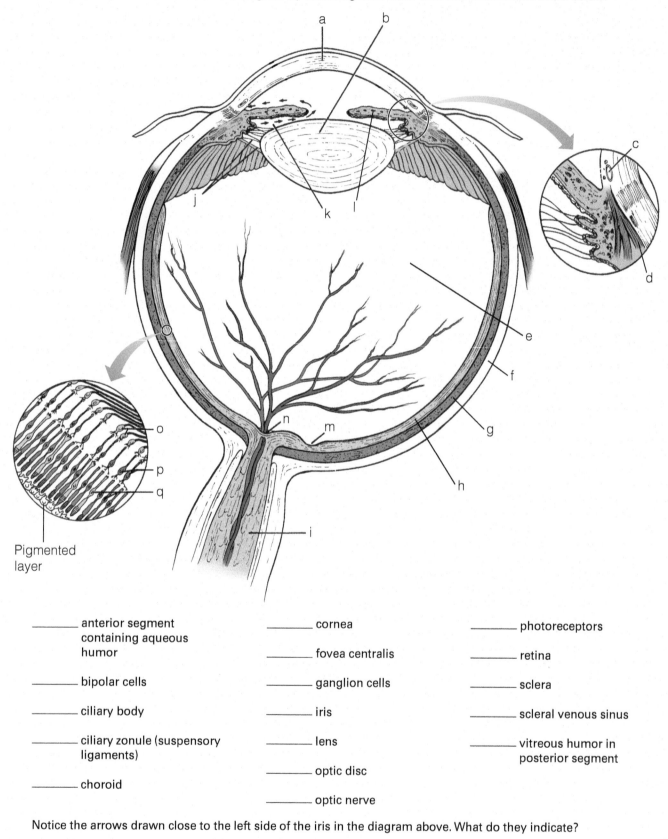

Pigmented layer

_____ anterior segment containing aqueous humor

_____ bipolar cells

_____ ciliary body

_____ ciliary zonule (suspensory ligaments)

_____ choroid

_____ cornea

_____ fovea centralis

_____ ganglion cells

_____ iris

_____ lens

_____ optic disc

_____ optic nerve

_____ photoreceptors

_____ retina

_____ sclera

_____ scleral venous sinus

_____ vitreous humor in posterior segment

Notice the arrows drawn close to the left side of the iris in the diagram above. What do they indicate?

_____

_____

_____

7. Match the key responses with the descriptive statements that follow.

Key: aqueous humor   cornea   optic disc   scleral venous sinus
          choroid   fovea centralis   retina   vitreous humor
          ciliary body   iris   sclera
          ciliary zonule   lens
          (suspensory ligament)

_____ 1. attaches the lens to the ciliary body

_____ 2. fluid filling the anterior segment of the eye

_____ 3. the blind spot

_____ 4. contains muscle that controls the size of the pupil

_____ 5. drains the aqueous humor from the eye

_____ 6. layer containing rods and cones

_____ 7. substance occupying the posterior segment of the eyeball

_____ 8. forms most of the pigmented vascular layer

_____ 9. tiny pit; contains only cones

_____ 10. important light-bending structure of the eye; shape can be modified

_____ 11. anterior transparent part of the fibrous layer—your "window on the world"

_____ 12. the white of the eye

8. The intrinsic eye muscles are under the control of which of the following? (Circle the correct response.)

autonomic nervous system   somatic nervous system

Dissection of the Cow (Sheep) Eye

9. What modification of the choroid that is *not* present in humans is found in the cow eye?

_____

What is its function? _____

_____

10. Describe the appearance of the retina. _____

_____

At what point is it attached to the posterior aspect of the eyeball? _____

Visual Tests and Experiments

11. Use terms from the key to complete the statements concerning near and distance vision. (Some terms may be used more than once.)

    Key: contracted   decreased   increased   lax   relaxed   taut

    During distance vision: The ciliary muscle is _____, the ciliary zonule (suspensory ligament) is _____, the convexity of the lens is _____, and light refraction is _____. During close vision: The ciliary muscle is _____, the ciliary zonule (suspensory ligament) is _____, lens convexity is _____, and light refraction is _____.

12. Explain why the part of the image hitting the blind spot is not seen. _____

13. Match the terms in column B with the descriptions in column A:

	Column A	Column B
_____	1. light bending	accommodation
_____	2. ability to focus for close (under 20 ft) vision	astigmatism
_____	3. normal vision	convergence
_____	4. inability to focus well on close objects (farsightedness)	emmetropia
_____	5. nearsightedness	hyperopia
_____	6. blurred vision due to unequal curvatures of the lens or cornea	myopia
_____	7. medial movement of the eyes during focusing on close objects	refraction

14. Record your Snellen eye test results below:

    Left eye (without glasses) _____ (with glasses) _____

    Right eye (without glasses) _____ (with glasses) _____

    Is your visual acuity normal, less than normal, or better than normal? _____

    Explain. _____

    _____

    Explain why each eye is tested separately when the Snellen eye chart is used. _____

    _____

    Explain 20/40 vision. _____

    _____

Explain 20/10 vision. _____

_____

15. Define *astigmatism:* _____

_____

16. Record the distance of your near point of accommodation as tested in the laboratory:

right eye _____ left eye _____

Is your near point within the normal range for your age? _____

17. How can you explain the fact that we see a great range of colors even though only three cone types exist?

_____

_____

18. In the experiment on the convergence reflex, what happened to the position of the eyeballs as the object was moved

closer to the subject's eyes? _____

What extrinsic eye muscles control the movement of the eyes during this reflex? _____

What is the value of this reflex? _____

_____

If these muscles were unable to function, what would be the visual result?

_____

19. Many college students struggling through mountainous reading assignments are told that they need glasses for "eyestrain." Why does looking at close objects cause more strain on the extrinsic and intrinsic eye muscles than does looking at far objects?

_____

_____

The Ear and Hearing and Balance: Anatomy

20. Select the terms from column B that apply to the column A descriptions. (Some terms are used more than once.)

Column A

Column B

_____, _____

anvil (incus)

_____ 1. collectively called the auditory ossicles

auricle

_____, _____

cochlea

_____, _____ 2. ear structures involved
with balance

endolymph

external acoustic meatus

_____ 3. transmits sound vibrations to the ossicles

hammer (malleus)

_____ 4. three circular passages, each in a different
plane of space

oval window

_____ 5. transmits the vibratory motion of the stirrup to
the fluid in the inner ear

perilymph

_____ 6. passage between the throat and the tympanic
cavity

pharyngotympanic (auditory) tube

round window

_____ 7. fluid contained within the membranous
labyrinth

semicircular canals

stirrup (stapes)

_____ 8. involved in equalizing pressure in the middle
ear with atmospheric pressure

tympanic membrane

vestibule

21. Identify all indicated structures and ear regions that are provided with leader lines or brackets in the following diagram.

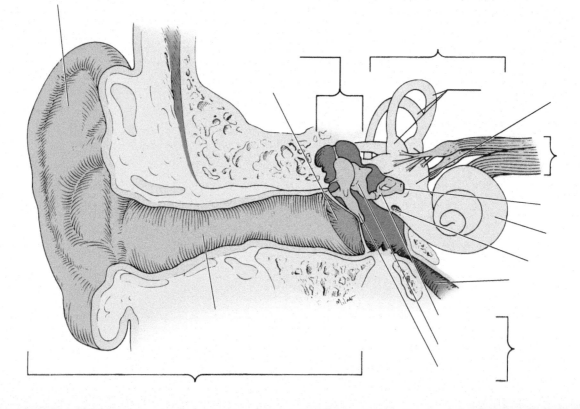

22. Match the membranous labyrinth structures listed in column B with the descriptive statements in column A. (Some terms are used more than once.)

Column A	Column B
_____ 1. contains the spiral organ of Corti	ampulla
_____, _____ 2. sites of the maculae	basilar membrane
_____ 3. hair cells of the spiral organ of Corti rest on this membrane	cochlear duct
	cochlear nerve
_____ 4. gel-like membrane overlying the hair cells of the spiral organ of Corti	cupula
_____ 5. contains the crista ampullaris	otoliths
_____, _____	saccule
_____ 6. function in static equilibrium	semicircular ducts
_____, _____, _____,	tectorial membrane
_____ 7. function in dynamic equilibrium	utricle
_____ 8. carries auditory information to the brain	vestibular nerve
_____ 9. gelatinous cap overlying hair cells of the crista ampullaris	
_____ 10. grains of calcium carbonate in the maculae	

23. Describe how sounds of different frequency (pitch) are differentiated in the cochlea. _____

_____

_____

24. Explain the role of the endolymph of the semicircular canals in activating the receptors during angular motion.

_____

_____

_____

25. Explain the role of the otoliths in perception of static equilibrium (head position). _____

_____

_____

_____

Hearing and Balance Tests

26. Was the auditory acuity measurement made during the experiment on page 211 the same or different for both ears?

    _____ What factors might account for a difference in the acuity of the two ears?

    _____

    _____

27. During the sound localization experiment on page 212, in which position(s) was the sound least easily located?

    _____

    How can this observation be explained? _____

    _____

28. When the tuning fork handle was pressed to your forehead during the Weber test, where did the sound seem to originate?

    _____

    Where did it seem to originate when one ear was plugged with cotton? _____

    How do sound waves reach the cochlea when conduction deafness is present? _____

    _____

29. The Rinne test evaluates an individual's ability to hear sounds conducted by air or bone. Which is typical of normal

    hearing? _____

30. Define *nystagmus:* _____

    _____

31. What does the Romberg test determine? _____

    _____

    Was the degree of sway greater with the eyes open or closed? _____

    Why? _____

    _____

32. Normal balance, or equilibrium, depends on input from a number of sensory receptors. Name them.

    _____

Chemical Senses: Location and Anatomy of Olfactory and Taste Receptors

33. Describe the cellular makeup and the location of the olfactory epithelium. _____

    _____

34. Name three sites where receptors for taste are found, and circle the predominant site:

_____, _____, and

_____

35. Describe the cellular makeup and arrangement of a taste bud. (Use a diagram, if helpful.)

_____

_____

Taste and Smell Experiments

36. Taste and smell receptors are both classified as _____ because they both respond to

_____

37. Why is it impossible to taste substances if the tongue is dry? _____

_____

38. Name three factors that influence our appreciation of foods. Substantiate each choice with an example from the laboratory experience.

1. _____   Substantiation _____

   _____

   _____

2. _____   Substantiation _____

   _____

   _____

3. _____   Substantiation _____

   _____

   _____

Expand on your explanation and choices by explaining why a cold, greasy hamburger is unappetizing to most people.

_____

_____

39. How palatable is food when you have a cold? _____

Explain. _____

_____

Functional Anatomy of the Endocrine Glands

Pre-Lab Quiz

1. Define *hormone*. _____

2. Circle True or False. The anterior pituitary gland is also referred to as the master endocrine gland because it controls the activity of many other endocrine glands.

3. The pancreas produces two hormones that are responsible for regulating blood sugar levels. Name the hormone that increases blood glucose levels. _____

4. Circle True or False. The gonads are considered to be both endocrine and exocrine glands.

5. Circle the correct term. <u>Pancreatic islets</u> / <u>Acinar cells</u> form the endocrine portion of the pancreas.

T
he **endocrine system** is the second major controlling system of the body. Acting with the nervous system, it helps coordinate and integrate the activity of the body's cells. However, the nervous system uses nerve impulses to bring about rapid control, whereas the more slowly acting endocrine system employs chemical "messengers," or **hormones,** which are released into the blood to be transported throughout the body. The major endocrine organs include the *pituitary gland, thyroid gland, parathyroid glands, adrenal glands, pancreas, gonads (ovaries and testes), thymus,* and *pineal gland.*

Although some hormone-producing glands (the anterior pituitary, thyroid, adrenals, parathyroids) have a purely endocrine function, others (the pancreas and gonads) have "mixed" functions—both endocrine and exocrine. In addition, there are varied numbers of hormone-producing cells within the intestine, stomach, kidney, and placenta, organs whose functions are primarily nonendocrine. Only the major endocrine organs are considered here.

Gross Anatomy and Basic Function of the Endocrine Glands

OBJECTIVE 1 List the hormones produced by the major endocrine organs, and discuss the general function of each. Additionally, describe the major pathology resulting from hyper- or hyposecretion of each.

Pituitary Gland

The *pituitary gland* is located in the sella turcica of the sphenoid bone. It has two functional areas, the **posterior pituitary** (nervous tissue) and the **anterior pituitary** (glandular tissue).

Posterior Pituitary Hormones

The posterior pituitary is not an endocrine gland in a strict sense because it does not produce the hormones it releases. Instead, it stores two hormones transported to it along axons from the hypothalamus. One of these hormones, **oxytocin,** stimulates powerful uterine contractions during birth and causes milk ejection in the lactating mother. The second, **antidiuretic hormone (ADH),** causes the kidneys to reabsorb more water from the forming urine, thereby reducing urine output, conserving body water, and increasing blood pressure.

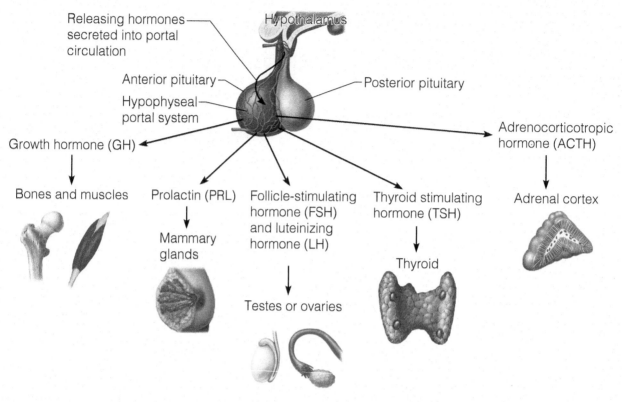

Figure 18.1 Hormones of the anterior pituitary and their major target organs. Neurons of the hypothalamus secrete releasing hormones, which stimulate secretion of hormones from the anterior pituitary. The releasing hormones are secreted into a capillary network that connects via portal veins to a second capillary bed in the anterior lobe of the pituitary gland.

Anterior Pituitary Hormones

The anterior pituitary, or adenohypophysis, secretes a number of hormones (**Figure 18.1**). Four of these are **tropic** hormones. Tropic hormones stimulate target organs that are also endocrine glands to secrete their hormones. Target organ hormones then produce their effects on other body organs and tissues. The tropic hormones include the following:

- The **gonadotropins—follicle-stimulating hormone (FSH)** and **luteinizing hormone (LH)**—regulate gamete production and hormonal activity of the gonads (ovaries and testes). (See Exercise 27.)

- **Adrenocorticotropic hormone (ACTH)** regulates the endocrine activity of the cortex portion of the adrenal gland.

- **Thyroid-stimulating hormone (TSH),** also called **thyrotropic hormone,** influences the growth and activity of the thyroid gland.

The other hormones produced by the anterior pituitary are not directly involved in regulating other endocrine glands of the body:

- **Growth hormone (GH),** a general metabolic hormone, plays an important role in determining body size. It exerts its main effects on muscle and long bone growth.

- **Prolactin (PRL)** stimulates breast development and promotes and maintains milk production by the mother's breast after childbirth. Its function in males is unknown.

The anterior pituitary controls the activity of so many other endocrine glands that it has often been called the *master*

endocrine gland. However, the anterior pituitary is not all-powerful, because release of its hormones is controlled by *releasing* or *inhibiting hormones* produced by the hypothalamus. These hypothalamic hormones are liberated into the blood of the *portal circulation,* which connects the blood supplies of the hypothalamus and anterior pituitary.

Thyroid Gland

The *thyroid gland* is composed of two lobes joined by a central mass, or isthmus. It is located in the throat, just inferior to the Adam's apple. It produces two major hormones, thyroid hormone and calcitonin.

Thyroid hormone is actually two active hormones—T_4 (thyroxine) and T_3 (triiodothyronine). Its primary function is to control the rate of body metabolism and cellular oxidation, so thyroid hormone affects virtually every cell in the body.

Calcitonin decreases blood calcium levels by stimulating calcium deposit in the bones. It acts antagonistically to parathyroid hormone, the hormonal product of the parathyroid glands.

Activity 1

Examining the Microscopic Structure of the Thyroid Gland

1. Go to station 1 at the demonstration area and scan the thyroid under low power, noting the **follicles,** spherical sacs containing a pink-stained material *(colloid).* Stored

T_3 and T_4 are attached to the protein colloidal material stored in the follicles as **thyroglobulin** and are released gradually to the blood. The **parafollicular cells** you see between the follicles produce calcitonin.

When the thyroid gland is actively secreting, the follicles appear small, and the colloidal material has a ruffled border. When the thyroid is hypoactive or inactive, the follicles are large and plump, and the follicular epithelium appears squamouslike. What is the physiological state of the tissue you have been viewing?

_____

_____

Activity 2

Palpating the Thyroid Gland

Try to palpate your thyroid gland by placing your fingers against your windpipe. As you swallow, the thyroid gland will move up and down on the sides and front of the windpipe.

Parathyroid Glands

The *parathyroid glands* are embedded in the posterior surface of the thyroid gland. Typically, there are two small oval glands on each lobe, but there may be more, and some may be located in other regions of the neck. They secrete **parathyroid hormone (PTH),** the most important regulator of calcium phosphate ion homeostasis of the blood. When blood calcium levels decrease below a certain critical level, the parathyroids release PTH, which causes release of calcium from bone matrix and prods the kidney to reabsorb more calcium (and less phosphate) from the filtrate. If blood calcium levels fall too low, **tetany,** prolonged muscle spasm, can cause respiratory paralysis and may be fatal.

Adrenal Glands

The two bean-shaped *adrenal,* or *suprarenal, glands* are located atop the kidneys. Anatomically, the **adrenal medulla** develops from neural tissue and is directly controlled by sympathetic nervous system neurons. The medullary cells respond to this stimulation by releasing **epinephrine** (80%) or **norepinephrine** (20%), which act with the sympathetic nervous system to produce the "fight-or-flight" response to stressors.

The **adrenal cortex** produces three major groups of steroid hormones, collectively called **corticosteroids.** The **mineralocorticoids,** chiefly **aldosterone,** regulate water and electrolyte balance in the extracellular fluids, mainly by regulating sodium ion reabsorption by kidney tubules. The **glucocorticoids** (cortisone and cortisol) help the body to resist long-term stressors.

The **sex hormones** produced by the adrenal cortex are chiefly androgens (male sex hormones), but some estrogens (female sex hormones) are produced as well. The sex hormones are produced throughout life in relatively insignificant amounts.

Pancreas

The *pancreas,* located partially behind the stomach in the abdomen, acts both as an exocrine and an endocrine gland.

It produces digestive enzymes, its exocrine product, as well as insulin and glucagon, important hormones concerned with regulating blood sugar levels.

Elevated blood glucose levels stimulate release of **insulin,** which decreases blood sugar levels, primarily by accelerating the uptake of glucose into the body cells. The common disease diabetes mellitus is caused either by insufficient insulin release or by insulin resistance.

Glucagon acts antagonistically to insulin. Its release is stimulated by low blood glucose levels, and its action is basically hyperglycemic. It stimulates the liver, its primary target organ, to break down its glycogen stores to glucose and to release the glucose to the blood.

Activity 3

Examining the Microscopic Structure of the Pancreas to Identify Alpha and Beta Cells

1. At station 2 at the demonstration area, observe pancreas tissue under low power to identify the roughly circular **pancreatic islets** *(islets of Langerhans),* the endocrine portions of the pancreas. The islets are scattered amid the more numerous acinar cells and stain differently (usually lighter), which makes their identification possible. (See Plate 38 in the Histology Atlas.)

2. Examine the cells of an islet under high power. Notice that the islet cells are densely packed and have no definite arrangement. In contrast, the cuboidal acinar cells are arranged around secretory ducts. The pancreas tissue you are viewing has been treated with special stains so that it is possible to distinguish the **alpha cells,** which produce glucagon, from the **beta cells,** which synthesize insulin. With these specific stains, the beta cells are larger and stain gray-blue, and the alpha cells are smaller and appear bright pink. What is the product of the alpha cells?

OBJECTIVE 2   Describe and explain the effects of hyperinsulinism.

Activity 4

Observing the Effects of Hyperinsulinism

Many people with diabetes mellitus need injections of insulin to maintain blood sugar (glucose) homeostasis. Adequate levels of blood glucose are essential for proper functioning of the nervous system; thus, insulin administration must be carefully controlled. If blood glucose levels fall sharply, the patient will go into insulin shock.

A small fish will be used to demonstrate the effects of hyperinsulinism. Because the action of insulin on the fish parallels that in the human, this experiment should provide valid information concerning its effect in humans.

1. Prepare two finger bowls. Using a wax marker, mark one A and the other B. To finger bowl A, add 100 ml of the commercial insulin solution. To finger bowl B, add 200 ml of 20% glucose solution.

Text continues on next page. →

18

2. Place a small fish in finger bowl A, and observe its actions carefully as the insulin diffuses into its bloodstream through the capillary circulation of its gills.

Approximately how long did it take for the fish to become comatose?

_____

What types of activity did you observe in the fish before it became comatose?

_____

_____

3. When the fish is comatose, carefully transfer it to finger bowl B, and observe its actions. What happens to the fish after it is transferred?

_____

_____

_____

Approximately how long did it take for this recovery?

_____

4. After you have made and recorded all observations, carefully return the fish to the aquarium.

The Gonads

The female *gonads,* or *ovaries,* are paired, almond-sized organs located in the pelvic cavity. In addition to producing the female sex cells (ova), they produce two groups of steroid hormones, estrogens and progesterone. The endocrine and exocrine functions of the ovaries do not begin until puberty, when the anterior pituitary gonadotropic hormones prod the ovary into action. The result is rhythmic ovarian cycles in which ova develop and hormone levels rise and fall. **Estrogens** are responsible for development of the secondary sex characteristics of the female at puberty (primarily maturation of the reproductive organs and development of the breasts) and act with progesterone to bring about cyclic changes of the uterine lining called the menstrual cycle. The estrogens also help prepare the mammary glands to produce milk (lactation).

Progesterone, as already noted, acts with estrogen to bring about the menstrual cycle. During pregnancy it quiets the uterine muscle and helps to prepare the breast tissue for lactation.

The paired oval *testes* of the male are suspended in a pouchlike sac, the scrotum, outside the pelvic cavity. Besides the male sex cells (sperm), the testes produce the male sex hormone, **testosterone.** Testosterone promotes the maturation of the reproductive system accessory structures, brings about the development of the secondary sex characteristics, and is responsible for the male sexual drive, or libido. As in females, the endocrine and exocrine functions of the testes begin at puberty.

Thymus

The *thymus* is situated in the superior thorax, posterior to the sternum and overlying the heart. It is large in the infant, begins to atrophy at puberty, and by old age it is relatively inconspicuous. The thymus produces a hormone called **thymosin,** which helps direct the maturation of a unique population of white blood cells called T lymphocytes or T cells. T lymphocytes are responsible for the cellular immunity aspect of body defense; that is, rejection of foreign grafts, tumors, or virus-infected cells.

Pineal Gland

The small, pinecone-shaped *pineal gland* hangs from the roof of the third ventricle of the brain. Its major endocrine product is **melatonin,** which appears to be involved in the sleep-wake cycle. Melatonin levels peak at night, making us drowsy, and are lowest around noon. Recent evidence suggests that melatonin has anti-aging properties. Melatonin appears to play a role in the production of antioxidants.

OBJECTIVE 3 Identify and name the major endocrine glands when provided with an appropriate diagram.

Activity 5

Identifying the Endocrine Organs

Locate the endocrine organs on **Figure 18.2**, and complete the labeling of that figure. Also locate these organs on the anatomical charts or torso.

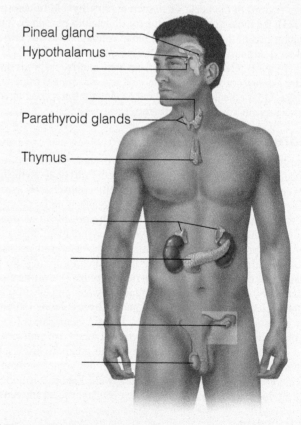

Pineal gland
Hypothalamus

Parathyroid glands

Thymus

Figure 18.2 Human endocrine organs.

REVIEW SHEET
Functional Anatomy
of the Endocrine Glands

Name _____ Lab Time/Date _____

Gross Anatomy and Basic Function of the Endocrine Glands

1. The endocrine and nervous systems are major regulating systems of the body. However, the nervous system has been compared to an airmail delivery system, and the endocrine system to the Pony Express. Briefly explain this comparison.

_____

_____

2. Define *hormone:* _____

_____

3. Identify the endocrine organ described by the following statements:

_____ 1. located in the throat; bilobed gland connected by an isthmus

_____ 2. found atop the kidney

_____ 3. a mixed gland, located close to the stomach and small intestine

_____ 4. found in the roof of the third ventricle of the brain

_____ 5. ride "horseback" on the thyroid gland

_____ 6. found in the pelvic cavity of the female, concerned with ova and female hormone production

4. Although the pituitary gland is often referred to as the master gland of the body, the hypothalamus exerts some control over the pituitary gland. How does the hypothalamus control both anterior and posterior pituitary functioning?

_____

_____

5. Name the hormone whose production in *inadequate* amounts results in the following conditions. (Use your textbook as necessary.)

_____ 1. poor development of secondary sex characteristics

_____ 2. tetany

_____ 3. diabetes mellitus

_____ 4. abnormally small stature, normal proportions

_____ 5. myxedema (a lower-than-normal metabolic rate)

6. For each statement describing hormonal effects, identify the hormone(s) involved by choosing a number from key A, and note the hormone's site of production with a letter from key B. More than one hormone may be involved in some cases.

Key A:

1. ACTH
2. ADH
3. aldosterone
4. calcitonin
5. epinephrine
6. estrogens
7. FSH
8. glucagon
9. GH
10. insulin

11. LH
12. oxytocin
13. progesterone
14. prolactin
15. PTH
16. testosterone
17. T$_4$/T$_3$
18. TSH
19. thymosin

Key B:

a. adrenal cortex
b. adrenal medulla
c. anterior pituitary
d. hypothalamus
e. ovaries
f. pancreas
g. parathyroid glands
h. posterior pituitary
i. testes
j. thyroid gland
k. thymus

_____, _____ 1. basal metabolism hormone

_____, _____ and _____, _____ 2. regulate blood calcium levels

_____, _____ 3. helps mature T lymphocytes

_____, _____ 4. drive development of secondary sexual characteristics

_____, _____; _____, _____; _____, _____; and _____, _____ 5. regulate the function of another endocrine gland

_____, _____ 6. mimic the sympathetic nervous system

_____, _____ and _____, _____ 7. regulate blood glucose levels; produced by the same "mixed" gland

_____, _____ and _____, _____ 8. directly responsible for regulating the menstrual cycle

_____, _____ and _____, _____ 9. help maintain salt and water balance in the body fluids

_____, _____ 10. involved in milk ejection

Observing the Effects of Hyperinsulinism

7. Briefly explain what was happening within the fish's body when the fish was immersed in the insulin solution.

_____

_____

8. What is the mechanism of the recovery process you observed? _____

_____

9. What would you do to help a friend who had accidentally taken an overdose of insulin? _____

_____ Why? _____

_____

10. What is a glucose tolerance test? (Use an appropriate reference, as necessary, to answer this question.)

_____

_____

Materials

☐ Models and charts of blood cells

☐ Safety glasses (student-provided)

☐ Demonstration area: Five stations of microscopes set up under oil of human blood smears. A pointer to each of the formed elements in order:

Station 1: Neutrophil pointed out; surrounded by erythrocytes

Station 2: Eosinophil

Station 3: Basophil

Station 4: Lymphocyte

Station 5: Monocyte

General Supply Area*

☐ Plasma (obtained from an animal hospital or prepared by centrifuging animal [e.g., cattle or sheep] blood obtained from a biological supply house)

☐ Wide-range pH paper

☐ Test tubes and test tube racks

☐ Heparinized animal blood (if desired by the instructor) obtained from a biological supply house or animal hospital (e.g., dog blood) or EDTA-treated red cells (reference cells[†]) with blood type labels obscured (available from Immunocor, Inc.)

☐ Clean microscope slides

☐ Sterile lancets

☐ Alcohol swabs (wipes)

☐ Absorbent cotton balls

☐ Disposable gloves

☐ Bucket or large beaker containing 10% household bleach solution for slide and glassware disposal

☐ Spray bottles containing 10% bleach solution

☐ Disposable autoclave bag

Because many blood tests are to be conducted in this exercise, it is advisable to set up a number of appropriately labeled supply areas for the various tests, as designated next.

Hematocrit Supply Area

☐ Heparinized capillary tubes

☐ Microhematocrit centrifuge and reading gauge (if the reading gauge is not available, millimeter ruler may be used)

Text continues on next page. →

Pre-Lab Quiz

1. Circle True or False. There are no special precautions that I need to observe when performing today's lab.

2. Three types of formed elements found in blood include erythrocytes, leukocytes, and:
   a. electrolytes
   b. fibers
   c. platelets
   d. sodium salts

3. The least numerous but largest of all agranulocytes is the:
   a. basophil
   b. lymphocyte
   c. monocyte
   d. neutrophil

4. _____ are the leukocytes responsible for releasing histamine and other mediators of inflammation.
   a. Basophils
   b. Eosinophils
   c. Monocytes
   d. Neutrophils

5. Circle the correct term. When determining the hematocrit / hemoglobin concentration, you will centrifuge whole blood in order to allow the formed elements to sink to the bottom of the sample.

6. Circle True or False. If an individual is transfused with the wrong type blood, the recipient's antibodies react with the donor's antigens, eventually clumping and hemolyzing the donated RBCs.

In this exercise, you will study plasma and formed elements of blood and conduct various hematologic tests. These tests are useful diagnostic tools because blood composition reflects the status of many body functions and malfunctions.

⚠ Your instructor will decide whether to use animal blood for testing or to have students test their own blood in accordance with the educational goals of the student group. For example, for students in the nursing or laboratory technician curricula, learning how to safely handle human blood or other human wastes is essential. If human blood is being tested—yours or that obtained from a clinical agency—wear gloves and safety glasses, and *observe all precautions provided in your text for disposal of human waste*. Immerse all soiled glassware in household bleach solution immediately after use, and place all disposable items (lancets, cotton balls, alcohol swabs, etc.) in a disposable autoclave bag so that they can be sterilized before disposal.

Composition of Blood

OBJECTIVE 1 State the average percentage of plasma and formed elements in whole blood.

Blood is a rather viscous substance that varies from bright red to a dull brick red, depending on the amount of oxygen it is carrying. The circulatory system of the average adult contains about 5.5 liters of blood.

Blood is classified as a type of connective tissue because it consists of a nonliving fluid matrix (**plasma**) in which living cells and cell fragments (**formed elements**) are suspended. The fibers typical of a connective tissue matrix become visible in blood only when clotting occurs. They then appear as fibrin threads, which form the framework for clot formation.

(Materials list continued)
☐ Capillary tube sealer or modeling clay

Hemoglobin Determination Supply Area
☐ Tallquist hemoglobin scales and test paper

Coagulation Time Supply Area
☐ Capillary tubes (nonheparinized)
☐ Fine triangular file

Blood Typing Supply Area
☐ Blood typing sera (anti-A, anti-B, and anti-Rh [D])
☐ Rh typing box

☐ Wax marker
☐ Toothpicks
☐ Clean microscope slides
☐ Medicine dropper

Notes to the Instructor: *Bloodstained glassware is to be soaked for 2 hours (or longer) in 10% bleach solution and then drained. Glassware and the disposable autoclave bag are to be autoclaved for 15 min at 121°C and 15 pounds pressure to ensure sterility. After autoclaving, the disposable autoclave bag may be discarded in any disposal facility and the glassware washed with laboratory detergent and reprepared for use. These instructions apply as well to any bloodstained glassware or disposable items used in other experimental procedures.

† The blood in these kits (each containing four blood cell types—A1, A2, B, and O—individually supplied in 10-ml vials) is used to calibrate cell counters and other automated clinical laboratory equipment. This blood has been carefully screened and can be safely used by students for blood typing and determining hematocrits. It is not usable for hemoglobin determinations or coagulation studies.

More than 100 different substances are dissolved or suspended in plasma (**Figure 19.1**), which is over 90% water. The composition of the blood varies continuously as cells remove or add substances to the blood. Three types of formed elements are present in blood. The most numerous are the **erythrocytes,** or **red blood cells (RBCs),** which are literally sacs of hemoglobin molecules that transport oxygen (and a small amount of carbon dioxide). **Leukocytes,** or **white blood cells (WBCs),** are part of the body's nonspecific defenses and the immune system, and **platelets** function in hemostasis (blood clot formation). Formed elements normally account for about 45% of whole blood, plasma for the remaining 55%.

O B J E C T I V E   2   Describe the composition and functions of plasma.

Activity 1

Determining the Physical Characteristics of Plasma

Go to the general supply area, and carefully pour a few milliliters of plasma into a test tube. Also obtain some wide-range pH paper, and then return to your laboratory bench to make the following simple observations.

pH of Plasma

Test the pH of the plasma with wide-range pH paper. Record the pH observed.

_____

Color and Clarity of Plasma

Hold the test tube up to a source of natural light. Note and record its color and degree of transparency. Is it clear, translucent, or opaque?

Color _____

Degree of transparency _____

Consistency

While wearing gloves, dip your finger and thumb into the plasma, and then press them firmly together for a few seconds. Gently pull them apart. How would you describe the consistency of plasma? Slippery, watery, sticky, or granular? Record your observations.

_____

O B J E C T I V E   3   Identify each of the formed elements when presented with a microscopic preparation or a photo, and cite their relative percentages and functions.

Activity 2

Examining the Formed Elements of Blood Microscopically

In this section, you observe blood cells on already prepared (purchased) blood slides. Go to the demonstration area where several formed elements are pointed out. Examine each slide in order as you read the following descriptions of cell types, and find each one on Figure 19.1 and in Plates 50–55 in the Histology Atlas.

Erythrocytes

At station 1, observe the erythrocytes, the cells that are the most numerous on this slide (see Plate 50 in the Histology Atlas). Erythrocytes average 7.5 μm in diameter and vary in color from a salmon red to pale pink, depending on the effectiveness of the stain. Notice that they have a biconcave disc shape and appear paler in the center than at the edge.

Red blood cells differ from the other blood cells in that they are anucleate when mature. As a result, they are unable to reproduce and have a limited life span of 100 to 120 days, after which they begin to fragment.

19

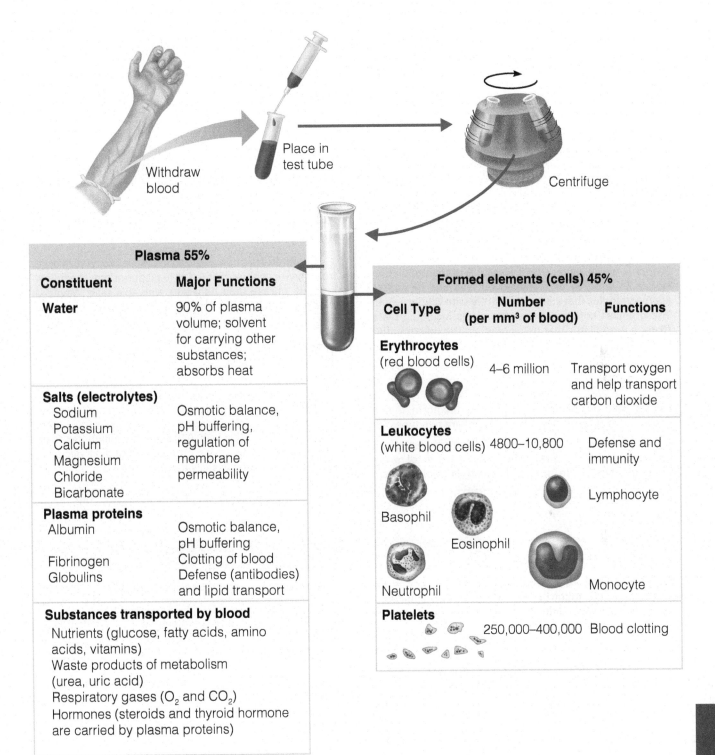

Figure 19.1 The composition of blood.

Leukocytes

Leukocytes, or white blood cells, are more typical cells than the erythrocytes because they contain a nucleus. Much less numerous than the red blood cells, white blood cells are protective, pathogen-destroying cells that are transported to all parts of the body in the blood or lymph. They are classified into two major groups, depending on whether or not they contain conspicuous granules in their cytoplasm.

Granulocytes make up the first group. The granules in their cytoplasm stain differentially with Wright's stain, and they have peculiar nuclei, which often consist of lobes of nuclear material connected by thin strands of nucleoplasm. There are three types of granulocytes:

• **Neutrophil:** Still at the first microscope, turn your attention to the cell at the end of the pointer, a neutrophil. Neutrophils represent 50% to 70% of the leukocyte population.

Text continues on next page. →

19

Typically their nucleus consists of three to seven lobes, and their pale lilac cytoplasm contains very fine cytoplasmic granules, which take up both the acidic (red) and basic (blue) dyes (*neutrophil* = neutral loving). Neutrophils function as active phagocytes, and their number increases explosively during acute infections. Compare to views in Plate 51 in the Histology Atlas.

- **Eosinophil:** Go to station 2 to study the eosinophil, which represents 2% to 4% of the leukocytes. Observe its nucleus, which is generally figure-8 or bilobed in shape, and its large cytoplasmic granules (elaborate lysosomes) that stain red-orange with Wright's stain. Eosinophils increase in number during allergies and parasite infections. Compare to Plate 54 in the Histology Atlas.

- **Basophil:** At station 3, view the rarest of the WBCs, a basophil, which represents 0.5% to 1% of the population. Notice its large U- or S-shaped nucleus and its coarse, sparse granules that stain deep purple with Wright's stain. The granules contain several chemicals including histamine, a vasodilator that helps mediate the inflammatory response. Compare to Plate 55 in the Histology Atlas.

Agranulocytes, the second group, contain no observable cytoplasmic granules. Although found in the bloodstream, the WBCs are much more abundant in lymphoid tissues. Their nuclei tend to be closer to the norm, that is, spherical, oval, or kidney-shaped. There are two types:

- **Lymphocyte:** At station 4, observe the smallest of the leukocytes, which is approximately the size of a red blood cell. Notice the large dark blue to purple, generally spherical or slightly indented nucleus. Sparse cytoplasm appears as a thin blue rim around the nucleus. Lymphocytes, which function as "warriors" of the immune system, represent 25% to 45% of the WBC population. Compare to Plate 52 in the Histology Atlas.

- **Monocyte:** At station 5, view a monocyte, the largest of the leukocytes, which is approximately twice the size of red blood cells. Monocytes represent 3% to 8% of leukocytes. The dark blue nucleus is generally kidney-shaped, and its abundant cytoplasm stains gray-blue. It functions as an active phagocyte (the "long-term cleanup team"), increasing dramatically in number during chronic infections such as tuberculosis. See also Plate 53 in the Histology Atlas.

Students are often asked to list the leukocytes in order from the most abundant to the least abundant. The following silly phrase may help you with this task: *N*ever *l*et *m*onkeys *e*at *b*ananas (neutrophils, lymphocytes, monocytes, eosinophils, basophils).

Platelets

Also at station 5, notice the small clusters of dark-staining, irregularly shaped bodies that appear much smaller than the other formed elements; these are platelets. Platelets are cell fragments of large multinucleate cells called **megakaryocytes.** The normal platelet count in blood ranges from 150,000 to 400,000 per cubic millimeter. Platelets are needed for the clotting process that occurs in plasma when blood vessels are ruptured.

Hematologic Tests

OBJECTIVE 4 Conduct and state the norms and importance of the following hematologic tests: hematocrit, hemoglobin determination, clotting time, and blood typing.

When a person enters a hospital as a patient, several hematologic (blood) tests are routinely done to determine general level of health. You will be conducting a few of these tests in this exercise.

! Materials such as cotton balls, lancets, and alcohol swabs are used in nearly all of the following diagnostic tests. These supplies are at the general supply area. Dispose properly of all supplies (glassware to the "bleach bucket" and disposable items to the autoclave bag) immediately after use.

Other necessary supplies and equipment are at specific supply areas marked according to the test with which they are used. Because nearly all of the tests require a finger stab, if you will be using your own blood it might be wise to read quickly through the tests to determine when more than one test can be done from the same finger stab. A little preplanning will save you the discomfort of having to puncture your finger several times.

An alternative to using your own blood is using heparinized blood samples supplied by your instructor. The purpose of using heparinized tubes is to prevent the blood from clotting. Thus blood collected and stored in such tubes will be suitable for all tests *except* coagulation time testing.

Total White and Red Blood Cell Counts

The hand-counting technique for determining total white and red blood cell counts, typically done in student labs, is outdated because most clinical agencies now have computerized equipment for performing blood counts. Hence we will not do this test during this lab session. It is important, however, to know the typical blood count values of healthy individuals and to understand what abnormal counts might indicate.

Averaging 4800 to 10,800 cells per cubic millimeter, white blood cells are an important part of the body's defense system, so it is essential to note any abnormalities in them. **Leukocytosis,** an abnormally high WBC count, may indicate bacterial or viral infection, hemorrhage, or poisoning by drugs or chemicals. An abnormally low white blood cell count (**leukopenia**) may indicate measles, infectious hepatitis or cirrhosis, tuberculosis, or excessive antibiotic or X-ray therapy. A person with leukopenia lacks the usual protective mechanisms. **Leukemia,** a malignant disorder of the lymphoid tissues characterized by uncontrolled cell division of abnormal WBCs and a reduction in the number of RBCs and platelets, is detectable not only by a total WBC count but also by a differential WBC count (a count of the relative number of each WBC seen on the slide).

The red blood cell count, like the white blood cell count, determines the total number of this cell type per unit volume of blood. Normally the RBC count averages 4.2–5.4 million cells per cubic millimeter for women and 4.7–6.1 million cells per cubic millimeter for men. Because RBCs are absolutely necessary for oxygen transport, a doctor typically investigates any excessive change in their number immediately.

An increase in the number of RBCs (**polycythemia**) may result from bone marrow cancer or from living at high altitudes where less oxygen is available. A decrease in the number of RBCs results in anemia. (The term **anemia** simply indicates a decreased oxygen-carrying capacity of blood that may result from a decrease in RBC number or size or a decreased hemoglobin content of the RBCs.)

Hematocrit

The **hematocrit** is routinely done when anemia is suspected. Centrifuging whole blood spins the formed elements to the bottom of the tube, with plasma forming the top layer (see Figure 19.1). Because the blood cell population is mostly RBCs, the hematocrit is generally considered equal to the RBC volume, and this is the only value reported. However, the relative percentage of WBCs can be differentiated, and both WBC and plasma volume will be reported here. Normal hematocrit values for the man and woman, respectively, are 42–52% and 37–47%.

Activity 3

Determining the Hematocrit

The hematocrit is determined by the micromethod, so only a drop of blood is needed. If possible (and if the centrifuge allows), all members of the class should prepare their capillary tubes at the same time so the centrifuge can be properly balanced and run only once.

1. Obtain two heparinized capillary tubes, capillary tube sealer or modeling clay, a lancet, alcohol swabs, and some cotton balls.

2. If you are using your own blood, open the alcohol packet, and scrub your third or fourth finger with the swab. Swing (circumduct) your arm for 10 to 15 seconds. This will dry the alcohol and cause your fingers to become engorged with blood. Then open the lancet packet and grasp the lancet by its blunt end. Quickly jab the pointed end into the prepared finger to produce a free flow of blood. Wipe away the first few drops with a cotton ball, and holding the red-line-marked end of the capillary tube to the blood drop, allow it to fill at least three-fourths full by capillary action (**Figure 19.2a**). If the blood is not flowing freely, the end of the capillary tube will not be completely submerged in the blood during filling, air will enter, and you will have to prepare another sample.

If you are using instructor-provided blood, simply immerse the red-marked end of the capillary tube in the blood sample, and fill it three-quarters full as just described.

3. Plug the blood-containing end by pressing it into the capillary tube sealer or clay (Figure 19.2b). Prepare a second tube in the same manner.

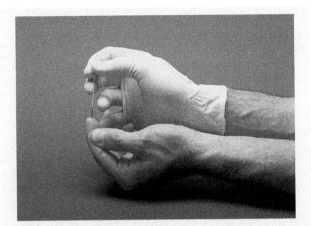

(a)

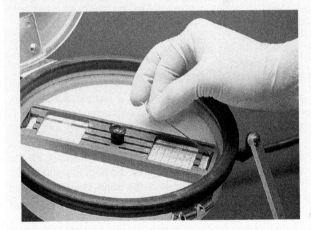

(b)

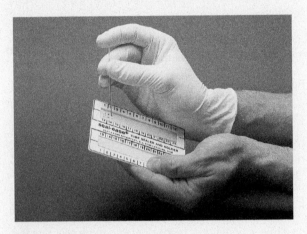

(c)

Figure 19.2 Steps in a hematocrit determination.
(a) Load a heparinized capillary tube with blood.
(b) Plug the blood-containing end of the tube with clay. (c) Place the tube in a microhematocrit centrifuge. (Centrifuge must be balanced.)

Text continues on next page. →

19

4. Place the prepared tubes opposite one another in the radial grooves of the microhematocrit centrifuge with the sealed ends abutting the rubber gasket at the centrifuge periphery (Figure 19.2c). This loading procedure balances the centrifuge and prevents blood from spraying everywhere by centrifugal force. *Make a note of the numbers of the grooves your tubes are in.* When all the tubes have been loaded, make sure the centrifuge is properly balanced, and secure the centrifuge cover. Turn the centrifuge on, and set the timer for 4 or 5 minutes.

5. Determine the percentage of RBCs, WBCs, and plasma by using the microhematocrit reader. The RBCs are the bottom layer, the plasma is the top layer, and the WBCs are the buff-colored layer between the two. If the reader is not available, use a millimeter ruler to measure the length of the filled capillary tube occupied by each element, and compute its percentage by using the following formula:

$$\frac{\text{Length of the column composed of the element (mm)}}{\text{Length of the original column of whole blood (mm)}} \times 100$$

Record your calculations below.

% RBC _____ % WBC _____ % plasma _____

Usually WBCs constitute 1% of the total blood volume. How do your blood values compare to this figure and to the normal percentages for RBCs and plasma?

_____

As a rule, a hematocrit is considered a more accurate test for determining the RBC composition of the blood than the total RBC count. A hematocrit within the normal range generally indicates a normal RBC number, whereas an abnormally high or low hematocrit is cause for concern.

Hemoglobin Concentration

A person can be anemic even with a normal RBC count. Because hemoglobin is the RBC protein responsible for oxygen transport, perhaps the most accurate way of measuring the oxygen-carrying capacity of the blood is to determine its hemoglobin content. Oxygen, which combines with the heme (iron-containing portion) of the hemoglobin molecule, is picked up by the blood cells in the lungs and unloaded in the tissues. Thus, the more hemoglobin molecules the RBCs contain, the more oxygen they will be able to transport. Normal hemoglobin content in men is slightly higher (13 to 18 g) than in women (12 to 16 g).

Activity 4

Determining Hemoglobin Concentration

Several techniques have been developed to estimate the hemoglobin content of blood, ranging from the old, rather inaccurate Tallquist method to expensive colorimeters, which are precisely calibrated and yield highly accurate results. Directions for the Tallquist method are provided here.

1. Obtain a Tallquist hemoglobin scale, lancets, alcohol swabs, and cotton balls.

2. Use instructor-provided *animal* blood, or prepare your finger as previously described. (For best results, make sure the alcohol evaporates before puncturing your finger.) Place one good-sized drop of blood on the special absorbent paper provided with the color chart. The blood stain should be larger than the holes on the color chart.

3. *As soon as* the blood has dried and lost its glossy appearance, match its color, under natural light, with the color standards by moving the specimen under the comparison chart so that the blood stain appears at all the various openings. (Do not allow the blood to dry to a brown color, because this will result in an inaccurate reading.) If the color of your blood sample is intermediate between two color standards, it may be necessary to estimate the percentage of hemoglobin.

4. Record your results as the percentage of hemoglobin concentration and as grams per 100 ml of blood below.

_____ g/100 ml blood _____ %

5. Dispose of the blood-stained paper in the autoclave bag.

Coagulation Time

Blood clotting, or **coagulation,** is a protective mechanism that minimizes blood loss when blood vessels are ruptured. Many substances normally present in the plasma, as well as some released by platelets and injured tissues, are involved. Basically hemostasis proceeds as follows (**Figure 19.3**): The injured tissues and platelets release **tissue factor, TF** and PF_3 respectively, which trigger the clotting mechanism, or cascade. Tissue factor and PF_3 interact with other blood clotting factors and calcium ions to form **prothrombin activator,** which in turn converts **prothrombin** (present in plasma) to **thrombin.** Thrombin then acts enzymatically to polymerize the soluble **fibrinogen** proteins (present in plasma) into insoluble **fibrin,** which forms a meshwork of strands that traps the RBCs and forms the basis of the clot. Normally, blood removed from the body clots within 2 to 6 minutes.

Activity 5

Determining Coagulation Time

1. Obtain a *nonheparinized* capillary tube, a lancet, cotton balls, a triangular file, and alcohol swabs.

2. Clean and prick a finger to produce a free flow of blood. Discard the lancet in the disposal container.

3. Place one end of the capillary tube in the blood drop, and hold the opposite end at a lower level to collect the sample.

4. Lay the capillary tube on a paper towel.

Record the time. _____

5. At 30-sec intervals, make a small nick on the tube close to one end with the triangular file, and then carefully break the tube. Slowly separate the ends to see if a gel-like thread of fibrin spans the gap. When this occurs, record below and on the data sheet the time it took for coagulation to occur. Are your results within the normal time range?

_____

6. Dispose of the capillary tube and used supplies in the disposable autoclave bag.

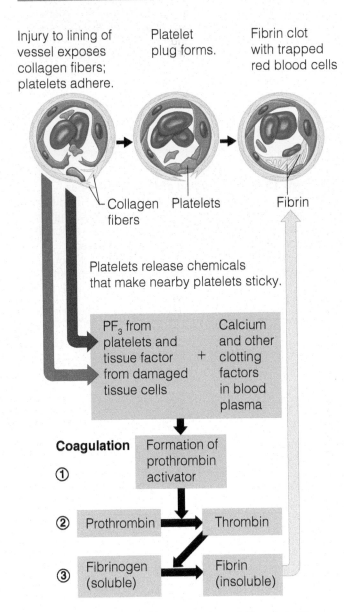

Figure 19.3 Events of hemostasis and blood clotting.
Steps ①–③ are the major phases of coagulation.

Blood Typing

OBJECTIVE 5   Discuss the reason for transfusion reactions resulting from administration of mis-matched blood.

Blood typing is a system for classifying blood based on specific glycoproteins present on the outer surface of the RBC plasma membrane. Such proteins are called **antigens,** or **agglutinogens,** and are genetically determined. Antigens of the ABO blood groups are accompanied by plasma proteins called **antibodies (agglutinins).** These antibodies act against RBCs carrying antigens that are not present on the person's own RBCs. If donor blood does not match the recipient's blood, then the recipient's antibodies react with the donor's blood antigens. This causes the RBCs to clump, agglutinate, and eventually hemolyze. It is because of this phenomenon (a transfusion reaction) that a person's blood must be carefully typed before a blood transfusion. **Note:** Development of antibodies in the ABO system does not require previous exposure to a foreign antigen. For example, a type A individual has naturally occurring anti-B antibody (Table 19.1).

Several blood typing systems exist, but the factors routinely typed for are antigens of the ABO and Rh blood groups, which are most commonly involved in transfusion reactions. The basis of the ABO typing is shown in Table 19.1.

Individuals whose red blood cells carry the Rh antigen are Rh positive (approximately 85% of the U.S. population); those lacking the antigen are Rh negative. Unlike ABO blood groups, neither Rh-positive (Rh$^+$) nor Rh-negative (Rh$^-$) blood carries preformed anti-Rh antibodies. This is understandable in the case of the Rh-positive individual. However, Rh-negative persons who receive transfusions of Rh-positive blood become sensitized by the Rh antigens of the donor RBCs, and their systems begin to produce anti-Rh antibodies. On later exposures to Rh-positive blood, typical transfusion reactions occur, resulting in the clumping and hemolysis of the donor blood cells.

Note: Although the blood of dogs and other mammals does react with some of the human agglutinins (present in the antisera), the reaction is not as pronounced and varies with the animal blood used. Hence, the most accurate and predictable blood typing results are obtained with human blood.

Activity 6

Typing for ABO and Rh Blood Groups

1. Obtain two clean microscope slides, a wax pencil, anti-A, anti-B, and anti-Rh typing sera, toothpicks, lancets, alcohol swabs, medicine dropper, and the Rh typing box.

2. Divide slide 1 into two equal halves with the wax marking pencil. Label the lower left-hand corner "anti-A" and the lower right-hand corner "anti-B." Mark the bottom of slide 2 "anti-Rh."

3. Place one drop of anti-A serum on the *left* side of slide 1. Place one drop of anti-B serum on the *right* side of slide 1. Place one drop of anti-Rh serum in the center of slide 2.

Text continues on next page. →

19

4. If you are using your own blood, cleanse your finger with an alcohol swab, pierce the finger with a lancet, and wipe away the first drop of blood. Obtain 3 drops of freely flowing blood, placing one drop on each side of slide 1 and a drop on slide 2.

If using instructor-provided animal blood, EDTA-treated blood, or samples from a simulated blood testing kit, use a medicine dropper to place one drop of blood on each side of slide 1 and a drop of blood on slide 2.

⚠ 5. Quickly mix each blood-antiserum sample with a *fresh* toothpick. Then dispose of the toothpicks, lancet, and used alcohol swab in the autoclave bag.

6. Place slide 2 on the Rh typing box, and rock it gently back and forth. (A slightly higher temperature is required for precise Rh typing than for ABO typing.)

7. After 2 minutes, observe all three blood samples for evidence of clumping. The agglutination that occurs in the positive test for the Rh factor is fine and difficult to see. Record your observations in the Activity 6 chart.

8. Interpret your ABO results in light of the information in **Figure 19.4**. If you observed clumping on slide 2, you are Rh positive. If not, you are Rh negative.

9. Record your blood type at the top of the Activity 6 chart.

10. Put used slides in the bleach-containing bucket at the general supply area; put disposable supplies in the autoclave bag.

Before leaving the laboratory, obtain a spray bottle containing bleach solution. Spray your laboratory bench with the bleach solution and wipe dry with a paper towel.

Activity 6: Blood Typing Result	Type: _____	
Result	**Observed (+)**	**Not observed (−)**
Presence of clumping with anti-A		
Presence of clumping with anti-B		
Presence of clumping with anti-Rh		

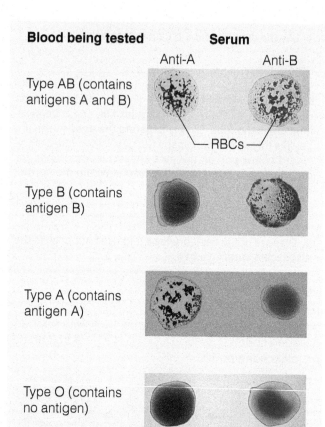

Blood being tested   **Serum**

Type AB (contains antigens A and B)

Type B (contains antigen B)

Type A (contains antigen A)

Type O (contains no antigen)

Figure 19.4 Blood typing of ABO blood types.
When serum containing anti-A or anti-B antibodies (agglutinins) is added to a blood sample, agglutination will occur between the agglutinin and the corresponding antigen (agglutinogen)—A or B. As illustrated, agglutination occurs with both sera in blood group AB, with anti-B serum in blood group B, with anti-A serum in blood group A, and with neither serum in blood group O.

Table 19.1	ABO Blood Groups				
			% of U.S. population		
ABO blood type	**Antigens present on RBC membranes**	**Antibodies present in plasma**	**White**	**Black**	**Asian**
A	A	Anti-B	40	27	28
B	B	Anti-A	11	20	27
AB	A and B	None	4	4	5
O	Neither	Anti-A and anti-B	45	49	40

Name _____ LabTime/Date _____

Composition of Blood

1. What is the blood volume of an average-sized adult? _____ liters

2. What determines whether blood is bright red or a dull brick-red? _____

   _____

3. Use the key to identify the cell type(s) or blood elements that fit the following descriptive statements. (Some terms may be used more than once.)

   Key: basophil   formed elements   monocyte
           eosinophil   lymphocyte   neutrophil
           erythrocyte   megakaryocyte   plasma

   _____ 1. its name means "neutral-loving"; a phagocyte

   _____, _____, and _____ 2. granulocytes

   _____ 3. also called a red blood cell

   _____, _____ 4. agranulocytes

   _____ 5. ancestral cell of platelets

   _____ 6. basophils, eosinophils, erythrocytes, lymphocytes, megakaryocytes, monocytes, and neutrophils are all examples of these

   _____ 7. number rises during parasite infections

   _____ 8. releases a vasodilator; the least abundant WBC

   _____ 9. transports oxygen

   _____ 10. primarily water, noncellular; the fluid matrix of blood

   _____ 11. phagocyte in chronic infections

   _____, _____, _____,

   _____, _____ 12. the five types of white blood cells

4. List four classes of nutrients normally found in plasma: _____, _____,

   _____, and _____

   Name two gases: _____ and _____

   Name three electrolytes: _____, _____, and _____

5. Describe the consistency and color of the plasma you observed in the laboratory.

_____

6. What is the average life span of a red blood cell? How does its anucleate condition affect this life span?

_____

_____

7. From memory, describe the structural characteristics of each of the following blood cell types as accurately as possible, and note the percentage of each in an individual's total population of white blood cells.

eosinophils _____

_____

neutrophils _____

_____

lymphocytes _____

_____

basophils _____

_____

monocytes _____

_____

8. Correctly identify the blood pathologies described in column A by matching them with selections from column B:

Column A	Column B
_____ 1. abnormal increase in the number of WBCs	anemia
_____ 2. abnormal increase in the number of RBCs	leukocytosis
_____ 3. condition of too few RBCs or of RBCs with hemoglobin deficiencies	leukopenia
_____ 4. abnormal decrease in the number of WBCs	polycythemia

Hematologic Tests

9. Broadly speaking, why are hematologic studies of blood so important in the diagnosis of disease?

_____

_____

10. In the chart that follows, record information from the blood tests you conducted. Complete the chart by recording values for healthy male adults and indicating the significance of high or low values for each test.

Test	Student test results	Normal values (healthy male adults)	Significance	
			High values	Low values
Total WBC count	—			
Total RBC count	—			
Hematocrit				
Hemoglobin determination				
Coagulation time				

11. Define *hematocrit:* _____

12. If you had a high hematocrit, would you expect your hemoglobin determination to be high or low?

_____ Why? _____

_____

13. If your blood clumped with both anti-A and anti-B sera, your ABO blood type would be _____. To what ABO blood

groups could you give blood? _____ From which ABO donor types could you receive blood? _____

Which ABO blood type is most common? _____ Least common? _____

14. Explain why an Rh-negative person does not have a transfusion reaction on the first exposure to Rh-positive blood but

does have a reaction on the second exposure. _____

_____

_____

What happens when an ABO blood type is mismatched for the first time? _____

_____

15. Assume that the blood of two patients has been typed for ABO blood type.

Typing results
Mr. Adams:

Blood drop
and anti-A serum

Blood drop
and anti-B serum

Typing results
Mr. Calhoon:

Blood drop
and anti-A serum

Blood drop
and anti-B serum

On the basis of these results, Mr. Adams has type _____ blood, and Mr. Calhoon has type _____ blood.

Could Mr. Adams safely receive a blood transfusion from Mr. Calhoon? _____

Could Mr. Calhoon safely receive a blood transfusion from Mr. Adams? _____

Materials

- ☐ X-ray image of human thorax and X-ray viewing box (if available)
- ☐ Torso model or laboratory chart showing heart anatomy
- ☐ Heart model (three-dimensional)
- ☐ Red and blue pencils
- ☐ Three-dimensional models of cardiac and skeletal muscle
- ☐ Demonstration area: Compound microscope set up with a longitudinal section cardiac muscle; pointer on an intercalated disc
- ☐ Preserved sheep heart, pericardial sacs intact (if possible)
- ☐ Dissecting tray and instruments
- ☐ Pointed glass rods for probes
- ☐ Disposable gloves
- ☐ Spray bottle containing 10% bleach solution

Pre-Lab Quiz

1. The heart is enclosed in a double-walled sac called the:
   - a. apex
   - b. mediastinum
   - c. pericardium
   - d. thorax

2. What is the name of the two receiving chambers of the heart?
   _____

3. The left ventricle discharges blood into the _____, from which all systemic arteries of the body diverge to supply the body tissues.
   - a. aorta
   - b. pulmonary artery
   - c. pulmonary vein
   - d. vena cava

4. Circle the correct term. The right atrioventricular valve, or tricuspid / mitral, valve prevents backflow into the right atrium when the right ventricle is contracting.

5. The functional blood supply of the heart itself is provided by the:
   - a. aorta
   - b. carotid arteries
   - c. coronary arteries
   - d. pulmonary trunk

6. Two microscopic features of cardiac cells that help distinguish them from other types of muscle cells are branching and:
   - a. intercalated discs
   - b. myosin fibers
   - c. sarcolemma
   - d. striations

The major function of the **cardiovascular system** is transportation. Using blood as the transport vehicle, the system carries oxygen, digested foods, cell wastes, electrolytes, and many other substances vital to the body's homeostasis to and from the body cells. The propulsive force is the beating heart, which is essentially a muscular pump equipped with one-way valves. As the heart contracts, it forces blood into a closed system of large and small plumbing tubes (blood vessels) within which the blood circulates. This exercise deals with the structure of the heart. Exercise 21 considers the anatomy of blood vessels.

Gross Anatomy of the Human Heart

OBJECTIVE 1 Describe the location of the heart in the body.

The **heart,** a cone-shaped organ approximately the size of a fist, is located within the **mediastinum,** the medial cavity of the thorax. It is flanked laterally by the lungs, posteriorly by the vertebral column, and anteriorly by the sternum (**Figure 20.1**). Its more pointed **apex** extends slightly to the left and rests on the diaphragm, approximately at the level of the fifth intercostal space. Its broader **base,** from which the great vessels emerge, lies beneath the second rib and points toward the right shoulder. In the body, the right ventricle of the heart forms most of its anterior surface.

If you press just below the left nipple, you can feel the apical pulse of your beating heart. Verify the relationships described above on an X-ray image or on Figure 20.1.

The heart is enclosed within a double-walled serous sac called the **pericardium.** The loosely fitting outer part of this sac is referred to as the **fibrous pericardium.** This fibrous layer protects the heart and anchors it to

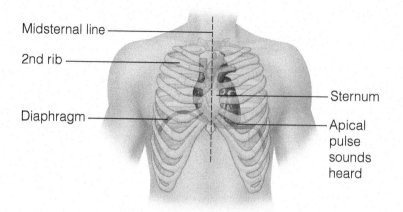

Figure 20.1 Location of the heart in the thorax.

surrounding structures, such as the diaphragm and sternum. Below the fibrous pericardium is the two-layer **serous pericardium.** Its **parietal layer** lines the inside of the fibrous pericardium. At the base of the heart, the parietal layer reflects back to cover the external heart as the **visceral layer,** or **epicardium.** Serous fluid produced by these membranes allows the heart to beat in a relatively frictionless environment.

The walls of the heart are composed of three layers:

• **Epicardium:** The outer layer, which is also the visceral pericardium.

• **Myocardium:** The middle layer. It is the thickest layer and is composed mostly of cardiac muscle.

• **Endocardium:** The inner lining of the heart that is made of simple squamous epithelium. It covers the heart valves and is continuous with the inner lining of the great vessels.

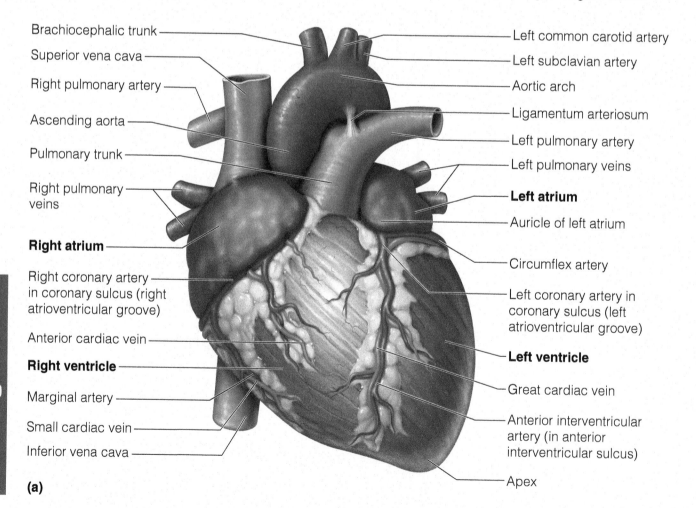

(a)

Figure 20.2 Anatomy of the human heart. (a) External anterior view.

Heart Chambers

The heart has four chambers: two superior **atria** and two inferior **ventricles** (**Figure 20.2**). The septum that divides the heart longitudinally is referred to as the **interatrial** or **interventricular septum,** depending on which chambers it partitions. Functionally, the atria are receiving chambers and are relatively ineffective as pumps. The right atrium receives oxygen-poor blood from the body via the **superior** and **inferior venae cavae.** Four **pulmonary veins** deliver oxygen-rich blood from the lungs to the left atrium.

The inferior ventricles, which form the bulk of the heart, are the discharging chambers. They force blood out of the heart into the large arteries that emerge from its base. The right ventricle pumps blood into the **pulmonary trunk,** which sends blood to the lungs to be oxygenated. The left ventricle discharges blood into the **aorta,** from which all systemic arteries of the body diverge to supply the body tissues. This is a much longer circuit than the pulmonary circuit, and the left ventricle walls are much thicker than those of the right ventricle. Discussions of the heart's pumping action usually refer to the activity of the ventricles.

Heart Valves

Four valves enforce a one-way blood flow through the heart chambers. The **atrioventricular (AV) valves,** located between the atrium and ventricle on each side, prevent backflow into the atria when the ventricles are contracting. The **semilunar (SL) valves** are located between a ventricle and a great vessel on each side.

- **Right atrioventricular (AV) valve** *(tricuspid valve):* Has three cusps (Figure 20.2b) anchored to the **papillary muscles** of the ventricular wall by cords called **chordae tendineae** (literally, "heart strings").

- **Left atrioventricular (AV) valve:** *(mitral valve or bicuspid valve):* Has two cusps anchored to the papillary muscles by chordae tendineae.

- **Pulmonary semilunar valve:** Has three cusps located between the right ventricle and the pulmonary trunk.

- **Aortic semilunar valve:** Has three pocketlike cusps located between the left ventricle and the aorta.

When the heart is relaxing, blood flows passively into the atria and then into the ventricles. At first, the AV valve flaps hang limply into the ventricular chambers, and then they are carried passively toward the atria by the accumulating blood. When the ventricles contract and compress the blood in their chambers, the intraventricular pressure rises, forcing the valve flaps superiorly, which closes the AV valves. The chordae tendineae anchor the flaps in a closed position that prevents backflow into the atria during ventricular contraction.

The SL valve cusps are forced open and flatten against the walls of the artery as the ventricles pump their blood into the large arteries during systole. However, when the

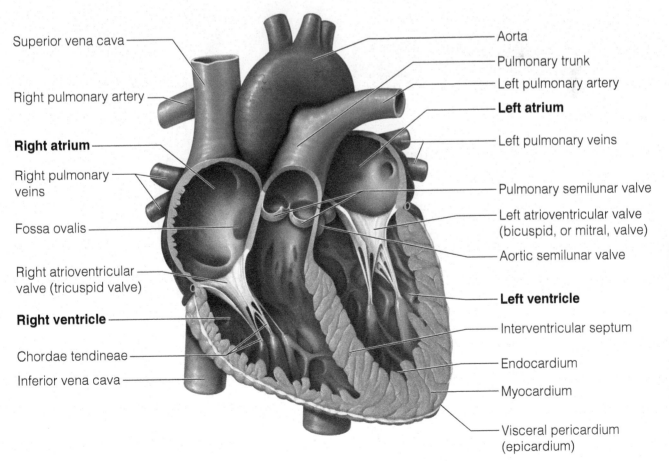

(b)

Figure 20.2 *(continued)* **(b)** Frontal section showing interior chambers and valves.

ventricles relax and blood flows backward toward the heart, the cusps fill with blood, closing the semilunar valves. This prevents the backflow of blood from the great vessels into the ventricles.

OBJECTIVE 2 Identify the major anatomical areas and structures of the heart when provided with a heart model, diagram, or sheep heart.

Activity 1

Using the Heart Model to Study Heart Anatomy

When you have pinpointed in Figure 20.2 all the structures described so far, observe the human heart model, and identify again the same structures without referring to the figure. Notice how much thicker the myocardium of the left ventricle is than that of the right ventricle. Compare the *shape* of the left ventricular cavity to the shape of the right ventricular cavity. Record your observations on the lines below.

_____

_____

_____

Pulmonary, Systemic, and Cardiac Circulations

OBJECTIVE 3 Trace the pathway of blood through the heart, and compare the pulmonary and systemic circulations.

Pulmonary and Systemic Circulations

The heart is a double pump. The right side serves as the **pulmonary circulation** pump, sending the carbon dioxide–rich blood entering its chambers to the lungs to unload carbon dioxide and pick up oxygen and then back to the left side of the heart (**Figure 20.3**). Gas exchange is the sole purpose of the pulmonary circuit. The second circuit, the **systemic circulation**, carries oxygen-rich blood from the left heart through the body tissues and back to the right heart. It supplies the functional blood supply to all body tissues.

Activity 2

Tracing the Path of Blood Through the Heart

Trace the pathway of blood through the heart by adding arrows to the frontal section diagram (Figure 20.2b). Use red arrows for the oxygen-rich blood and blue arrows for the less oxygen-rich blood.

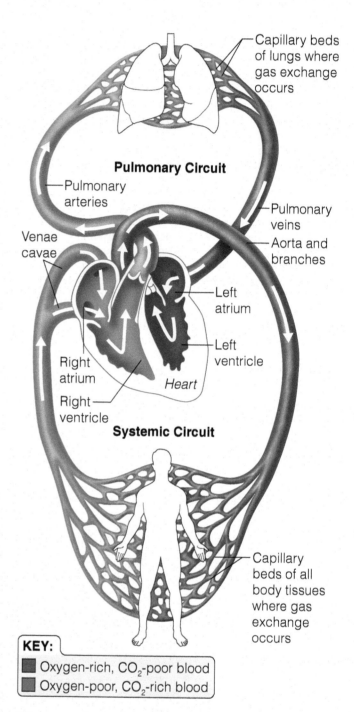

KEY:

■ Oxygen-rich, CO_2-poor blood
■ Oxygen-poor, CO_2-rich blood

Figure 20.3 The systemic and pulmonary circuits. The heart is a double pump that serves two circulations. The right side of the heart pumps blood through the pulmonary circuit to the lungs and back to the left heart. (For simplicity, the actual number of two pulmonary arteries and four pulmonary veins has been reduced to one each.) The left heart pumps blood via the systemic circuit to all body tissues and back to the right heart. Notice that blood flowing through the pulmonary circuit gains oxygen and loses carbon dioxide. Blood flowing through the systemic circuit loses oxygen and picks up carbon dioxide.

Cardiac Circulation

OBJECTIVE 4 Name and follow the functional blood supply of the heart.

Even though the heart chambers are bathed with blood almost continuously, this blood does not nourish the myocardium. The blood supply that nourishes the heart is provided by the right and left coronary arteries (see Figure 20.2a). The **coronary arteries** branch from the base of the aorta and encircle the heart in the **coronary sulcus (atrioventricular groove)** at the junction of the atria and ventricles. They then branch over the heart's surface, the right coronary artery supplying the posterior surface of the ventricles and the lateral aspect of the right side of the the heart, largely through its **posterior interventricular** and **marginal artery** branches. The left coronary artery supplies the anterior ventricular walls and the laterodorsal part of the left side of the heart via the **anterior interventricular artery** and the **circumflex artery.** The coronary arteries and their branches are compressed during systole and fill when the heart is relaxed.

The myocardium is drained by several **cardiac veins,** which empty into the **coronary sinus** (an enlarged vessel on the backside of the heart). The coronary sinus, in turn, empties into the right atrium. In addition, several **anterior cardiac veins** empty directly into the right atrium.

Microscopic Anatomy of Cardiac Muscle

OBJECTIVE 5 Describe the microscopic structure of cardiac muscle, and indicate the importance of intercalated discs.

Cardiac muscle is found in only one place—the heart. Because the heart acts as a blood pump, propelling blood to all tissues

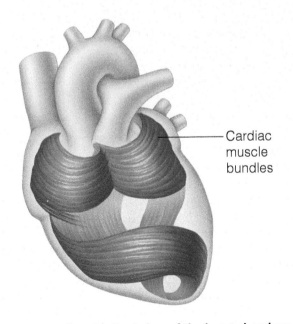

Figure 20.4 Longitudinal view of the heart chambers showing the spiral arrangement of the cardiac muscle fibers.

of the body, cardiac muscle is very important to life. Cardiac muscle is involuntary, ensuring a constant blood supply.

The cardiac cells are arranged in spiral or figure-8-shaped bundles (**Figure 20.4**). When the heart contracts, its internal chambers become smaller (or are temporarily obliterated), forcing the blood upward into the large arteries leaving the heart.

Activity 3

Examining Cardiac Muscle Cells

1. Observe the three-dimensional model of cardiac muscle, examining its branching cells and the areas where the cells interdigitate, the **intercalated discs.** These two structural features provide a continuity to cardiac muscle not seen in other muscle tissues and allow coordinated heart activity.

2. Compare the model of cardiac muscle to the model of skeletal muscle. Note the similarities and differences between the two kinds of muscle tissue.

3. Go to the microscope at the demonstration area, and observe a longitudinal section of cardiac muscle under high power. Identify the nucleus, striations, intercalated discs (pointed out), and sarcolemma of the individual cells, and then compare your observations to **Figure 20.5**.

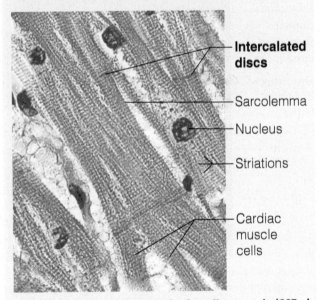

Figure 20.5 Photomicrograph of cardiac muscle (665×).

DISSECTION

The Sheep Heart

Dissecting a sheep heart is valuable because it is similar in size and structure to the human heart. Also, dissection allows you to view structures in a way not possible with models and diagrams. Refer to **Figure 20.6** as you proceed with the dissection.

Text continues on next page. →

20

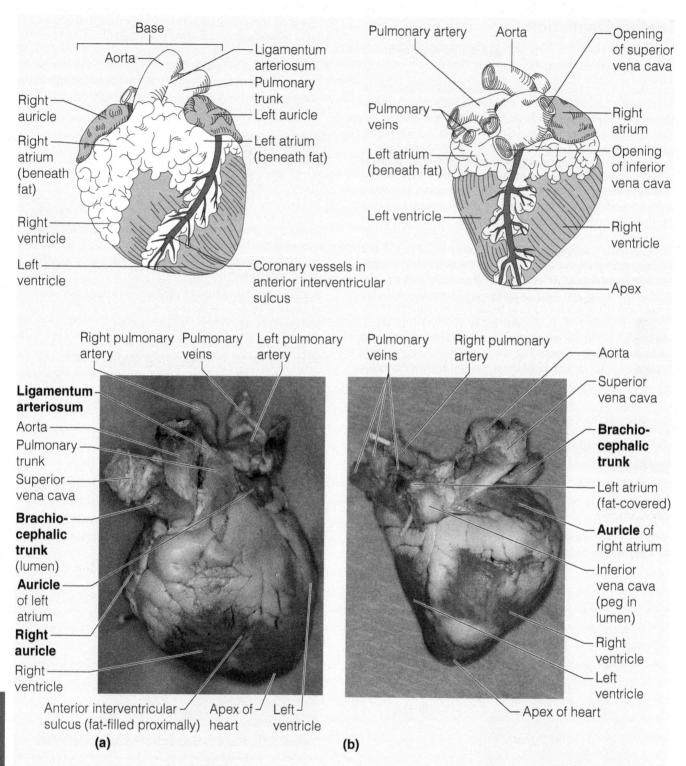

Figure 20.6 Anatomy of the sheep heart. (a) Anterior view. **(b)** Posterior view. Diagrammatic views at top; photographs at bottom.

1. Obtain a preserved sheep heart, a dissecting tray, dissecting instruments, a glass probe, and gloves. Rinse the sheep heart in cold water. Now you are ready to make your observations.

2. Observe the texture of the pericardium. Also, find its point of attachment to the heart. Where is it attached?

3. If the serous pericardial sac is still intact, slit open the parietal pericardium and cut it from its attachments. Observe the epicardium (visceral layer). Using a sharp scalpel, carefully pull a little of this serous membrane away from the myocardium. How do its position, thickness, and apposition to the heart differ from those of the parietal layer?

_____

_____

_____

_____

4. Examine the external surface of the heart. Notice the accumulation of adipose tissue, which in many cases marks the separation of the chambers and the location of the coronary arteries. Carefully scrape away some of the fat with a scalpel to expose the coronary blood vessels.

5. Identify the base and apex of the heart, and then identify the two wrinkled **auricles,** earlike flaps of tissue projecting from the atrial chambers. The balance of the heart muscle is ventricular tissue. To identify the left ventricle, compress the ventricular chambers on each side of the longitudinal fissures carrying the coronary blood vessels. The side that feels thicker and more solid is the left ventricle. The right ventricle is much thinner and feels somewhat flabby when compressed. This difference reflects the greater demand placed on the left ventricle, which must pump blood through the much longer systemic circulation. Hold the heart in its anatomical position (Figure 20.6a), with the anterior surface uppermost. In this position, the left ventricle composes the entire apex and the left side of the heart.

6. Identify the pulmonary trunk and the aorta leaving the superior aspect of the heart. The pulmonary trunk is more anterior, and you may see it divide into the right and left pulmonary arteries if it has not been cut too close to the heart. The thicker-walled aorta, which branches almost immediately, is located just beneath the pulmonary trunk. The first branch of the sheep aorta, the **brachiocephalic trunk,** can be identified unless the aorta has been cut immediately as it leaves the heart. The brachiocephalic trunk splits to form the right carotid and subclavian arteries, which supply the right side of the head and right forelimb, respectively.

Carefully clear away the fat between the pulmonary trunk and the aorta to expose the **ligamentum arteriosum,** a remnant of the **ductus arteriosus.** (In the fetus, the ductus arteriosus allows blood to pass directly from the pulmonary trunk to the aorta, thus bypassing the nonfunctional fetal lungs.)

7. Cut through the wall of the aorta until you see the aortic semilunar valve. Identify the two openings into the coronary arteries just above the valve. Insert a probe into one of these holes to see if you can follow the course of a coronary artery across the heart.

8. Turn the heart to view its posterior surface. The heart will appear as shown in Figure 20.6b. Notice that the right and left ventricles appear equal-sized in this view. Try to identify the four thin-walled pulmonary veins entering the left atrium. (It may or may not be possible to locate the pulmonary veins from this vantage point, depending on how they were cut as the

heart was removed.) Identify the superior and inferior venae cavae entering the right atrium. Compare the approximate diameter of the superior vena cava with that of the aorta.

Which is larger? _____

Which has thicker walls? _____

Why do you suppose these differences exist?

_____

_____

_____

_____

OBJECTIVE 6   Explain the operation of the heart valves.

9. Insert a probe into the superior vena cava, and use scissors to cut through its wall so that you can see the interior of the right atrium. Do not extend your cut entirely through the right atrium or into the ventricle. Observe the right atrioventricular valve.

How many flaps does it have? _____

Pour some water into the right atrium and allow it to flow into the ventricle. _Slowly and gently_ squeeze the right ventricle to watch the closing action of this valve. (If you squeeze too vigorously, you'll get a face full of water!) Drain the water from the heart before continuing.

10. Return to the pulmonary trunk and cut through its anterior wall until you can see the pulmonary semilunar valve. Pour some water into the base of the pulmonary trunk to observe the closing action of this valve. How does its action differ from that of the atrioventricular valve?

_____

_____

_____

_____

_____

11. After observing semilunar valve action, drain the heart once again. Return to the superior vena cava, and continue the cut made in its wall through the right atrium and right atrioventricular valve into the right ventricle.

Text continues on next page. →

20

12. Next, make a longitudinal incision through the aorta, and continue it into the left ventricle. Again notice how much thicker the myocardium of the left ventricle is than that of the right ventricle. Compare the *shape* of the left ventricular cavity to the shape of the right ventricular cavity.

_____

_____

_____

_____

Are the chordae tendineae observed in the right ventricle

also present in the left ventricle? _____

Count the number of cusps in the left atrioventricular valve. How does this compare with the number seen in the right atrioventricular valve?

_____

_____

How do the sheep valves compare with their human counterparts?

_____

13. Continue your incision from the left ventricle superiorly into the left atrium. Reflect the cut edges of the atrial wall, and try to locate the entry points of the pulmonary veins into the left atrium. Follow the pulmonary veins to the heart exterior with a probe. Notice how thin-walled these vessels are.

14. Dispose of the organic debris, and clean the dissecting tray and instruments with detergent and water. Wash the lab bench with bleach solution before leaving the laboratory.

20

EXERCISE

20

REVIEW SHEET
Anatomy of the Heart

Name _____ Lab Time/Date _____

Gross Anatomy of the Human Heart

1. An anterior view of the heart is shown here. Identify each structure by writing its name on the corresponding leader line:

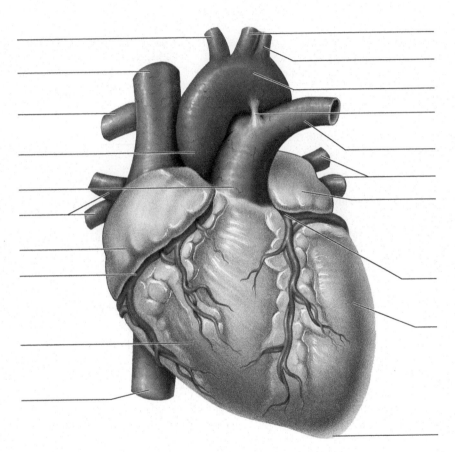

2. What is the function of the fluid that fills the pericardial sac? _____

_____

3. Match the terms in the key to the descriptions provided below. (Some terms may be used more than once.)

Key:

_____ 1. drains blood into the right atrium

atria

_____ 2. superior heart chambers

coronary arteries

_____ 3. inferior heart chambers

coronary sinus

_____ 4. visceral pericardium

endocardium

_____ 5. receiving chambers of the heart

epicardium

_____ 6. layer composed of cardiac muscle

myocardium

_____ 7. provide nutrient blood to the heart muscle

ventricles

_____ 8. lining of the heart chambers

_____ 9. actual "pumps" of the heart

4. What is the function of the valves found in the heart? _____

_____

5. Can the heart function with leaky valves? (Consider this: can a water pump function with leaky valves?) _____

6. What is the role of the chordae tendineae? _____

_____

Pulmonary, Systemic, and Cardiac Circulations

7. A simple schematic of a so-called general circulation is shown below. What part of the circulation is missing from this diagram?

_____

Correctly draw the diagram as best you can to make it depict a complete systemic/pulmonary circulation, and rename "general circulation" as the correct subcirculation.

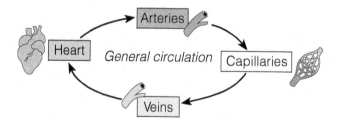

8. Differentiate clearly between the roles of the pulmonary and systemic circulations. _____

_____

_____

9. Complete the following scheme of circulation in the human body:

Right atrium through the right atrioventricular valve to the _____ through the _____

_____ valve to the pulmonary trunk to the _____ to the capillary beds of the lungs to

the _____ to the _____ of the heart through the _____ valve to the

_____ through the _____ valve to the _____ to the systemic arteries to

the _____ of the _____ tissues to the systemic veins to the _____ and

_____ entering the right atrium of the heart.

10. If the left atrioventricular valve does not close properly, which circulation is affected? _____

11. Why might a thrombus (blood clot) in the anterior descending branch of the left coronary artery cause sudden death?

_____

_____

Microscopic Anatomy of Cardiac Muscle

12. Add the following terms to the photo of cardiac muscle at the right:

    intercalated disc

    nucleus of cardiac muscle fiber

    striations

    cardiac muscle fiber

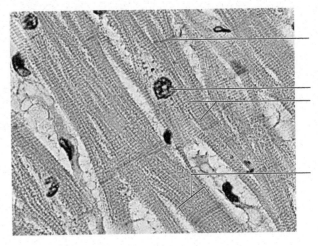

13. What role does the unique structure of cardiac muscle play in its function? (**Note:** Before attempting a response,

    describe the unique anatomy.) _____

_____

_____

_____

Dissection of the Sheep Heart

14. During the sheep heart dissection, you were asked initially to identify the right and left ventricles without cutting into the heart. During this procedure, what differences did you observe between the two chambers?

_____

_____

How would you say this structural difference reflects the relative functions of these two heart chambers?

_____

_____

_____

15. Semilunar valves prevent backflow into the _____; AV valves prevent backflow into the

_____. Using your own observations, explain how the operation of the semilunar

valves differs from that of the AV valves. _____

_____

_____

_____

16. A remnant of the fetal structure is observable in the heart. What was it called in the fetal heart, where was it located, and what purpose did it serve as a functioning fetal structure?

_____

_____

Anatomy of Blood Vessels

Materials

☐ Anatomical charts of human arteries and veins (or a three-dimensional model of the human circulatory system)

☐ Anatomical charts of the following specialized circulations: pulmonary circulation, fetal circulation, hepatic portal circulation, arterial supply and cerebral arterial circle of the brain (or a brain model showing this circulation)

☐ Demonstration area: Microscope slides showing cross sections of an artery and vein set up for student viewing

Pre-Lab Quiz

1. Circle the correct term. <u>Arteries</u> / <u>Veins</u> drain tissues and return blood to the heart.

2. Circle True or False. It is through the walls of capillaries that actual gas exchange takes place between tissue cells and blood.

3. The _____ is the largest artery of the body.
   a. aorta   b. carotid artery   c. femoral artery   d. subclavian artery

4. Circle the correct term. The largest branch of the abdominal aorta, the <u>renal</u> / <u>superior</u> mesenteric artery, supplies most of the small intestine and the first half of the large intestine.

5. Located in the lower limb, the _____ is the longest vein in the body.
   a. external iliac   b. fibular   c. great saphenous   d. internal iliac

6. Circle the correct term. In the developing fetus, the umbilical <u>artery</u> / <u>vein</u> carries blood rich in nutrients and oxygen to the fetus.

The blood vessels form a closed transport system. As the heart contracts, blood is propelled into the large arteries leaving the heart. It moves into successively smaller arteries and then to the arterioles, which feed the capillary beds in the tissues. Capillary beds are drained by the venules, which in turn empty into veins that finally empty into the great veins entering the heart.

Arteries, carrying blood away from the heart, and veins, which return blood to the heart, are simply conducting vessels. Only the tiny capillaries that branch throughout the tissues directly serve the needs of the body's cells. It is through the capillary walls that exchanges are made between tissue cells and blood. Respiratory gases, nutrients, and wastes move along diffusion gradients.

In this exercise, you will examine the microscopic structure of blood vessels and identify the major arteries and veins of the systemic circulation and other special circulations.

Microscopic Structure of the Blood Vessels

OBJECTIVE 1   Describe the tunics of blood vessel walls. State the function of each layer, and discuss how it is/may be modified to serve the differing functional requirements of arteries, veins, and capillaries.

Except for the tiny capillaries, the walls of blood vessels have three coats, or *tunics* (**Figure 21.1**).

- **Tunica intima:** Lines the lumen of a vessel and is a single thin layer of *endothelium* (squamous cells underlain by a scant amount of connective tissue). Its cells fit closely together, forming an extremely smooth blood vessel lining that helps decrease resistance to blood flow.

- **Tunica media:** Is the bulky middle coat made primarily of smooth muscle and elastic tissue. The smooth muscle, controlled by the sympathetic nervous system, is active in changing the diameter of blood vessels. The change in blood vessel diameter alters resistance to blood flow and blood pressure.

- **Tunica externa:** Is the outermost tunic and is composed of fibrous connective tissue. Its function is to support and protect the vessel.

Figure 21.1 Structure of arteries, veins, and capillaries.
(a) Light photomicrograph of a muscular artery and the
corresponding vein in cross section (85×). See also Plate 21
in the Histology Atlas. **(b)** The walls of arteries and veins
are composed of three tunics: the tunica intima, tunica
media, and tunica externa. Capillaries—between arteries
and veins in the circulatory pathway—are composed only
of the tunica intima. Notice that the tunica media is thick
in arteries and relatively thin in veins.

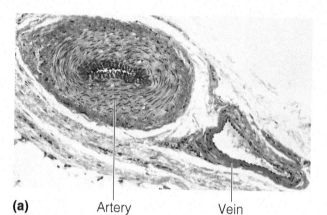

(a)   Artery   Vein

Artery

Tunica intima
• Endothelium
• Loose connective tissue

Vein

Tunica media
• Smooth muscle
• Elastic fibers

Tunica externa
• Collagen fibers

Valve

Lumen   Arteriole   Capillary
network   Venule   Lumen

Basement membrane
Endothelial cells

(b)   **Capillary**

The walls of arteries tend to be thicker than those of veins. The tunica media in particular is much heavier and contains much more smooth muscle and elastic tissue. This structural difference reflects a functional difference in the two types of vessels. Because arteries are closer to the pumping action of the heart, they must be able to expand as blood is propelled into them and then recoil passively as the blood flows off into the circulation during diastole, and their walls must be strong and resilient enough to withstand such pressure fluctuations.

By contrast, veins are far removed from the heart in the circulatory pathway and are essentially low-pressure vessels. Thus, veins may be thinner walled without jeopardy. However, because the pressure in veins tends to be too low to force blood back to the heart and the blood returning to the heart often

flows against gravity, structural modifications are needed to ensure that venous return equals cardiac output. Thus, the lumens of veins tend to be substantially larger than those of corresponding arteries, and there are valves in larger veins that prevent backflow of blood. The skeletal muscle "pump" also promotes venous return; as the skeletal muscles surrounding the veins contract and relax, the blood is "milked" through the veins toward the heart. Pressure changes that occur in the thorax during breathing also aid the return of blood to the heart.

The transparent walls of the tiny capillaries are only one cell layer thick, consisting of just the endothelium underlain by a small amount of fine connective tissue (i.e., just the tunica intima). Because of this exceptional thinness, exchanges occur easily between the blood and tissue cells.

OBJECTIVE 2 Recognize a cross-sectional view of an artery and a vein.

Activity 1

Examining the Microscopic Structure of Arteries and Veins

1. Go to the demonstration area to examine a slide showing a cross-sectional view of blood vessels.

2. Using Figure 21.1a as a guide, scan the section to identify a thick-walled artery. Often, but not always, its lumen will appear scalloped because of the constriction of its walls by the elastic tissue of the media.

3. Identify a vein. Its lumen may be elongated or irregularly shaped and collapsed, and its walls will be considerably thinner.

Major Systemic Arteries of the Body

OBJECTIVE 3 Identify the major arteries arising from the aorta, and name the body region supplied by each.

The **aorta** is the largest artery of the body. Extending upward as the **ascending aorta** from the left ventricle, it arches posteriorly and to the left at the **aortic arch** and then courses downward as the **thoracic aorta** through the thoracic cavity. It passes through the diaphragm to enter the abdominal cavity as the **abdominal aorta,** just anterior to the vertebral column.

Figure 21.2 depicts the relationship of the aorta and its major branches in schematic form. As you locate the arteries on this figure and the ones that follow, be aware of ways to make your memorization task easier. In many cases the name

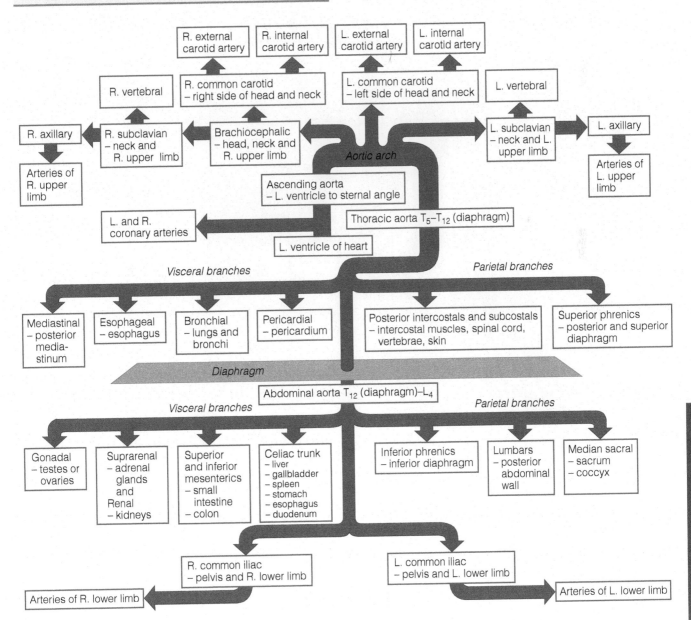

Figure 21.2 Schematic of the systemic arterial circulation. (Notice that a few of the arteries listed here are not discussed in the exercise; L. = left, R. = right.)

of the artery reflects the body region traveled through (axillary, subclavian, brachial, popliteal), the organ served (renal, hepatic), or the bone followed (tibial, femoral, radial, ulnar).

Ascending Aorta

The only branches of the ascending aorta are the **right** and the **left coronary arteries,** which supply the myocardium. The coronary arteries are described in Exercise 20 in conjunction with heart anatomy.

Aortic Arch and Thoracic Aorta

The **brachiocephalic** (literally, "arm-head") **trunk** is the first branch of the aortic arch (**Figure 21.3**). The other two major arteries branching off the aortic arch are the **left common** **carotid artery** and the **left subclavian artery.** The brachiocephalic artery splits and divides into the **right common carotid artery** and the **right subclavian artery.**

Arteries Serving the Head and Neck

The common carotid artery on each side divides to form an **internal carotid artery,** which serves the brain, and an **external carotid artery.** The external carotid artery supplies the tissues external to the skull in the neck and head.

The right and left subclavian arteries each give off several branches to the head and neck. The first of these is the **vertebral artery,** which runs up the posterior neck to supply the cerebellum, brain stem, and the posterior cerebral hemispheres. In the armpit, the subclavian artery becomes the axillary artery, which serves the upper limb.

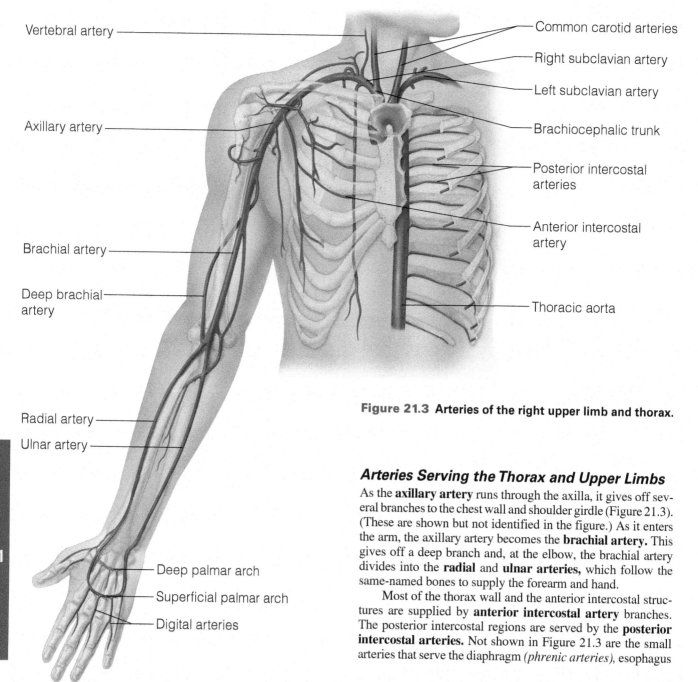

Vertebral artery

Axillary artery

Brachial artery

Deep brachial artery

Radial artery

Ulnar artery

Deep palmar arch

Superficial palmar arch

Digital arteries

Common carotid arteries

Right subclavian artery

Left subclavian artery

Brachiocephalic trunk

Posterior intercostal arteries

Anterior intercostal artery

Thoracic aorta

Figure 21.3 Arteries of the right upper limb and thorax.

Arteries Serving the Thorax and Upper Limbs

As the **axillary artery** runs through the axilla, it gives off several branches to the chest wall and shoulder girdle (Figure 21.3). (These are shown but not identified in the figure.) As it enters the arm, the axillary artery becomes the **brachial artery.** This gives off a deep branch and, at the elbow, the brachial artery divides into the **radial** and **ulnar arteries,** which follow the same-named bones to supply the forearm and hand.

Most of the thorax wall and the anterior intercostal structures are supplied by **anterior intercostal artery** branches. The posterior intercostal regions are served by the **posterior intercostal arteries.** Not shown in Figure 21.3 are the small arteries that serve the diaphragm (*phrenic arteries),* esophagus

21

(esophageal arteries), and bronchi *(bronchial arteries).* However, Figure 21.2 indicates these vessels.

Abdominal Aorta

Although several small branches of the descending aorta serve the thorax, its more major branches serve the abdominal organs and the lower limbs.

Arteries Serving Abdominal Organs

The **celiac trunk** is an unpaired artery that divides almost immediately into three branches (**Figure 21.4a**): the **left gastric artery** supplying the stomach, the **splenic artery** supplying the spleen, and the **common hepatic artery**, which gives off branches to the stomach, small intestine, and pancreas. The common hepatic artery becomes the **hepatic artery proper** as it runs to serve the liver.

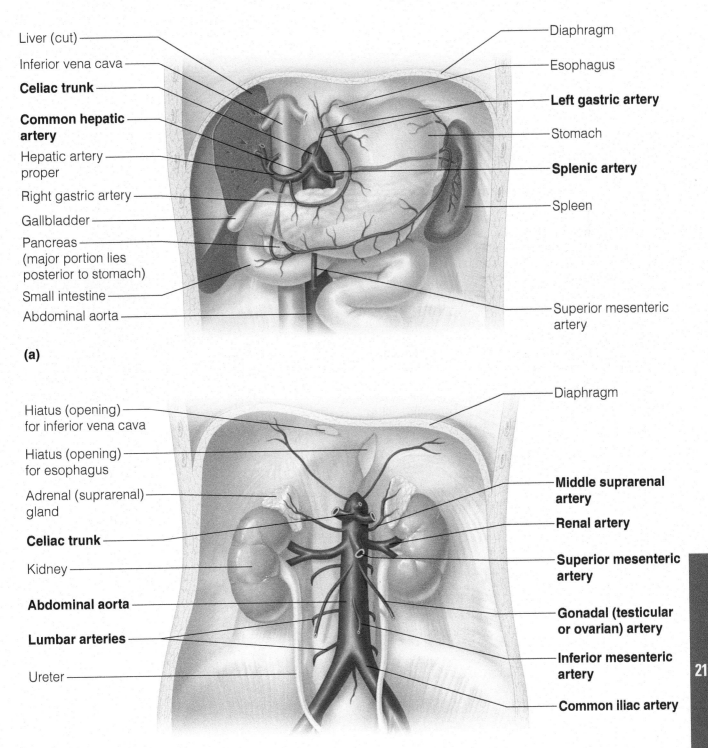

(a)

(b)

Figure 21.4 Arteries of the abdomen. (a) The celiac trunk and its major branches.
(b) Major branches of the abdominal aorta.

21

The largest branch of the abdominal aorta, the **superior mesenteric artery,** supplies most of the small intestine and the first half of the large intestine.

The paired **renal arteries** supply the kidneys, and the **gonadal arteries,** arising from the ventral aortic surface just below the renal arteries, serve the gonads (Figure 21.4b). They are called **ovarian arteries** in the female and **testicular arteries** in the male. Because these vessels travel through the inguinal canal to supply the testes, they are much longer in males than in females.

The final major branch of the abdominal aorta is the **inferior mesenteric artery,** which supplies the distal half of the large intestine. Near this, four pairs of lumbar arteries arise from the aorta and supply the posterior abdominal wall (lumbar region).

In the pelvic region, the descending aorta divides into the two large **common iliac arteries,** which serve the pelvis, lower abdominal wall, and the lower limbs.

Arteries Serving the Lower Limbs

Each of the common iliac arteries extends for about 2 inches into the pelvis before it divides into the internal and external iliac arteries (**Figure 21.5**). The **internal iliac artery** supplies the gluteal muscles, and the adductor muscles of the medial thigh, as well as the genitals.

The **external iliac artery** supplies the anterior abdominal wall and the lower limb. In the thigh, its name changes to **femoral artery.** Proximal branches of the femoral artery supply the head of the femur and the hamstring muscles. Slightly lower, the femoral artery gives off a deep branch, the **deep femoral artery,** which supplies the posterior thigh (knee flexor muscles). At the knee, the femoral artery briefly becomes the **popliteal artery;** its subdivisions—the **anterior** and **posterior tibial arteries**—supply the leg and foot. The anterior tibial artery supplies the extensor muscles and terminates with the **dorsalis pedis artery.** The dorsalis pedis supplies the dorsum of the foot and continues on as the **arcuate artery.** The dorsalis pedis is often palpated in patients with circulation problems of the leg to determine the circulatory efficiency to the limb as a whole.

☐ Palpate your own dorsalis pedis artery.

Check the box when you have completed this task.

Activity 2

Locating Arteries on an Anatomical Chart or Model

Now that you have identified the arteries on Figures 21.2–21.5, attempt to locate and name them (without referring to these figures) on a large anatomical chart or three-dimensional model of the vascular system.

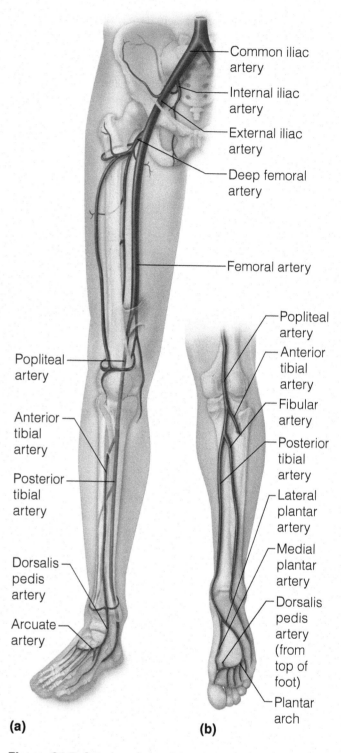

(a)   (b)

Figure 21.5 Arteries of the right pelvis and lower limb.

Major Systemic Veins of the Body

OBJECTIVE 4 Identify the major veins draining into the venae cavae, and indicate the body areas drained.

Arteries are generally located in deep, well-protected body areas. However, veins tend to follow a more superficial course and are often easily seen on the body surface. Most deep veins parallel the course of the major arteries, and in many cases the naming of the veins and arteries is identical except for identifying the vessels as veins. Veins draining the head and upper extremities empty into the **superior vena cava,** and those draining the lower body empty into the **inferior vena cava. Figure 21.6** is a schematic of the systemic veins and their relationship to the venae cavae to get you started.

Veins Draining into the Inferior Vena Cava

The inferior vena cava, a much longer vessel than the superior vena cava, returns blood to the heart from all body regions below the diaphragm. It begins in the lower abdominal region with the

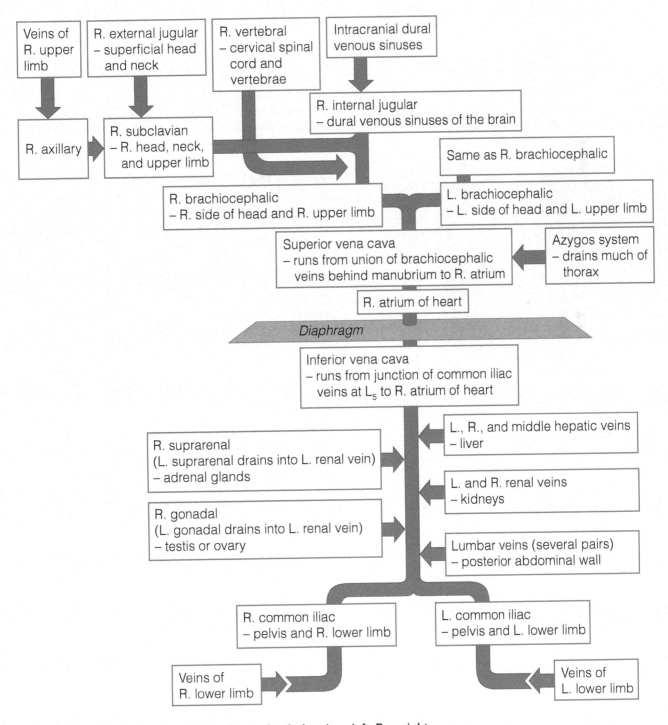

Figure 21.6 Schematic of systemic venous circulation. L. = left, R. = right.

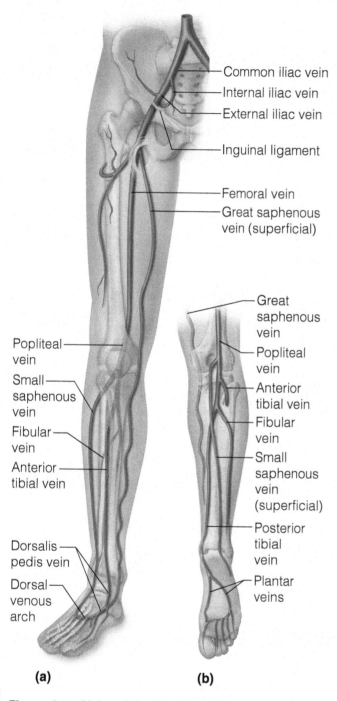

(a)   **(b)**

Figure 21.7 Veins of the right lower limb. (a) Anterior view. **(b)** Posterior view.

union of the paired **common iliac veins** (**Figure 21.7**), which drain venous blood from the legs and pelvis.

Veins of the Lower Limbs

Each common iliac vein is formed by the union of the **internal iliac vein,** draining the pelvis, and the **external iliac vein,** which receives venous blood from the lower limb (Figure 21.7). Veins of the leg include the **anterior** and **posterior tibial veins,** which serve the calf and foot. The anterior tibial vein is a continuation of the **dorsalis pedis vein** of the foot. The posterior tibial vein is formed by the union of the **medial** and **lateral plantar veins** and ascends deep in the calf muscles. It joins with the **fibular vein** at the knee to produce the **popliteal vein,** which crosses the back of the knee. The popliteal vein becomes the **femoral vein** in the thigh. The femoral vein in turn becomes the external iliac vein in the inguinal region.

The **great saphenous vein,** a superficial vein, is the longest vein in the body. Beginning in common with the **small saphenous vein** from the **dorsal venous arch,** it extends up the medial side of the leg, knee, and thigh to empty into the femoral vein. The small saphenous vein drains the calf muscle and then empties into the popliteal vein at the knee (Figure 21.7b).

Veins of the Abdomen

Moving superiorly in the abdominal cavity (**Figure 21.8**), the inferior vena cava receives blood from the posterior abdominal wall via several pairs of **lumbar veins,** and from the right ovary or testis via the **right gonadal vein.** (The **left gonadal vein** drains into the left renal vein superiorly.) The paired **renal veins** drain the kidneys. Just above the right renal vein, the **right suprarenal vein** (receiving blood from the adrenal gland on the same side) drains into the inferior vena cava, but its partner, the **left suprarenal vein,** empties into the left renal vein inferiorly. The **right** and **left hepatic veins** drain the liver. The unpaired veins draining the digestive tract organs empty into a special vessel, the **hepatic portal vein,** which carries blood to the liver to be processed before it enters the systemic venous system. (The hepatic portal system is discussed separately on page 269.)

Veins Draining into the Superior Vena Cava

Veins draining into the superior vena cava are named from the superior vena cava distally, but remember that the flow of blood is in the *opposite* direction.

Veins of the Head and Neck

The **right** and **left brachiocephalic veins** drain the head, neck, and upper extremities and unite to form the superior vena cava (**Figure 21.9**). Notice that although there is only one brachiocephalic artery, there are two brachiocephalic veins.

Branches of the brachiocephalic veins include the internal jugular, vertebral, and subclavian veins. The **internal jugular veins** are large veins that drain the dural sinuses of the brain, and they receive blood from the head and neck as they move inferiorly. The **vertebral veins** (not shown in Figure 21.9) drain the posterior aspect of the head and neck. The **subclavian veins** receive venous blood from the upper limb. The **external jugular vein,** returning venous drainage of the extracranial (superficial) tissues of the head and neck, joins the subclavian vein near its origin.

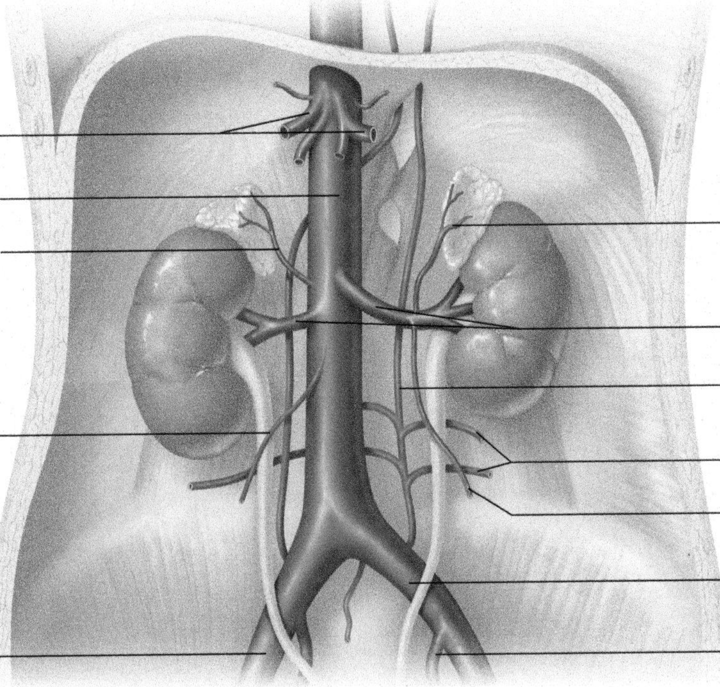
Hepatic veins
Inferior vena cava
Right suprarenal vein
Right gonadal vein
External iliac vein
Left suprarenal vein
Renal veins
Left ascending lumbar vein
Lumbar veins
Left gonadal vein
Common iliac vein
Internal iliac vein

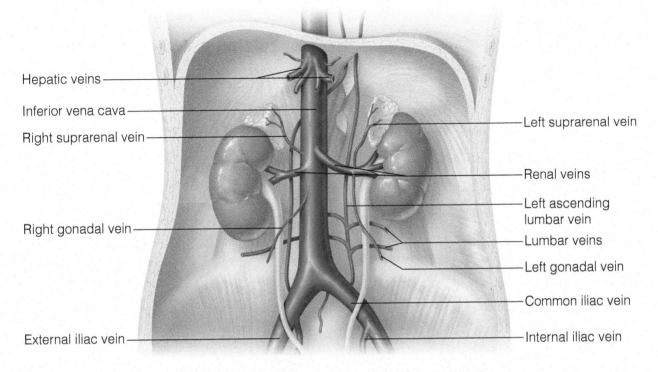

Figure 21.8 Venous drainage of abdominal organs not drained by the hepatic portal vein.

Veins of the Upper Limb and Thorax

As the subclavian vein enters the axilla, it becomes the **axillary vein** and then the **brachial vein** as it runs the course of the humerus (Figure 21.9). The brachial vein is formed by the union of the deep **radial** and **ulnar veins** of the forearm. The superficial venous drainage of the arm includes the **cephalic vein** laterally, which empties into the axillary vein; the medial **basilic vein,** which enters the brachial vein; and the **median cubital vein,** which runs between the cephalic and basilic veins in the anterior elbow.

The **azygos vein,** which drains the right side of the thorax, enters the dorsal aspect of the superior vena cava just before that vessel enters the heart.

Activity 3

Identifying the Systemic Veins

Identify the important veins of the systemic circulation on the large anatomical chart or model without referring to the figures.

Special Circulations

OBJECTIVE 5 Discuss the unique features of the special circulations studied.

Pulmonary Circulation

The pulmonary circulation (discussed previously with heart anatomy on page 250) differs in many ways from systemic circulation because it does not serve the metabolic needs of the body tissues. It functions instead to bring blood into close contact with the air sacs of the lungs to permit gas exchanges that rid the blood of excess carbon dioxide and replenish its supply of vital oxygen.

Pulmonary circulation begins with the large **pulmonary trunk,** which leaves the right ventricle and divides into the **right** and **left pulmonary arteries** about 2 inches above its origin (**Figure 21.10**). The pulmonary arteries plunge into the lungs, where they subdivide into **lobar arteries** (three on the right and two on the left), which accompany the main bronchi into the lungs. The lobar arteries branch extensively within the lungs and finally end in the capillary networks surrounding the air sacs of the lungs. Diffusion of the respiratory gases occurs across the walls of the air sacs (alveoli) and **pulmonary capillaries.** The pulmonary capillary beds are drained by venules, which converge to form larger and larger veins and finally the four **pulmonary veins** (two leaving each lung), which return the blood to the left atrium of the heart.

Activity 4

Identifying Vessels of the Pulmonary Circulation

In Figure 21.10, label all structures provided with leader lines using choices from the list provided in the figure.

Fetal Circulation

In a developing fetus, the lungs and digestive system are not yet functioning, and all nutrient, excretory, and gaseous

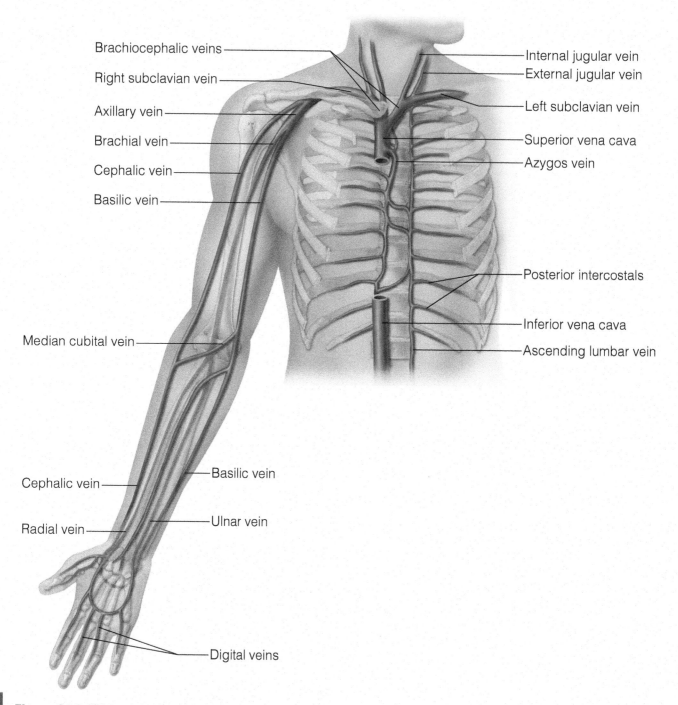

Brachiocephalic veins

Right subclavian vein

Axillary vein

Brachial vein

Cephalic vein

Basilic vein

Internal jugular vein

External jugular vein

Left subclavian vein

Superior vena cava

Azygos vein

Posterior intercostals

Inferior vena cava

Ascending lumbar vein

Median cubital vein

Cephalic vein

Radial vein

Basilic vein

Ulnar vein

Digital veins

Figure 21.9 Veins of the right upper limb and shoulder. For clarity, the abundant branching and anastomoses of these vessels are not shown.

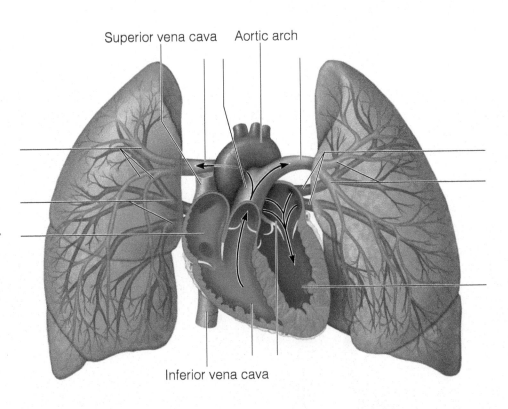

Superior vena cava   Aortic arch

Inferior vena cava

a. Left atrium

b. Pulmonary trunk

c. Right pulmonary artery

d. Left pulmonary artery

e. Left pulmonary veins

f. Lobar arteries (left lung)

g. Lobar arteries (right lung)

h. Right atrium

i. Right ventricle

j. Right pulmonary veins

k. Left ventricle

Figure 21.10 The pulmonary circulation.

exchanges occur through the placenta (**Figure 21.11**). Nutrients and oxygen move from the mother's blood into fetal blood, and carbon dioxide and other metabolic wastes move in the opposite direction.

Fetal blood travels through the umbilical cord, which contains three blood vessels: the **umbilical vein** carries blood rich in nutrients and oxygen to the fetus; the smaller **umbilical arteries** carry carbon dioxide and waste-laden blood from the fetus to the placenta. As newly oxygenated blood flows superiorly toward the fetal heart, some of this blood perfuses the liver, but most of it is shunted through the immature liver to the inferior vena cava via the **ductus venosus,** which carries the blood to the right atrium of the heart.

Because fetal lungs are nonfunctional and collapsed, two shunting mechanisms ensure that blood almost entirely bypasses the lungs. Some of the blood entering the right atrium moves into the left atrium through the **foramen ovale,** a flaplike opening in the interatrial septum. The left ventricle then pumps the blood out of the aorta to the systemic circulation. Blood that does enter the right ventricle and is pumped out of the pulmonary trunk encounters a second shunt, the **ductus arteriosus,** a short vessel connecting the pulmonary trunk and the aorta. Because the collapsed lungs present an extremely high-resistance pathway, blood tends to enter the systemic circulation through the ductus arteriosus.

The aorta carries blood to the tissues of the body; this blood ultimately finds its way back to the placenta via the umbilical arteries. At birth, or shortly after, the foramen ovale closes, the ductus arteriosus collapses, and the circulatory pattern becomes that of the adult.

Activity 5

Tracing the Pathway of Fetal Blood Flow

Figure 21.11 indicates the pathway of fetal blood flow with arrows. Appropriately label all specialized fetal circulatory structures provided with leader lines.

Hepatic Portal Circulation

The veins of the hepatic portal circulation (**Figure 21.12**) drain the digestive organs, spleen, and pancreas and deliver this blood to the liver via the **hepatic portal vein.** As blood percolates through the liver, some of the nutrients are stored or processed in various ways for release to the general circulation. The liver in turn is drained by the hepatic veins that enter the inferior vena cava.

The **inferior mesenteric vein,** draining the distal part of the large intestine, joins the **splenic vein,** which drains the spleen, pancreas, and stomach. The splenic vein and the **superior mesenteric vein,** which drains the small intestine and the proximal colon, unite to form the hepatic portal vein. The **left gastric vein,** which drains the lesser curvature of the stomach, drains directly into the hepatic portal vein.

Activity 6

Tracing the Hepatic Portal Circulation

Locate the vessels named in Figure 21.12.

21

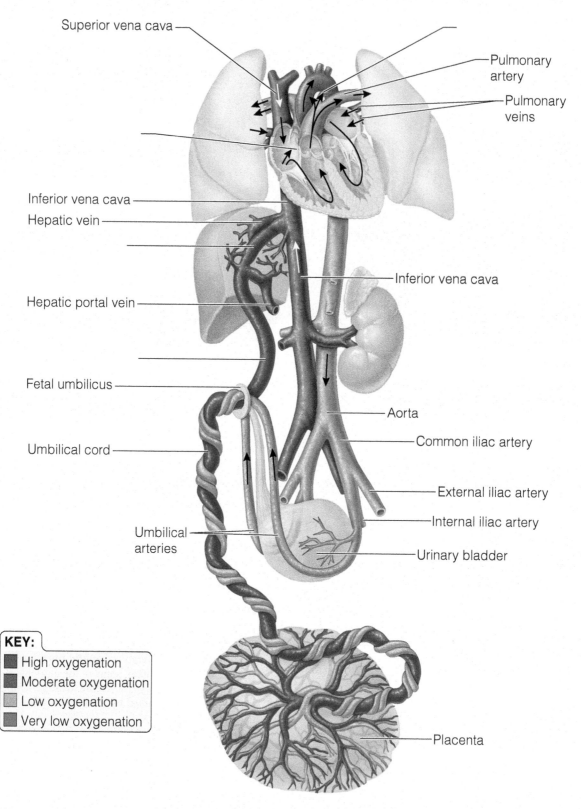

Superior vena cava

Pulmonary artery

Pulmonary veins

Inferior vena cava

Hepatic vein

Inferior vena cava

Hepatic portal vein

Fetal umbilicus

Aorta

Common iliac artery

Umbilical cord

External iliac artery

Internal iliac artery

Umbilical arteries

Urinary bladder

KEY:
■ High oxygenation
■ Moderate oxygenation
■ Low oxygenation
■ Very low oxygenation

Placenta

21

Figure 21.11 Schematic of the fetal circulation.

Arterial Supply of the Brain and the Cerebral Arterial Circle

A continuous blood supply to the brain is essential because oxygen deprivation for even a few minutes causes the delicate brain tissue to die. The brain is supplied by two pairs of arteries arising from the region of the aortic arch—the *internal carotid arteries* and the *vertebral arteries*. **Figure 21.13** is a diagram of the brain's arterial supply.

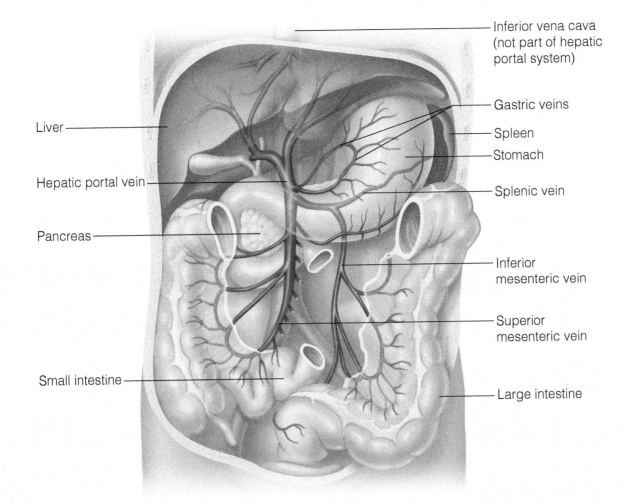

Inferior vena cava
(not part of hepatic
portal system)

Gastric veins

Spleen

Stomach

Splenic vein

Inferior
mesenteric vein

Superior
mesenteric vein

Large intestine

Liver

Hepatic portal vein

Pancreas

Small intestine

Figure 21.12 The hepatic portal circulation.

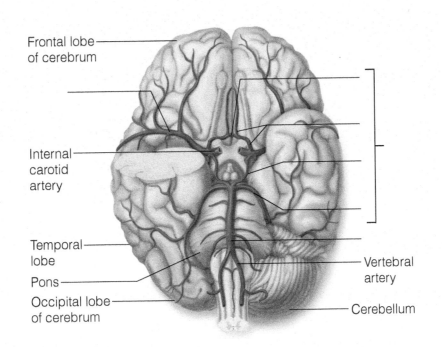

Frontal lobe
of cerebrum

Internal
carotid
artery

Temporal
lobe

Pons

Occipital lobe
of cerebrum

Vertebral
artery

Cerebellum

Figure 21.13 Arterial supply of the brain.

21

Activity 7

Tracing the Arterial Supply of the Brain

The internal carotid and vertebral arteries are labeled in Figure 21.13. As you read the description of the brain's blood supply that follows, complete the labeling of Figure 21.13.

The **internal carotid arteries,** branches of the common carotid arteries, take a deep course through the neck, entering the skull through the carotid canals of the temporal bone. Within the cranium, each divides into **anterior** and **middle cerebral arteries,** which supply the bulk of the cerebrum. The internal carotid arteries also contribute to the **cerebral arterial circle (circle of Willis),** an arterial network at the base of the brain surrounding the pituitary gland and the optic chiasma, by helping to form a **posterior communicating artery** on each side. The circle is completed by the **anterior communicating artery,** a short shunt connecting the right and left anterior cerebral arteries.

The paired **vertebral arteries** branch from the subclavian arteries and pass superiorly through the transverse processes of the cervical vertebrae to enter the skull through the foramen magnum. Within the skull, the vertebral arteries unite to form the single **basilar artery,** which runs superiorly along the ventral brain stem, giving off branches to the pons and cerebellum. At the base of the cerebrum, the basilar artery divides to form the **posterior cerebral arteries,** which supply the posterior part of the cerebrum and become part of the cerebral arterial circle by joining with the posterior communicating arteries.

The uniting of the anterior and posterior blood supplies via the cerebral arterial circle is a protective device that provides an alternate set of pathways for blood to reach the brain tissue in the case of impaired blood flow anywhere in the system.

REVIEW SHEET
Anatomy of Blood Vessels

Name _____ Lab Time/Date _____

Microscopic Structure of the Blood Vessels

1. Use the key choices to identify the blood vessel tunic described. (Some choices may be used more than once.)

   Key: tunica intima   tunica media   tunica externa

   _____ 1. most internal tunic

   _____ 2. bulky middle tunic contains smooth muscle and elastin

   _____ 3. its smooth surface decreases friction

   _____ 4. tunic of capillaries

   _____, _____, _____ 5. tunic(s) of arteries and veins

   _____ 6. tunic that is especially thick in arteries

   _____ 7. most superficial tunic

2. Servicing the capillaries is the basic function of the organs of the circulatory system. Explain this statement.

   _____

   _____

   _____

3. Cross-sectional views of an artery and of a vein are shown here. Identify each by labeling the appropriate leader line. Also respond to the related questions that follow.

   Which of these vessels may have valves? _____

   Which of these vessels depends on its elasticity to propel blood along? _____

   Which depends on the skeletal muscle pump and changes during breathing? _____ Explain this dependence.

   _____

   _____

4. Why are the walls of arteries relatively thicker than those of the corresponding veins? _____

_____

_____

_____

Major Systemic Arteries and Veins of the Body

5. Use the key on the right to identify the arteries or veins described on the left.

Key:

_____ 1. the arterial system has one of these; the venous system has two

_____ 2. these arteries supply the myocardium

_____ 3. the more anterior artery pair serving the brain

_____ 4. longest vein in the body

_____ 5. artery on the foot checked after leg surgery

_____ 6. serves the posterior thigh

_____ 7. arteries supplying the diaphragm

_____ 8. formed by the union of the radial and ulnar veins

_____, _____ 9. two superficial veins of the arm

_____ 10. artery serving the kidney

_____ 11. testicular or ovarian veins

_____ 12. artery that supplies the distal half of the large intestine

_____ 13. drains the pelvic organs and lower limbs

_____ 14. what the external iliac vein drains into in the pelvis

_____ 15. major artery serving the arm

_____ 16. supplies most of the small intestine

_____ 17. what the femoral artery becomes at the knee

_____ 18. an arterial trunk that has three major branches, which run to the liver, spleen, and stomach

_____ 19. major artery serving the skin and scalp of the head

_____, _____ 20. two veins that join, forming the popliteal vein

_____ 21. artery generally used to take the pulse at the wrist

anterior tibial

basilic

brachial

brachiocephalic

celiac trunk

cephalic

common carotid

common iliac

coronary

deep femoral

dorsalis pedis

external carotid

femoral

gonadal

great saphenous

inferior mesenteric

internal carotid

internal iliac

fibular

phrenic

popliteal

posterior tibial

radial

renal

subclavian

superior mesenteric

vertebral

6. The human arterial and venous systems are diagrammed on this page and the next. Identify all indicated blood vessels.

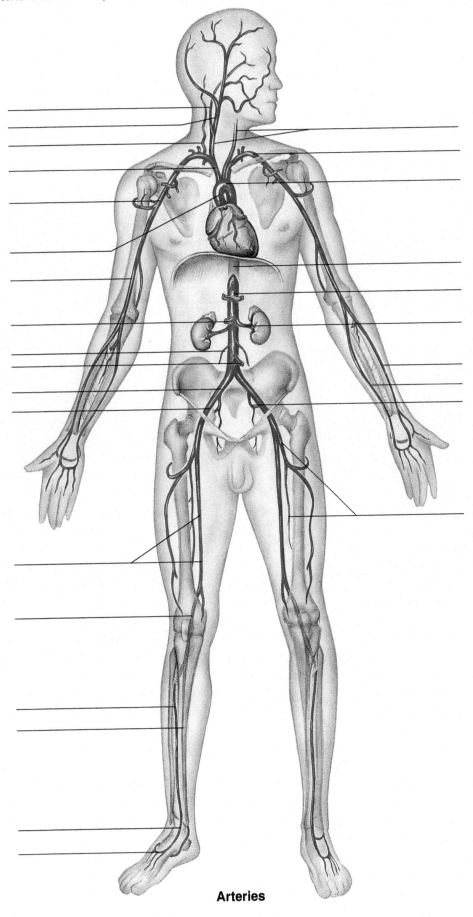

Arteries

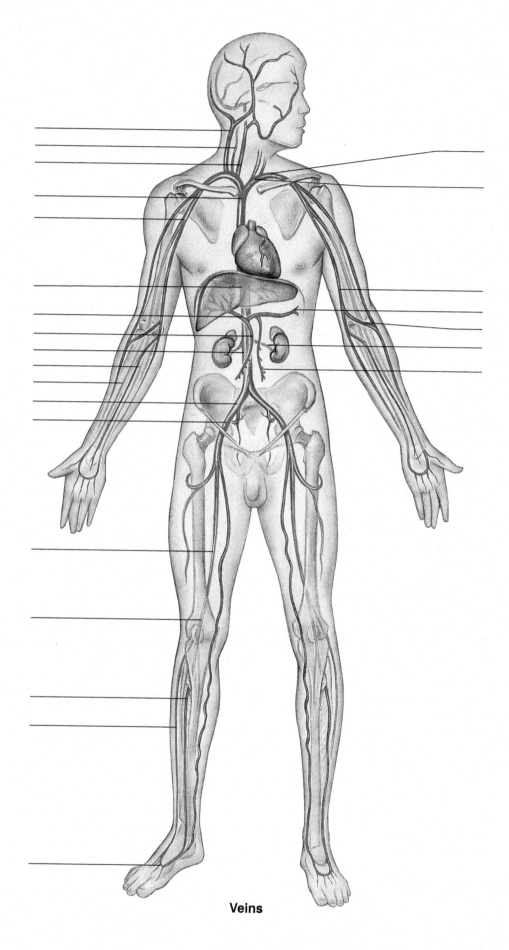

Veins

7. Trace the blood flow for the following situations:

a. From the capillary beds of the left thumb to the capillary beds of the right thumb: _____

_____

_____

_____

_____

_____

_____

b. From the pulmonary vein to the pulmonary artery by way of the right side of the brain: _____

_____

_____

_____

_____

_____

_____

_____

_____

_____

Special Circulations

Pulmonary Circulation

8. Trace the pathway of a carbon dioxide gas molecule in the blood from the inferior vena cava until it leaves the blood-stream. Name all structures (vessels, heart chambers, and others) it passes through en route.

_____

_____

_____

9. Trace the pathway of an oxygen gas molecule from an alveolus of the lung to the right atrium of the heart. Name all

structures through which it passes. _____

_____

_____

10. Most arteries of the adult body carry oxygen-rich blood, and the veins carry oxygen-depleted, carbon dioxide–rich blood.

How are the pulmonary arteries and veins different? _____

_____

_____

Hepatic Portal Circulation

11. What is the source of blood in the hepatic portal system? _____

_____

12. Why is this blood carried to the liver before it enters the systemic circulation? _____

_____

13. The hepatic portal vein is formed by the union of the _____, which drains the

_____, _____, _____, and the

_____ (via the interior mesenteric vein), and the _____, which drains

the _____ and _____. The _____ vein,

which drains the lesser curvature of the stomach, empties directly into the hepatic portal vein.

14. Trace the flow of a drop of blood from the small intestine to the right atrium of the heart, noting all structures it

encounters or passes through on the way. _____

_____

_____

Arterial Supply of the Brain and the Cerebral Arterial Circle

15. Branches of the internal carotid and vertebral arteries cooperate to form a ring of blood vessels encircling the pituitary

gland, at the base of the brain. What name is given to this communication network? _____

What is its function? _____

_____

16. What portion of the brain is served by the anterior and middle cerebral arteries? _____

_____

Both the anterior and middle cerebral arteries arise from the _____ arteries.

17. Trace the usual pathway of a drop of blood from the aorta to the left occipital lobe of the brain, noting all structures

through which it flows. Aorta $\longrightarrow$ _____ $\longrightarrow$ _____ $\longrightarrow$

_____ $\longrightarrow$ _____ $\longrightarrow$ left

occipital lobe.

Fetal Circulation

18. The failure of two of the fetal bypass structures to become obliterated after birth can cause congenital heart disease, in which the youngster would have improperly oxygenated blood. Which two structures are these?

_____ and _____

19. For each of the following structures, indicate its function in the fetus. Circle the blood vessel that carries the most oxygen-rich blood.

Structure	Function in fetus
Umbilical artery	
Umbilical vein	
Ductus venosus	
Ductus arteriosus	
Foramen ovale	

20. What organ serves as a respiratory/digestive/excretory organ for the fetus? _____

EXERCISE 22

Human Cardiovascular Physiology—Blood Pressure and Pulse Determinations

Materials

- ☐ Stethoscope
- ☐ Sphygmomanometer
- ☐ Watch (or clock) with a second hand
- ☐ Felt marker
- ☐ Step stools (16 in. and 20 in. in height)
- ☐ Cot (if available)
- ☐ Alcohol swabs

Pre-Lab Quiz

1. Circle the correct term. According to general usage, <u>systole</u> / <u>diastole</u> refers to ventricular relaxation.

2. A graph illustrating the pressure and volume changes during one heartbeat is called the:
   a. blood pressure
   b. cardiac cycle
   c. conduction system of the heart
   d. electrical events of the heartbeat

3. Circle True or False. When ventricular systole begins, intraventricular pressure increases rapidly, closing the atrioventricular (AV) valves.

4. The average heart beats approximately _____ times per minute.
   a. 50
   b. 75
   c. 100
   d. 125

5. What device will you use today to measure your subject's blood pressure? _____

6. In reporting a blood pressure of 120/90, which number represents the *diastolic* pressure? _____

During this exercise, we will investigate pulse, heart sounds, and blood pressure, all of which reflect the heart and blood vessels in action. The discussion of the cardiac cycle below will help you to understand and interpret the physiological measurements taken during the lab.

Cardiac Cycle

OBJECTIVE 1 Define *systole, diastole,* and *cardiac cycle,* and describe the events of the cardiac cycle.

In a healthy heart, the atria contract simultaneously. Then, as they begin to relax, the ventricles contract. However, in general usage, the terms **systole** and **diastole** refer to contraction and relaxation, respectively, of the ventricles.

The **cardiac cycle** includes events of one complete heartbeat. During the cardiac cycle, both atria and ventricles contract and then relax, and a predictable sequence of changes in blood volume and pressure occurs within the heart. **Figure 22.1** shows the events of the cardiac cycle for the left side of the heart. Pressure changes in the right side of the heart are less dramatic, but the same relationships apply.

Let's start our discussion of the cardiac cycle with the heart in complete relaxation (diastole). Pressure in the heart is very low, and blood is flowing passively from the pulmonary and systemic circulations into the atria and on through to the ventricles. The semilunar valves are closed, and the AV valves are open. Then atrial contraction occurs and atrial pressure increases, forcing blood remaining in their chambers into the ventricles. Then ventricular systole begins, and pressure in the ventricles rises rapidly, closing the AV valves. When ventricular pressure exceeds that of the large arteries leaving the heart, the semilunar valves are forced open, and the blood in the ventricles gushes through those valves. During this phase, the pressure in the aorta reaches approximately 120 mm Hg. While the ventricles are contracting, the atria relax; as their chambers fill with blood, atrial pressure gradually rises. At the end of the ventricular systole, the ventricles

281

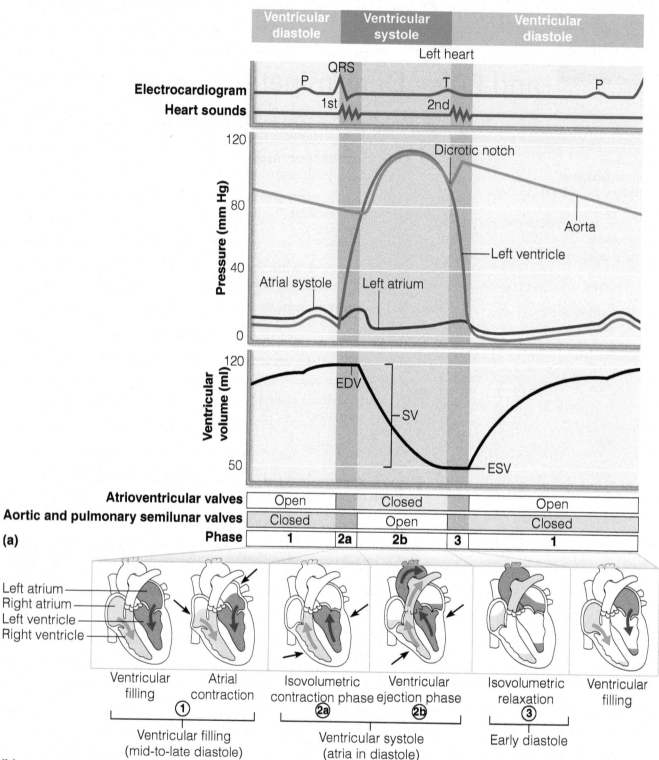

	Ventricular diastole	Ventricular systole	Ventricular diastole

Left heart

Electrocardiogram
Heart sounds

Pressure (mm Hg)

Ventricular volume (ml)

Atrial systole
Left atrium
Dicrotic notch
Aorta
Left ventricle

EDV
SV
ESV

Atrioventricular valves	Open	Closed	Open
Aortic and pulmonary semilunar valves	Closed	Open	Closed
Phase	1	2a	2b	3	1

(a)

Left atrium
Right atrium
Left ventricle
Right ventricle

Ventricular filling — Atrial contraction ①
Ventricular filling (mid-to-late diastole)

Isovolumetric contraction phase ②a — Ventricular ejection phase ②b
Ventricular systole (atria in diastole)

Isovolumetric relaxation ③ — Ventricular filling
Early diastole

(b)

Figure 22.1 Summary of events occurring in the heart during the cardiac cycle. (a) Events in the left side of the heart. An electrocardiogram tracing is superimposed on the graph (top) so that pressure and volume changes can be related to electrical events occurring at any point. The P wave indicates depolarization of the atria; the QRS wave is depolarization of the ventricles (which hides the repolarization wave of the atria); the T wave is repolarization of the ventricles. Time occurrence of heart sounds, due to valve closures, is also indicated. *EDV = end diastolic volume (volume in ventricle just *before* it begins to contract); SV = stroke volume, ESV = end systolic volume (volume in ventricle just after it has contracted and ejected blood). **(b)** Events of phases 1 through 3 of the cardiac cycle are depicted in diagrammatic views of the heart.

22

relax; the semilunar valves snap shut, preventing backflow, and the pressure within the ventricles begins to drop. When intraventricular pressure is again less than atrial pressure, the AV valves are forced open, and the ventricles again begin to fill with blood. Atrial and aortic pressures decrease, and the ventricles rapidly refill, completing the cycle. The average heart beats approximately 70 to 76 beats per minute, so the length of the cardiac cycle is about 0.8 second. (This value was obtained by dividing 60 seconds by the number of beats per minute.)

Study Figure 22.1 carefully to make sure you understand what has been discussed before continuing on with the exercise.

Heart Sounds

OBJECTIVE 2   Relate heart sounds to events of the cardiac cycle.

Two distinct sounds can be heard during each cardiac cycle. These **heart sounds** are commonly described by the monosyllables "lub" and "dup"; the sequence is lub-dup, pause, lub-dup, pause, and so on. The first heart sound (lub) occurs as the AV valves close at the beginning of systole. The second heart string (dup) occurs as the semilunar valves close at the end of systole. Figure 22.1a indicates the timing of heart sounds in the cardiac cycle and in relation to an electrocardiogram (ECG).

Activity 1

Auscultating Heart Sounds

In this activity, you will auscultate (listen to) your partner's heart sounds with an ordinary stethoscope.

1. Obtain a stethoscope and some alcohol swabs. Heart sounds are best auscultated if the subject's outer clothing is removed, so a male subject is preferable.

2. Clean the earpieces of the stethoscope with an alcohol swab. Allow the alcohol to dry. Notice that the earpieces are angled. For comfort, angle the earpieces in a *forward* direction when you place them into your ears.

3. Put on the stethoscope. Place the diaphragm of the stethoscope on your partner's thorax, just medial to the left nipple at the fifth intercostal space. Listen carefully for heart sounds. The first sound will be a longer, louder (more booming) sound than the second, which is short and sharp. After listening for a couple minutes, try to time the pause between the second sound of one heartbeat and the first sound of the subsequent heartbeat.

How long is this interval? _____ sec

How does it compare to the interval between the first and second sounds of a single heartbeat?

_____

_____

The Pulse

OBJECTIVE 3   Define *pulse,* and accurately determine a subject's apical and radial pulse.

The term **pulse** refers to the alternating surges of pressure (expansion and then recoil) in an artery that occur with each beat of the left ventricle. Normally the pulse rate equals the heart rate, and the pulse averages 70 to 76 beats per minute in the resting state.

Conditions other than pulse *rate* are also useful clinically. Can you feel it strongly—does the blood vessel expand and recoil (sometimes visibly) with the pressure waves—or is it difficult to detect? Is it regular like the ticking of a clock, or does it seem to skip beats? Record your observations.

_____

_____

_____

_____

_____

Activity 2

Taking an Apical Pulse

With the subject sitting quietly, one student, using a stethoscope, should determine the apical pulse (by counting the heartbeats) while at the same time another student should count the radial pulse rate (inside the wrist). Position the stethoscope over the fifth left intercostal space. The person taking the radial pulse will determine the starting point for the count and give the stop-count signal exactly 1 minute later. Record your values below.

apical count _____ beats/min

radial count _____ pulses/min

pulse deficit _____ pulses/min

The apical pulse may be slightly faster than the radial because of a slight lag in time as the blood rushes from the heart into the large arteries where it can be palpated. However, any large difference between the values observed, referred to as a **pulse deficit,** may indicate a weakened heart that is unable to pump sufficient blood into the arterial tree or abnormal heart rhythms. Apical pulse counts are routinely ordered for people with cardiac disease.

22

Activity 3

Palpating Superficial Pulse Points

The pulse may be felt easily on any artery close to the body surface when the artery is compressed over a bone or firm tissue. Palpate the following pulse or pressure points on your partner (or yourself) by placing the fingertips of the first two fingers of one hand over the artery. (**Note:** Never use your thumb when measuring a pulse, because your thumb has a faint pulse of its own.) It helps to compress the artery firmly as you begin your palpation and then immediately ease up on the pressure slightly. In each case, notice the regularity of the pulse and assess its force. **Figure 22.2** illustrates the superficial pulse points to be palpated. Check off the boxes as you locate each pulse point.

☐ **Common carotid artery:** At the side of the neck

☐ **Superficial temporal artery:** Anterior to the ear

☐ **Facial artery:** Clench the teeth, and palpate the pulse just anterior to the masseter muscle (in line with the corner of the mouth).

☐ **Brachial artery:** In the antecubital fossa, at the point where it splits into the radial and ulnar arteries

☐ **Radial artery:** At the lateral aspect of the wrist, just above the thumb

☐ **Femoral artery:** In the groin

☐ **Popliteal artery:** At the back of the knee

☐ **Posterior tibial artery:** Just above the medial malleolus

☐ **Dorsalis pedis artery:** On the dorsum of the foot

Which pulse point had the greatest amplitude (force)?

_____

Which had the least? _____

Can you offer any explanation for this? _____

_____

_____

_____

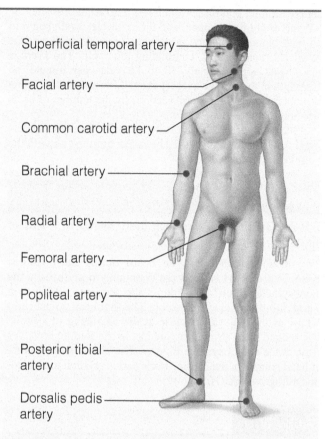

Superficial temporal artery

Facial artery

Common carotid artery

Brachial artery

Radial artery

Femoral artery

Popliteal artery

Posterior tibial artery

Dorsalis pedis artery

Figure 22.2 Body sites where the pulse is most easily palpated.

Because of its easy accessibility, the pulse is most often taken on the radial artery. With your partner sitting quietly, practice counting the radial pulse for 1 minute. Do three counts, and average the results.

count 1 _____ count 2 _____

count 3 _____ average _____

Blood Pressure Determinations

OBJECTIVE 4 Define *blood pressure* and *pulse,* and accurately determine a subject's pulse with a sphygmomanometer.

Blood pressure is the pressure the blood exerts against the inner blood vessel walls; it is generally measured in the arteries. Because the heart alternately contracts and relaxes, the rhythmic flow of blood into the arteries causes the blood pressure to rise and fall during each beat. Thus you must take two blood pressure readings: the **systolic pressure,** which is the pressure in the arteries at the peak of ventricular ejection, and the **diastolic pressure,** the pressure during ventricular relaxation. Blood pressures are reported in millimeters of mercury (mm Hg), with the systolic pressure appearing first; 120/80 translates to 120 over 80, or a systolic pressure of 120 mm Hg and a diastolic pressure of 80 mm Hg. However, normal blood pressure varies considerably from one person to another.

Activity 4

Using a Sphygmomanometer to Measure Arterial Blood Pressure Indirectly

The **sphygmomanometer,** commonly called a *blood pressure cuff,* is an instrument used to measure blood pressure by the auscultatory method (**Figure 22.3**). It consists of an inflatable cuff with an attached pressure gauge. The cuff is inflated to stop blood flow to the forearm. As cuff pressure is gradually released, the examiner listens with a stethoscope over the brachial artery (Figure 22.3c).

1. Work in pairs to obtain radial artery blood pressure readings. Obtain a stethoscope, alcohol swabs, and a sphygmomanometer. Clean the earpieces of the stethoscope with the alcohol swabs, and check the cuff for the presence of trapped air by compressing it against the laboratory table. (A partially inflated cuff will produce erroneous measurements.)

2. The subject should sit in a comfortable position with one arm resting on the laboratory table (approximately at heart level if possible). Wrap the cuff snugly around the subject's arm, just above the elbow, with the inflatable area on the medial arm surface. The cuff may be marked with an arrow; if so, position the arrow over the brachial artery (Figure 22.3a). Secure the cuff by tucking the distal end under the wrapped portion or by bringing the Velcro areas together.

3. Palpate the brachial pulse, and lightly mark its position with a felt pen. Don the stethoscope, and place its diaphragm over the pulse point.

⚠ *Do not keep the cuff inflated for more than 1 minute.* If you have any trouble obtaining a reading within this time, deflate the cuff, wait 1 or 2 minutes, and try again. (A prolonged interruption of blood flow can cause fainting.)

4. Inflate the cuff to approximately 160 mm Hg pressure to stop blood flow into the forearm. Then slowly release the pressure valve. Watch the pressure gauge as you listen for the first soft thudding sounds of the blood spurting through the partially blocked artery. These characteristic sounds, called the **sounds of Korotkoff,** indicate the resumption of blood flow into the forearm. Make a mental note of this pressure (record as the systolic pressure), and continue to release the cuff pressure. You will notice first an increase, then a muffling, of the sound. Record as the diastolic pressure, the pressure at which the sounds disappear and the blood flows freely (Figure 22.3d). Make two blood pressure determinations, and record your results.

First trial: Second trial:

systolic pressure _____   systolic pressure _____

diastolic pressure _____ diastolic pressure _____

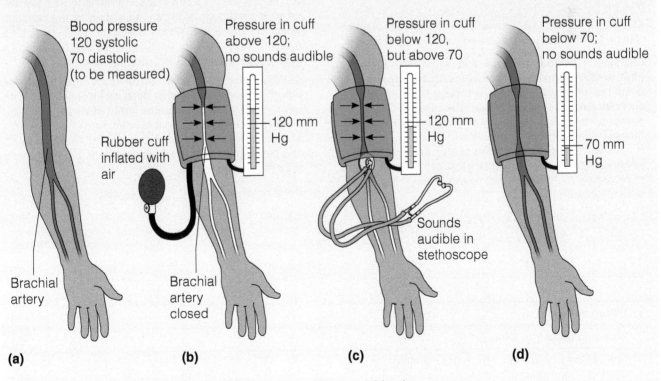

(a)   (b)   (c)   (d)

Figure 22.3 Procedure for measuring blood pressure. (Assume a blood pressure of 120/70.)

22

Activity 5

Observing the Effect of Various Factors on Blood Pressure and Heart Rate

Arterial blood pressure (BP) is directly proportional to cardiac output (CO, amount of blood pumped out of the left ventricle per minute) and peripheral resistance (PR) to blood flow; that is,

$$BP = CO \times PR$$

Peripheral resistance is increased by blood vessel constriction (most importantly the arterioles), by an increase in blood viscosity or volume, and by a loss of elasticity of the arteries (seen in arteriosclerosis). Any factor that increases either the cardiac output or the peripheral resistance causes an almost immediate reflex rise in blood pressure. Here we investigate two factors that alter blood pressure—posture and exercise.

For the following tests, one student should act as the subject and two as examiners (one taking the radial pulse and the other auscultating the brachial blood pressure). A fourth student collects and records the data. Leave the sphygmomanometer cuff on the subject's arm throughout the experiments (in a deflated state, of course) so that, at the proper times, the blood pressure can be taken quickly. In each case, take the measurements at least twice.

Posture

To monitor circulatory adjustments to changes in position, take blood pressure and pulse measurements under the conditions noted in the Activity 5 Posture chart below. Also record your results on that chart.

Exercise

OBJECTIVE 5 Investigate the effects of exercise on blood pressure, pulse, and cardiovascular fitness.

Changes in blood pressure and pulse during and after exercise provide a good yardstick for measuring overall cardiovascular fitness. Although there are more accurate tests to evaluate fitness, the *Harvard Step Test* described here is a quick way to compare the relative fitness level of a group of people.

You will be working in groups of four, duties assigned as indicated previously, except that student 4, in addition to recording the data, will act as the timer and call the cadence (rhythm).

⚠ Any student with a known heart problem should refuse to be the subject.

All four students may act as the subject in turn, if desired, but the bench stepping is to be performed *at least twice* in each group—once with a well-conditioned person acting as the subject, and once with a poorly conditioned subject.

Bench stepping is the following series of movements repeated sequentially:

1. Place one foot on the step.

2. Step up with the other foot so that both feet are on the platform. Straighten the legs and the back.

3. Step down with the other foot.

4. Bring the other foot down.

The pace for the stepping will be set by the "timer" (student 4), who will repeat "Up-2-3-4, up-2-3-4" at such a pace that each "up-2-3-4" sequence takes 2 sec (so there are 30 cycles/min).

1. Student 4 should obtain the step (20-in. height for male subject, or 16 in. for a female subject) while baseline measurements are being obtained on the subject.

2. Once the baseline pulse and blood pressure measurements have been recorded in the Activity 5 Exercise chart (page 287), the subject is to stand quietly at attention for 2 min to allow his or her blood pressure to stabilize before beginning to step.

3. The subject is to bench step for as long as possible, up to a maximum of 5 min, according to the cadence called by the timer. Watch the subject for crouching (posture must remain erect). If he or she is unable to keep the pace up for 15 sec, stop the test.

4. When the subject is stopped by the pacer for crouching, stops voluntarily because he or she is unable to continue, or has completed 5 min of bench stepping, he or she is to sit down. At this point, record the duration of exercise (in seconds), and measure the blood pressure and pulse immediately and thereafter at 1-min intervals for 3 min post-exercise.

Duration of exercise: _____ sec

Activity 5: Cardiovascular Responses to Changes in Posture				BP = blood pressure	
	Trial 1			Trial 2	
	BP	Pulse		BP	Pulse
Sitting quietly					
Reclining (after 2 to 3 min)					
Immediately on standing from the reclining position ("at attention" stance)					
After standing for 3 min					

5. Calculate the subject's *index of physical fitness* using the following formula:

$$\text{Index} = \frac{\text{duration of exercise in seconds} \times 100}{2 \times \text{sum of the 3 pulse counts in recovery}}$$

Interpret scores according to the following scale:

below 55	poor physical condition
55 to 62	low average
63 to 71	average
72 to 79	high average
80 to 89	good
90 and over	excellent

6. Record the test values on the Activity 5 exercise chart, and repeat the testing and recording procedure with the second subject.

When did you notice a greater elevation of blood pressure and pulse?

_____

Explain: _____

_____

Was there a sizeable difference between the after-exercise values for well-conditioned and poorly conditioned individuals?

_____ Explain: _____

_____

Activity 5: Cardiovascular Responses to Changes in Exercise			BP = blood pressure P = pulse							
			Interval Following Test							
	Baseline		Immediately		1 min		2 min		3 min	
Harvard Step Test for 5 min at 30 cycles/min	BP	P	BP	P	BP	P	BP	P	BP	P
Well-conditioned individual										
Poorly conditioned individual										

Skin Color as an Indicator of Local Circulatory Dynamics

Skin color reveals with surprising accuracy the state of the local circulation.

For example, massive hemorrhage may be internal and hidden (thus, not obvious), but it will still threaten the blood delivery to vital organs. One of the earliest responses of the body to such a threat is constriction of the skin's blood vessels, which reduces blood flow to the skin and diverts it into the circulatory mainstream to serve other, more vital tissues.

As a result, the skin, particularly that of the extremities, becomes pale, cold, and eventually moist with perspiration, indicating that the circulation is dangerously inadequate.

The experiments on local circulation outlined below consider a number of factors that affect blood flow to the tissues.

OBJECTIVE 6   Indicate factors affecting or determining blood flow and skin color.

Activity 6

Examining the Effect of Local Chemical and Physical Factors on Skin Color

The local blood supply to the skin (indeed, to any tissue) is influenced by (1) local metabolites, (2) the oxygen supply, (3) local temperature, and (4) substances released by injured tissues, to name a few. The following simple experiments examine two of these factors. Each experiment should be conducted by students in groups of three or four. One student will act as the subject; the others will conduct the tests and make and record observations.

Vasodilation and Flushing of the Skin Due to Lack of Oxygen

1. Obtain a blood pressure cuff (sphygmomanometer) and stethoscope. You will also need a watch with a second hand.

2. The subject should roll up the sleeves as high as possible and then lay the forearms side by side on the bench top.

22

Text continues on next page. →

3. Observe the general color of the subject's forearm skin, and the normal contour and size of the veins. Notice whether skin color is similar bilaterally. Record your observations:

_____

_____

_____

4. Apply the blood pressure cuff to one arm, and inflate it to 250 mm Hg. Keep it inflated for 1 min. During this period, repeat the observations made in the previous step, and record the results:

_____

_____

5. Release the pressure in the cuff (leaving the deflated cuff in position), and again record the forearm skin color and the condition of the forearm veins. Make this observation immediately after deflating and then again 30 sec later.

Immediately after deflating _____

_____

30 sec after deflating _____

_____

The above observations constitute your baseline information. Now conduct the following tests.

6. Instruct the subject to raise the cuffed arm above his or her head and to clench the fist as tightly as possible. While the hand and forearm muscles are tightly contracted, rapidly inflate the cuff to 240 mm Hg or more. This maneuver partially empties the hand and forearm of blood and stops most blood flow to the hand and forearm. Once the cuff has been inflated, the subject is to relax the fist and return the forearm to the bench top so it can be compared to the other forearm.

7. Leave the cuff inflated for exactly 1 min. During this interval, compare the skin color in the "ischemic" (blood-deprived) hand to that of the "normal" (noncuffed-limb) hand. After 1 min, quickly release the pressure.

What are the subjective effects* of stopping blood flow to the arm and hand for 1 min?

_____

_____

*Subjective effects are sensations—such as pain, coldness, warmth, tingling, and weakness—experienced by the subject. They are "symptoms" of a change in function.

What are the objective effects (actual color of skin and condition of veins)?

_____

_____

How long does it take for the subject's ischemic hand to regain its normal color?

_____

Effects of Venous Congestion

With another subject, conduct the following simple experiment: Raise one arm above the head, and let the other hang by the side for 1 min. After 1 min, quickly lay both arms on the bench top, and compare their color.

Color of raised arm _____

Color of dependent arm _____

From this and the preceding observations, analyze the factors that determine tint of color and intensity of skin color. Record your conclusions.

_____

_____

_____

_____

Effect of Mechanical Stimulation of Blood Vessels of the Skin

With moderate pressure, draw the blunt end of your pen across the skin of a subject's forearm. Wait 3 min to observe the effects, and then repeat with firmer pressure.

What changes in skin color do you observe with light-to-moderate pressure?

_____

With heavy pressure? _____

The redness, or *flare*, observed after mechanical stimulation of the skin results from a local inflammatory response promoted by *chemical mediators* released by injured tissues. These mediators stimulate increased blood flow into the area and cause the capillaries to leak fluid into the local tissues. (**Note:** People differ considerably in skin sensitivity. Those most sensitive will show **dermographism,** a condition in which the direct line of stimulation will swell quite obviously. This excessively swollen area is called a *wheal*.)

REVIEW SHEET

Human Cardiovascular Physiology—Blood Pressure and Pulse Determinations

Name _____   LabTime/Date _____

Cardiac Cycle

1. Using the terms to the right of the diagram and the letter choices on the diagram, correctly identify each valve closing and opening, chamber pressures, volume lines, heart sounds, and each period of the cardiac cycle.

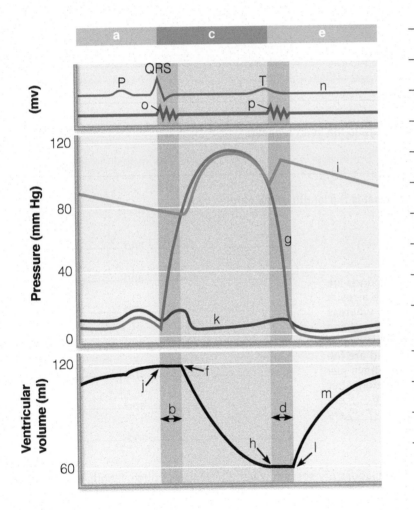

_____ 1. aortic pressure

_____ 2. atrial pressure (left)

_____ 3. ECG

_____ 4. first heart sound

_____ 5. second heart sound

_____ 6. ventricular pressure (left)

_____ 7. ventricular volume

_____ 8. aortic (semilunar) valve closes

_____ 9. aortic (semilunar) valve opens

_____ 10. AV and semilunar valves are closed (2 letters)

_____ 11. AV valve closes

_____ 12. AV valve opens

_____ 13. ventricular diastole (2 letters)

_____ 14. ventricular systole

2. Define the following terms:

   systole: _____

   diastole: _____

   cardiac cycle: _____

3. Answer the following questions concerning events of the cardiac cycle:

When are the AV valves closed? _____

Open? _____

What event within the heart causes the AV valves to open? _____

_____

What causes them to close? _____

When are the semilunar valves closed? _____

Open? _____

What event causes the semilunar valves to open? _____

To close? _____

At what point in the cardiac cycle is the pressure in the heart highest? _____

Lowest? _____

4. If an individual's heart rate is 80 beats/min, what is the length of the cardiac cycle?_____

Heart Sounds

5. Complete the following statements:

    The monosyllables describing the heart sounds are ___1___ and ___1___. The first heart sound is a result of closure of the ___2___ and ___2___ valves, whereas the second is a result of closure of the ___3___ and ___3___ valves. The heart chambers that have just been filled when you hear the first heart sound are the ___4___ and ___4___, and the chambers that have just emptied are the ___5___ and ___5___. Immediately after the second heart sound, the ___6___ and ___6___ are filling with blood, and the ___7___ and ___7___ are empty.

1. _____ and _____

2. _____ and _____

3. _____ and _____

4. _____ and _____

5. _____ and _____

6. _____ and _____

7. _____ and _____

6. As you listened to the heart sounds during the laboratory session, what differences in pitch, length, and amplitude

(loudness) of the two sounds did you observe? _____

_____

_____

7. No one expects you to be a full-fledged physician on such short notice, but on the basis of what you have learned about heart sounds, how might abnormal sounds be used to diagnose heart problems? (Use your textbook as necessary.)

_____

_____

_____

The Pulse

8. Define *pulse:* _____

_____

9. Identify the artery palpated at each of the following pressure points:

at the wrist _____   on the dorsum of the foot _____

in front of the ear _____   at the side of the neck _____

in the groin _____   above the medial malleolus _____

10. How would you tell by simple observation whether bleeding is arterial *or* venous? _____

_____

Blood Pressure Determinations

11. Define *blood pressure:* _____

12. Identify the phase of the cardiac cycle to which each of the following apply:

systolic pressure _____ diastolic pressure _____

13. What is the name of the instrument used to compress the artery and record pressures in the auscultatory method of

determining blood pressure? _____

14. What are sounds of Korotkoff? _____

_____

What causes the systolic sound? _____

_____

The disappearance of sound? _____

15. Interpret 145/85. _____

_____

16. In Exercise 21, you learned about the relative positions of veins and arteries. Based on this knowledge, how would you expect venous pressures to compare to arterial pressures?

_____

Why? _____

Observing the Effect of Various Factors on Blood Pressure and Heart Rate

17. What effect do the following have on blood pressure? (Indicate increase by I and decrease by D.)

_____ 1. increased diameter of the arterioles   _____ 4. hemorrhage

_____ 2. increased blood viscosity   _____ 5. arteriosclerosis

_____ 3. increased cardiac output   _____ 6. increased pulse rate

18. In which position (sitting, reclining, or standing) is the blood pressure normally the highest?

_____ The lowest? _____

What immediate changes in blood pressure did you observe when the subject stood up after having been in the sitting

or reclining position? _____

What changes in the blood vessels might account for the change? _____

_____

_____

After the subject stood for 3 minutes, what changes in blood pressure did you observe? _____

_____

How do you account for this change? _____

19. What was the effect of exercise on blood pressure? _____

On pulse? _____ Do you think these effects reflect changes in cardiac output *or* in

peripheral resistance? _____

Skin Color as an Indicator of Local Circulatory Dynamics

20. Describe normal skin color and the appearance of the veins in the subject's forearm before any testing was conducted.

_____

21. What changes occurred when the subject emptied the forearm of blood (by raising the arm and making a fist) and the

flow was blocked with the cuff? _____

Materials

- ☐ Human torso model
- ☐ Respiratory organ system model and/or chart of the respiratory system
- ☐ Preserved inflatable lung preparation (obtained from a biological supply house) or sheep pluck fresh from the slaughterhouse
- ☐ Source of compressed air*
- ☐ 2-foot length of laboratory rubber tubing
- ☐ Dissecting tray
- ☐ Disposable gloves
- ☐ Disposable autoclave bag
- ☐ Demonstration area:

  Station 1: Cross section of trachea set up for viewing under low power of a microscope

  Station 2: Lung tissue set up for microscopic viewing

*If a compressed air source is not available, cardboard mouthpieces that fit the cut end of the rubber tubing should be available for student use. Disposable autoclave bags should also be provided for discarding the mouthpiece.

Pre-Lab Quiz

1. Circle True or False. Four processes—pulmonary ventilation, external respiration, transport of respiratory gases, and internal respiration—must all occur in order for the respiratory system to function fully.

2. The upper respiratory structures include the nose, the larynx, and the:
   a. epiglottis
   b. lungs
   c. pharynx
   d. trachea

3. Circle the correct term. The <u>thyroid cartilage</u> / <u>oropharynx</u> is the largest and most prominent of the laryngeal cartilages.

4. Air flows from the larynx to the trachea, and then enters the:
   a. left and right lungs
   b. left and right main bronchi
   c. pharynx
   d. tertiary bronchi

5. Complete the sentence. _____, tiny balloonlike expansions of the alveolar sacs, are composed of a single thin layer of squamous epithelium. They are the main structural and functional units of the lung and the actual sites of gas exchange.

6. Circle the correct term. Fissures divide the lungs into lobes, three on the right and <u>two</u> / <u>three</u> on the left.

B ody cells require a continuous supply of oxygen. As the cells use oxygen, they release carbon dioxide, a waste product that the body must get rid of. The major role of the respiratory system, our focus in this exercise, is to supply the body with the oxygen it needs and dispose of carbon dioxide. To fulfill this role, at least four distinct processes, collectively referred to as *respiration*, must occur.

OBJECTIVE 1 Define *pulmonary ventilation, external respiration, transport of respiratory gases,* and *internal respiration.*

Pulmonary ventilation: The movement of air into and out of the lungs. More simply called *ventilation,* or *breathing.*

External respiration: Gas exchanges to and from the pulmonary circuit blood that occur in the lungs (oxygen loading and carbon dioxide unloading).

Transport of respiratory gases: Transport of respiratory gases between the lungs and tissue cells of the body using blood as the transport vehicle.

Internal respiration: Exchange of gases to and from the blood capillaries of the systemic circulation (oxygen unloading and carbon dioxide loading).

Only the first two processes are the tasks of the respiratory system, but all four must occur for the respiratory system to "do its job." Hence, the respiratory and circulatory systems are irreversibly linked.

Upper Respiratory System Structures

OBJECTIVE 2 Identify the major structures of the upper respiratory system on a diagram or model, and describe their functions.

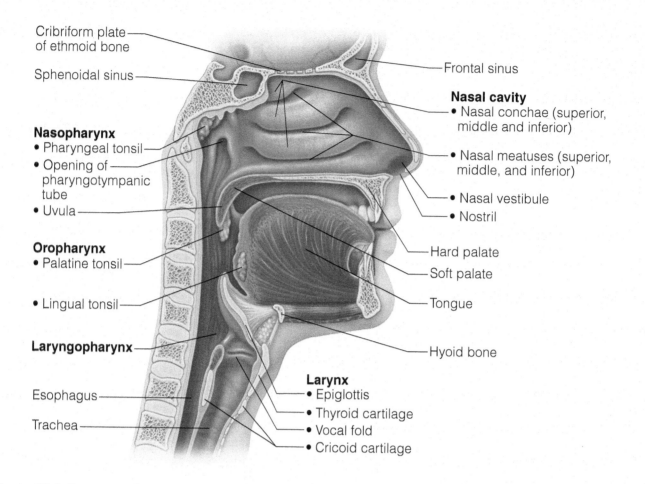

Figure 23.1 Structures of the upper respiratory tract (sagittal section).

The upper respiratory system structures—the nose, pharynx, and larynx—are shown in **Figure 23.1** and described next. As you read through the descriptions, identify each structure in the figure.

Air generally passes into the respiratory tract through the **nostrils** (also called **nares**), and enters the **nasal cavity.** It then flows posteriorly over three pairs of lobelike structures, the **inferior, superior,** and **middle nasal conchae,** which increase the air turbulence. As the air passes through the nasal cavity, it is warmed, moistened, and filtered by the nasal mucosa. The air that flows directly beneath the superior part of the nasal cavity may stimulate the olfactory receptors in the mucosa of that region.

The nasal cavity is surrounded by the **paranasal sinuses** in the frontal, sphenoid, ethmoid, and maxillary bones. These sinuses act as resonance chambers in speech. Their mucosae, like that of the nasal cavity, warm and moisten the incoming air.

The nasal passages are separated from the oral cavity below by a partition composed anteriorly of the **hard palate** and posteriorly by the **soft palate.**

Of course, air may also enter the body via the mouth. From there it passes through the oral cavity to move into the pharynx posteriorly, where the oral and nasal cavities are joined temporarily.

Commonly called the *throat,* the funnel-shaped **pharynx** connects the nasal and oral cavities to the larynx and esophagus inferiorly. It has three named parts (Figure 23.1):

1. The **nasopharynx** lies posterior to the nasal cavity and is continuous with it. Because it lies above the soft palate, it serves only as an air passage. High on its posterior wall are the *pharyngeal tonsils,* paired masses of lymphoid tissue. The *pharyngotympanic* or *auditory tubes,* which allow middle ear pressure to become equalized to atmospheric pressure, drain into the nasopharynx.

2. The **oropharynx** lies posterior to the oral cavity. It extends from the soft palate to the epiglottis of the larynx inferiorly, so it serves as a common conduit for food and air. In its lateral walls are the *palatine tonsils.* The *lingual tonsil* covers the base of the tongue.

3. The **laryngopharynx,** like the oropharynx, accommodates both ingested food and air. It extends to the larynx, where the common pathway divides into the respiratory and digestive channels. From the laryngopharynx, air enters the lower respiratory passageways by passing through the larynx (voice box) into the trachea below.

The **larynx** (Figure 23.1) is made up of nine cartilages, most quite small. The largest are the shield-shaped **thyroid cartilage,** whose anterior protrusion is commonly called the *Adam's apple,* and the more inferior ring-shaped **cricoid cartilage.** All laryngeal cartilages are composed of hyaline cartilage except the **epiglottis,** a flaplike elastic cartilage superior to the opening of the larynx. The epiglottis forms a lid over the larynx when we swallow. This closes off the respiratory passageway and routes the incoming food or drink into the esophagus, or food chute, posteriorly. (Check the box when you have completed the following task.)

☐ Palpate your larynx by placing your hand on the anterior neck surface approximately halfway down its length. Swallow. Can you feel the cartilaginous larynx rising?

If anything other than air enters the larynx, a cough reflex attempts to expel the substance. This reflex operates only when a person is conscious, *so never try to feed or pour liquids down the throat of an unconscious person.*

The mucous membrane of the larynx is thrown into a pair of folds called the **vocal folds,** or **true vocal cords,** which vibrate with expelled air for speech. The slitlike passageway between the vocal folds is called the **glottis.**

Identifying the Upper Respiratory System Organs

Before continuing, identify all the respiratory organs described previously on a torso model or anatomical chart.

Lower Respiratory System Structures

OBJECTIVE 3   Identify lower respiratory system organs, and describe the structure of each.

Air entering the **trachea** travels down its length (about 11 cm) to the level of the fifth thoracic vertebra. There the passageway divides into the right and left **main,** or **primary, bronchi (Figure 23.2).**

The trachea is lined with a ciliated mucus-secreting epithelium, as are many other respiratory system passageways. The cilia propel mucus (produced by goblet cells) loaded with dust particles, bacteria, and other debris away from the lungs and toward the throat, where it can be spat out or swallowed. The walls of the trachea are reinforced with C-shaped cartilages, with the incomplete portion of the rings facing toward the esophagus. The open parts of these cartilages allow the esophagus to expand anteriorly when a large piece of food is swallowed. The solid portions reinforce the trachea walls to keep its passageway open regardless of the pressure changes that occur during breathing.

The main bronchi plunge into their respective lungs at an indented area called the **hilum** (see **Figure 23.3b**). The right

main bronchus is wider, shorter, and more vertical than the left, and inhaled foreign objects are more likely to become lodged in it. Inside the lungs, the primary bronchi divide further into smaller and smaller branches (the secondary, tertiary, on down), finally becoming the **bronchioles.** Each bronchiole divides into many **terminal bronchioles.** Each terminal bronchiole branches into two or more **respiratory bronchioles** (see Figure 23.2b). All but the tiniest branches have cartilage in their walls, usually small plates of hyaline cartilage. As the respiratory tubes get smaller and smaller, the relative amount of smooth muscle in their walls increases, and the amount of cartilage declines and finally disappears. The continuous branching of the respiratory passageways in the lungs is often referred to as the **respiratory tree** (see Figure 23.2 and 23.3b).

The respiratory bronchioles in turn subdivide into **alveolar ducts,** which end in alveolar sacs that rather resemble clusters of grapes. **Alveoli,** tiny balloonlike expansions along the alveolar sacs, are composed of a single thin layer of squamous epithelium overlying a wispy connective tissue layer. The external surfaces of the alveoli are densely spiderwebbed

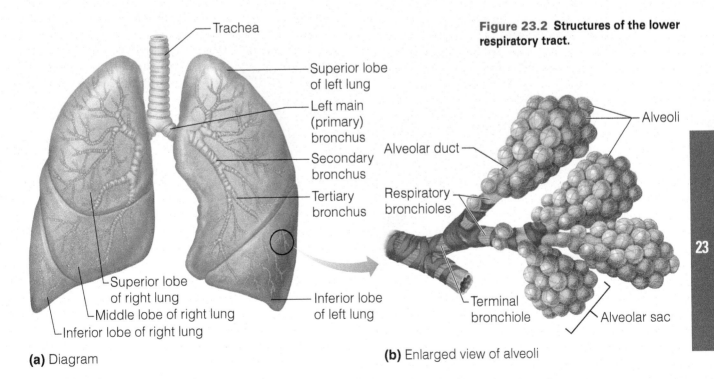

Figure 23.2 Structures of the lower respiratory tract.

Trachea

Superior lobe of left lung

Left main (primary) bronchus

Secondary bronchus

Tertiary bronchus

Superior lobe of right lung

Middle lobe of right lung

Inferior lobe of right lung

Inferior lobe of left lung

Alveolar duct

Respiratory bronchioles

Alveoli

Terminal bronchiole

Alveolar sac

(a) Diagram

(b) Enlarged view of alveoli

23

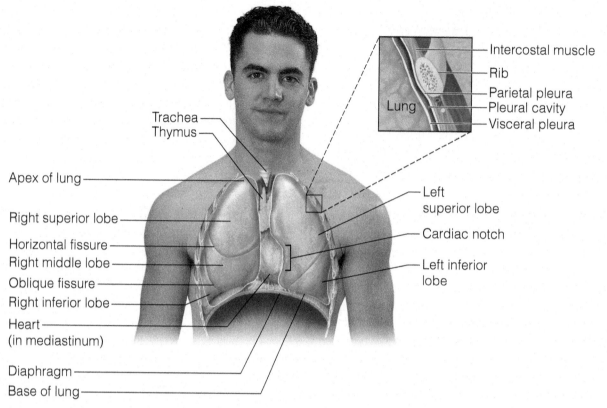

(a) Anterior view. The lungs flank mediastinal structures laterally.

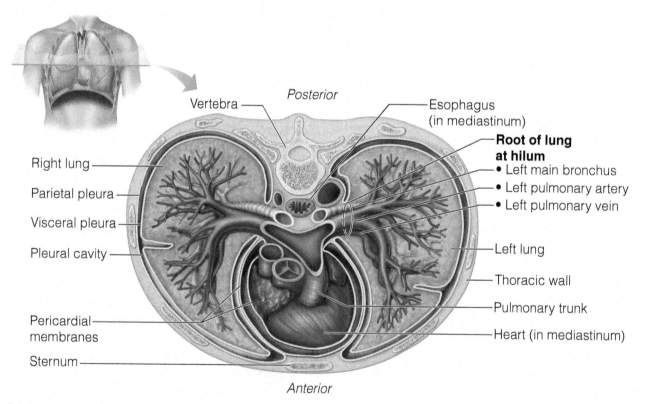

(b) Transverse section through the thorax, viewed from above.

Figure 23.3 Anatomical relationships of organs in the thoracic cavity. (a) Anterior view of the thoracic organs. The inset at upper right depicts the pleura and the pleural cavity. (b) Transverse section through the superior part of the thorax, showing the branching respiratory passageways in the lungs and the main organs in the mediastinum. **Note:** The size of the pleural cavity is exaggerated for clarity.

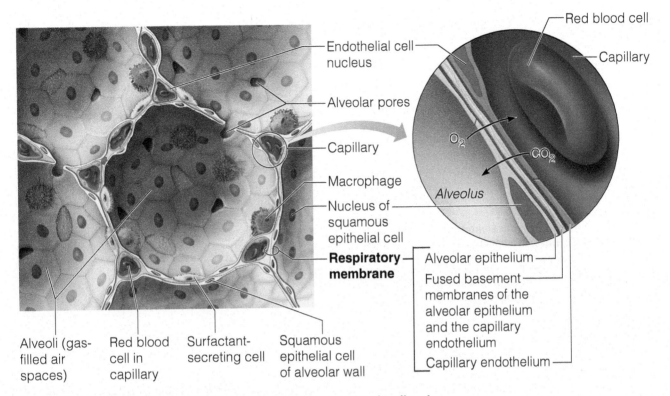

Endothelial cell nucleus

Alveolar pores

Capillary

Macrophage

Nucleus of squamous epithelial cell

Respiratory membrane

Red blood cell

Capillary

O_2

CO_2

Alveolus

Alveolar epithelium

Fused basement membranes of the alveolar epithelium and the capillary endothelium

Capillary endothelium

Alveoli (gas-filled air spaces)

Red blood cell in capillary

Surfactant-secreting cell

Squamous epithelial cell of alveolar wall

Figure 23.4 Diagrammatic view of the relationship between the alveoli and pulmonary capillaries involved in gas exchange.

with pulmonary capillaries (**Figure 23.4**). Together, the alveolar and capillary walls and their fused basement membranes form the **respiratory membrane.**

Because gas exchanges occur by simple diffusion across the respiratory membrane, the alveolar sacs, alveolar ducts, and respiratory bronchioles are referred to as **respiratory zone structures.** All other respiratory passageways serve as access or exit routes to and from these gas exchange chambers and are called **conducting zone structures.**

The Lungs and Their Pleural Coverings

The paired lungs are soft, spongy organs that occupy the entire thoracic cavity except for the *mediastinum,* which houses the heart, bronchi, esophagus, and other organs (Figure 23.3). Each lung is connected to the mediastinum by a *root* containing its vascular supply and bronchial attachments. All structures distal to the primary bronchi are inside the lungs. A lung's *apex,* its narrower superior aspect, is just deep to the clavicle, and its *base,* the inferior surface, rests on the diaphragm. The medial surface of the left lung has a recess that accommodates the heart. Fissures divide the lungs into a number of *lobes*—two in the left lung and three in the right. Other than the respiratory passageways and air spaces that make up their bulk, the lungs are mostly elastic connective tissue, which allows them to recoil passively during expiration.

Each lung is enclosed in a double-layered serous membrane sac called the **pleura.** The outer layer, the **parietal**

pleura, is attached to the thoracic walls and the **diaphragm.** The inner layer, covering the lung tissue, is the **visceral pleura.** The two pleural layers are separated by the *pleural cavity.* The pleural layers produce lubricating serous fluid that causes them to adhere closely to one another, holding the lungs to the thoracic wall and allowing them to move easily against one another during the movements of breathing.

Identifying the Lower Respiratory System Organs

Before proceeding, be sure to locate all the lower respiratory structures described on the torso model, thoracic cavity structures model, or an anatomical chart.

23

Activity 3

Demonstrating Lung Inflation in a Sheep Pluck

A *sheep pluck* includes the larynx, trachea with attached lungs, the heart, and portions of the major blood vessels found in the mediastinum (aorta, pulmonary artery and vein, venae cavae).

Put on disposable gloves, obtain a fresh sheep pluck (or a preserved pluck of another animal), and identify the lower respiratory system organs. Once you have completed your observations, insert a hose from an air compressor (vacuum pump) into the trachea and alternately allow air to flow in and out of the lungs. Notice how the lungs inflate. This observation is educational in a preserved pluck, but it is a spectacular sight in a fresh

one. Another advantage of using a fresh pluck is that it changes color (becomes redder) as hemoglobin in trapped RBCs becomes loaded with oxygen.

If air compressors are not available, you may obtain the same effect by using a length of laboratory rubber tubing to blow into the trachea. Do not inhale through the tubing. Obtain a cardboard mouthpiece, and fit it into the cut end of the laboratory tubing before attempting to inflate the lungs.

⚠ Dispose of the mouthpiece and gloves in the autoclave bag immediately after use.

OBJECTIVE 4   Recognize the microscopic structure of tissue of the trachea and lungs.

Activity 4

Examining Prepared Slides of Trachea and Lung Tissue

1. Go to station 1 at the demonstration area to examine a slide of a cross section of the tracheal wall. Identify the smooth muscle layer, the hyaline cartilage supporting rings, and the pseudostratified ciliated epithelium. Using **Figure 23.5a** and Plates 27 and 28 in the Histology Atlas as a guide, also try to identify a few goblet cells in the epithelium.

2. Next, at station 2, examine a slide of lung tissue. The alveolus is the main structural and functional unit of

the lung and is the actual site of gas exchange. Identify the thin squamous epithelium of the alveolar walls (Figure 23.5b). See also Plate 26 in the Histology Atlas.

How does the structure of the alveolar walls aid in their

role of gas exchange? _____

_____

_____

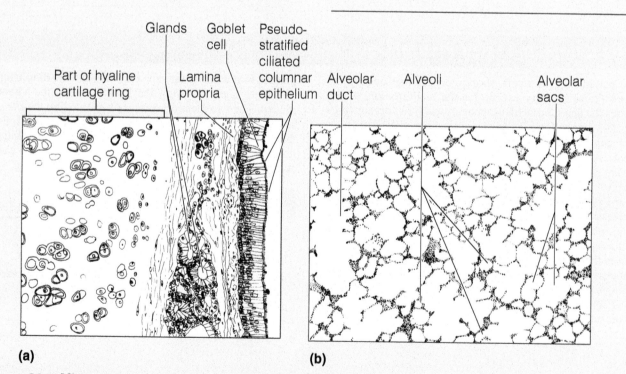

Glands   Goblet   Pseudo-
cell   stratified
ciliated
Part of hyaline   Lamina   columnar   Alveolar   Alveoli   Alveolar
cartilage ring   propria epithelium duct   sacs

(a)   **(b)**

Figure 23.5 Microscopic structure of (a) a portion of the trachea, cross-sectional view, and (b) alveoli.

REVIEW SHEET
Anatomy of the Respiratory System

Name _____   Lab Time/Date _____

Upper and Lower Respiratory System Structures

1. Complete the labeling of the diagram of the upper respiratory structures (sagittal section).

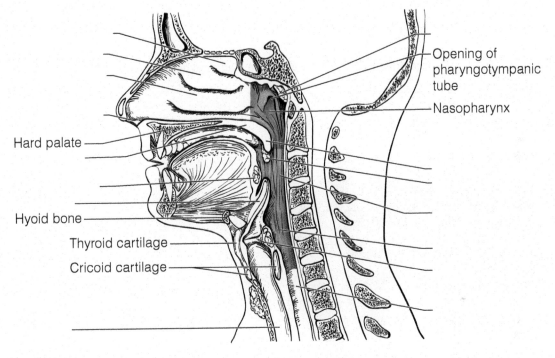

Opening of
pharyngotympanic
tube

Nasopharynx

Hard palate

Hyoid bone

Thyroid cartilage

Cricoid cartilage

2. What is the significance of the fact that the human trachea is reinforced with cartilage rings?

_____

Of the fact that the rings are incomplete posteriorly? _____

_____

3. Name the specific cartilages in the larynx that are described below:

   1. forms the Adam's apple _____   3. broader anteriorly _____

   2. a "lid" for the larynx _____

4. Trace a molecule of oxygen from the nostrils (nares) to the pulmonary capillaries of the lungs:

   Nostrils ⟶ _____

   _____

   _____ ⟶ pulmonary capillaries

5. What is the function of the pleural membranes? _____

_____

_____

6. Name two functions of the nasal cavity mucosa: _____

7. The following questions refer to the main, or primary, bronchi:

   Which is longer? _____ Larger in diameter? _____ More horizontal? _____

   The more common site where a foreign object that has entered the respiratory passageways is likely to become

   lodged? _____

8. Correctly label all structures provided with leader lines on the diagrams below.

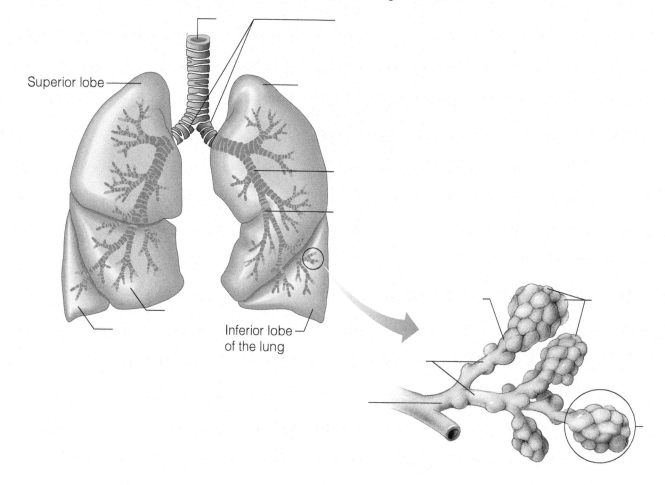

Superior lobe

Inferior lobe
of the lung

9. Match the terms in column B to the descriptions in column A.

Column A	Column B
_____ 1. pleural layer covering the lung tissue	alveolus
_____ 2. "floor" of the nasal cavity	bronchiole
_____ 3. food and fluid passageway inferior to the laryngopharynx	concha
_____ 4. flaps over the glottis during swallowing of food	epiglottis
_____ 5. contains the vocal cords	esophagus
_____ 6. the part of the conducting pathway between the larynx and the primary bronchi	glottis
_____ 7. pleural layer lining the walls of the thorax	larynx
_____ 8. site from which oxygen enters the pulmonary blood	palate
_____ 9. opening between the vocal folds	parietal pleura
_____ 10. increases air turbulence in the nasal cavity	primary bronchi
	trachea
	visceral pleura

10. Define *external respiration:* _____

_____

internal respiration: _____

_____

Demonstrating Lung Inflation in a Sheep Pluck

11. Does the lung inflate part by part or as a whole, like a balloon? _____

What happened when the pressure was released? _____

What type of tissue ensures this phenomenon? _____

Examining Prepared Slides of Lung and Tracheal Tissue

12. The tracheal epithelium is ciliated and has goblet cells. What is the function of each of these modifications?

cilia: _____

goblet cells: _____

13. The tracheal epithelium is said to be "pseudostratified." Why? _____

_____

_____

14. On the diagram below, identify alveolar epithelium, capillary endothelium, alveoli, and red blood cells. Bracket the respiratory membrane.

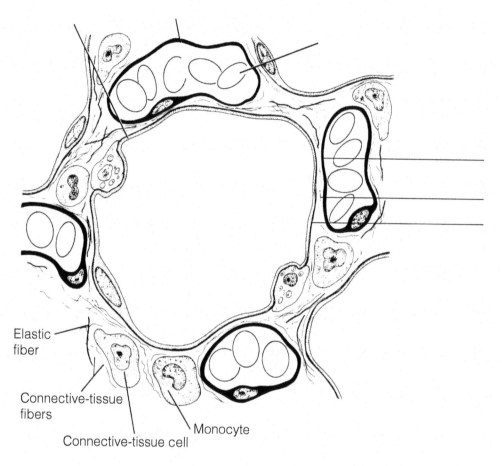

Elastic
fiber

Connective-tissue
fibers

Connective-tissue cell

Monocyte

15. Why does oxygen move from the alveoli into the pulmonary capillary blood? _____

_____

_____

16. What structural characteristic of the alveoli makes them an ideal site for the diffusion of gases?

_____

24

Respiratory System Physiology

Materials

- ☐ Model lung (bell jar demonstrator)
- ☐ Tape measure
- ☐ Spirometer (nonrecording)
- ☐ Disposable mouthpieces
- ☐ Nose clips
- ☐ Alcohol swabs
- ☐ 70% ethanol solution in a battery jar
- ☐ Disposable autoclave bag
- ☐ Paper bag
- ☐ Pneumograph, recording attachments, and recording apparatus—kymograph or physiograph (if available)
- ☐ Table (on chalkboard) for recording class data
- ☐ Millimeter ruler

Pre-Lab Quiz

1. Circle the correct term. Inspiration / Expiration is the phase of pulmonary ventilation when air passes out of the lungs.

2. Which of the following processes does *not* occur during inspiration?
   a. Diaphragm moves to a flattened position.
   b. Gas pressure inside the lungs is lowered.
   c. Inspiratory muscles relax.
   d. Size of thoracic cavity increases.

3. During normal quiet breathing, about _____ ml of air moves into and out of the lungs with each breath.
   a. 250
   b. 500
   c. 1000
   d. 2000

4. Circle True or False. The neural centers that control respiratory rhythm and maintain a rate of 12–18 respirations per minute are located in the medulla and thalamus.

5. Circle the correct term. Changes in pH and oxygen concentrations in the blood are monitored by chemoreceptor regions in the medulla / aortic and carotid bodies.

Mechanics of Respiration

OBJECTIVE 1 Define *inspiration* and *expiration,* and explain the role of muscles and volume changes in the mechanical process of breathing.

Pulmonary ventilation, or **breathing,** consists of two phases: **inspiration,** when air is flowing into the lungs, and **expiration,** when air passes out of the lungs. As the inspiratory muscles contract, the size of the thoracic cavity increases. The diaphragm moves from its relaxed dome shape to a flattened position, increasing the superoinferior volume; and the external intercostals lift the rib cage, increasing the anteroposterior and lateral dimensions (**Figure 24.1**). The presence of serous fluid in the pleural cavity causes the lungs to adhere to the thoracic walls like flypaper; thus, the intrapulmonary volume also increases, lowering the air (gas) pressure inside the lungs. The gases then expand to fill the available space, creating a partial vacuum that causes airflow into the lungs—the act of inspiration.

During expiration, the inspiratory muscles relax, and the elastic lung tissue recoils. Thus, both the intrathoracic and intrapulmonary volumes decrease. As the gas molecules within the lungs are forced closer together, intrapulmonary pressure rises above atmospheric pressure. This causes gases to flow out of the lungs to equalize the pressure inside and outside the lungs—the act of expiration.

Inspiration **Expiration**

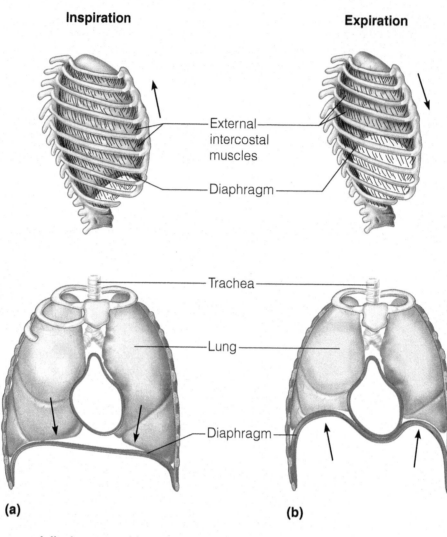

External intercostal muscles

Diaphragm

Trachea

Lung

Diaphragm

(a) **(b)**

Figure 24.1 Rib cage and diaphragm positions during breathing. (a) At the end of a normal inspiration: chest expanded, diaphragm depressed. **(b)** At the end of a normal expiration: chest depressed, diaphragm elevated.

Activity 1

Operating the Model Lung

Observe the model lung, which demonstrates the principles involved as gas flows into and out of the lungs. It is a simple device with a bottle "thorax," a rubber membrane "diaphragm," and balloon "lungs."

1. Go to the demonstration area, and work the model lung by moving the rubber diaphragm up and down. Notice the changes in balloon (lung) size as the volume of the thoracic cavity alternately increases and decreases. (The balloon will not fully inflate; it will just increase and decrease in size.) **Note:** This demonstration shows the effects of manipulating the diaphragm only. The lungs would show a more dramatic change if the action of the rib cage could also be shown.

2. Respond to the questions concerning these observations in question 1 in the Exercise 24 Review Sheet on page 309.

3. After observing the operation of the model lung, conduct the following tests on your lab partner. Use the tape measure to determine chest circumference by placing the tape around the chest as high up under the armpits as possible. Record the measurements in inches in the appropriate space for each of the conditions.

Quiet breathing:

Inspiration _____ Expiration _____

Forced breathing:

Inspiration _____ Expiration _____

Do the results agree with what you expected on the basis

of what you have learned so far? _____

24

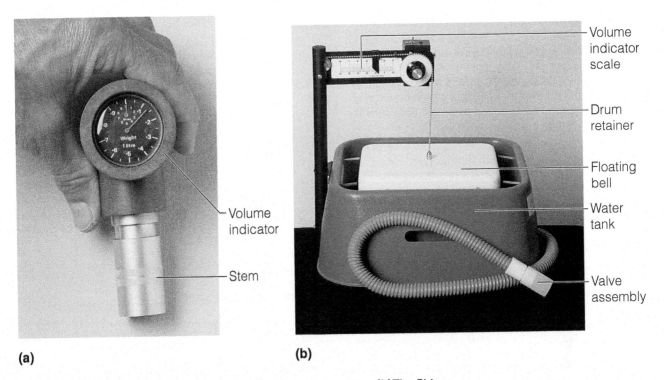

(a)   **(b)**

Figure 24.2 Spirometers. (a) The Wright handheld dry spirometer. **(b)** The Phipps and Bird "wet" spirometer.

Respiratory Volumes and Capacities—Spirometry

OBJECTIVE 2   Define and provide volume amounts for the various respiratory volumes investigated in the laboratory.

A person's size, sex, age, and physical condition can all produce variations in respiratory volumes. Normal quiet breathing moves about 500 ml of air into and out of the lungs with each breath. As you have seen in the first activity, we can usually forcibly inhale or exhale much more air than is exchanged in normal quiet breathing. (Figure 24.3 on page 306 shows a tracing of the various respiratory volumes and their relationships to each other.)

Respiratory volumes are measured with an apparatus called a **spirometer.** There are two major types of spirometers, which give comparable results—the handheld dry, or

wheel, spirometers (such as the Wright spirometer illustrated in **Figure 24.2a**) and "wet" spirometers, such as the Phipps and Bird spirometer (Figure 24.2b). The more sophisticated wet spirometer consists of a plastic or metal *bell* that air can be added to or removed from and that rests in a rectangular or cylindrical tank. The tank contains water and has a tube running through it to carry air above the water level and into the floating bottomless bell, which is inverted over the water-containing tank and connected to a volume indicator.

In nonrecording spirometers, such as those used in the next activity, an indicator moves as air is *exhaled,* and only expired air volumes can be measured directly.

OBJECTIVE 3   Demonstrate proper usage of a spirometer.

Activity 2

Measuring Respiratory Volumes

1. Before using the spirometer, count and record the subject's normal respiratory rate.

Respirations per minute _____

2. Identify the parts of the spirometer you will be using by comparing it to the illustration in Figure 24.2a or 24.2b. Examine the spirometer volume indicator *before beginning* to make sure you know how to read the scale. Work in pairs, with one person acting as the subject while the other records the volume measured. The subject should stand up straight during testing. **Note:** Reset the indicator to zero before beginning each trial.

Obtain a disposable cardboard mouthpiece. Insert it in the open end of the valve assembly (attached to the flexible tube) of the wet spirometer or over the fixed stem of the handheld dry spirometer. Before beginning, the subject should practice exhaling through the mouthpiece without exhaling through the nose, or prepare to use the nose clips (clean them first with an alcohol swab). If you are using the handheld spirometer, make sure its dial faces upward so that the volumes can be easily read during the tests.

Text continues on next page. →

24

3. Ensure that the subject stands erect during testing. Run the test three times for each required measurement. Record the data, and then find the average volume figure for that measurement. After you have completed the trials and figured the averages, enter the average values on the table prepared on the chalkboard for tabulation of class data, and copy all averaged data onto the Exercise 24 Review Sheet.

4. Measure **tidal volume (TV)**. The TV, or volume of air inhaled and exhaled with each normal respiration, is approximately 500 ml. To conduct the test, inhale a normal breath, and then exhale a normal breath of air into the spirometer mouthpiece. (Do not force the expiration!) Record the volume, and repeat the test twice more.

trial 1 _____ ml   trial 2 _____ ml

trial 3 _____ ml   average TV _____ ml

5. Measure **expiratory reserve volume (ERV)**. The expiratory reserve volume, the volume of air that can be forcibly exhaled after a normal expiration, ranges between 700 and 1200 ml.

Inhale and exhale normally two or three times. Then insert the spirometer mouthpiece and exhale forcibly as much of the additional air as you can. Record your results, and repeat the test twice more.

trial 1 _____ ml   trial 2 _____ ml

trial 3 _____ ml   average ERV _____ ml

6. Measure **vital capacity (VC)**. The VC, or total exchangeable air of the lungs (the sum of TV + IRV + ERV), is normally around 4500 ml, with a range of 3600 ml to 4800 ml.

Breathe in and out normally two or three times, and then bend over and exhale all the air possible. Then, as you raise yourself to the upright position, inhale as fully as possible. (It is very important to *strain* to inhale as much air as you possibly can.) Quickly insert the mouthpiece, and exhale as forcibly as you can. Record your results and repeat the test twice more.

trial 1 _____ ml   trial 2 _____ ml

trial 3 _____ ml   average VC _____ ml

7. Compute the **inspiratory reserve volume (IRV)**, or volume of air that can be forcibly inhaled following a normal inspiration. It can now be computed using the average values obtained for TV, ERV, and VC by plugging them into this equation:

$$IRV = VC - (TV + ERV)$$

Record your average IRV: _____ ml

The normal IRV is substantial, ranging from 1900 to 3100 ml. How does your computed value compare?

_____

Figure 24.3 is an idealized tracing of the respiratory volumes described and tested in this exercise. Reexamine it carefully. How closely do your test results compare to the values in that tracing?

_____

A respiratory volume that cannot be experimentally demonstrated here is residual volume (RV), the amount of air remaining in the lungs after a maximal expiratory effort. However, the presence of RV (usually about 1200 ml) is important because it allows gas exchange to go on continuously—even between breaths.

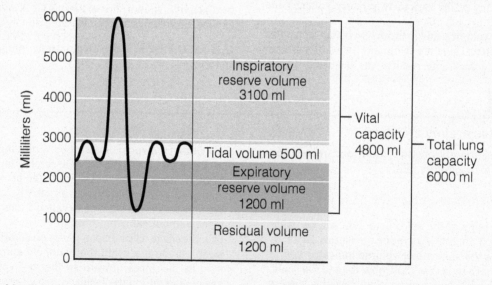

Figure 24.3 Idealized tracing of the various respiratory volumes of a healthy young adult male.

8. Finish recording for this subject. Before continuing with the next member of your group:

- Dispose of used cardboard mouthpieces in the autoclave bag.

- Swish the valve assembly (if removable) in the 70% ethanol solution, then rinse with tap water.

- Put a fresh mouthpiece into the valve assembly (or on the stem of the handheld spirometer). Using the procedures outlined previously, measure and record the respiratory volumes for all members of your group.

Factors Influencing Rate and Depth of Respiration

OBJECTIVE 4   Explain the relative importance of various chemical and mechanical factors causing respiratory variations.

The neural centers that control respiratory rhythm and depth are located in the medulla and pons. Although the medulla initiates the basic rate and rhythm of breathing, typically at a pace of 12 to 18 respirations/min, physical actions such as talking, yawning, coughing, and exercise can modify the rate and depth of respiration. So too can chemical factors such as changes in oxygen or carbon dioxide concentrations in the blood or changes in blood pH. Changes in carbon dioxide blood levels act directly on the medulla control centers, whereas changes in pH and oxygen levels are monitored by chemoreceptor regions in the aortic and carotid bodies, which in turn send input to the medulla. Experiments in this section test the relative importance of various physical and chemical factors in the process of respiration.

The **pneumograph,** an apparatus that records variations in breathing patterns, is the best means of observing respiratory variations. The chest pneumograph is a coiled rubber hose that is attached around the thorax. As the subject breathes, chest movements produce pressure changes within the pneumograph that are transmitted to a recorder.

Your instructor will demonstrate the method of setting up the pneumograph and discuss the interpretation of the results. Work in pairs so that one person can mark the record to identify the test for later interpretation. Ideally, the student being tested should face *away* from the recording apparatus.

Activity 3

Demonstrating Respiratory Variations

1. If the pneumograph apparatus is available, attach the pneumograph tubing firmly, but not restrictively, around the thoracic cage at the level of the sixth rib, leaving room for the chest to expand during testing. If the subject is female, position the tubing above the breasts to prevent slippage during testing. Set the pneumograph speed at 1 or 2, and the time signal at 10-second intervals. Record quiet breathing for 1 minute with the subject in a sitting position. If the pneumograph is not available, simply count the subject's breaths per minute.

Record breaths per minute. _____

2. The next step is to make a vital capacity tracing. (This will not be done if the pneumograph is not available. Use the VC measurement obtained earlier as your baseline.) Record a maximal inhalation followed by a maximal exhalation. This should agree with the vital capacity measurement obtained earlier and will provide a baseline for comparison during the rest of the pneumograph testing.

Stop the recording apparatus, and mark the graph appropriately to indicate tidal volume, expiratory reserve volume, inspiratory reserve volume, and vital capacity (the total of the three measurements). Also mark, with arrows, the direction the recording stylus moves during inspiration and during expiration.

Measure in millimeters (mm) the height of the vital capacity recording. Divide the vital capacity measurement

average recorded on the Exercise 24 Review Sheet by the millimeter measurement to obtain the volume (in milliliters of air) represented by 1 mm on the recording. For example, if your vital capacity reading is 4000 ml and the vital capacity tracing occupies a vertical distance of 40 mm on the pneumograph recording, then a vertical distance of 1 mm equals 100 ml of air.

Record your computed VC value. _____ ml air/mm

3. Record or count the subject's breathing as he or she performs activities from the list below. Make sure the record is marked accurately to identify each test conducted. Record your results on the Exercise 24 Review Sheet.

talking	swallowing water
yawning	coughing
laughing	lying down
standing	doing a math problem (concentrating)
running in place	

4. Without recording, have the subject breathe normally for 2 minutes and then inhale deeply and hold his or her breath for as long as he or she can.

Time the breath-holding interval. _____ sec

Text continues on next page. →

24

As the subject exhales, turn on the recording apparatus, and record the recovery period (time to return to normal breathing—usually slightly over 1 minute):

Time of recovery period. _____ sec

Did the subject have the urge to inspire *or* expire during breath holding?

_____

Without recording, repeat the above experiment, but this time the subject should exhale completely and forcefully *after* taking the deep breath. What was observed this time?

_____

_____

5. Have the subject hyperventilate (breathe deeply and forcefully at the rate of 1 breath/4 sec) for about 30 seconds.* Record, or visually count breaths per minute, both during and after hyperventilation. How does the pattern obtained during hyperventilation compare with that recorded during the vital capacity tracing?

_____

*A sensation of dizziness may develop. (As the carbon dioxide is washed out of the blood by overventilation, blood pH increases, leading to a fall in blood pressure and reduced cerebral circulation.) The subject may have no desire to breathe immediately after forced breathing is stopped. If the period of breathing cessation—apnea—is extended, cyanosis (bluish tint) of the lips may occur.

Is the respiratory rate after hyperventilation faster *or* slower than during normal quiet breathing?

_____

6. Repeat the previous test, but do not record or do a visual count until after hyperventilation. After hyperventilation, the subject is to hold the breath as long as possible. Can the breath be held for a longer or shorter time after hyperventilating?

_____

7. Without recording, have the subject breathe into a paper bag for 3 minutes; then record the person's breathing movements.

! During the bag-breathing exercise, the subject's partner should watch the subject carefully for any untoward reactions.

Is the breathing rate faster *or* slower than that recorded during normal quiet breathing?

_____

After hyperventilating? _____

! Dispose of the paper bag in the autoclave bag. Keep the pneumograph records to interpret results, and hand them in if requested by the instructor. By examining the test results, you should be able to determine which chemical factor, carbon dioxide or oxygen, has the greater effect on modifying the respiratory rate and depth.

EXERCISE

24

REVIEW SHEET
Respiratory System Physiology

Name _____ Lab Time/Date _____

Mechanics of Respiration

1. Base your answers to the following on your observations of the operation of the model lung.

   Under what *internal* conditions does air tend to flow into the lungs? _____

   _____

   Under what *internal* conditions does air tend to flow out of the lungs? Explain. _____

   _____

2. Activation of the diaphragm and the external intercostal muscles begins the inspiratory process. What results from

   the contraction of these muscles, and how is this accomplished? _____

   _____

   _____

   _____

3. What was the approximate increase in diameter of chest circumference during a quiet inspiration?

   _____ inches   During forced inspiration? _____ inches

   What temporary physiological advantage does the substantial increase in chest circumference during forced
   inspiration create?

   _____

   _____

4. The presence of a partial vacuum between the pleural membranes is necessary for proper inflation of the lungs. What
   would occur if an opening were made into the chest cavity, as with a puncture wound?

   _____

   _____

Respiratory Volumes and Capacities: Spirometry

5. Write the respiratory volume term and the normal value that is described by the following statements:

   Volume of air present in the lungs after a forceful expiration _____

   Volume of air that can be expired forcibly after a normal expiration _____

   Volume of air that is breathed in and out during a normal respiration _____

Volume of air that can be inspired forcibly after a normal inspiration _____

Volume of air corresponding to TV + IRV + ERV _____

6. Record experimental respiratory volumes as determined in the laboratory.

Average TV _____ ml   Average VC _____ ml

Average ERV _____ ml   Average IRV _____ ml

Factors Influencing Rate and Depth of Respiration

7. Where are the neural control centers of respiratory rhythm? _____ and _____

8. Based on pneumograph reading of respiratory variation, what was the rate of quiet breathing?

Initial testing _____ breaths/min

Record observations of how the initial pneumograph recording was modified during the various testing procedures described below. Indicate the respiratory rate, and include comments on the relative depth of the respiratory peaks observed.

Test performed	Observations
Talking	
Yawning	
Laughing	
Standing	
Running in place	
Swallowing water	
Coughing	
Lying down	
Concentrating	

9. Student data:

Breath-holding interval after a deep inhalation _____ sec   Length of recovery period _____ sec

Breath-holding interval after a forceful expiration _____ sec   Length of recovery period _____ sec

After breathing quietly and taking a deep breath (which you held), did you feel an urge to inspire or to expire?

_____

After exhaling and then holding your breath, did you want to inspire or expire? _____

10. Observations after hyperventilation: _____

_____

11. Blood CO_2 levels and blood pH are related. When blood CO_2 levels increase, the pH increases. Explain what changes might occur in the blood's pH if the breathing rate increased or decreased. _____

_____

12. Length of breath holding after hyperventilation: _____ sec

Why does hyperventilation produce apnea or a reduced respiratory rate?_____

_____

13. Observations for rebreathing breathed air: _____

_____

Why does rebreathing breathed air increase the respiratory rate? _____

_____

14. Do the following factors generally increase (indicate with I) or decrease (indicate with D) the respiratory rate and depth?

1. increase in blood CO_2 _____   3. increase in blood pH _____

2. decrease in blood O_2 _____   4. decrease in blood pH _____

Did it appear that CO_2 or O_2 had a greater effect on modifying the respiratory rate? _____

15. Where are sensory receptors sensitive to changes in O_2 levels in the blood located? _____

_____

25

Functional Anatomy of the Digestive System

Materials

Digestive System Anatomy
☐ Dissectible torso model
☐ Anatomical chart of the human digestive system
☐ Model of a villus (if available)
☐ Jaw model or human skull
☐ Demonstration area: Prepared microscope slides for student viewing under low power:
 Station 1: Cross section of the duodenum (small intestine)
 Station 2: Liver

Chemical and Physical Processes of Digestion

Enzyme Action Supply Area
☐ Test tubes and test tube rack
☐ Graduated cylinder
☐ Wax markers
☐ Hot plates
☐ 250-ml beakers
☐ Boiling chips
☐ Water bath set at 37°C (if not available, incubate at room temperature and double the time)
☐ Ice water bath
☐ Chart on chalkboard for recording class results
☐ Dropper bottle of 1% trypsin
☐ Dropper bottle of 1% BAPNA solution
☐ Dropper bottle of vegetable oil
☐ Bile salts (sodium taurocholate)
☐ Parafilm (small squares to cover the test tubes)

Physical Processes Supply Area
☐ Water pitcher
☐ Paper cups
☐ Stethoscope
☐ Alcohol swabs
☐ Disposable autoclave bag

Pre-Lab Quiz

1. The _____ lines the lumen of the alimentary canal and consists of epithelium, lamina propria, and muscularis mucosae.
 a. mucosa b. serosa c. submucosa

2. Circle the correct term. Approximately 10 in. long, the <u>esophagus</u> / <u>alimentary canal</u> conducts food from the pharynx to the stomach.

3. The _____ is located on the left side of the abdominal cavity and is hidden by the liver and diaphragm.
 a. gallbladder
 b. large intestine
 c. small intestine
 d. stomach

4. Circle True or False. Nearly all nutrient absorption occurs in the small intestine.

5. Circle the correct term. The <u>ascending colon</u> / <u>descending colon</u> traverses down the left side of the abdominal cavity and becomes the sigmoid colon.

6. A tooth consists of two major regions, the crown and the:
 a. dentin
 b. enamel
 c. gingiva
 d. root

The **digestive system** provides the body with the nutrients essential for health. The organs of this system ingest, digest, and absorb food and eliminate the undigested remains as feces.

The digestive system consists of a hollow tube extending from the mouth to the anus, into which a number of accessory organs or glands empty their secretions (**Figure 25.1**). Food within this tube, the *alimentary canal,* is technically outside the body because it has contact only with the cells lining the tract. Before ingested food is available to the body cells, it must be broken down *physically* (chewing, churning) and *chemically* (enzymatic hydrolysis) into its smaller diffusible molecules—a process called **digestion.** The digested end products can then pass through the epithelial cells lining the tract into the blood to be distributed to the body cells—a process termed **absorption.**

The organs of the digestive system are separated into two major groups: the **alimentary canal,** or **gastrointestinal (GI) tract,** and the **accessory digestive organs.** The alimentary canal consists of the mouth, pharynx, esophagus, stomach, small and large intestines, and anus. The accessory structures include the teeth and tongue, which participate in the mechanical breakdown of food; and the salivary glands, gallbladder, liver, and pancreas, which release their products into the alimentary canal. These individual organs are described shortly.

General Histologic Plan of The Alimentary Canal

OBJECTIVE 1 Describe the general histologic structure of the wall of the alimentary canal.

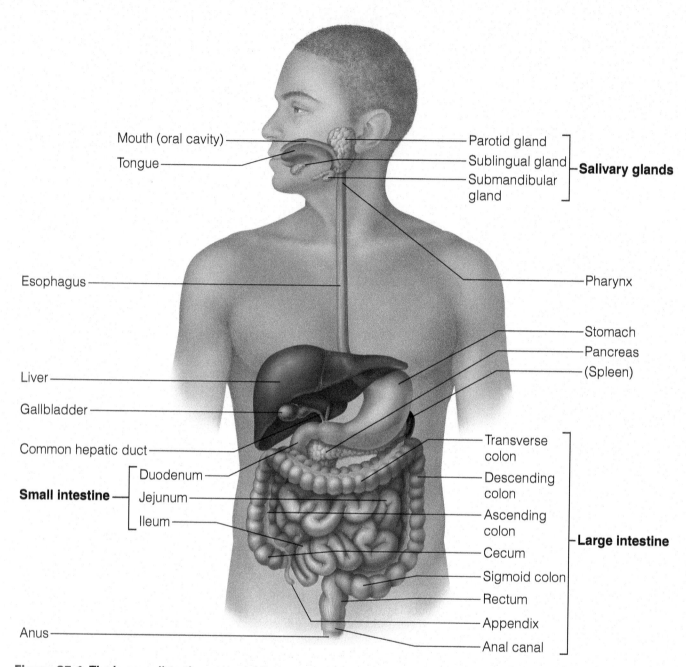

Figure 25.1 The human digestive system: Alimentary canal and accessory organs.
Liver and gallbladder are reflected superiorly and to the right side of the body.

Essentially the alimentary canal walls have four basic **tunics** (layers). From the lumen outward, these are the *mucosa,* the *submucosa,* the *muscularis externa,* and the *serosa* (Figure 25.2). Each tunic has a predominant tissue type and plays a specific role in digestion. Table 25.1 summarizes the characteristics of these layers.

Activity 1

Observing the Histologic Structure of the Alimentary Canal Wall

Go to the demonstration area where a cross section of the duodenum (part of the small intestine) is secured to the microscope stage. Identify the four basic tunics of the intestinal wall—that is, the **mucosa** (and its three sublayers), the **submucosa** (connective tissue layer deep to the mucosa), the **muscularis externa** (composed of circular and longitudinal smooth muscle layers), and the **serosa** (the outermost layer). Examine the large leaflike *villi,* which increase the surface area for absorption. Consult Figure 25.2 and Plate 33 in the Histology Atlas as you work.

What type of epithelium do you see here? _____

_____

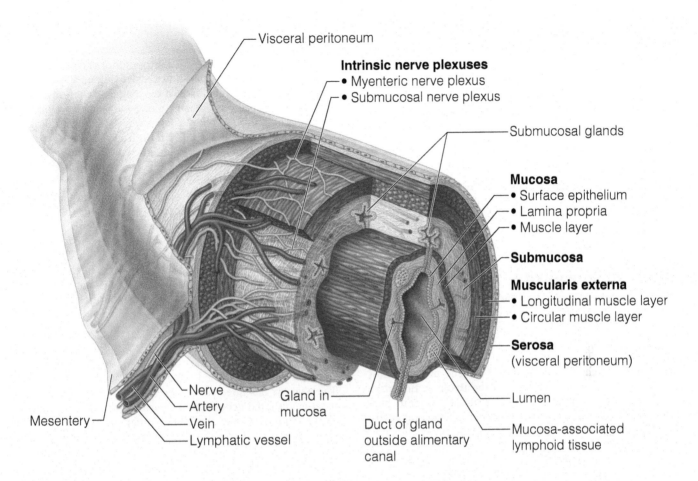

Figure 25.2 Basic structure of the alimentary canal wall. (See also Plate 33 in the Histology Atlas.)

Table 25.1	**Alimentary Canal Wall Layers (Figure 25.2)**		

Layer	Subdivision of the layer	Tissue type	Major functions (generalized for the layer)
Mucosa	Surface epithelium	Stratified squamous epithelium in the mouth, esophagus, and anus; simple columnar epithelium in the remainder of the canal	Secretion of mucus, digestive enzymes, and hormones; absorption of end products into the blood; protection against infectious disease.
	Lamina propria	Areolar connective tissue with blood vessels; many lymphoid follicles, especially as tonsils and mucosa-associated lymphoid tissue (MALT)	
	Muscle layer	A thin layer of smooth muscle	
Submucosa	N/A	Areolar and dense irregular connective tissue containing blood vessels, lymphatic vessels, and nerve fibers (submucosal nerve plexus)	Blood vessels absorb and transport nutrients. Elastic fibers help maintain the shape of each organ.
Muscularis externa	Circular layer Longitudinal layer	Inner layer of smooth muscle Outer layer of smooth muscle	Segmentation and peristalsis of digested food along the tract are regulated by the myenteric nerve plexus.
Serosa* (visceral peritoneum)	Visceral peritoneum	Single layer of flat, serous fluid producing cells	Reduces friction as the digestive system organs slide across one another.

*Since the esophagus is outside the peritoneal cavity, the serosa is replaced by an adventitia made of areolar connective tissue that binds the esophagus to surrounding tissues.

25

Organs of the Alimentary Canal

OBJECTIVE 2 Identify on a model or appropriate diagram the organs that make up the alimentary canal, and indicate the digestive role of each organ.

Activity 2

Identifying Alimentary Canal Organs

The pathway that food takes as it passes through the alimentary canal organs is described in the next sections. Identify each structure in Figure 25.1 and on the torso model as you work.

Mouth or Oral Cavity

Food enters the digestive tract through the **mouth, or oral cavity** (**Figure 25.3**). Within this mucosa-lined cavity are the gums, teeth, and tongue. The **lips (labia)** protect its anterior opening, the **cheeks** form its lateral walls, and the **palate,** its roof. The anterior part of the palate is called the **hard palate** because bone underlies it. The posterior **soft palate** is unsupported by bone, and the **uvula,** a fingerlike projection of the soft palate, extends inferiorly from its posterior edge. The soft palate rises to close off the oral cavity from the nasal and pharyngeal passages during swallowing. The muscular **tongue** occupies the floor of the oral cavity. A membrane, the **lingual frenulum,** secures the tongue to the floor of the mouth (Figure 25.3b). The space between the lips and cheeks and the teeth is the **vestibule;** the area that lies within the teeth and gums is the **oral cavity** proper.

On each side of the mouth at its posterior end are masses of lymphoid tissue, the **palatine tonsils** (Figure 25.3). The **lingual tonsil** covers the base of the tongue, posterior to the oral cavity proper. The tonsils, along with other lymphoid tissues, are part of the body's defense system. For histology of the palatine tonsils see Plate 25 in the Histology Atlas.

Three pairs of **salivary glands** duct their secretion, saliva, into the oral cavity. One component of saliva, salivary amylase, begins the digestion of starchy foods in the mouth. (The salivary glands are discussed in more detail on page 321.)

As food enters the mouth, it is mixed with saliva and masticated (chewed). The cheeks and lips help hold the food between the teeth, and the mobile tongue mixes the food with saliva during chewing and initiates swallowing. Thus the mechanical and chemical breakdown of food begins before the food has left the mouth. The surface of the tongue is covered with papillae, many of which contain taste buds (see Exercise 17).

Pharynx

From the mouth, food passes posteriorly into the pharynx, a common passageway for food, fluid, and air (Figure 25.3). The pharynx has three parts—the **nasopharynx** (behind the nasal cavity), the **oropharynx** (extends from the soft palate to the epiglottis), and the **laryngopharynx** (extends from the epiglottis to the base of the larynx), which is continuous with the esophagus.

The walls of the pharynx contain two layers of skeletal muscle: an inner longitudinal layer and an outer layer of circular constrictor muscles. These muscles initiate wavelike contractions that propel the food inferiorly into the esophagus.

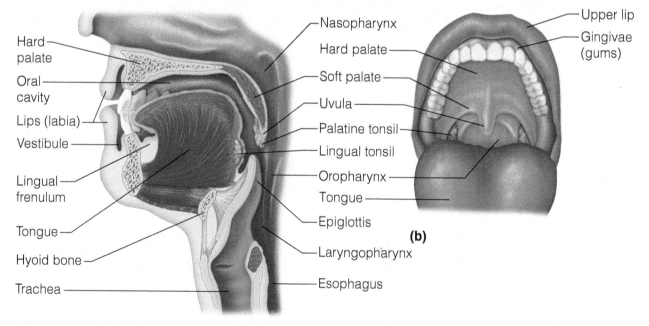

25

(a)

Figure 25.3 Anatomy of the mouth (oral cavity). (a) Sagittal section of the oral cavity and pharynx. **(b)** Anterior view of the oral cavity.

Esophagus

The **esophagus,** or gullet, extends from the pharynx through the diaphragm to the stomach. It is approximately 10 inches long in humans and is basically a food passageway that conducts food to the stomach by *peristalsis*. At its superior end its walls contain skeletal muscle; this is replaced by smooth muscle in the area nearing the stomach. The **cardioesophageal sphincter,** a thickening of the smooth muscle layer at the esophagus-stomach junction, controls food passage into the stomach (**Figure 25.4**).

Stomach

The **stomach** (Figures 25.1 and 25.4) is on the left side of the abdominal cavity and is hidden by the liver and diaphragm. Different regions of the saclike stomach are the **cardial region** (the area surrounding the opening through which food enters the stomach), the **fundus** (the expanded portion of the stomach, lateral to the cardiac region), the **body** (midpart of the stomach), and the **pylorus** (the terminal part of the stomach, which is continuous with the small intestine through the **pyloric sphincter**).

The concave medial surface of the stomach is the **lesser curvature;** its convex lateral surface is the **greater curvature.** Two mesenteries, called *omenta*, extend from these curvatures. The **lesser omentum** extends from the liver to the lesser curvature. The **greater omentum** extends from the greater curvature of the stomach, drapes downward over the abdominal contents to cover them in an apronlike fashion, and then attaches to the posterior body wall. **Figure 25.5** illustrates the omenta as well as the other peritoneal attachments of the abdominal organs.

The stomach is a temporary storage region for food as well as a site for food breakdown. It contains a third *obliquely* oriented layer of smooth muscle in its muscularis externa that allows it to churn, mix, and pummel the food, physically breaking it down to smaller fragments. *Gastric glands* of the mucosa secrete hydrochloric acid and hydrolytic enzymes. The mucosal glands also secrete a thick mucus that protects the stomach from being digested by its protein-digesting enzymes. Food processed in the stomach resembles a creamy mass (chyme), which enters the small intestine through the pyloric sphincter. For histology of the stomach, see Plates 31 and 32 in the Histology Atlas.

Small Intestine

OBJECTIVE 3   Describe structural specializations of the small intestine that contribute to its digestive role(s).

The **small intestine** is a convoluted tube about 2 meters (6 feet) long in a living person. It extends from the pyloric sphincter to the ileocecal valve. The small intestine is suspended by the fan-shaped **mesentery** from the posterior abdominal wall (Figure 25.5), and it lies, framed on both sides and superiorly by the large intestine, in the abdominal cavity. The small intestine has three regions (see Figure 25.1): (1) The **duodenum** extends from the pyloric sphincter for

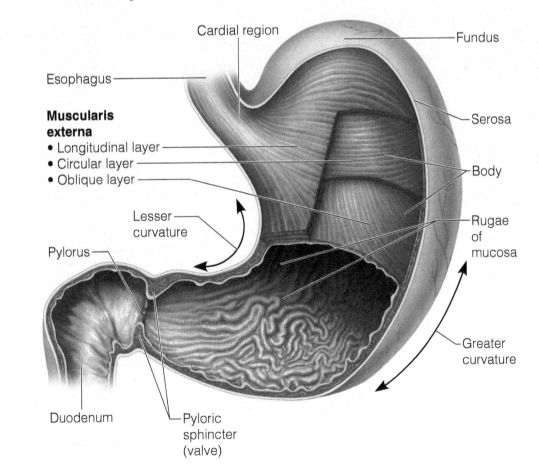

Figure 25.4 Gross anatomy of the stomach (frontal section).

Cardial region

Fundus

Esophagus

Muscularis externa
• Longitudinal layer
• Circular layer
• Oblique layer

Serosa

Body

Lesser curvature

Rugae of mucosa

Pylorus

Duodenum

Pyloric sphincter (valve)

Greater curvature

25

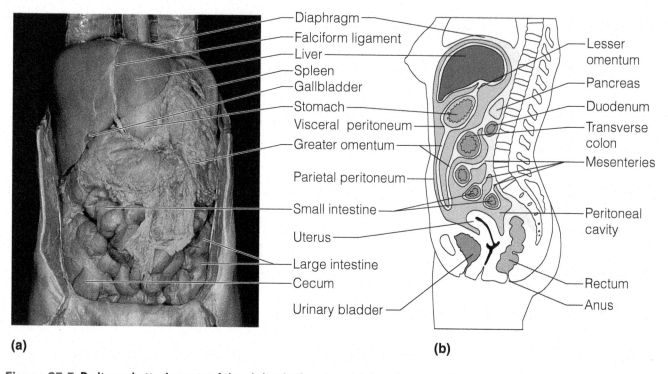

(a)

(b)

Figure 25.5 Peritoneal attachments of the abdominal organs. (a) Anterior view; the greater omentum is shown in its normal position covering the abdominal viscera. **(b)** Sagittal view of the abdominopelvic cavity of a female.

about 10 inches and curves around the head of the pancreas. (2) The **jejunum,** continuous with the duodenum, extends for about 8 feet. (3) The **ileum,** the terminal portion of the small intestine, is about 12 feet long and joins the large intestine at the **ileocecal valve.**

Brush border enzymes, enzymes bound to the microvilli of the columnar epithelial cells, and—more important—enzymes produced by the pancreas and ducted into the duodenum via the **pancreatic duct** complete the chemical breakdown process in the small intestine. Bile (formed in the liver) also enters the duodenum via the **bile duct** in the same area. At the duodenum, the ducts join to form the bulblike **hepatopancreatic ampulla** and empty their products into the duodenal lumen through an opening called the **duodenal papilla.**

Nearly all food absorption occurs in the small intestine, where three structural modifications that increase the absorptive area appear—microvilli, villi, and circular folds (**Figure 25.6**). **Microvilli** are microscopic projections of the surface plasma membrane of the columnar epithelial cells of the mucosa. **Villi** are the fingerlike projections of the mucosa that give it a velvety appearance and texture. The **circular folds (plicae circulares)** are deep folds of the mucosal and submucosal layers that force chyme to spiral through the intestine, mixing it and slowing its progress to allow time for digestion and absorption. Any residue remaining undigested at the end of the small intestine enters the large intestine through the ileocecal valve. Local collections of lymphoid nodules found in the submucosa called **Peyer's patches** increase along the length of the small intestine (see Plate 35 in the Histology Atlas).

Activity 3

Examining the Villus Model

If a villus model is available, identify the following cells or regions before continuing: epithelium, goblet cells, lamina propria, slips of the muscularis mucosae, capillary bed, and lacteal.

Large Intestine

The **large intestine** (**Figure 25.7**) is about 1.5 m (5 feet) long and extends from the ileocecal valve to the anus. It consists of the following subdivisions: the **cecum, appendix, colon, rectum,** and **anal canal.**

The colon has several regions. The **ascending colon** travels up the right side of the abdominal cavity and makes a right-angle turn at the **right colic (hepatic) flexure** to cross the abdominal cavity as the **transverse colon.** It then turns at the **left colic (splenic) flexure** and continues downward as the **descending colon,** where it becomes the S-shaped **sigmoid colon.** The sigmoid colon, rectum, and the anal canal lie in the pelvis and thus are not considered abdominal cavity structures.

The anal canal terminates in the **anus,** the opening to the body exterior. The anus, which has an external sphincter of skeletal muscle (the voluntary sphincter) and an internal sphincter of smooth muscle (the involuntary sphincter), is normally closed except during defecation when feces are eliminated from the body.

In the large intestine, the longitudinal muscle layer of the muscularis externa is reduced to three muscle bands. These

25

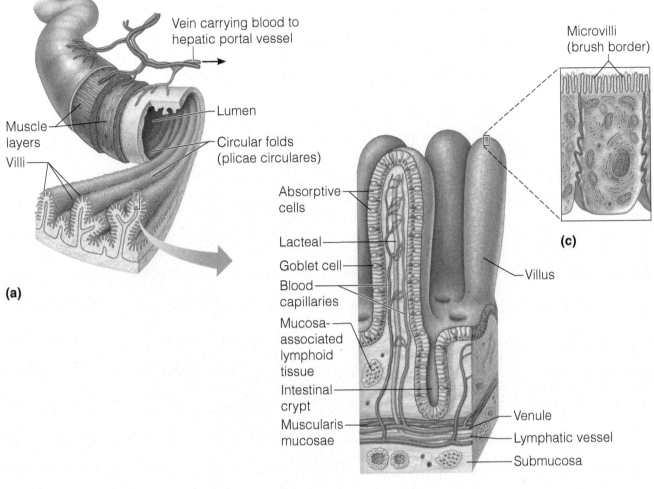

Figure 25.6 Structural modifications of the small intestine. (a) Several circular folds seen on the inner surface of the small intestine. **(b)** Enlargement of one villus extension of the circular fold. **(c)** Enlargement of an absorptive cell to show microvilli.

bands are shorter than the rest of the wall of the large intestine, so they cause the wall to pucker into small pocketlike sacs called **haustra.**

The major function of the large intestine is to compact and propel the fecal matter toward the anus and to eliminate it from the body. While it does that chore, it (1) provides a site for intestinal bacteria to manufacture some vitamins (B and K), which it then absorbs into the bloodstream; and (2) reclaims most of the remaining water (and some of the electrolytes) from undigested food, thus conserving body water.

Accessory Digestive Organs

OBJECTIVE 4   Name and indicate the function of each accessory digestive organ.

Teeth

Usually by the early 20s two sets of teeth have developed (**Figure 25.8**). The initial set, the **deciduous** (or **milk**) **teeth,** appears between the ages of 6 months and 2½ years. The child begins to shed the deciduous teeth around the age of 6, and a second set of teeth, the **permanent teeth,** gradually replaces them. During years 6 to 12, the child has mixed dentition—some permanent and some deciduous teeth. Generally, by the age of 12, all of the deciduous teeth have been shed.

Teeth are classified as **incisors, canines** (eye teeth), **premolars** (bicuspids), and **molars.** Teeth names reflect differences in relative structure and function. The chisel-shaped incisors are used in biting. Canines are fanglike, used for tearing or piercing food. Incisors, canines, and premolars typically have single roots. The lower molars have two roots but the upper molars usually have three. The premolars and molars have broad crowns with rounded cusps (grinding surfaces) specialized for the grinding of food.

Dentition is described by means of a **dental formula,** which specifies the numbers, types, and position of the teeth in one side of the jaw. (Because tooth arrangement is bilaterally symmetrical, it is necessary to indicate only one side of

25

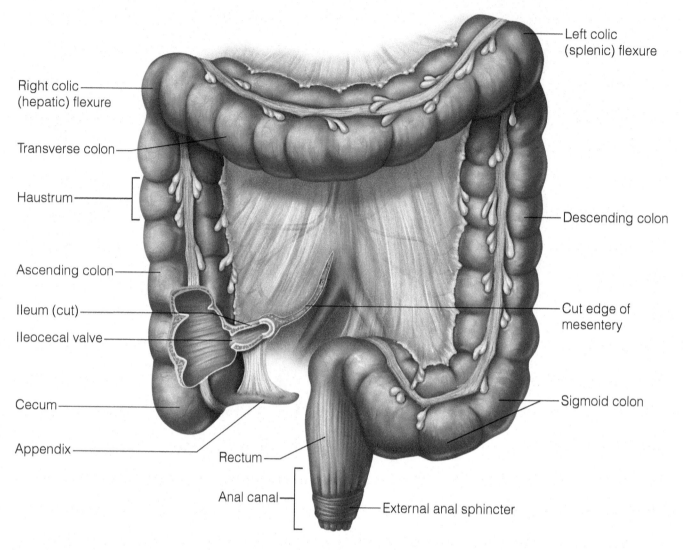

Right colic
(hepatic) flexure

Transverse colon

Haustrum

Ascending colon

Ileum (cut)

Ileocecal valve

Cecum

Appendix

Rectum

Anal canal

Left colic
(splenic) flexure

Descending colon

Cut edge of
mesentery

Sigmoid colon

External anal sphincter

Figure 25.7 The large intestine. A section of the cecum is removed to show the
ileocecal valve.

the jaw.) The complete dental formula for the deciduous teeth
from the medial to posterior aspect of each jaw is as follows:

$$\frac{\text{Upper teeth: 2 incisors, 1 canine, 0 premolars, 2 molars}}{\text{Lower teeth: 2 incisors, 1 canine, 0 premolars, 2 molars}} \times 2$$

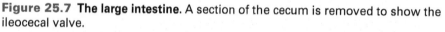

This formula is generally shortened to read as follows:

$$\frac{2,1,0,2}{2,1,0,2} \times 2 = 20 \text{ (number of deciduous teeth)}$$

The 32 permanent teeth are then described by the following
dental formula:

$$\frac{2,1,2,3}{2,1,2,3} \times 2 = 32 \text{ (number of permanent teeth)}$$

Although 32 is the usual number of permanent teeth, not
everyone develops a full set. In many people, the third molars,
commonly called *wisdom teeth,* never erupt.

OBJECTIVE 5   Name human deciduous and permanent teeth, and describe the basic anatomy of a tooth.

> ### Activity 4
>
> **Identifying Types of Teeth**
> Identify the four types of teeth (incisors, canines, premo-
> lars, and molars) on the jaw model or human skull.

A tooth consists of two major regions, the **crown** and the
root. A longitudinal section made through a tooth shows
the following basic anatomy (**Figure 25.9**). The enamel-
covered crown is the superior portion of the tooth visible
above the **gum,** or **gingiva.** Enamel is the hardest substance
in the body and is fairly brittle because it is heavily mineral-
ized with calcium salts (chiefly $CaPO_4$).

That part of the tooth embedded in the jaw is the root, and
the root and crown are connected by a constricted **neck.** The
outermost surface of the root is covered by **cement,** which is
similar to bone in composition. The cementum attaches the
tooth to the **periodontal membrane (ligament),** which holds
the tooth in the alveolar socket. **Dentin,** which comprises the
bulk of the tooth, is the bonelike material located deep to the
enamel and cement.

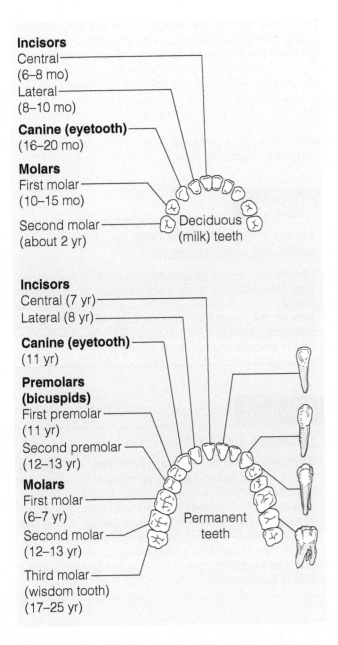

Incisors
Central (6–8 mo)
Lateral (8–10 mo)
Canine (eyetooth) (16–20 mo)
Molars
First molar (10–15 mo)
Second molar (about 2 yr)
Deciduous (milk) teeth

Incisors
Central (7 yr)
Lateral (8 yr)
Canine (eyetooth) (11 yr)
Premolars (bicuspids)
First premolar (11 yr)
Second premolar (12–13 yr)
Molars
First molar (6–7 yr)
Second molar (12–13 yr)
Third molar (wisdom tooth) (17–25 yr)
Permanent teeth

Figure 25.8 Human deciduous teeth and permanent teeth. (Approximate time of teeth eruption shown in parentheses.)

The **pulp cavity** occupies the core of the tooth. **Pulp,** connective tissue liberally supplied with blood vessels, nerves, and lymphatics, occupies this cavity and provides for tooth sensation and supplies nutrients to the tooth tissues. Where the pulp cavity extends into the root, it becomes the **root canal.**

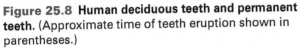
Activity 5

Studying Internal Tooth Anatomy

If the jaw model provided has a removable tooth that is sectioned longitudinally, identify as many of the structures detailed in Figure 25.9 as possible.

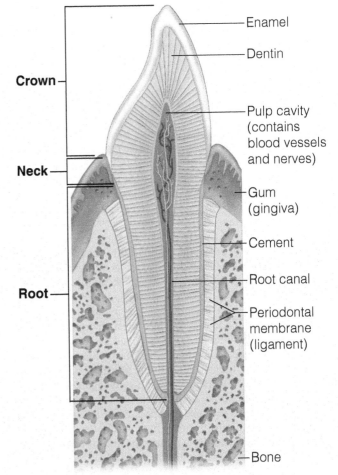

Crown
Neck
Root

Enamel
Dentin
Pulp cavity (contains blood vessels and nerves)
Gum (gingiva)
Cement
Root canal
Periodontal membrane (ligament)
Bone

Figure 25.9 Longitudinal section of a canine tooth.

Salivary Glands

Three pairs of major **salivary glands** (see Figure 25.1) empty their secretions into the oral cavity:

Parotid glands: Large glands located anterior to the ear and ducting via the parotid duct into the mouth over the second upper molar.

Submandibular glands: Located along the medial aspect of the mandible in the floor of the mouth, and ducting under the tongue close to the frenulum.

Sublingual glands: Small glands located most anteriorly in the floor of the mouth and emptying under the tongue via several small ducts (**Plate 37 in the Histology Atlas**).

Saliva is a mixture of mucus, which moistens the food and helps to bind it together into a mass, and a clear serous fluid containing the enzyme *salivary amylase*. Salivary amylase begins the digestion of starch.

Activity 6

Locating the Salivary Glands

Identify each of the salivary glands discussed previously on an anatomical chart or torso model. Also, attempt to follow their ducts to where they empty into the oral cavity.

Liver and Gallbladder

The **liver** (see Figure 25.1), the largest gland in the body, is located inferior to the diaphragm, more to the right side of the body. As noted earlier, it hides the stomach in a superficial view of abdominal contents. The human liver has four lobes and is suspended from the diaphragm and anterior abdominal wall by the **falciform ligament** (see Figure 25.5a).

The liver's digestive function is to produce bile, which leaves the liver through the **common hepatic duct** and then enters the duodenum via the **bile duct.** Bile has no enzymes but is important to fat digestion because of its emulsifying action (the physical breakdown of larger particles into smaller ones) on fat. This creates a larger surface area for fat-digesting enzymes (lipases) to work on. Without bile, little fat digestion or absorption occurs.

When digestive activity is not occurring, bile backs up in the **cystic duct** and enters the **gallbladder,** a small, green sac on the inferior surface of the liver. It is stored there until needed for the digestive process. While there, bile is concentrated by the removal of water and some ions.

The liver is very important in the initial processing of the nutrient-rich blood draining the digestive organs. Special phagocytic cells remove debris such as bacteria from the blood as it flows past, while the liver parenchyma cells pick up oxygen and nutrients. Much of the glucose transported to the liver from the GI tract is stored as glycogen in the liver for later use, and amino acids taken from the blood by the liver cells are used to make plasma proteins. The processed blood ultimately drains from the liver via the *hepatic vein.* In addition, bile, destined for the small intestine, is continuously being made by the hepatic cells.

Pancreas

The **pancreas** is a soft, triangular gland that extends across the posterior abdominal wall from the spleen to the duodenum (see Figure 25.1). Like the duodenum, it is a retroperitoneal organ (see Figure 25.5). The pancreas has both an endocrine function (it produces the hormones insulin and glucagon) and an exocrine (enzyme-producing) function.

(See Plate 38 in the Histology Atlas.) It produces a variety of hydrolytic enzymes, which it secretes in an alkaline fluid into the duodenum via the pancreatic duct. Pancreatic juice is very alkaline. Its high concentration of bicarbonate ion (HCO_3^-) neutralizes the acidic chyme entering the duodenum from the stomach, enabling the pancreatic and intestinal enzymes to operate at their optimal pH. (Optimal pH for digestive activity to occur in the stomach is very acidic and results from the presence of HCl. Optimal pH for the small intestine is slightly alkaline.)

Activity 7

Locating the Liver, Pancreas, and Associated Structures

Identify the liver, the gallbladder, and the common hepatic, bile, and cystic ducts on the anatomical chart or torso model before continuing. Notice the relationship of the liver to the diaphragm and stomach. Also identify the pancreas, pancreatic duct, and if possible, the hepatopancreatic ampulla and duodenal papilla.

Activity 8

Examining the Histology of the Liver

Go to station 2 at the demonstration area, and examine a slide of liver tissue. Identify as many of the structural features illustrated in Plate 39 in the Histology Atlas as possible. Notice the central canals and how the liver cells form cords that radiate from those canals. If possible, identify a triad—a region containing a branch of the hepatic artery, a branch of the hepatic portal vein, and a bile duct. The liver units, called lobules, are six-sided, and a triad is found at each corner.

Digestion of Foodstuffs: Enzymatic Action

OBJECTIVE 6 List and indicate the specific function of the major enzymes or enzyme groups produced by the salivary glands, stomach, small intestine, and pancreas. Summarize conditions promoting their optimal functioning.

Figure 25.10 is a flowchart of the progressive digestion and absorption of proteins, fats, and carbohydrates. It indicates the enzymes involved and their source, site of action, and path of absorption. Acquaint yourself with the flowchart before beginning these experiments, and refer to it as necessary during the laboratory session.

Enzymes are large protein molecules produced by body cells, that act as biological *catalysts.* The digestive enzymes are hydrolytic enzymes, or *hydrolases.* Their **substrates,** or the molecules on which they act, are organic food molecules which they break down by adding water to the molecular bonds, thus breaking the bonds between the building blocks, or monomers.

The hydrolytic enzymes are very specific in their action. Each enzyme hydrolyzes only one or a small group of substrate molecules, and certain environmental conditions are necessary for it to function optimally. Because digestive enzymes and bile actually function *outside* the body cells while in the digestive tract, their activity can also be studied in a test tube. Such in vitro studies provide a convenient laboratory environment for investigating the effect of such variations on enzyme activity.

In this laboratory session, we will examine factors that influence trypsin's digestion of proteins (trypsin is a pancreatic enzyme) and explore the role of bile made by the liver.

Protein Digestion by Trypsin

OBJECTIVE 7 Perform an appropriate chemical test to determine whether digestion of protein has occurred.

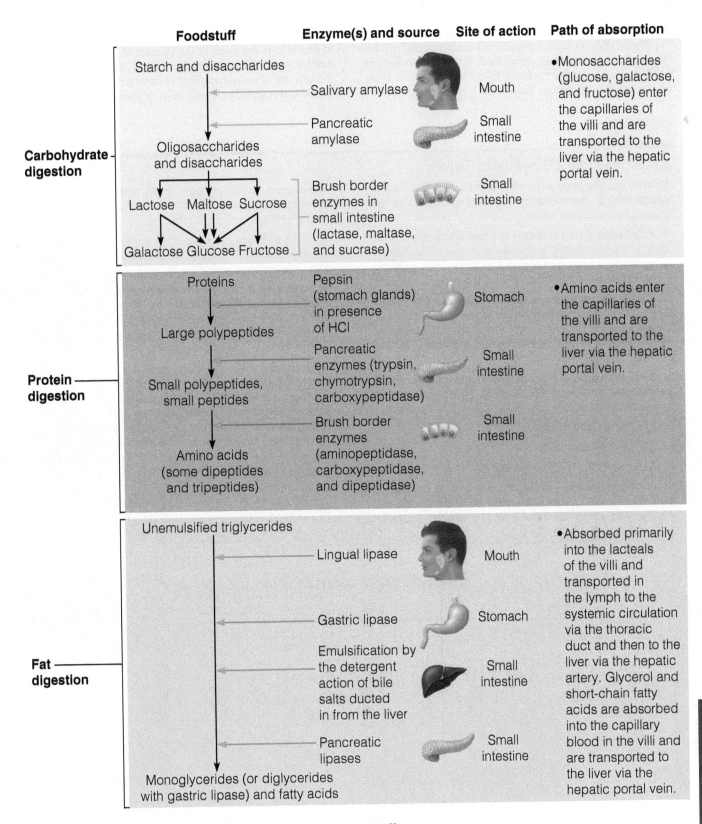

Figure 25.10 Flowchart of digestion and absorption of foodstuffs.

Trypsin hydrolyzes proteins to small fragments. BAPNA is a synthetic (human-made) protein substrate consisting of a dye covalently bound to an amino acid. Trypsin hydrolysis of BAPNA cleaves the dye molecule from the amino acid, causing the solution to change from colorless to bright yellow.

Because the covalent bond between the dye molecule and the amino acid is the same as the peptide bonds that link amino acids together, the appearance of a yellow color indicates the activity of an enzyme that is capable of cleaving peptide bonds and is direct evidence of hydrolysis.

Activity 9

Assessing Protein Digestion by Trypsin

Work in groups of three or four, with each person in the group taking responsibility for setting up some of the experimental samples.

1. From supply area 1, obtain five test tubes, a test tube rack, a dropper bottle of trypsin and one of BAPNA, a graduated cylinder, a wax pencil, a 250-ml beaker, boiling chips, and a hot plate and bring them to your bench.

2. One student should prepare the controls (tubes 1T and 2T), and two should prepare the experimental samples (tubes 3T to 5T). The fourth person can set up the samples for the next activity, "Demonstrating the Action of Bile on Fats."

- Mark each tube with a wax pencil, and load the tubes as indicated in **Figure 25.11**, using 3 drops of each indicated substance.

    1T—trypsin and water

    2T—BAPNA and water

    3T, 4T, and 5T—trypsin and BAPNA

- For experimental sample 3T, which is to be boiled before incubation, place a few boiling chips in the 250-ml beaker, add about 125 ml of water (or enough to cover the sample-containing part of the test tube), and bring the water to a boil on the hot plate. Place the specimen in the boiling water for 4 minutes.

- Place all tubes in a rack in the appropriate water bath for approximately 1 hour. Shake the rack occasionally to keep the contents well mixed.

3. Assess your results. The presence of a yellow color indicates a **positive hydrolysis test.** If the sample mixture remains clear, no detectable hydrolysis has occurred.

Record the color of the experimental tube in Figure 25.11.

Upon completing the experiments, each group should communicate its results to the rest of the class by recording them in a chart on the chalkboard. All members of the class should observe the **controls*** as well as the positive and negative results of all experimental samples. Additionally, all members of the class should be able to explain the tests used and the results anticipated and observed for each experiment.

*Controls are the specimens or standards against which experimental samples are compared.

Tube no.	1T	2T	3T		4T	5T
Additives (3 drops ea)	trypsin, water	BAPNA, water	trypsin	Boil trypsin 4 min, then add BAPNA. → boiled trypsin, BAPNA	trypsin, BAPNA	trypsin, BAPNA
Incubation condition	37°C	37°C	37°C		37°C	0°C
Color change						
Result: (+) or (−)						

Additive key: ■ Trypsin ▨ BAPNA ☐ Water

Figure 25.11 Summary table for trypsin digestion of protein.

The Action of Bile on Fats

OBJECTIVE 8   Describe the function(s) of bile in the digestive process.

The treatment that fats and oils go through during digestion in the small intestine is more complicated than that of carbohydrates or proteins—pretreatment with bile to physically emulsify the fats is required. Hence, two sets of reactions occur.

First: Fats/oils $\xrightarrow[\text{emulsification}]{\text{Bile}}$ minute fat/oil droplets

Then: Fat/oil droplets $\xrightarrow{\text{Lipase}}$ monoglycerides and fatty acids

In this activity, we will be investigating the emulsifying activity of bile.

Activity 10

Demonstrating the Action of Bile on Fats

1. From supply area 1, obtain two test tubes and a test tube rack, plus one dropper bottle of vegetable oil, bile salts, a wax marker, and two squares of Parafilm.

2. Although *bile,* a secretory product of the liver, is not an enzyme, it emulsifies fats, which provide a larger surface area for enzymatic activity. To demonstrate the action of bile on fats, mark one of the test tubes as #1 and the other as #2 with a wax marker, and prepare them as follows:

• To tube 1 add 10 drops of water and 2 drops of vegetable oil.

• To tube 2 add 10 drops of water, 2 drops of vegetable oil, and a pinch of bile salts.

• Cover each tube with a small square of Parafilm, shake vigorously, and allow the tubes to stand at room temperature.

After 10–15 minutes, observe both tubes. If emulsification has not occurred, the oil will be floating on the surface of the water. If emulsification has occurred, the fat droplets will be suspended throughout the water, forming an emulsion.

In which tube has emulsification occurred?

_____

Physical Processes: Mechanisms of Food Propulsion and Mixing

OBJECTIVE 9   Identify the alimentary canal organs involved in physical processes of digestion.

Although enzyme activity is very important in the overall food breakdown process, foods must also be processed physically (churning and chewing), and moved by mechanical means along the tract if digestion and absorption are to be completed. Both skeletal and smooth muscles are involved in digestion. This fact is demonstrated by the simple activities that follow.

Activity 11

Observing Movements and Auscultating the Sounds of Digestion

1. From supply area 2, obtain a pitcher of water, a stethoscope, a paper cup, an alcohol swab, and an autoclave bag to prepare for the following observations.

2. While swallowing a mouthful of water, consciously notice the movement of your tongue, which initiates the voluntary *buccal phase* of deglutition (swallowing). Record your observations.

_____

_____

_____

3. Repeat the swallowing process while your laboratory partner watches movements of your larynx that are visible externally. (This movement is more obvious in men, who have larger Adam's apples.) Record your observations.

_____

What do these movements accomplish?_____

_____

_____

_____

4. Before donning the stethoscope, your lab partner should clean the earpieces with an alcohol swab. Then, he or she should place the diaphragm of the stethoscope over your abdominal wall, approximately 1 inch below the xiphoid process and slightly to the left, to listen for sounds as you again take two or three swallows of water. There should be two audible sounds—one when the water splashes against the cardioesophageal sphincter, and the second when the peristaltic wave (the propulsive movement of the involuntary *pharyngeal–esophageal phase*) arrives at the sphincter and the sphincter opens, allowing water to gurgle into the stomach. Determine, as

Text continues on next page. →

25

accurately as possible, the time interval between these two sounds, and record it below.

Interval between arrival of water at the sphincter and the opening of the sphincter:

_____ sec

This interval gives a fair indication of the time it takes for the peristaltic wave to travel down the 10-inch-long esophagus. (Actually the time interval is slightly less than it seems, because pressure causes the sphincter to relax before the peristaltic wave reaches it.)

⚠ Dispose of the used paper cup in the autoclave bag.

Segmentation and Peristalsis

OBJECTIVE 10 Compare and contrast segmentation and peristalsis as mechanisms of propulsion.

Although several types of movements occur in the digestive tract, segmentation and peristalsis are most important as mixing and propulsive mechanisms.

Segmental movements are local constrictions of the organ wall that occur rhythmically. They serve mainly to mix the foodstuffs with digestive juices. However, segmentation is also important in propelling food through the small intestine.

Peristaltic movements are the major means of propelling food through most of the digestive viscera. Essentially they are waves of contraction followed by waves of relaxation that squeeze foodstuffs through the alimentary canal. They are superimposed on segmental movements.

REVIEW SHEET

Functional Anatomy
of the Digestive System

Name _____ Lab Time/Date _____

General Histological Plan of the Alimentary Canal

1. The basic structural plan of the digestive tube has been presented. Fill in the table below to complete the information listed.

Wall layer	Subdivisions of the layer	Major functions
Mucosa		
Submucosa	N/A	
Muscularis externa		
Serosa		

Organs of the Alimentary Canal

2. The tubelike digestive system canal that extends from the mouth to the anus is the _____ canal.

3. How is the muscularis externa of the stomach modified? _____

_____

How does this modification relate to the stomach's function? _____

_____

4. Using the key letters, match the items in column B with the descriptive statements in column A. (Some responses may be used more than once.)

Column A

_____ 1. structure that suspends the small intestine from the posterior body wall

_____, _____, _____ 2. three modifications of the small intestine that increase the surface area for absorption

_____ 3. large collections of lymphoid tissue found in the submucosa of the small intestine

_____ 4. deep folds of the mucosa and submucosa that extend completely or partially around the circumference of the small intestine

_____, _____ 5. regions that break down foodstuffs mechanically

_____ 6. mobile organ that initiates swallowing

_____ 7. conduit that serves the respiratory and digestive systems

_____ 8. lies posterior to the trachea; conveys food from the pharynx to the stomach

_____ 9. surface projections of a mucosal epithelial cell

_____ 10. valve at the junction of the small and large intestines

_____ 11. primary region of enzymatic digestion

_____ 12. membrane securing the tongue to the floor of the mouth

_____ 13. area between the teeth and lips/cheeks

_____ 14. wormlike sac that outpockets from the cecum

_____ 15. carbohydrate (starch) digestion begins here

_____ 16. two-layered serous membrane attached to the greater curvature of the stomach

_____ 17. organ distal to the small intestine

_____ 18. valve preventing movement of chyme from the duodenum into the stomach

_____ 19. posterosuperior boundary of the oral cavity

_____ 20. location of the hepatopancreatic sphincter through which pancreatic secretions and bile pass

_____ 21. outermost layer of a digestive organ in the abdominal cavity

_____ 22. principal site for the synthesis of vitamins (B, K) by bacteria

_____ 23. distal end of the alimentary canal

_____ 24. bone-supported part of roof of the mouth

Column B

a. anus

b. appendix

c. esophagus

d. lingual frenulum

e. greater omentum

f. hard palate

g. haustra

h. ileocecal valve

i. large intestine

j. lesser omentum

k. mesentery

l. microvilli

m. oral cavity

n. parietal peritoneum

o. Peyer's patches

p. pharynx

q. circular folds

r. pyloric valve

s. rugae

t. small intestine

u. soft palate

v. stomach

w. tongue

x. vestibule

y. villi

z. visceral peritoneum

5. Correctly identify all structures depicted in the diagram below.

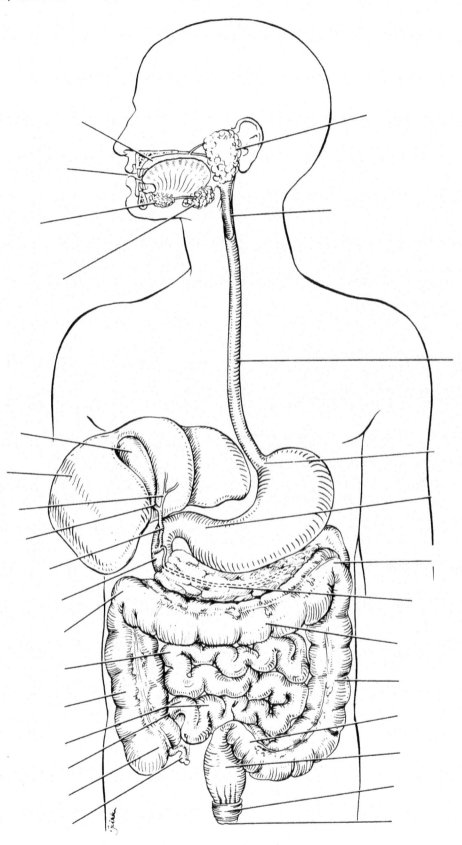

Accessory Digestive Organs

6. Use the key terms to identify each tooth area described below. (Some terms may be used more than once.)

_____ 1. visible portion of the tooth

_____ 2. material covering the tooth root

_____ 3. hardest substance in the body

_____ 4. attaches the tooth to bone and surrounding alveolar structures

_____ 5. portion of the tooth embedded in bone

_____ 6. forms the major portion of tooth structure; similar to bone

_____ 7. area of tooth below the dentin

_____ 8. site of blood vessels, nerves, and lymphatics

_____ 9. portion of the tooth covered with enamel

Key:

cement

crown

dentin

enamel

gingiva

periodontal membrane

pulp

root

7. In humans, the number of deciduous teeth is _____; the number of permanent teeth is _____.

8. The dental formula for permanent teeth is $\dfrac{2,1,2,3}{2,1,2,3}$. Explain what this means: _____

_____

9. What teeth are the "wisdom teeth"? _____

_____

10. Various types of glands form a part of the alimentary tube wall or release their secretions into it by means of ducts. Match the glands listed in column B with the function/locations described in column A.

Column A

_____ 1. produce(s) a product containing amylase that begins starch breakdown in the mouth

_____ 2. produce(s) a whole spectrum of enzymes and an alkaline fluid that is secreted into the duodenum

_____ 3. produce(s) bile that it secretes into the duodenum via the bile duct

_____ 4. produce(s) HCl and pepsinogen

Column B

gastric glands

liver

pancreas

salivary glands

11. What is the role of the gallbladder? _____

Digestion of Foodstuffs: Enzymatic Action

12. Match the following definitions with the proper choices from the key.

    Key:

    _____ 1. increases the rate of a chemical reaction without becoming
    part of the product

    catalyst

    _____ 2. provides a standard of comparison for test results

    control

    _____ 3. biological catalyst: protein in nature

    enzyme

    _____ 4. substance on which a catalyst works

    substrate

13. The enzymes of the digestive system are classified as hydrolases. What does this mean?

    _____

    _____

14. Fill in the following chart about the various digestive system enzymes described in this exercise.

Enzyme	Organ producing it	Site of action	Substrate(s)	Optimal pH
Salivary amylase				
Trypsin				
Lipase (pancreatic)				

15. Name the end products of digestion for the following types of foods:

    proteins: _____ carbohydrates: _____

    fats: _____ and _____

16. In the exercise concerning trypsin function, how could you tell protein hydrolysis occurred? _____

    Why was tube 1T necessary? _____

    Why was tube 2T necessary? _____

    Why was 37°C the optimal incubation temperature? _____

    Why did very little, if any, digestion occur in test tube 3T? _____

    _____

    Why did very little, if any, digestion occur in test tube 5T? _____

    _____

    Trypsin is a protein-digesting enzyme similar to pepsin, the protein-digesting enzyme in the stomach. Would trypsin

    work well in the stomach? _____ Why or why not? _____

17. In the procedure concerning the action of bile salts, how did the appearance of tubes 1 and 2 differ? _____

_____

Explain the difference. _____

_____

18. Pancreatic and intestinal enzymes operate optimally at a pH that is slightly alkaline, yet the chyme entering the duodenum from the stomach is very acid. How is the proper pH for the functioning of the pancreatic-intestinal enzymes ensured?

_____

_____

19. Assume you have been chewing a piece of bread for 5 or 6 minutes. How would you expect its taste to change during

this interval? _____

Why? _____

20. In the space below, draw the pathway of a peanut butter sandwich (peanut butter = protein and fat; bread = starch) from the mouth to the site of absorption of its breakdown products, noting where digestion occurs and what specific enzymes are involved.

Physical Processes: Mechanisms of Food Propulsion and Mixing

21. Match the items in the key to the descriptive statements that follow.

Key:

_____ 1. blocks off nasal passages during swallowing

buccal

_____ 2. voluntary phase of swallowing

cardioesophageal

_____ 3. propulsive waves of smooth muscle contraction

peristalsis

_____ 4. sphincter that opens when food or fluids exert pressure on it

pharyngeal–esophageal

_____ 5. movement that mainly serves to mix foodstuffs

segmental

_____ 6. forces food into the pharynx

tongue

_____ 7. involuntary phase of swallowing

uvula

Materials

- ☐ Human dissectible torso model and/or anatomical chart of the human urinary system
- ☐ Three-dimensional model of the cut kidney and of a nephron (if available)
- ☐ Dissecting tray and instruments
- ☐ Pig or sheep kidney, doubly or triply injected
- ☐ Disposable gloves
- ☐ Demonstration area: Longitudinal section of the kidney set up for microscopic examination under low power; pointer on a glomerulus
- ☐ Student samples of urine collected in sterile containers at the beginning of the lab or "normal" artificial urine provided by the instructor
- ☐ Numbered "pathologic" urine specimens provided by the instructor
- ☐ Wide-range pH paper
- ☐ Urinometer
- ☐ Disposable gloves
- ☐ Disposable autoclave bags
- ☐ Laboratory buckets containing 10% bleach solution
- ☐ Combination dipsticks (Multistix preferred)

Pre-Lab Quiz

1. Circle the correct term. In its excretory role, the urinary system is primarily concerned with the removal of <u>carbon-containing</u> / <u>nitrogenous</u> wastes from the body.

2. The _____ perform(s) the excretory and homeostatic functions of the urinary system.
   a. kidneys
   b. ureters
   c. urinary bladder
   d. all of the above

3. Circle the correct term. As the renal artery approaches a kidney, it is divided into branches known as the <u>segmental arteries</u> / <u>afferent arterioles</u>.

4. What do we call the anatomical units responsible for urine production?

5. This knot of coiled capillaries, found in the kidneys, forms the filtrate. It is the:
   a. arteriole
   b. glomerulus
   c. podocyte
   d. tubule

6. Circle True or False. During tubular reabsorption, components of the filtrate move from the bloodstream into the tubule.

Metabolism of nutrients by the body produces wastes that must be removed from the body. Although excretory processes involve several organ systems (the lungs excrete carbon dioxide, and skin glands excrete salts and water), it is mainly the **urinary system** that removes nitrogenous wastes from the body. The kidney also maintains the electrolyte, acid-base, and fluid balances of the blood and is thus a major, if not *the* major, homeostatic organ of the body.

To properly do its job, the kidney acts first as a blood "filter," and then as a blood "processor." It allows toxins, metabolic wastes, and excess ions to leave the body in the urine, while retaining needed substances and returning them to the blood.

Gross Anatomy of the Human Urinary System

OBJECTIVE 1 Identify, on an appropriate model or diagram, the urinary system organs and describe the function of each.

The paired kidneys and ureters and the single urinary bladder and urethra make up the urinary system (**Figure 26.1**). The kidneys perform the functions described above and manufacture urine in the process. The remaining organs of the system provide temporary storage or transportation channels for urine.

Activity 1

Identifying Urinary System Organs

Examine the human torso model, a large anatomical chart, or a three-dimensional model of the urinary system to locate and study the anatomy and relationships of the urinary organs.

1. Locate the paired **kidneys** on the dorsal body wall in the superior lumbar region. Notice that the right kidney is slightly lower than the left kidney

Text continues on next page. →

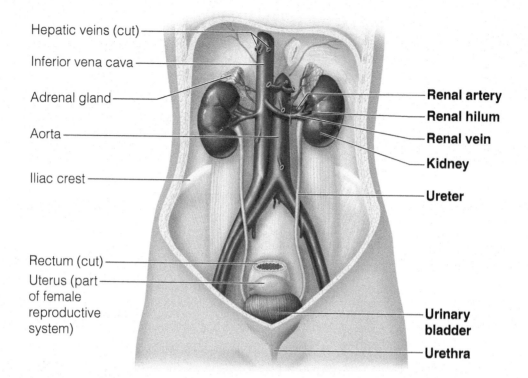

Hepatic veins (cut)
Inferior vena cava
Adrenal gland
Aorta
Iliac crest
Rectum (cut)
Uterus (part of female reproductive system)

Renal artery
Renal hilum
Renal vein
Kidney
Ureter
Urinary bladder
Urethra

Figure 26.1 Organs of the female urinary system. Anterior view.

because it is "crowded" by the liver. In a living person, fat deposits (the *perirenal fat capsules*) hold the kidneys in place in a retroperitoneal position against the muscles of the posterior trunk wall.

2. Observe the **renal arteries** as they diverge from the descending aorta and plunge into the indented medial region (**hilum**) of each kidney. Note also the **renal veins**, which drain the kidneys (circulatory drainage) and the two

ureters, which drain urine from the kidneys and conduct it by peristalsis to the bladder for temporary storage.

3. Locate the **urinary bladder,** and notice where the two ureters enter this organ. Also identify the single **urethra,** which drains the bladder. The triangular region of the bladder, which is outlined by these three openings (two ureteral and one urethral orifice), is the **trigone** (**Figure 26.2**). If possible, identify the two sphincter

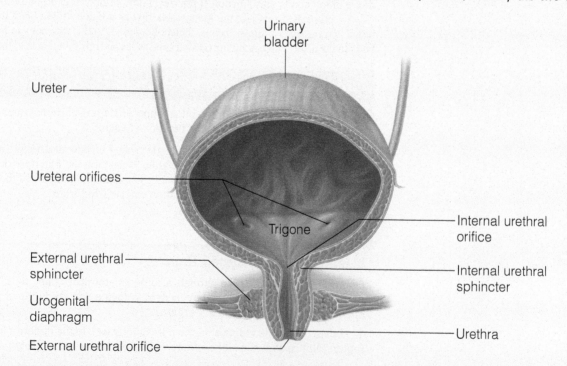

Urinary bladder
Ureter
Ureteral orifices
Trigone
External urethral sphincter
Urogenital diaphragm
External urethral orifice

Internal urethral orifice
Internal urethral sphincter
Urethra

Figure 26.2 Basic structure of the female urinary bladder and urethra.

muscles that control the outflow of urine from the bladder. The more superior **internal urethral sphincter** is an involuntary sphincter composed of smooth muscle. The **external urethral sphincter** consists of skeletal muscle and is voluntarily controlled.

4. Follow the course of the urethra to the body exterior. In the male, it is approximately 20 cm (8 inches) long, travels the length of the **penis,** and opens at its tip. Its three named regions are the *prostatic, membranous,* and *spongy (penile) urethrae* (described in more detail in Exercise 27). The male urethra has a dual function: it conducts urine to the body exterior, and it provides a passageway for semen ejection from the body. Thus, in the man, the urethra is part of both the urinary and reproductive systems. In women, the urethra is very short, approximately 4 cm (1½ inches) long, and it serves only to transport urine. Its external opening, the **external urethral orifice,** lies anterior to the vaginal opening.

OBJECTIVE 2   Identify the major anatomical areas of a dissected kidney.

DISSECTION

Gross Internal Anatomy of the Pig or Sheep Kidney

1. Obtain a preserved sheep or pig kidney, dissecting tray, and instruments. Observe the kidney to identify the **fibrous capsule,** a smooth transparent membrane that adheres tightly to the surface of the kidney and prevents infections in surrounding areas from spreading to the kidneys.

2. Find the ureter, renal vein, and renal artery at the hilum (indented) region. The renal vein has the thinnest wall and will be collapsed. The ureter is the largest of these structures and has the thickest wall.

3. In preparation for dissection, don gloves. Make a cut through the longitudinal axis (frontal section) of the kidney, and locate the regions described next and shown in **Figure 26.3**.

Text continues on next page. →

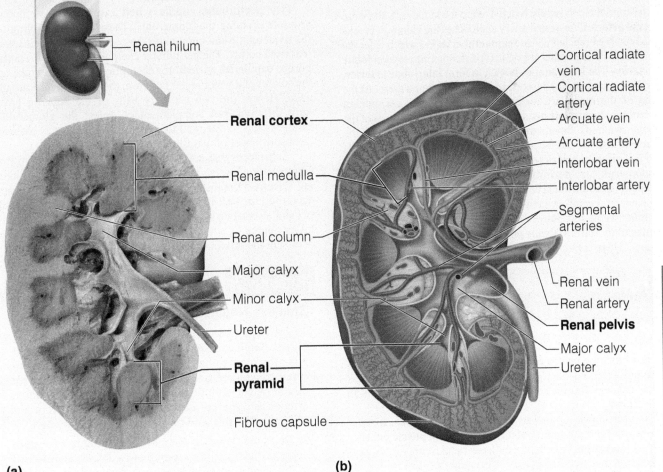

(a)   **(b)**

Figure 26.3 Internal anatomy of the kidney. Frontal sections. **(a)** Photograph of a right kidney. **(b)** Diagrammatic view showing the larger blood vessels supplying the kidney tissue.

Renal cortex: The superficial kidney region, which is lighter in color. If the kidney is doubly injected with latex, you will see a predominance of red and blue latex specks in this region indicating its rich blood supply.

Medullary region: Deep to the cortex; a darker, reddish brown color. The medulla is segregated into triangular areas that have a striped appearance—the **renal (medullary) pyramids.** The base of each pyramid faces toward the cortex. Its more pointed **apex** points to the innermost kidney region.

Renal columns: Areas of tissue, more like the cortex in appearance, which separate the renal pyramids.

Renal pelvis: Medial to the hilum; a relatively flat, basin-like cavity that is continuous with the **ureter,** which exits from the hilum region. Fingerlike extensions of the pelvis form cuplike areas called **calyces** that enclose the apexes of the renal pyramids. The calyces collect urine draining continuously from the pyramidal tips into the pelvis.

4. If the kidney is doubly or triply injected, follow the renal blood supply from the renal artery to the **glomeruli.**

5. Now obtain a three-dimensional model of a cut kidney and reidentify the structures described in steps 2–4.

OBJECTIVE 3   Trace the blood supply of the kidney from the renal artery to the renal vein.

The arterial blood supply is delivered to the kidneys by the large **renal arteries.** As a renal artery approaches the kidney, it breaks up into five branches called **segmental arteries,** which enter the hilum. Each segmental artery, in turn, divides into several **lobar arteries.** The lobar arteries branch to form **interlobar arteries,** which ascend toward the cortex in the renal column areas. At the top of the medullary region, these arteries give off arching branches, the **arcuate arteries,** which curve over the bases of the renal pyramids. Small **cortical radiate arteries** branch off the arcuate arteries and ascend into the cortex, giving off the individual **afferent arterioles,** which provide the capillary networks (**glomeruli** and **peritubular capillary beds**) that supply the nephrons, or functional units, of the kidney. Blood draining from the nephron capillary networks in the cortex enters the **cortical radiate veins** and then drains through the **arcuate veins** and the **interlobar veins** to finally enter the **renal vein** in the pelvis region. (There are no lobar or segmental veins.)

Functional Microscopic Anatomy of the Kidney

OBJECTIVE 4   Describe the anatomy of a nephron.

Each kidney contains over a million nephrons, the anatomical units responsible for forming urine. **Figure 26.4** depicts the structure and the relative positioning of the nephrons in the kidney.

Each nephron consists of two main structures: a *renal corpuscle* and a *renal tubule.* Each **renal corpuscle** consists of a **glomerulus** (a knot of capillaries) and a cup-shaped hollow structure that completely surrounds the glomerulus, the **glomerular (Bowman's) capsule.** Its inner wall consists of specialized cells called **podocytes,** with long branching processes called *foot processes.* Podocytes cling to each other

and to the endothelial wall of the glomerular capillaries, forming a very porous membrane around the glomerulus.

The **renal tubule,** which makes up the rest of the nephron, is about 3 cm (1.25 inches) long. As it extends from the glomerular capsule, it coils and drops down into a long hairpin loop and then again coils and twists before entering a collecting duct. In order from the glomerular capsule, the anatomical areas of the renal tubule are the **proximal convoluted tubule, nephron loop (loop of Henle),** and the **distal convoluted tubule.**

Most nephrons, called **cortical nephrons,** are located entirely within the cortex. However, parts of the nephron loops of the **juxtamedullary nephrons** (located close to the cortex-medulla junction) penetrate well into the medulla. The **collecting ducts,** each of which receives urine from many nephrons, run downward through the renal pyramids to empty the urine product into the calyces and pelvis of the kidney.

Nephron function depends on some unique features of the renal circulation. There are two distinct capillary beds, the *glomerulus* and the *peritubular capillary bed.* Because the **glomerulus** is (1) fed and drained by arterioles (arterioles are high-resistance vessels as opposed to venules) and (2) the feeder **afferent arteriole** is larger in diameter than the **efferent arteriole** draining the bed, it is a high-pressure bed along its entire length. The high hydrostatic pressure created by these two anatomical features forces out fluid and blood components smaller than proteins from the glomerulus into the glomerular capsule. That is, it forms the filtrate which is processed by the nephron tubule.

The **peritubular capillary bed** arises from the efferent arteriole draining the glomerulus. These capillaries cling to the renal tubule and empty into the cortical radiate veins that leave the cortex. The peritubular capillaries are *low-pressure* porous capillaries adapted for absorption and readily take up the solutes and water reclaimed from the filtrate by the tubule cells. Hence, the two capillary beds of the nephron have very different, but complementary, roles: the glomerulus produces the filtrate, and the peritubular capillaries reclaim (reabsorb) most of that filtrate.

Substances that are almost entirely reabsorbed from the filtrate include water, glucose, and amino acids. Various ions are selectively reabsorbed or allowed to go out in the urine according to what is required to maintain appropriate blood pH and electrolyte balance. Wastes are reabsorbed to a much lesser degree or not at all. The bulk of tubular reabsorption occurs in the proximal convoluted tubule.

Activity 2

Studying Nephron Structure

1. Obtain a nephron model, and bring it to your lab bench. Begin your study of nephron structure by identifying the glomerulus, glomerular capsule, proximal and distal convoluted tubules, and the nephron loop on the model. Also identify the arcuate and cortical radiate arteries and the corresponding veins, the afferent and efferent arterioles, and the peritubular capillary bed.

2. Go to the demonstration area to continue your study of nephron structure by examining a longitudinal section of the kidney. Scan the slide under low power.

Text continues on page 338. →

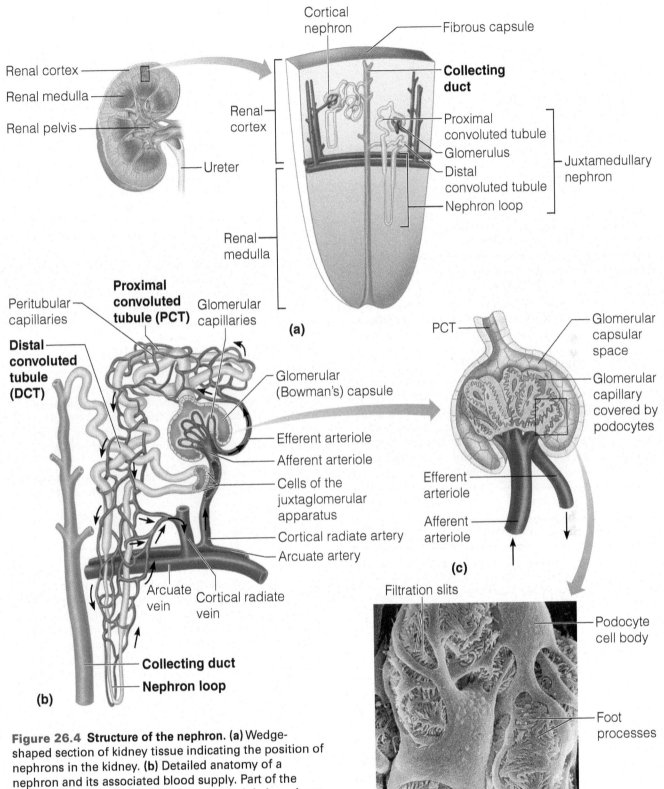

(a)

(b)

(c)

(d)

Figure 26.4 Structure of the nephron. (a) Wedge-shaped section of kidney tissue indicating the position of nephrons in the kidney. **(b)** Detailed anatomy of a nephron and its associated blood supply. Part of the distal convoluted tubule and afferent arteriole have been sectioned to reveal the location of the juxtaglomerular apparatus. **(c)** Diagrammatic view of the relationship of the visceral layer of the glomerular capsule to the glomerular capillaries. **(d)** Scanning electron micrograph of podocytes clinging to the glomerular capillaries.

26

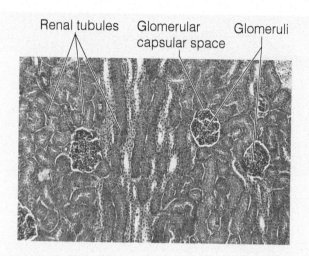

Renal tubules   Glomerular   Glomeruli
                 capsular space

Figure 26.5 Microscopic structure of kidney tissue. Low-power view of the renal cortex (60×). See also Plate 41 in the Histology Atlas.

3. Take a close look at the cortical area. Identify a glomerulus (pointed-out structure), which appears as a ball of tightly packed material containing many small nuclei (**Figure 26.5**). Notice the vacant-appearing region corresponding to the lumen of the glomerular capsule that surrounds it.

4. The balance of the kidney tissue consists of renal tubules. Note that the renal tubules are cut at various angles. Also try to pick out the thin-walled nephron loop portion of the tubules and a section of the proximal convoluted tubule, which has dense microvilli.

Urinalysis

Blood composition depends largely on three factors: diet, cellular metabolism, and urinary output. In 24 hours, the kidneys filter approximately 150 to 180 liters of blood plasma into their tubules, where it is processed. In the same period, urine output is 1.0 to 1.8 liters.

Characteristics of Urine

OBJECTIVE 5   List the physical characteristics and normal pH and specific gravity ranges of urine.

Freshly voided urine is usually clear and pale to deep yellow in color. This normal yellow color is due to *urochrome*, a pigment arising from the body's breakdown of hemoglobin. As a rule, the greater the solute concentration, the deeper the yellow color. Abnormal urine color may be due to certain foods, such as beets, to various drugs, to bile, or to blood.

The odor of freshly voided urine is slightly aromatic, but bacterial action gives it an ammonia-like odor when left standing. Certain diseases may alter the characteristic odor of urine. For example, the urine of a person with uncontrolled diabetes mellitus (and elevated levels of ketones) smells fruity, like acetone.

The pH of urine ranges from 4.5 to 8.0, but its average value, 6.0, is slightly acidic. Diet may markedly influence the pH of the urine. For example, a high-protein diet increases the

acidity of urine, while a vegetarian diet increases the alkalinity of the urine. A bacterial infection of the urinary tract may also result in urine with a high pH.

Specific gravity is the relative weight of a specific volume of liquid compared with an equal volume of distilled water. The specific gravity of distilled water is 1.000, because 1 ml weighs 1 g. Because urine contains dissolved solutes, it weighs more than water, and its customary specific gravity ranges from 1.001 to 1.030. Urine with a specific gravity of 1.001 contains few solutes and is very dilute. Dilute urine is common when a person drinks large amounts of water, uses diuretics, or suffers from chronic renal failure. Conditions that produce urine with a high specific gravity include limited fluid intake, fever, and kidney inflammation, called *pyelonephritis*. If urine becomes excessively concentrated, some of the solutes begin to precipitate or crystallize, forming **kidney stones,** or **renal calculi.**

Solutes normally found in urine (in order of *decreasing* concentration) include urea; sodium,* potassium, phosphate, and sulfate ions; creatinine; and uric acid. Much smaller but highly variable amounts of calcium, magnesium, and bicarbonate ions are also found in urine.

Abnormal Urinary Constituents

Abnormal urinary constituents are substances not normally present in the urine when the body is operating properly. These include glucose, ketone bodies, blood proteins (primarily albumin), red blood cells, hemoglobin, white blood cells (pus), and bile. Table 26.1 names abnormal urinary constituents and possible conditions in which they might appear.

OBJECTIVE 6   Conduct dipstick tests to determine the presence of abnormal substances in the urine specimens.

Activity 3

Analyzing Urine Samples

In this part of the exercise, you will use combination dipsticks and perform a number of tests to determine the characteristics of normal urine as well as to identify abnormal urinary components. You will investigate both "normal" urine—yours or a normal sample provided by your instructor—designated as the *standard urine specimen* in Table 26.2 *and* an unknown urine specimen provided by your instructor. Record the number of your unknown specimen in Table 26.2. Then conduct the following tests on both samples and record your results by circling the appropriate description or by adding data to complete Table 26.2.

⚠ *Obtain and wear disposable gloves throughout this laboratory session.* Although the instructor-provided urine samples are actually artificial urine, you should nonetheless observe the techniques of safe handling of body fluids as part of your learning process.

Text continues on next page. →

---

*Sodium ions appear in relatively high concentration in the urine because of reduced urine volume, not because large amounts are being secreted. Sodium is the major positive ion in the plasma; under normal circumstances, most of it is actively reabsorbed.

Table 26.1   Abnormal Urinary Constituents

Substance	Name of condition	Possible causes
Glucose	Glycosuria	Diabetes mellitus
Ketone bodies	Ketonuria	Excessive formation and accumulation of ketone bodies, as in starvation and untreated diabetes mellitus
Proteins	Proteinuria (also called albuminuria)	Nonpathologic: Excessive physical exertion, pregnancy Pathologic: Glomerulonephritis, hypertension
Pus (WBCs and bacteria)	Pyuria	Urinary tract infection
RBCs	Hematuria	Bleeding in the urinary tract (due to trauma, kidney stones, infection)
Hemoglobin	Hemoglobinuria	Various: Transfusion reaction, hemolytic anemia
Bile pigments	Bilirubinuria	Liver disease (hepatitis)

Table 26.2   Urinalysis Results*

Observation or test	Normal values	Standard urine specimen	Unknown specimen (#)
Physical Characteristics			
Color	Pale yellow	Yellow: pale medium dark other _____	Yellow: pale medium dark other _____
Transparency	Transparent	Clear Slightly cloudy Cloudy	Clear Slightly cloudy Cloudy
Odor	Characteristic	Describe _____ _____	Describe _____ _____
pH	4.5–8.0	_____	_____
Specific gravity	1.001–1.030	_____	_____
Organic Components			
Glucose	Negative	Record results: _____	Record results: _____
Albumin	Negative	Record results: _____	Record results: _____
Ketone bodies	Negative	Record results: _____	Record results: _____
RBCs/hemoglobin	Negative	Record results: _____	Record results: _____
Bilirubin	Negative	Record results: _____	Record results: _____

*In recording urinalysis data, circle the appropriate description if provided; otherwise, record the results you observed.

When you have completed the laboratory procedures (1) dispose of the gloves and used pH paper strips in the autoclave bag; (2) put used glassware in the bleach-containing laboratory bucket; and (3) wash the lab bench down with 10% bleach solution.

Determining Physical Characteristics of Urine

1. Assess the color, transparency, and odor of your "normal" sample and one of the numbered pathologic samples, and circle the appropriate descriptions in Table 26.2.

2. Obtain a roll of wide-range pH paper to determine the pH of each sample. Use a fresh piece of paper for each test, and dip the strip into the urine to be tested two or three times before comparing the color obtained with the chart on the dispenser. Record your results in Table 26.2. You will be using one of the combination dipsticks (e.g., Multistix) later; recheck this pH determination then.

3. To determine specific gravity, obtain a urinometer cylinder and float. Mix the urine well, and fill the urinometer cylinder about two-thirds full with urine.

Text continues on next page. →

26

4. Examine the urinometer float to determine how to read its markings. In most cases, the scale has numbered lines separated by a series of unnumbered lines. The numbered lines give the reading for the first two decimal places. You must determine the third decimal place by reading the lower edge of the meniscus—the curved surface representing the urine-air junction—on the stem of the float.

5. Carefully lower the urinometer float into the urine. Make sure it is floating freely before attempting to take the reading. Record the specific gravity of both samples in the table. *Do not dispose of this urine if the samples that you have are less than 200 ml in volume* because you will need to make more determinations.

Determining Organic Constituents in Urine

Combination dipsticks will be used for all of the tests in this section, so you should be prepared to take the readings on several factors (pH, protein [albumin], glucose, ketones, and blood/hemoglobin) at the same time. Generally speaking, results for all of these tests may be read *during* the second minute after immersion, but readings taken after 2 minutes have passed should be considered inaccurate. Pay careful attention to the directions for method and time of immersion and disposal of excess urine from the strip, regardless of the dipstick used.

Glucose

Conduct the dipstick test according to the instructions on the vial. Record the results in Table 26.2.

Albumin

Use a combination dipstick, and conduct the determinations as indicated on the vial. Record your results.

Ketones

Use a combination dipstick, and conduct the determinations as indicated on the vial. Record your results.

Blood/Hemoglobin

Test your urine samples for the presence of hemoglobin by using a combination dipstick according to the directions on the vial. Usually a short drying period is required before the reading is made, so read the directions carefully. Record your results.

Verify your conclusions on the unknown specimen with your instructor before cleaning your bench with bleach solution and leaving the laboratory.

REVIEW SHEET
Functional Anatomy
of the Urinary System

Name _____   Lab Time/Date _____

Gross Anatomy of the Human Urinary System

1. What is the function of the fat cushion that surrounds the kidneys in life? _____

   _____

2. Complete the labeling of the diagram to correctly identify the urinary system organs. Then respond to the questions that follow.

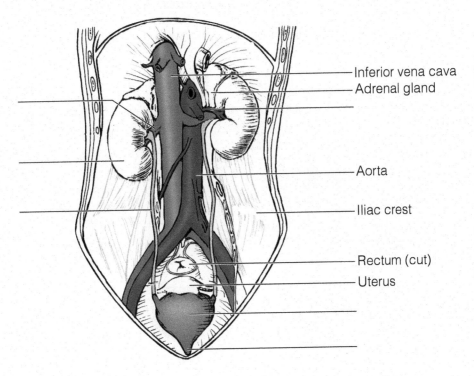

- Inferior vena cava
- Adrenal gland

- Aorta

- Iliac crest

- Rectum (cut)
- Uterus

Which of the structures identified above is applicable to the following statements?

_____   1. maintains water and electrolyte balance of the blood

_____   2. serves as a storage area for urine

_____   3. transports urine to the body exterior

_____   4. transports arterial blood to the kidney

_____   5. produces urine

_____   6. transports urine to the urinary bladder

_____   7. is shorter in women than in men

Gross Internal Anatomy of the Pig or Sheep Kidney

3. Match the appropriate structure in column B to its description in column A. (Some responses may be used more than once.)

Column A

Column B

_____ 1. smooth membrane clinging tightly to the kidney surface

cortex

_____ 2. portion of the kidney containing mostly collecting ducts

medulla

_____ 3. portion of the kidney containing the bulk of the nephron structures

calyx

_____ 4. superficial region of kidney tissue

renal column

_____ 5. basinlike area of the kidney, continuous with the ureter

fibrous capsule

_____ 6. an extension of the pelvis that encircles the apex of a pyramid

renal pelvis

_____ 7. area of cortexlike tissue running between the renal pyramids

Functional Microscopic Anatomy of the Kidney

4. Match each of the lettered structures on the diagram of the nephron (and associated renal blood supply) on the left with the terms on the right:

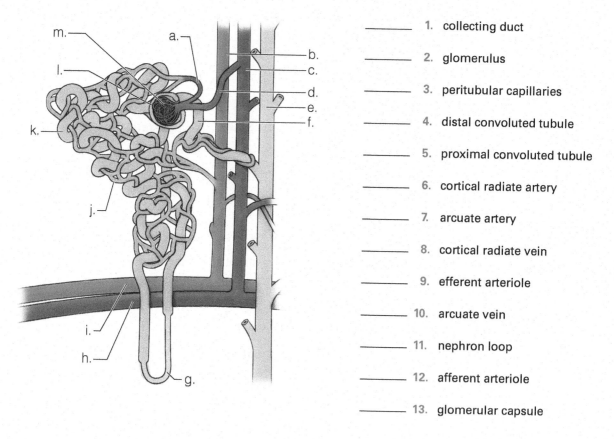

_____ 1. collecting duct

_____ 2. glomerulus

_____ 3. peritubular capillaries

_____ 4. distal convoluted tubule

_____ 5. proximal convoluted tubule

_____ 6. cortical radiate artery

_____ 7. arcuate artery

_____ 8. cortical radiate vein

_____ 9. efferent arteriole

_____ 10. arcuate vein

_____ 11. nephron loop

_____ 12. afferent arteriole

_____ 13. glomerular capsule

5. Using the terms provided in question 4, identify the following:

_____ 1. site of filtrate formation

_____ 2. primary site of tubular reabsorption

_____ 3. structure that conveys the processed filtrate (urine) to the renal pelvis

_____ 4. blood supply that directly receives substances from the tubular cells

_____ 5. its inner (visceral) membrane forms part of the filtration membrane

6. Explain why the glomerulus is such a high-pressure capillary bed. _____

   How does the high pressure help the glomerulus form filtrate? _____

   _____

7. What structural modification of certain tubule cells enhances their ability to reabsorb substances from the filtrate?

   _____

8. Trace a drop of blood from the time it enters the kidney in the renal artery until it leaves the kidney through the renal vein.

   Renal artery ⟶ _____

   _____ ⟶ renal vein

9. Trace the anatomical pathway of a molecule of creatinine (metabolic waste) from the glomerular capsule to the urethra. Note each microscopic and/or gross structure it passes through in its travels, and include the names of the subdivisions of the renal tubule.

   Glomerular capsule ⟶ _____

   _____

   _____ ⟶ urethra

Urinalysis: Characteristics of Urine

10. What is the normal volume of urine excreted in a 24-hour period? _____

11. List three nitrogenous wastes that are routinely found in urine:

    _____

    List three substances that are absent from the urine of healthy individuals:

    _____

    List two substances that are routinely found in filtrate but *not* in the urine product:

    _____

12. Explain why urinalysis is a routine part of any good physical examination. _____

    _____

13. What substance is responsible for the normal yellow color of urine? _____

14. Which has a greater specific gravity: 1 ml of urine or 1 ml of distilled water? _____

    Explain. _____

    _____

15. Explain the relationship between the color, specific gravity, and volume of urine. _____

    _____

Abnormal Urinary Constituents

16. How does a urinary tract infection influence urine pH? _____

17. Several specific terms have been used to indicate the presence of abnormal urine constituents. Identify which urine abnormalities listed in column A might be caused by each of the conditions listed in column B.

Column A		Column B
_____ 1. blood in the urine		albuminuria
_____ 2. hemolytic anemia		glycosuria
_____ 3. eating a 5-lb box of candy at one sitting		hematuria
_____ 4. pregnancy		hemoglobinuria
_____ 5. starvation		ketonuria
_____ 6. urinary tract infection		pyuria

18. What are renal calculi, and what conditions favor their formation? _____

    _____

19. What change would you expect to occur in a urine sample that has been stored at room temperature? _____

    _____

Anatomy of the Reproductive System

☐ Models or large laboratory charts of the male and female reproductive tracts

☐ Ovary model

☐ Demonstration area: Prepared microscope slides set up for microscopic examination

  Station 1: Human sperm (oil-immersion)

  Station 2: Ovary

Pre-Lab Quiz

1. Circle the correct term. The paired oval testes lie in the <u>scrotal sac</u> / <u>prostate</u> outside the abdominopelvic cavity, where they are kept slightly cooler than body temperature.

2. After sperm are produced, they enter the first part of the duct system, the:
   a. ductus deferens   c. epididymis
   b. ejaculatory duct   d. urethra

3. Circle the correct term. The <u>interstitial cells</u> / <u>seminiferous tubules</u> produce testosterone, the hormonal product of the testis.

4. The endocrine products of the ovaries are estrogen and:
   a. luteinizing hormone   c. prolactin
   b. progesterone   d. testosterone

5. Circle the correct term. The <u>labia majora</u> / <u>clitoris</u> are/is homologous to the penis.

6. Circle the correct term. A developing egg is ejected from the ovary at the appropriate stage of maturity in an event known as <u>menstruation</u> / <u>ovulation</u>.

The **reproductive system** is unique. Most simply stated, its biological function is to perpetuate the species. The reproductive role of the male is to manufacture sperm and to deliver them to the female reproductive tract. The female, in turn, produces eggs. If the time is suitable, the combination of sperm and egg produces a fertilized egg. Once fertilization has occurred, the female uterus provides a nurturing, protective environment in which the embryo, later called the fetus, develops until birth.

Gross Anatomy of the Human Male Reproductive System

OBJECTIVE 1   Identify structures of the male reproductive system on an appropriate model or diagram, and give the function of each.

The primary sex organs of the male are the **testes,** the male **gonads,** which have both an exocrine (sperm production) and an endocrine (testosterone production) function. All other reproductive structures are ducts or sources of secretions, which aid in the safe delivery of the sperm to the body exterior or female reproductive tract.

Activity 1

Identifying Male Reproductive Organs

As the following organs and structures are described, locate them on **Figure 27.1**, and then identify them on a model of the male reproductive system or on a large laboratory chart.

Text continues on next page. →

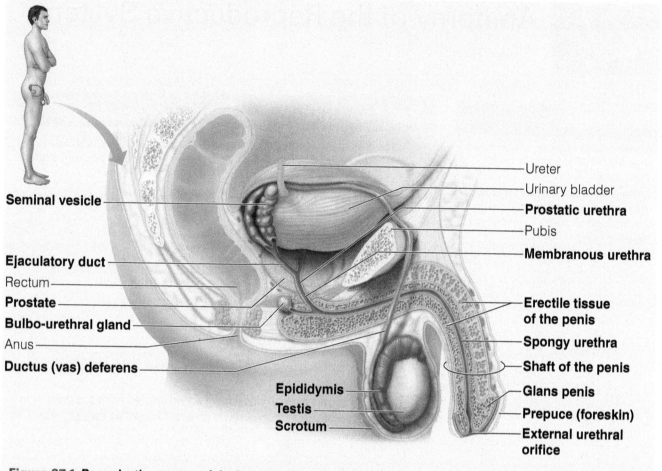

Figure 27.1 Reproductive system of the human male, sagittal view.

The paired oval testes lie in the **scrotal sac** outside the abdominopelvic cavity. The temperature there is slightly lower than body temperature, a requirement for producing viable sperm.

OBJECTIVE 2   Trace the pathway of sperm from the testis to the external environment.

The accessory structures forming the *duct system* are the epididymis, the ductus deferens, the ejaculatory duct, and the

urethra. Identify the **epididymis,** an elongated structure running up the posterolateral aspect of the testis and capping its superior aspect. The epididymis forms the first portion of the duct system and provides a site for immature sperm to mature. Follow the **ductus deferens** (sperm duct) as it runs superiorly from the epididymis, passes through the inguinal canal into the pelvic cavity, and arches over the superior aspect of the urinary bladder. The ductus deferens (also called the *vas deferens*) is enclosed along with blood vessels and nerves in a connective tissue sheath called the **spermatic cord.** The end of the ductus

Table 27.1	Accessory Glands of the Male Reproductive System (Figure 27.1)	
Accessory gland	**Location**	**Secretion**
Seminal glands (seminal vesicles)	Paired glands located posterior to the urinary bladder. The duct of each gland merges with a ductus deferens to form the ejaculatory duct.	A thick, light yellow, alkaline secretion containing fructose (a simple sugar) and other substances that nourish or activate the sperm passing through the tract. Its secretion has the largest contribution to the volume of semen.
Prostate	Single gland that encircles the urethra inferior to the bladder.	A milky fluid secreted into the urethra that plays a role in activating sperm.
Bulbo-urethral glands	Paired tiny glands that drain into the intermediate part of the urethra.	A clear mucus that lubricates the tip of the penis for copulation and neutralizes traces of urine in the urethra prior to ejaculation.

deferens empties into the **ejaculatory duct.** Contraction of the ejaculatory duct propels the sperm through the prostate gland to the **prostatic urethra,** which in turn empties into the **membranous urethra** and then into the **spongy (penile) urethra,** which runs through the length of the penis to the body exterior.

The *accessory glands* include the paired seminal glands (vesicles), prostate, and bulbo-urethral glands. These glands produce **seminal fluid,** the liquid medium in which sperm leave the body. Table 27.1 summarizes the locations and secretions of accessory glands.

The **penis,** part of the external genitalia of the male along with the scrotal sac, is the copulatory organ of the male.

Designed to deliver sperm into the female reproductive tract, it consists of a shaft, which terminates in an enlarged tip, the **glans.** The skin covering the penis is loosely applied, and it reflects downward to form a fold of skin, the **prepuce,** or **foreskin,** around the proximal end of the glans. (The foreskin is sometimes removed in the surgical procedure called *circumcision.*) Internally, the penis consists primarily of three elongated cylinders of erectile tissue that fill with blood during sexual excitement. This causes the penis to enlarge and become rigid so that it may serve as a penetrating device. This event is called **erection.**

Microscopic Anatomy of the Testes and Sperm

Testis

OBJECTIVE 3 Name the exocrine and endocrine products of the testis.

Each testis is covered by a dense connective tissue capsule called the **tunica albuginea** (literally, "white tunic"). Extensions of this sheath enter the testis, dividing it into a number of lobes, each of which houses one to four highly coiled **seminiferous tubules,** the sperm-forming factories (**Figure 27.2**). The seminiferous tubules of each lobe empty the sperm into another set of tubules, the **rete testis,** at the mediastinum of the testis. Sperm traveling through the rete testis then enter the epididymis, located on the exterior

aspect of the testis. Lying in the connective tissue between the seminiferous tubules are the **interstitial cells,** which produce testosterone, the hormonal product of the testes.

Sperm

OBJECTIVE 4 Relate sperm structure to sperm function.

During sperm formation, all the excess cytoplasm is sloughed off the developing sperm, and what remains is compacted into the three regions. At the risk of oversimplifying, these regions are the *head,* the *midpiece,* and the *tail* (**Figure 27.3b**), which correspond roughly to the activating and genetic region, the metabolic region, and the locomotor region, respectively. The mature sperm is a streamlined cell equipped with an organ of locomotion that enables it to move long distances in jig time to get to the egg.

The sperm head contains the DNA of the chromosomes. Essentially it *is* the nucleus of the spermatid. Anterior to the nucleus is the **acrosome,** which contains enzymes involved in sperm penetration of the egg.

In the midpiece of the sperm is a centriole that produces the filaments that form the sperm tail. Wrapped tightly around the centriole are mitochondria that provide the ATP needed for the whiplike movements of the tail filaments.

Activity 2

Viewing Sperm Microscopically

Go to station 1 of the demonstration area and view a prepared slide of human sperm with the oil immersion lens. Do not touch the focusing knobs. Compare what you see to the photograph of sperm in Figure 27.3a and Plate 47 in the Histology Atlas. Identify the head, acrosome, and tail regions. Draw and appropriately label two or three sperm in the space below.

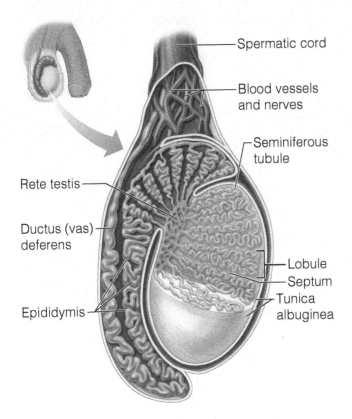

Spermatic cord

Blood vessels and nerves

Seminiferous tubule

Rete testis

Ductus (vas) deferens

Lobule

Septum

Tunica albuginea

Epididymis

Figure 27.2 Sagittal section of the testis and associated epididymis. See also Plates 44 and 46 in the Histology Atlas.

Text continues on next page. →

27

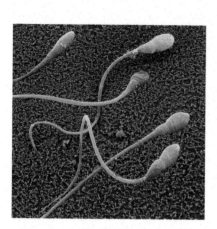

(a) Scanning electron micrograph of mature sperm (1525×)

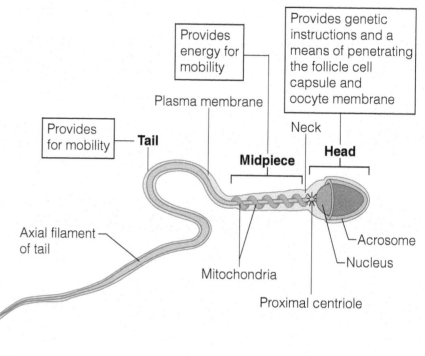

Provides energy for mobility

Provides genetic instructions and a means of penetrating the follicle cell capsule and oocyte membrane

Plasma membrane

Provides for mobility

Tail

Neck

Midpiece

Head

Axial filament of tail

Acrosome

Nucleus

Mitochondria

Proximal centriole

(b) Diagrammatic view of sperm

Figure 27.3 Structure of a sperm.

Deformed sperm (for example, sperm with multiple heads or tails) are sometimes present in such preparations. Did you observe any?

_____ If so, describe them. _____

_____

_____

Gross Anatomy of the Human Female Reproductive System

OBJECTIVE 5 Identify the structures of the female reproductive system when provided with an appropriate model or diagram, and explain the function of each.

The **ovaries** (female gonads) are the primary sex organs of the female. Like the testes of the male, the ovaries produce both an exocrine product (eggs, or ova) and endocrine products (estrogens and progesterone). The accessory structures of the female reproductive system transport, house, nurture, or otherwise serve the needs of the reproductive cells and/or the developing fetus.

The reproductive structures of the female are generally considered in terms of internal organs and external organs, or external genitals.

27

Activity 3

Identifying Female Reproductive Organs

As you read the descriptions of these structures, locate them on **Figure 27.4** and **Figure 27.5** and then on the female reproductive system model or large laboratory chart.

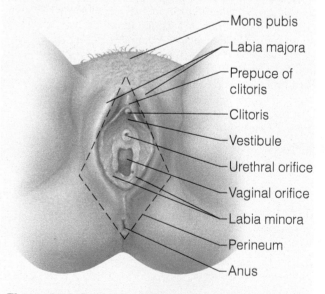

Mons pubis

Labia majora

Prepuce of clitoris

Clitoris

Vestibule

Urethral orifice

Vaginal orifice

Labia minora

Perineum

Anus

Figure 27.4 External genitalia of the human female.

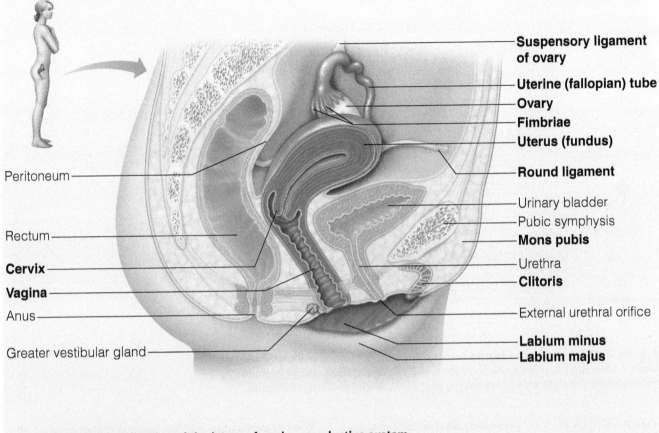

Figure 27.5 Sagittal section of the human female reproductive system.

Labels (left side, top to bottom):
Peritoneum
Rectum
Cervix
Vagina
Anus
Greater vestibular gland

Labels (right side, top to bottom):
Suspensory ligament of ovary
Uterine (fallopian) tube
Ovary
Fimbriae
Uterus (fundus)
Round ligament
Urinary bladder
Pubic symphysis
Mons pubis
Urethra
Clitoris
External urethral orifice
Labium minus
Labium majus

The **external genitalia** consist of the mons pubis, the labia majora and minora, the clitoris, the urethral and vaginal orifices, and greater vestibular glands. The **mons pubis** is a rounded fatty area overlying the pubic symphysis. Running inferiorly and posteriorly from the mons pubis are two elongated, hair-covered skin folds, the **labia majora,** which are homologous to the scrotum of the male. These enclose two smaller hair-free folds, the **labia minora.** (Terms indicating only one of the two folds in each case are *labium majus* and *minus,* respectively.) The labia minora, in turn, enclose a region called the **vestibule,** which contains the clitoris, most anteriorly, followed by the urethral orifice and the vaginal orifice. The diamond-shaped region between the anterior end of the labial folds, the ischial tuberosities laterally, and the anus posteriorly is called the perineum.

The small protruding **clitoris** is homologous to the male penis and likewise is composed of highly sensitive erectile tissue and is hooded by a prepuce. The urethral orifice, posterior to the clitoris, is the outlet for the urinary system and has no reproductive function in the female. The vaginal opening is flanked by the pea-sized, mucus-secreting **greater vestibular glands.** These glands (not illustrated) lubricate the distal end of the vagina during sexual intercourse.

OBJECTIVE   6   Identify the fundus, body, and cervix regions of the uterus.

The internal female organs include the vagina, uterus, uterine tubes, ovaries, and the structures that suspend these organs in the pelvic cavity (Figure 27.5). The **vagina** extends for approximately 10 cm (4 inches) from the vestibule to the uterus superiorly. It serves as a copulatory organ and birth canal and permits the menstrual flow to pass. The pear-shaped **uterus,** situated between the bladder and the rectum, is a muscular organ with its narrow end, the **cervix,** directed inferiorly. The major portion of the uterus is the **body;** its superior rounded region above the entrance of the uterine tubes is the **fundus.** A fertilized egg is implanted in the uterus, which houses the embryo or fetus during its development.

The **uterine,** or **fallopian, tubes** enter the superior part of the uterus and extend for about 10 cm (4 inches) toward the **ovaries** in the peritoneal cavity. The distal ends of the tubes are funnel-shaped and have fingerlike projections called **fimbriae.** Unlike the male duct system, there is no actual contact between the female gonad and the initial part of the female duct system—the uterine tube.

The internal female organs are all retroperitoneal, except the ovaries. They are supported and suspended somewhat freely by folds of peritoneum. The peritoneum takes an undulating course. The fold that encloses the uterine tubes and uterus and secures them to the lateral body walls is the **broad ligament.** The **round ligaments** and the **uterosacral ligaments (Figure 27.6)** also help attach the uterus to the body wall. The ovaries are supported medially by the **ovarian ligament** (extending from the uterus to the ovary) and laterally by the **suspensory ligaments.**

27

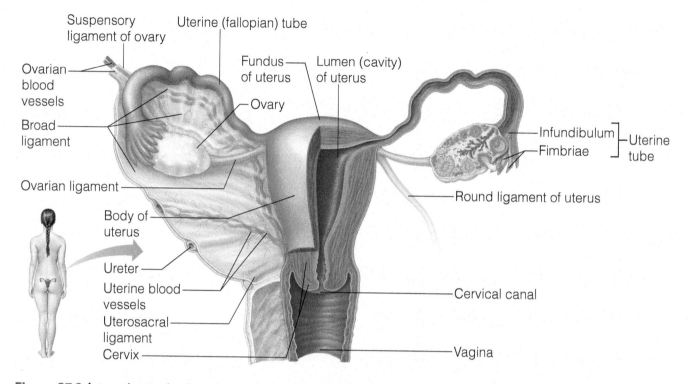

Figure 27.6 Internal reproductive organs of a female, posterior view. The posterior walls of the vagina, uterus, uterine tubes, and the broad ligament have been removed on the right side to reveal the shape of the lumen of these organs.

OBJECTIVE 7 Name the exocrine and endocrine products of the ovary.

Within the ovaries, the female gametes (eggs) begin their development in saclike structures called *follicles* (**Figure 27.7**). The growing follicles also produce *estrogens.*

When a developing egg has reached the appropriate stage of maturity, it is ejected from the ovary in an event called **ovulation.** The ruptured follicle is then converted to a *corpus luteum,* which secretes progesterone (and some estrogens).

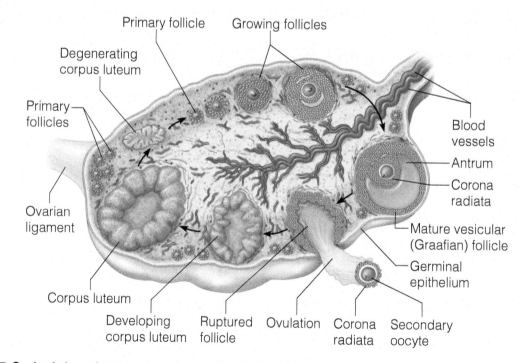

Figure 27.7 Sagittal view of a human ovary showing the developmental stages of an ovarian follicle.

Conducting a Microscopic Study of the Ovary

Because many different stages of ovarian development exist within the ovary at any one time, a single microscopic preparation will contain follicles at many different stages of development. Go to station 2 of the demonstration area where a cross section of ovary tissue has been set up for viewing, and identify the following structures. Refer to Figure 27.7 and **Figure 27.8** as you work.

Germinal epithelium: Outermost layer of the ovary.

Primary follicle: One or a few layers of cuboidal follicle cells surrounding the larger central developing ovum.

Secondary (growing) follicles: Follicles consisting of several layers of follicle cells surrounding the central developing ovum and beginning to show evidence of fluid accumulation in a central cavity. Secrete estrogens.

Vesicular (Graafian) follicle: At this stage of development, the follicle has a large antrum containing fluid. The developing ovum is pushed to one side of the follicle and is surrounded by a capsule of several layers of follicle cells called the **corona radiata** (radiating crown). When the immature ovum (secondary oocyte) is released, it enters the uterine tubes with its corona radiata intact.

Corpus luteum: A solid glandular structure or a structure containing a scalloped lumen that develops from

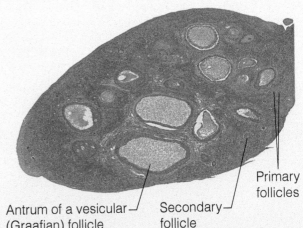

Antrum of a vesicular (Graafian) follicle

Secondary follicle

Primary follicles

Figure 27.8 Photomicrograph of a mammalian ovary showing follicles in different developmental phases (2.5×). (See also Plates 19, 20, and 49 in the Histology Atlas.)

the ovulated follicle. Produces both estrogens and progesterone.

Now examine the ovary model to reidentify the same structures on a model.

27

REVIEW SHEET
Anatomy of the Reproductive System

Name _____ Lab Time/Date _____

Gross Anatomy of the Human Male Reproductive System

1. List the two principal functions of the testis: _____

2. Identify all indicated structures or portions of structures on the diagrammatic view of the male reproductive system below.

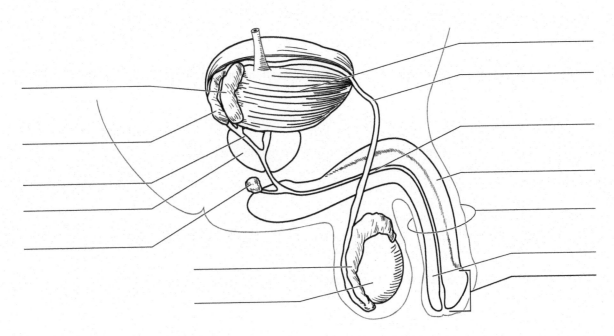

3. How might enlargement of the prostate interfere with urination or the man's reproductive ability?

_____

_____

4. Match the terms in column B to the descriptive statements in column A.

Column A

_____ 1. copulatory organ/penetrating device

_____ 2. produces sperm

_____ 3. duct conveying sperm to the ejaculatory duct; in the spermatic cord

_____ 4. a urine and semen conduit

_____ 5. sperm maturation site

_____ 6. location of the testis in adult males

_____ 7. hoods the glans penis

_____ 8. portion of the urethra between the prostate and the penis

_____ 9. empties a secretion into the prostatic urethra

_____ 10. empties a secretion into the membranous urethra

Column B

bulbo-urethral gland

epididymis

glans penis

membranous urethra

spongy urethra

penis

prepuce

prostate

prostatic urethra

seminal gland

scrotum

testis

ductus deferens

5. Why are the testes located in the scrotum? _____

_____

6. Describe the composition of semen, and name all structures contributing to its formation. _____

_____

_____

7. Of what importance is the fact that seminal fluid is alkaline? _____

_____

8. Using the following terms, trace the pathway of sperm from the testes to the urethra: rete testis, epididymis, seminiferous tubule, ductus deferens.

_____ $\longrightarrow$ _____ $\longrightarrow$ _____ $\longrightarrow$ _____

Gross Anatomy of the Human Female Reproductive System

9. Below is a diagram of a frontal section of a portion of the female reproductive system. Identify all indicated structures.

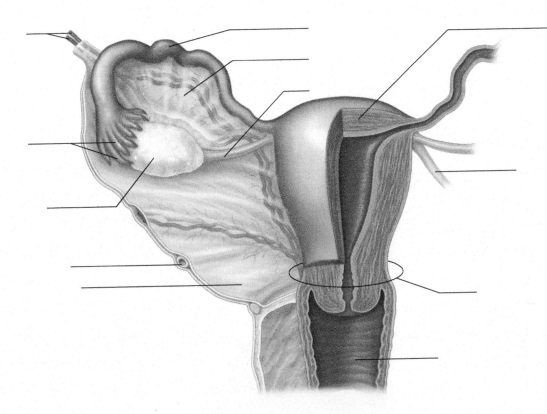

10. Identify the female reproductive system structures described below:

_____ 1. site of fetal development

_____ 2. copulatory canal

_____ 3. "fertilized egg" typically formed here

_____ 4. becomes erectile during sexual excitement

_____ 5. duct extending superolaterally from the uterus

_____ 6. produces eggs, estrogens, and progesterone

_____ 7. fingerlike ends of the uterine tube

11. Name the structures composing the external genitals, or vulva, of the female. _____

_____

_____

12. Put the following vestibular–perineal structures in their proper order from the anterior to the posterior aspect: vaginal orifice, anus, urethral opening, and clitoris.

Anterior limit: _____ → _____ → _____ → _____

13. Name the male structure that is homologous to the female structures named below.

labia majora_____ clitoris_____ ovaries_____

14. Assume a couple has just consummated the sex act and the man's sperm have been deposited in the woman's vagina. Trace the pathway of the sperm through the female reproductive tract.

_____

15. Define *ovulation:* _____

Microscopic Anatomy of Selected Male and Female Reproductive Organs

16. The testis is divided into a number of lobes by connective tissue. Each of these lobes contains one to four_____

_____, which converge on a tubular region called the _____

17. On the diagram showing the sagittal section of the human testis, correctly identify all structures provided with leader lines.

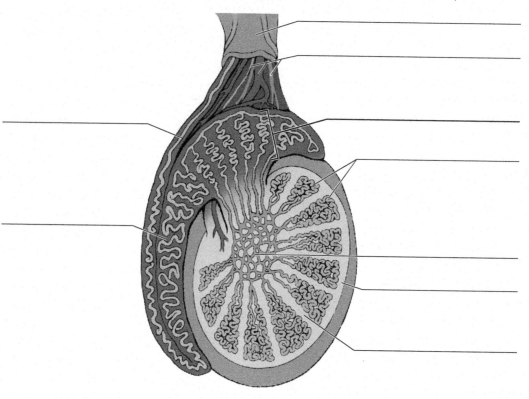

18. In the female reproductive system, what is a follicle? _____

_____

How are primary and vesicular follicles anatomically different? _____

_____

_____

_____

What is a corpus luteum? _____

_____

19. What hormones are produced by the corpus luteum? _____

Histology Atlas

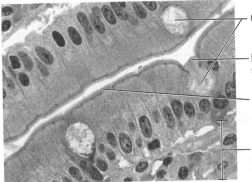

PLATE 1 Simple columnar epithelium containing goblet cells, which are secreting mucus (400×). (Exercise 5, page 40)

Goblet cells

Mucus secretion

Microvilli (brush border)

Underlying connective tissue

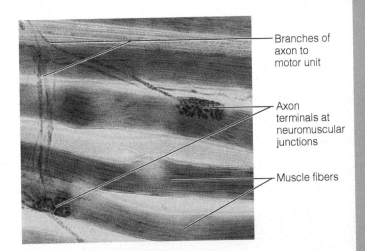

Branches of axon to motor unit

Axon terminals at neuromuscular junctions

Muscle fibers

PLATE 4 Part of a motor unit (150×). (Exercise 11, page 125)

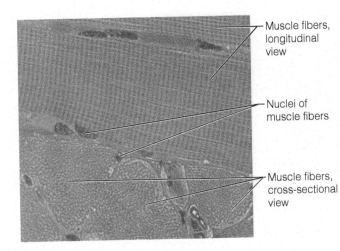

Muscle fibers, longitudinal view

Nuclei of muscle fibers

Muscle fibers, cross-sectional view

PLATE 2 Skeletal muscle, transverse and longitudinal views shown (400×). (Exercise 5, page 46; Exercise 11, page 123)

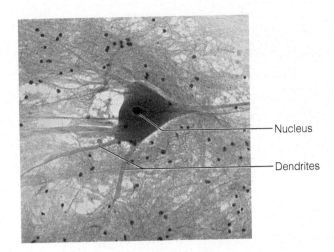

Nucleus

Dendrites

PLATE 5 Light micrograph of a multipolar neuron (200×). (Exercise 5, page 46; Exercise 13, pages 152–153)

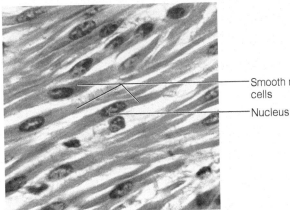

Smooth muscle cells

Nucleus

PLATE 3 Smooth muscle cells (430×). (Exercise 5, page 46)

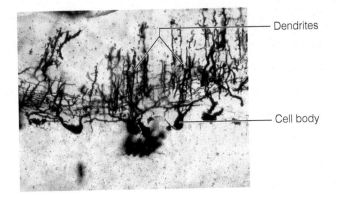

Dendrites

Cell body

PLATE 6 Silver-stained Purkinje cells of the cerebellum (125×). (Exercise 13, pages 153–154)

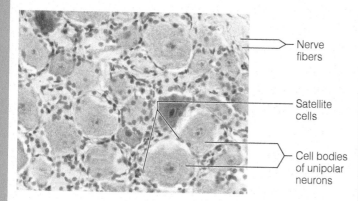

PLATE 7 Dorsal root ganglion displaying neuron cell bodies and satellite cells (200×). (Exercise 13, page 154)

Nerve fibers

Satellite cells

Cell bodies of unipolar neurons

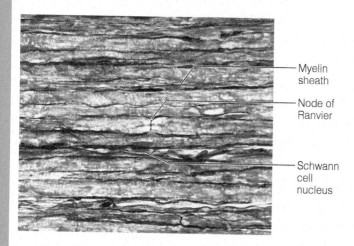

Myelin sheath

Node of Ranvier

Schwann cell nucleus

PLATE 8 Longitudinal view of myelinated axons (500×). (Exercise 13, page 154)

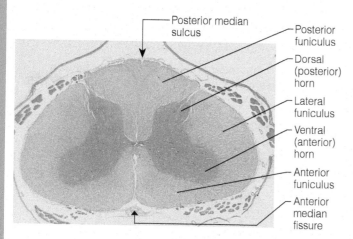

Posterior median sulcus

Posterior funiculus

Dorsal (posterior) horn

Lateral funiculus

Ventral (anterior) horn

Anterior funiculus

Anterior median fissure

PLATE 9 Adult spinal cord, cross-sectional view (12×). (Exercise 15, pages 184–185)

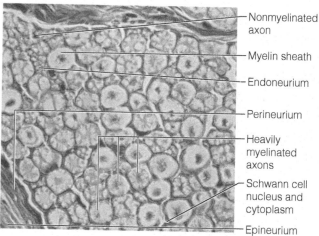

Nonmyelinated axon

Myelin sheath

Endoneurium

Perineurium

Heavily myelinated axons

Schwann cell nucleus and cytoplasm

Epineurium

PLATE 10 Cross section of a portion of a peripheral nerve (250×). Heavily myelinated fibers are identified by a centrally located axon surrounded by an unstained ring of myelin. (Exercise 13, page 156)

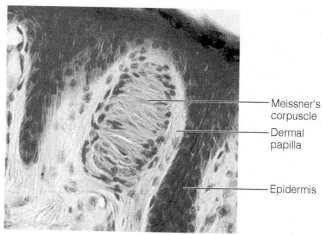

Meissner's corpuscle

Dermal papilla

Epidermis

PLATE 11 Meissner's corpuscle in a dermal papilla (275×). (Exercise 6, page 58)

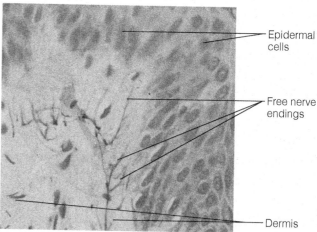

Epidermal cells

Free nerve endings

Dermis

PLATE 12 Free nerve endings at dermal–epidermal junction (400×). (Exercise 6, page 58)

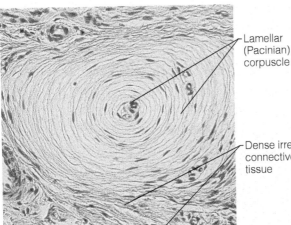

Lamellar (Pacinian) corpuscle

Dense irregular connective tissue

PLATE 13 Cross section of a lamellar (Pacinian) corpuscle in the dermis (125×). (Exercise 6, page 58)

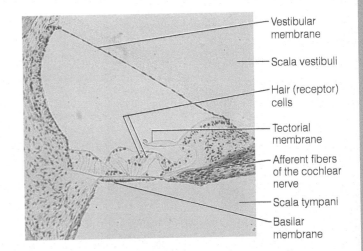

Vestibular membrane

Scala vestibuli

Hair (receptor) cells

Tectorial membrane

Afferent fibers of the cochlear nerve

Scala tympani

Basilar membrane

PLATE 16 The spiral organ of Corti (150×). (Exercise 17, page 211)

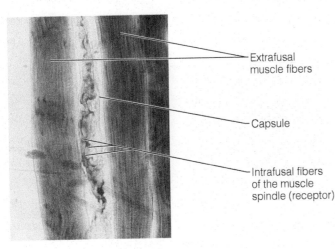

Extrafusal muscle fibers

Capsule

Intrafusal fibers of the muscle spindle (receptor)

PLATE 14 Longitudinal section of a muscle spindle (325×).

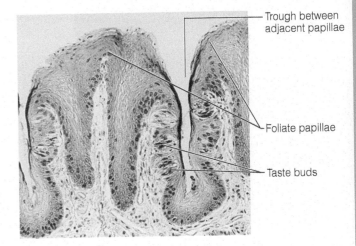

Trough between adjacent papillae

Foliate papillae

Taste buds

PLATE 17 Location of taste buds on lateral aspects of foliate papillae of tongue (150×). (Exercise 17, page 216)

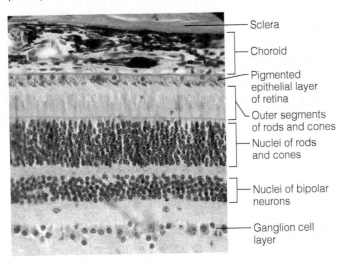

Sclera

Choroid

Pigmented epithelial layer of retina

Outer segments of rods and cones

Nuclei of rods and cones

Nuclei of bipolar neurons

Ganglion cell layer

PLATE 15 Structure of the retina of the eye (250×). (Exercise 17, page 204)

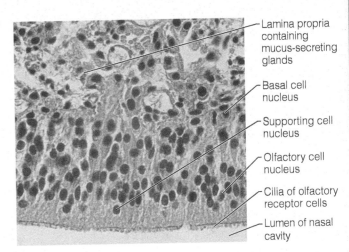

Lamina propria containing mucus-secreting glands

Basal cell nucleus

Supporting cell nucleus

Olfactory cell nucleus

Cilia of olfactory receptor cells

Lumen of nasal cavity

PLATE 18 Olfactory epithelium. From lamina propria to nasal cavity, the general arrangement of cells in this pseudostratified epithelium: basal cells, olfactory receptor cells, and supporting cells (350×). (Exercise 17, page 215)

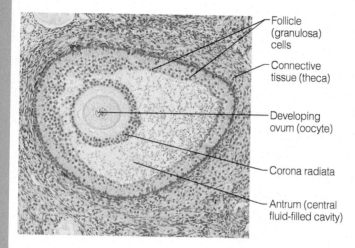

PLATE 19 lines:
- Follicle (granulosa) cells
- Connective tissue (theca)
- Developing ovum (oocyte)
- Corona radiata
- Antrum (central fluid-filled cavity)

PLATE 19 A vesicular (Graafian) follicle of ovary (140×). (Exercise 27, page 351)

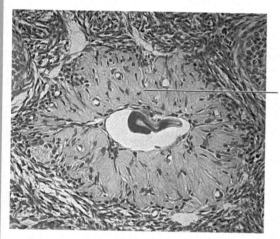

- Corpus luteum

PLATE 20 Glandular corpus luteum of an ovary (125×). (Exercise 27, page 351)

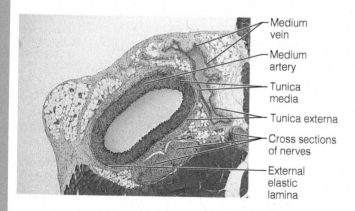

- Medium vein
- Medium artery
- Tunica media
- Tunica externa
- Cross sections of nerves
- External elastic lamina

PLATE 21 Cross-sectional view of an artery, a vein, and nerves (25×). (Exercise 21, page 260)

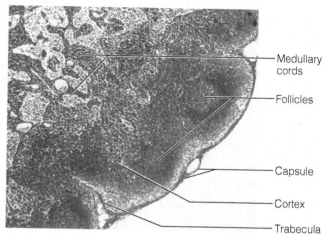

- Medullary cords
- Follicles
- Capsule
- Cortex
- Trabecula

PLATE 22 Main structural features of a lymph node (15×).

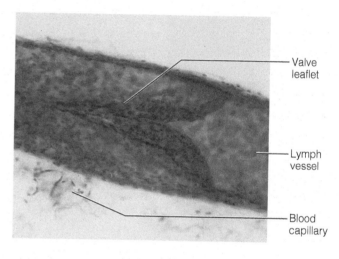

- Valve leaflet
- Lymph vessel
- Blood capillary

PLATE 23 Lymphatic vessel (140).

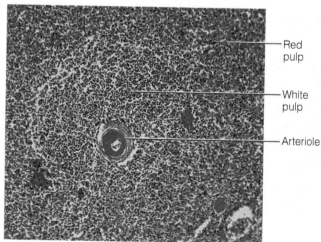

- Red pulp
- White pulp
- Arteriole

PLATE 24 Microscopic portion of spleen showing red and white pulp regions (50×).

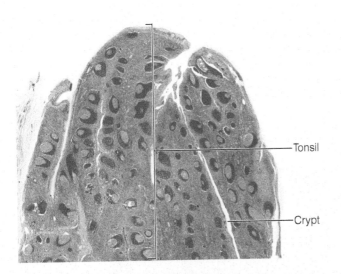

PLATE 25 Histology of a palatine tonsil. The exterior surface is covered with epithelium that invaginates deeply to form crypts (7×). (Exercise 25, page 316)

Tonsil

Crypt

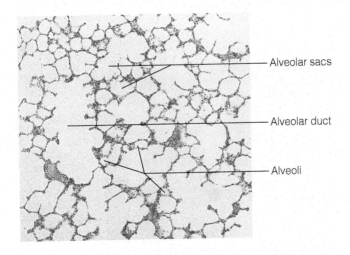

Alveolar sacs

Alveolar duct

Alveoli

PLATE 26 Photomicrograph of part of the lung showing alveoli and alveolar ducts and sacs (25×). (Exercise 23, page 298)

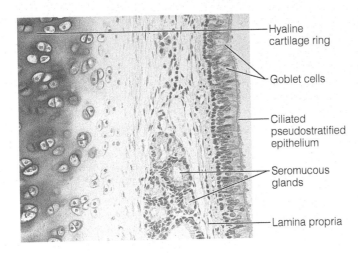

Hyaline cartilage ring

Goblet cells

Ciliated pseudostratified epithelium

Seromucous glands

Lamina propria

PLATE 27 Cross section through the trachea showing the ciliated pseudostratified epithelium, glands, and part of the supporting ring of hyaline cartilage (125×). (Exercise 23, page 298)

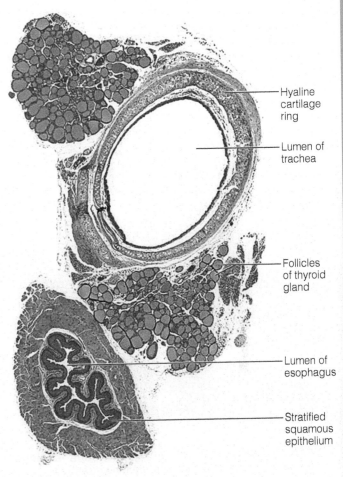

Hyaline cartilage ring

Lumen of trachea

Follicles of thyroid gland

Lumen of esophagus

Stratified squamous epithelium

PLATE 28 Cross section through trachea and esophagus (10×). (Exercise 23, page 298)

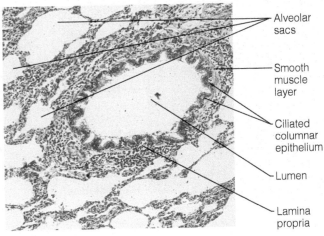

Alveolar sacs

Smooth muscle layer

Ciliated columnar epithelium

Lumen

Lamina propria

PLATE 29 Bronchiole, cross-sectional view (50×).

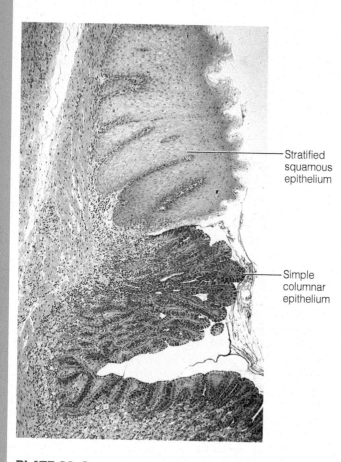

Stratified
squamous
epithelium

Simple
columnar
epithelium

PLATE 30 Gastroesophageal junction showing simple
columnar epithelium of stomach meeting stratified
squamous epithelium of esophagus (50×).

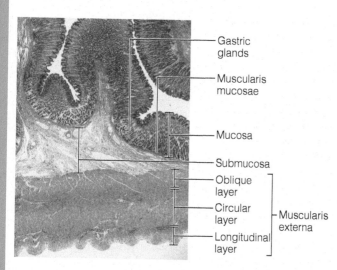

Gastric
glands

Muscularis
mucosae

Mucosa

Submucosa

Oblique
layer

Circular
layer   } Muscularis
               externa

Longitudinal
layer

PLATE 31 Stomach. Longitudinal view through wall
showing four tunics (25×). (Exercise 25, page 317)

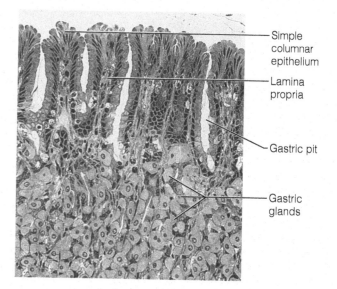

Simple
columnar
epithelium

Lamina
propria

Gastric pit

Gastric
glands

PLATE 32 Detailed structure of gastric glands and pits
(175×). (Exercise 25, page 317)

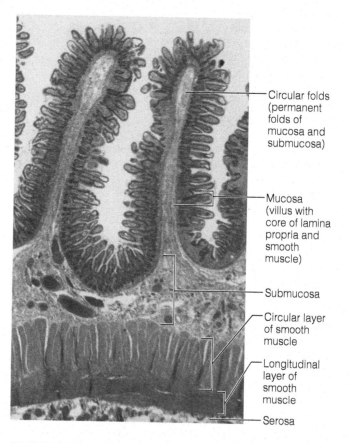

Circular folds
(permanent
folds of
mucosa and
submucosa)

Mucosa
(villus with
core of lamina
propria and
smooth
muscle)

Submucosa

Circular layer
of smooth
muscle

Longitudinal
layer of
smooth
muscle

Serosa

PLATE 33 Cross section through wall of small intestine
showing circular folds and the arrangement of layers,
or tunics (38×). Villi of mucosa are large and obvious.
(Exercise 25, pages 314–315)

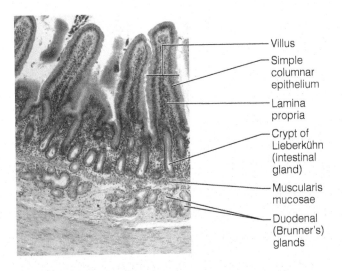

Villus

Simple columnar epithelium

Lamina propria

Crypt of Lieberkühn (intestinal gland)

Muscularis mucosae

Duodenal (Brunner's) glands

PLATE 34 Cross-sectional view of duodenum showing villi and duodenal glands (15×).

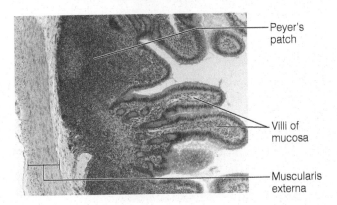

Peyer's patch

Villi of mucosa

Muscularis externa

PLATE 35 Cross section through ileum, showing Peyer's patches (15×). (Exercise 25, page 318)

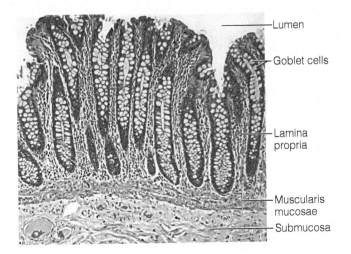

Lumen

Goblet cells

Lamina propria

Muscularis mucosae

Submucosa

PLATE 36 Large intestine. Cross-sectional view showing the abundant goblet cells of the mucosa (80×).

Mucous cells   Serous demilunes

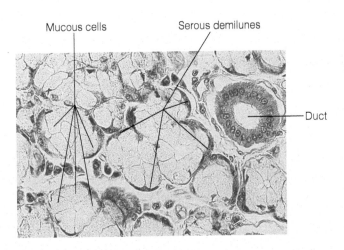

Duct

PLATE 37 Sublingual salivary glands (225×). (Exercise 25, page 321)

Acinar (exocrine) tissue   Islets (endocrine tissue)

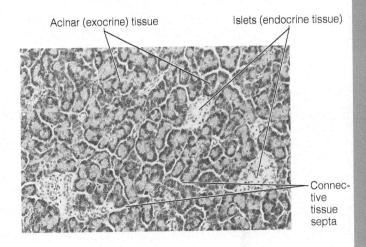

Connective tissue septa

PLATE 38 Pancreas tissue. Exocrine and endocrine (islets) areas clearly visible (100×). (Exercise 18, page 231; Exercise 25, page 322)

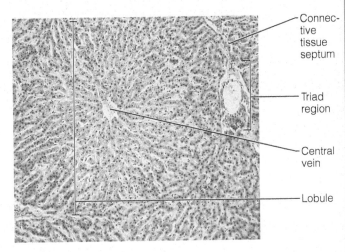

Connective tissue septum

Triad region

Central vein

Lobule

PLATE 39 Pig liver. Structure of liver lobules (35×). (Exercise 25, page 322)

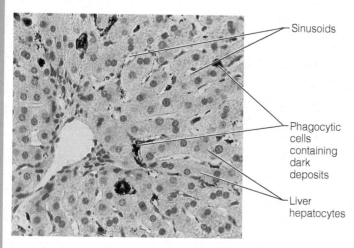

Sinusoids

Phagocytic cells containing dark deposits

Liver hepatocytes

PLATE 40 Liver stained to show location of phagocytic cells lining sinusoids (325×).

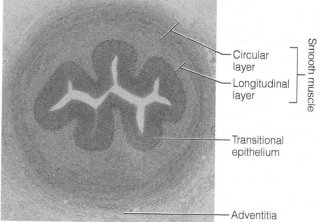

Circular layer

Longitudinal layer

Smooth muscle

Transitional epithelium

Adventitia

PLATE 43 Cross section of ureter (35×).

Renal tubules

Lumen of the glomerular capsule

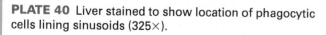
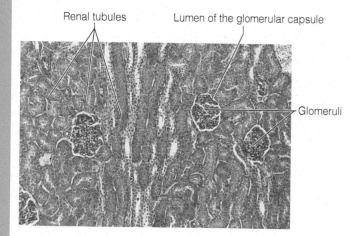

Glomeruli

PLATE 41 Renal cortex of kidney (60×). (Exercise 26, page 338)

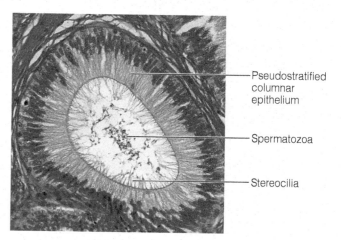

Pseudostratified columnar epithelium

Spermatozoa

Stereocilia

PLATE 44 Cross section of epididymis (165×). Stereocilia of the epithelial lining are obvious. (Exercise 27, page 347)

Cuboidal epithelium of the renal tubule

Lumen of the glomerular capsule

Glomerulus

Parietal layer of the glomerular capsule

Juxtaglomerular cells

Macula densa

PLATE 42 Detailed structure of a glomerulus (300×).

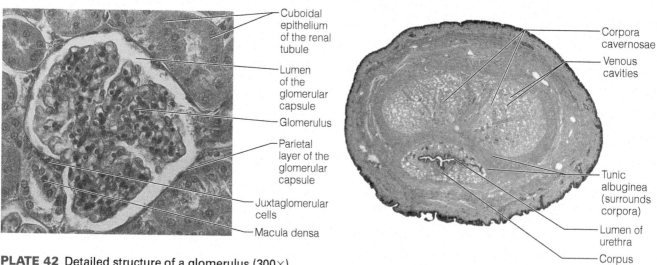

Corpora cavernosae

Venous cavities

Tunic albuginea (surrounds corpora)

Lumen of urethra

Corpus spongiosum

PLATE 45 Penis, transverse section (2.5×).

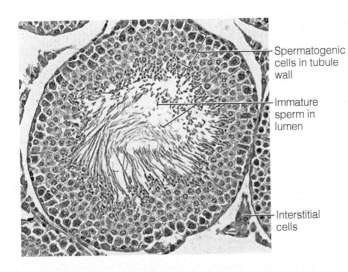

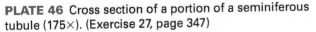

PLATE 46 Cross section of a portion of a seminiferous tubule (175×). (Exercise 27, page 347)

- Spermatogenic cells in tubule wall
- Immature sperm in lumen
- Interstitial cells

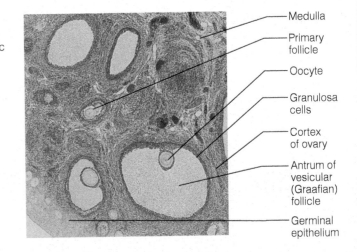

PLATE 49 The ovary, showing its follicles in various stages of development (45×). (Exercise 27, page 351)

- Medulla
- Primary follicle
- Oocyte
- Granulosa cells
- Cortex of ovary
- Antrum of vesicular (Graafian) follicle
- Germinal epithelium

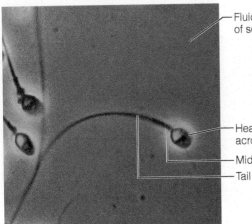

PLATE 47 Semen, the product of ejaculation, consisting of sperm and fluids secreted by the accessory glands (particularly the prostate and seminal vesicles) (1400×). (Exercise 27, page 347)

- Fluid medium of semen
- Head with acrosome — Sperm
- Midpiece
- Tail

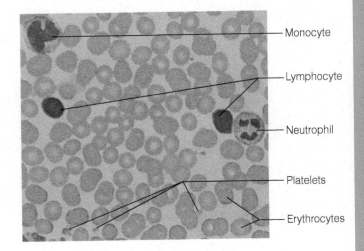

PLATE 50 Human blood smear (800×). (Exercise 19, page 236)

- Monocyte
- Lymphocyte
- Neutrophil
- Platelets
- Erythrocytes

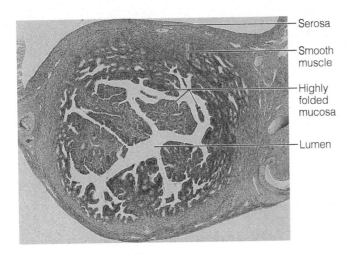

PLATE 48 Cross-sectional view of the uterine tube (25×).

- Serosa
- Smooth muscle
- Highly folded mucosa
- Lumen

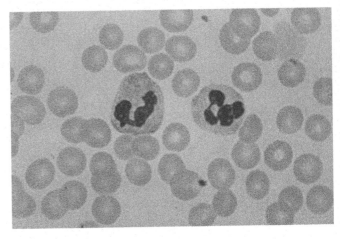

PLATE 51 Two neutrophils surrounded by erythrocytes (1500×). (Exercise 19, page 238)

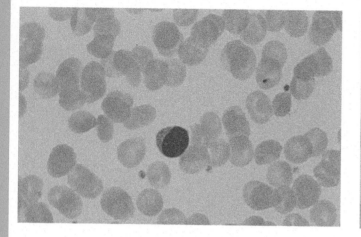

PLATE 52 Lymphocyte surrounded by erythrocytes (1125×). (Exercise 19, page 238)

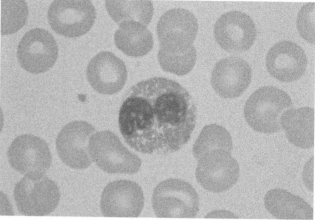

PLATE 54 An eosinophil surrounded by erythrocytes (1750×). (Exercise 19, page 238)

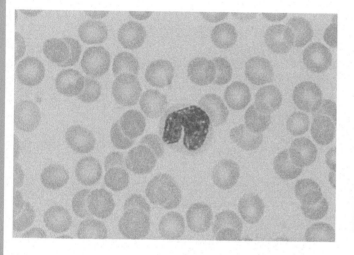

PLATE 53 Monocyte surrounded by erythrocytes (925×). (Exercise 19, page 238)

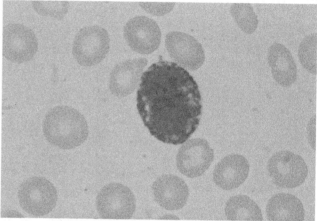

PLATE 55 A basophil surrounded by erythrocytes (1750×). (Exercise 19, page 238)

The Microscope

Materials

- ☐ Compound microscope
- ☐ Millimeter ruler
- ☐ Prepared slides of the letter *e* or newsprint
- ☐ Immersion oil in a dropper bottle
- ☐ Lens paper
- ☐ Prepared slide of grid ruled in millimeters (grid slide)
- ☐ Prepared slide of three crossed colored threads
- ☐ Clean microscope slide and coverslip
- ☐ Toothpicks (flat-tipped)
- ☐ Physiologic saline in a dropper bottle
- ☐ Methylene blue stain (dilute) in a dropper bottle
- ☐ Filter paper
- ☐ Forceps
- ☐ Beaker containing fresh 10% household bleach solution for wet mount disposal
- ☐ Disposable autoclave bag

Note to the Instructor: The slides and coverslips used for viewing cheek cells are to be soaked for 2 hours (or longer) in 10% bleach solution and then drained. The slides, coverslips, and disposable autoclave bag (containing used toothpicks) are to be autoclaved for 15 min at 121°C and 15 pounds pressure to ensure sterility. After autoclaving, the disposable autoclave bag may be discarded in any disposal facility and the glassware washed with laboratory detergent and reprepared for use. These instructions apply as well to any bloodstained glassware or disposable items used in other experimental procedures.

Objectives

1. Identify the parts of the microscope, and list the function of each.
2. Describe and demonstrate the proper techniques for care of the microscope.
3. Define *total magnification* and *resolution*.
4. Demonstrate proper focusing technique.
5. Define *parfocal*, *field*, and *depth of field*.
6. Estimate the size of objects in a field.

With the invention of the microscope, biologists gained a valuable tool to observe and study structures (such as cells) that are too small to be seen by the unaided eye. As a result, many of the theories basic to the understanding of biological sciences have been established. This exercise will familiarize you with the workhorse of microscopes—the compound microscope—and provide you with the necessary instructions for its proper use.

Care and Structure of the Compound Microscope

The **compound microscope** is a precision instrument and should always be handled with care. At all times you must observe the following rules for its transport, cleaning, use, and storage:

- When transporting the microscope, hold it in an upright position, with one hand on its arm and the other supporting its base. Avoid jarring the instrument when setting it down.

- Use only special grit-free lens paper to clean the lenses. Clean all lenses before and after use.

- Always begin the focusing process with the lowest-power objective lens in position, changing to the higher-power lenses as necessary.

- Never use the coarse adjustment knob with the high-power or oil immersion lenses.

- Always use a coverslip with temporary (wet mount) preparations.

- Before putting the microscope in the storage cabinet, remove the slide from the stage, rotate the lowest-power objective lens into position, and replace the dust cover.

- Never remove any parts from the microscope; inform your instructor of any mechanical problems that arise.

Activity 1

Identifying the Parts of a Microscope

1. Obtain a microscope, and bring it to the laboratory bench. (Use the proper carrying technique!)

☐ Record the number of your microscope in the **Microscope Summary Chart**.

Compare your microscope with the illustration in **Figure A.1**, and identify the microscope parts described in **Table A.1**.

Microscope Summary Chart

	Microscope # _____		Magnification of Ocular Lens _____ ×	
	Scanning	**Low power**	**High power**	**Oil immersion**
Magnification of objective lens	×	×	×	×
Total magnification	×	×	×	×
Detail observed				
Field diameter	mm µm	mm µm	mm µm	mm µm
Working distance	mm	mm	mm	mm

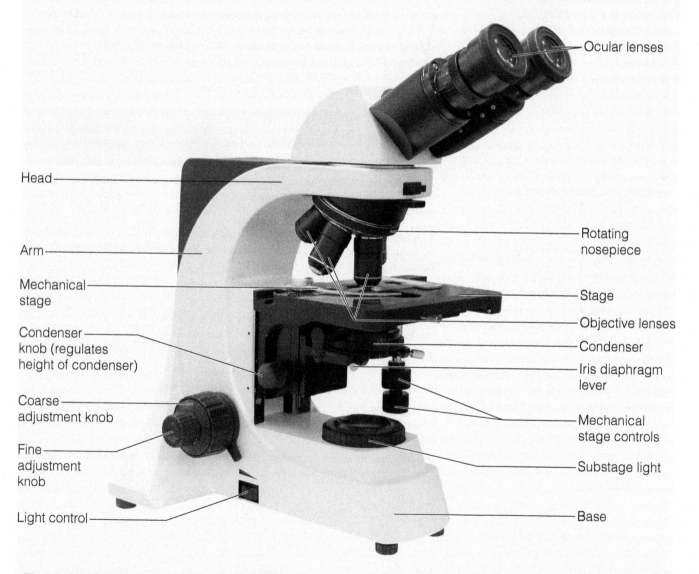

Figure A.1 Compound microscope and its parts.

Table A.1	Parts of the Microscope
Microscope part	**Description and function**
Base	The bottom of the microscope. Provides a sturdy flat surface to support and steady the microscope.
Substage light	Located in the base. The light from the lamp passes directly upward through the microscope.
Light control knob	Located on the base or arm. This dial allows you to adjust the intensity of the light passing through the specimen.
Stage	The platform that the slide rests on while being viewed. The stage has a hole in it to allow light to pass through the stage and through the specimen.
Mechanical stage	Holds the slide in position for viewing and has two adjustable knobs that control the precise movement of the slide.
Condenser	Small nonmagnifying lens located beneath the stage that concentrates the light on the specimen. The condenser may have a knob that raises and lowers the condenser to vary the light delivery. Generally, the best position is close to the inferior surface of the stage.
Iris diaphragm lever	The iris diaphragm is a shutter within the condenser that can be controlled by a lever to adjust the amount of light passing through the condenser. The lever can be moved to close the diaphragm and improve contrast. If your field of view is too dark, you can open the diaphragm to let in more light.
Coarse adjustment knob	This knob allows you to make large adjustments to the height of the stage to initially focus your specimen.
Fine adjustment knob	This knob is used for precise focusing once the initial coarse focusing has been completed.
Head	Attaches to the nosepiece to support the objective lens system. It also provides for attachment of the eyepieces which house the ocular lenses.
Arm	Vertical portion of the microscope that connects the base and the head.
Nosepiece	Rotating mechanism connected to the head. Generally, it carries three or four objective lenses and permits positioning of these lenses over the hole in the stage.
Objective lenses	These lenses are attached to the nosepiece. Usually, a compound microscope has four objective lenses: scanning (4×), low-power (10×), high-power (40×), and oil immersion (100×) lenses. Typical magnifying powers for the objectives are listed in parentheses.
Ocular lens(es)	Binocular microscopes will have two lenses located in the eyepieces at the superior end of the head. Most ocular lenses have a magnification power of 10×. Some microscopes will have a pointer and/or reticle (micrometer), which can be positioned by rotating the ocular lens.

2. Examine the objectives carefully; note their relative lengths and the numbers inscribed on their sides. On most microscopes, the low-power (l.p.) objective lens is the shortest and typically has a magnification of 10×. The high-power (h.p.) objective lens is of intermediate length and has a magnification range from 40× to 50×, depending on the microscope. The oil immersion objective lens is usually the longest of the objectives and has a magnifying power of 95× to 100×. Note that some microscopes lack the oil immersion lens but have a very low magnification lens called the **scanning lens**. A scanning lens is a very short objective lens with a magnification of 4× or 5×.

☐ Record the magnification of each objective lens of your microscope in the first row of the Microscope Summary Chart. Also, cross out the column relating to a lens that your microscope does not have.

3. Rotate the low-power objective until it clicks into position, and turn the coarse adjustment knob about 180 degrees. Notice how far the stage (or objective) travels during this adjustment. Move the fine adjustment knob 180 degrees, noting again the distance that the stage (or the objective) moves.

Magnification and Resolution

The microscope is an instrument of magnification. In the compound microscope, magnification is achieved through the interplay of two lenses—the ocular lens and the objective lens. The objective lens magnifies the specimen to produce a **real image** that is projected to the ocular. This real image is magnified by the ocular lens to produce the **virtual image** seen by your eye (**Figure A.2**).

The **total magnification** of any specimen being viewed is equal to the power of the ocular lens multiplied by the power of the objective lens used. For example, if the ocular lens magnifies 10× and the objective lens being used magnifies 45×, the total magnification is 450× (10 × 45).

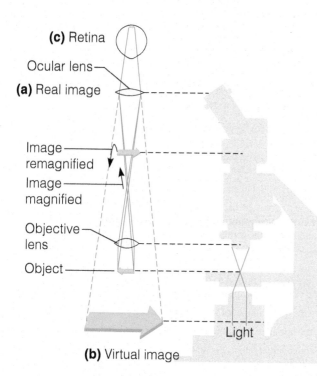

(c) Retina
Ocular lens
(a) Real image
Image remagnified
Image magnified
Objective lens
Object
Light
(b) Virtual image

Figure A.2 Image formation in light microscopy.
(a) Light passing through the objective lens forms a real image. **(b)** The real image serves as the object for the ocular lens, which remagnifies the image and forms the virtual image. **(c)** The virtual image passes through the lens of the eye and is focused on the retina.

Activity 2

Determining Total Magnification
Determine the total magnification you may achieve with each of the objectives on your microscope and record the figures on the second row of the Microscope Summary Chart on page 368.

The compound light microscope has certain limitations. Although the level of magnification is almost limitless, the **resolution** (or resolving power), the ability to discriminate two close objects as separate, is not. The human eye can resolve objects about 100 µm apart, but the compound microscope has a resolution of 0.2 µm under ideal conditions. Objects closer than 0.2 µm are seen as a single fused image.

Resolving power (RP) is determined by the amount and physical properties of the visible light that enters the microscope. In general, the more light delivered to the objective lens, the greater the resolution. The size of the objective lens aperture (opening) decreases with increasing magnification, allowing less light to enter the objective. Thus, you will probably find it necessary to increase the light intensity at the higher magnifications.

Activity 3

Viewing Objects Through the Microscope

1. Obtain a millimeter ruler, a prepared slide of the letter *e* or newsprint, a dropper bottle of immersion oil, and some lens paper. Adjust the condenser to its highest position and switch on the light source of your microscope. (If the light source is not built into the base, use the curved surface of the mirror to reflect the light up into the microscope.)

2. Secure the slide on the stage so that the letter *e* is centered over the light beam passing through the stage. If you are using a microscope with spring clips, make sure the slide is secured at both ends. If your microscope has a mechanical stage, open the jaws of its slide retainer (holder) by using the control lever (typically) located at the rear left corner of the mechanical stage. Insert the slide squarely within the confines of the slide retainer. Check to see that the slide is resting on the stage (and not on the mechanical stage frame) before releasing the control lever.

3. With your lowest power (scanning or low-power) objective in position over the stage, use the coarse adjustment knob to bring the objective and stage as close together as possible.

4. Look through the ocular and adjust the light for comfort. Now use the coarse adjustment knob to focus slowly away from the *e* until it is as clearly focused as possible. Complete the focusing with the fine adjustment knob.

5. Sketch the letter in the circle just as it appears in the **field** (the area you see through the microscope).

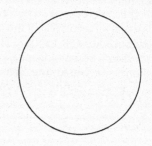

What is the total magnification? _____ ×

How far is the bottom of the objective from the specimen? In other words, what is the **working distance**? Use a millimeter ruler held vertically to make this measurement and record it here and in the Microscope Summary Chart on page 368.

_____ mm

How has the apparent orientation of the *e* changed in terms of top to bottom, right to left, and so on?

_____

_____

6. Move the slide slowly away from you on the stage as you view it through the ocular. In what direction does the image move?

_____

Move the slide to the left. In what direction does the image move?

_____

At first, this change in orientation will confuse you, but with practice you will learn to move the slide in the desired direction with no problem.

7. Without touching the focusing knobs, increase the magnification by rotating the next higher magnification lens (low-power or high-power) into position over the stage. Make sure it clicks into position. Using the fine adjustment only, sharpen the focus.* What new details become clear?

_____

_____

What is the total magnification now? _____ ×

As best you can, measure the distance between the objective and the slide (the working distance), and record it on the chart.

Why should you *not* use the coarse focusing knob when you are focusing with the higher-powered objective lenses?

_____

_____

Is the image larger or smaller? _____

Approximately how much of the letter *e* is visible now?

_____

Is the field larger or smaller? _____

Why is it necessary to center your object (or the portion of the slide you wish to view) before changing to a higher power?

_____

Move the iris diaphragm lever while observing the field. What happens?

_____

Is it more desirable to increase *or* to decrease the light when changing to a higher magnification?

_____ Why? _____

_____

8. If you have just been using the low-power objective, repeat the steps given in direction 7 using the high-power objective lens. Record the total magnification, approximate working distance, and information on detail observed on the Microscope Summary Chart on page 368.

9. Without touching the focusing knob, rotate the high-power lens out of position so that the area of the slide over the opening in the stage is unobstructed. Place a drop of immersion oil over the *e* on the slide, and rotate the oil immersion lens into position. Set the condenser at its highest point (closest to the stage), and open the diaphragm fully. Adjust the fine focus and fine-tune the light for the best possible resolution.

Is the field again decreased in size? _____

What is the total magnification with the oil immersion lens?

_____ ×

Is the working distance less *or* greater than it was when the high-power lens was focused?

_____

Compare your observations on the relative working distances of the objective lenses with the illustration in **Figure A.3**. Explain why it is desirable to begin the focusing process in low power.

_____

_____

_____

*Today most good laboratory microscopes are **parfocal**; that is, the slide should be in focus (or nearly so) at the higher magnifications once you have properly focused in l.p. If you are unable to swing the objective into position without raising the objective, your microscope is not parfocal. Consult with your instructor.

Text continues on next page. →

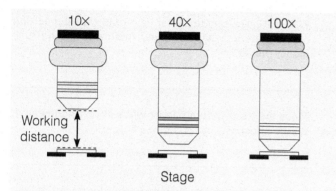

Figure A.3 Relative working distances of the 10×, 40×, and 100× objectives.

10. Rotate the oil immersion lens slightly to the side, and remove the slide. Clean the oil immersion lens carefully with lens paper, and then clean the slide in the same manner with a fresh piece of lens paper.

Diameter of the Microscope Field

By now you should know that the size of the microscope field decreases with increasing magnification. For future microscope work, it will be useful to determine the diameter of each of the microscope fields. This information will allow you to make a fairly accurate estimate of the size of the objects you view in any field. For example, if you have calculated the field diameter to be 4 mm and the object being observed extends across half this diameter, you can estimate the length of the object to be approximately 2 mm.

Microscopic specimens are usually measured in micrometers and millimeters, both units of the metric system. You can get an idea of the relationship and meaning of these units from **Table A.2**. The table on the inside back cover provides a more detailed treatment.

Table A.2	Comparing Metric Units of Length	
Metric unit	**Abbreviation**	**Equivalent**
Meter	m	about 39.37 in.
Centimeter	cm	10^{-2} m
Millimeter	mm	10^{-3} m
Micrometer (or micron)	μm (μ)	10^{-6} m
Nanometer	nm (mμ)	10^{-9} m

Activity 4

Determining the Diameter of the Microscope Field

1. Return the letter *e* slide to the supplies area, and obtain a grid slide (a slide prepared with graph paper ruled in millimeters). Each of the squares in the grid is 1 mm on each side. Use your lowest-power objective to bring the grid lines into focus.

2. Move the slide so that one grid line touches the edge of the field on one side, and then count the number of squares you can see across the diameter of the field. If you can see only part of a square, as in the accompanying diagram, estimate the part of a millimeter that the partial square represents.

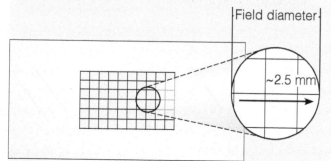

For future reference, record this figure in the appropriate space marked "field size" on the Microscope Summary Chart on page 368. (If you have been using the scanning lens, repeat the procedure with the low-power objective lens.) Complete the chart by computing the approximate diameter of the high-power and immersion fields. Say the diameter of the low-power field (total magnification of 50×) is 2 mm. You would compute the diameter of a high-power field with a total magnification of 100× as follows:

$$2 \text{ mm} \times 50 = Y(\text{diameter of h.p. field}) \times 100$$

$$100 \text{ mm} = 100Y$$

$$1 \text{ mm} = Y(\text{diameter of the h.p. field})$$

The formula is:

Diameter of the l.p. field (mm) × total magnification of the l.p. field = diameter of field Y × total magnification of field Y

3. Estimate the length (longest dimension) of the following microscopic objects. *Base your calculations on the field sizes you have determined for your microscope.*

a. Object seen in low-power field:

approximate length:

_____ mm

b. Object seen in high-power field:

approximate length:

_____ mm

or _____ μm

c. Object seen in oil immersion field:

approximate length:

_____ μm

4. If an object viewed with the oil immersion lens looked like the field depicted just below, could you determine its approximate size from this view?

If not, then how could you determine it?

_____

_____

_____

Perceiving Depth

Any microscopic specimen has depth as well as length and width; it is rare indeed to view a tissue slide with just one layer of cells. Normally you can see two or three cell thicknesses. Therefore, it is important to learn how to determine relative depth with your microscope.*

Activity 5

Perceiving Depth

1. Return the grid slide, and obtain a slide with colored crossed threads. Focusing at low magnification, locate the point where the three threads cross each other.

2. Use the iris diaphragm lever to greatly reduce the light, thus increasing the contrast. Focus down with the coarse adjustment until the threads are out of focus, and then slowly focus upward again, noting which thread comes into clear focus first. This one is the lowest, or most inferior, thread. (You will see two or even all three threads, so you must be very careful in determining which one comes into clear focus first.) Record your observations:

_____ thread over _____

Continue to focus upward until the uppermost thread is clearly focused. Again record your observation.

_____ thread over _____

Which thread is uppermost? _____

Lowest? _____

*In microscope work, the **depth of field** (the depth of the specimen clearly in focus) is greater at lower magnifications.

Activity 6

Preparing and Observing a Wet Mount

1. Obtain the following: a clean microscope slide and coverslip, a flat-tipped toothpick, a dropper bottle of physiological saline, a dropper bottle of methylene blue stain, forceps, and filter paper.

2. Place a drop of physiological saline in the center of the slide. Using the flat end of the toothpick, *gently* scrape the inner lining of your cheek. Agitate the end of the toothpick containing the cheek scrapings in the drop of saline (**Figure A.4a**).

3. Add a tiny drop of the methylene blue stain to the preparation. (These epithelial cells are nearly transparent and thus difficult to see without the stain, which colors the nuclei of the cells and makes them look much darker than the cytoplasm.) Stir again, and then dispose of the toothpick as described below.

 Immediately discard the used toothpick in the disposable autoclave bag provided at the supplies area.

4. Hold the coverslip with the forceps so that its bottom edge touches one side of the fluid drop (Figure A.4b), then *carefully* lower the coverslip onto the preparation (Figure A.4c). *Do not just drop the coverslip,* or you will trap large air bubbles under it, which will obscure the cells. *Always use a coverslip with a wet mount* to prevent soiling the lens if you should misfocus.

5. Examine your preparation carefully. The coverslip should be closely apposed to the slide. If there is excess fluid around its edges, you will need to remove it. Obtain a piece of filter paper, fold it in half, and use the folded edge to absorb the excess fluid.

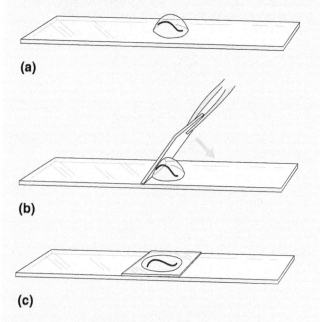

(a)

(b)

(c)

Figure A.4 Procedure for preparing a wet mount.
(a) Place the object in a drop of water (or saline) on a clean slide, **(b)** hold a coverslip at a 45° angle with forceps, and **(c)** lower it carefully over the water and the object.

 Before continuing, discard the filter paper in the disposable autoclave bag.

6. Place the slide on the stage, and locate the cells in low power. You will probably want to dim the light with the iris diaphragm to provide more contrast for viewing the lightly stained cells. Furthermore, a wet mount will dry out quickly in bright light, because a bright light source is hot.

7. Cheek epithelial cells are very thin, six-sided cells. In the cheek, they provide a smooth, tilelike lining, as shown in **Figure A.5.**

8. Make a sketch of the epithelial cells that you observe.

Approximately how wide are the cheek epithelial cells?

_____ mm

Why do *your* cheek cells look different from those illustrated in Figure A.5? (Hint: What did you have to *do* to your cheek to obtain them?)

_____

_____

 9. When you complete your observations, dispose of your wet mount preparation in the beaker of bleach solution.

10. Before leaving the laboratory, make sure all other materials are properly discarded or returned to the appropriate laboratory station. Clean the microscope lenses, and put the dust cover on the microscope before you return it to the storage cabinet.

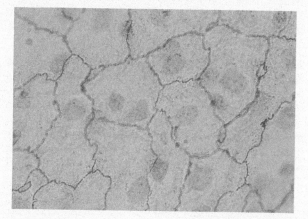

Figure A.5 Epithelial cells of the cheek cavity (surface view, 710×).

Credits

Illustrations

All illustrations by Imagineering STA Media Services, unless otherwise noted.

Exercise 1 1.2–1.4: Precision Graphics.

Exercise 5 5.2a–c,e,f, 5.3a–d,f,g, 5.4a–c, 5.5: Precision Graphics.

Exercise 13 13.5: Electronic Publishing Services.

Exercise 14 14.5: Electronic Publishing Services. 14.8: Precision Graphics.

Exercise 15 15.3: Precision Graphics.

Exercise 17 17.3: Precision Graphics. 17.8: Precision Graphics.

Exercise 20 20.6a,b: Precision Graphics.

Exercise 21 21.2: Precision Graphics. 21.6: Precision Graphics.

Exercise 25 25.1: Electronic Publishing Services. 25.11: Precision Graphics.

Exercise 27 27.3b: Precision Graphics.

Appendices A.2–A.4: Precision Graphics.

Photographs

Exercise 1 1.3, 1.6b: John Wilson White/ Pearson Education.

Exercise 2 2.1, 2.2, 2.3b: Elena Dorfman/ Pearson Education. 2.3b: Pearson Education. 2.5: Racobovt/Shutterstock.

Exercise 3 3.3, 3.RS.7: William Karkow/ Pearson Education.

Exercise 4 4.1: Richard Megna/ Fundamental Photographs.

Exercise 5 5.2a,d: William Karkow/ Pearson Education. 5.2b,f, 5.3c,f,g: Allen Bell, University of New England/Pearson Education. 5.2c: Ed Reschke/Photolibrary/ Getty Images 5.2e, 5.3b, 5.4a: Nina Zanetti/ Pearson Education. 5.3a: PAL 3.0/Pearson Education. 5.3d: Lisa Lee/Pearson Education. 5.3e: Steve Downing/Pearson Education. 5.4b: Ed Reschke/Photolibrary/ Getty Images. 5.4c, 5.5: Biophoto Associates/Science Source.

Exercise 6 6.1b: William Karkow/Pearson Education. 6.3, 6.RS.2: Marian Rice.

Exercise 7 7.3c: William Karkow/Pearson Education. 7.RS.2: Allen Bell, University of New England/Pearson Education.

Exercise 9 Table 9.4: From A Stereoscopic Atlas of Human Anatomy, by David L. Bassett, M.D.

Exercise 10 10.4: John Wilson White/ Pearson Education.

Exercise 11 11.3b: Lisa Lee/Pearson Education. 11.5: Victor P. Eroschenko/ Pearson Education.

Exercise 12 12.3b: Karen Krabbenhoft/ Pearson Education.

Exercise 13 13.1b: William Karkow/ Pearson Education.

Exercise 14 14.1b: A. Glauberman/ Science Source. 14.2, 14.3a, 14.7: Karen Krabbenhoft, PAL 3.0, Pearson Education. 14.4a: From A Stereoscopic Atlas of Human Anatomy, by David L. Bassett, M.D. 14.8: Sharon Cummings/Pearson Education. 14.9, 14.10: Elena Dorfman/ Pearson Education.

Exercise 16 16.3, 16.4, 16.5: Richard Tauber/Pearson Education.

Exercise 17 17.4b: From A Stereoscopic Atlas of Human Anatomy, by David L. Bassett, M.D. 17.5: Elena Dorfman/ Pearson Education. 17.11: Richard Tauber/ Pearson Education. 17.16c: PAL 3.0, Pearson Science/Pearson Education.

Exercise 19 19.2: Elena Dorfman/Pearson Education. 19.4, 19.RS.1: Jack Scanlan/ Pearson Education.

Exercise 20 20.5, 20.RS.3: William Karkow/Pearson Education. 20.6: Wally Cash/Pearson Education.

Exercise 21 21.1a: Ed Reschke/ Photolibrary/Getty Images

Exercise 23 23.3a: Richard Tauber/ Pearson Education.

Exercise 24 24.2: Elena Dorfman/Pearson Education.

Exercise 25 25.5a: From A Stereoscopic Atlas of Human Anatomy, by David L. Bassett, M.D.

Exercise 26 26.3: Karen Krabbenhoft/ Pearson Education. 26.4d: Professor P.M. Motta & M. Castellucci/Science Source. 26.5: Victor P. Eroschenko/Pearson Education.

Exercise 27 27.3a: Juergen Berger/Science Source. 27.8: Lisa Lee/Pearson Education.

Histology Atlas Plates 1, 6, 7, 21, 31, 34, 35: Nina Zanetti, Pearson Education. Plates 2, 4, 9, 10, 12–14, 16–19, 27, 29, 32, 36–43, 46, 48–53: Victor P. Eroschenko, Pearson Education. Plate 3, 25: Biophoto Associates/Science Source. Plate 5: Michael Abbey/Science Source. Plates 8, 20: Eroschenko's Interactive Histology. Plate 11: Kilgore College Biology Dept., Kilgore, Texas. Plate 15: David B. Fankhauser, University of Cincinnati, Clermont College. Plate 22: LUMEN Histology, Loyola University Medical Education Network. Plate 23: Astrid & Hanns-Frieder Micheler/Science Source. Plate 24: Danny Gohel. Plate 26: Marian Rice. Plate 28: Deltagen. Plate 30: Roger C. Wagner, Dept. of Biological Sciences, University of Delaware. Plate 33: Inner-space Imaging/Science Source. Plate 44: Michael W. Davidson and Florida State University, in collaboration with Optical Microscopy at the National High Magnetic Field Laboratory. Plate 45: Harry Plymale. Plate 47: J. Walsh/Science Photo Library. Plate 54: Pearson PH College. Plate 55: J. O. Ballard, Professor of Medicine & Pathology, Penn State University College of Medicine.

Appendices A.1: Vereshchagin Dmitry/ Shutterstock. A.5: Victor P. Eroschenko/ Pearson Education.

Index